OXFORD HISPANIC STUDIES

General Editor

PAUL JULIAN SMITH

Poets of Contemporary Latin America

History and the Inner Life

WILLIAM ROWE

OXFORD
UNIVERSITY PRESS

OXFORD
UNIVERSITY PRESS

Great Clarendon Street, Oxford OX2 6DP

Oxford University Press is a department of the University of Oxford.
It furthers the University's objective of excellence in research, scholarship,
and education by publishing worldwide in

Oxford New York

Athens Auckland Bangkok Bogotá Buenos Aires Calcutta
Cape Town Chennai Dar es Salaam Delhi Florence Hong Kong Istanbul
Karachi Kuala Lumpur Madrid Melbourne Mexico City Mumbai
Nairobi Paris São Paulo Singapore Taipei Tokyo Toronto Warsaw

and associated companies in Berlin Ibadan

Oxford is a registered trade mark of Oxford University Press
in the UK and in certain other countries

Published in the United States
by Oxford University Press Inc., New York

© William Rowe 2000

The moral rights of the author have been asserted
Database right Oxford University Press (maker)

First published 2000

British Library Cataloguing in Publication Data

Data available

Library of Congress Cataloging in Publication Data

Rowe, William.
Poets of contemporary Latin America: history and the inner life/William Rowe.
p. cm.—(Oxford Hispanic studies)
Includes bibliographical references and index.
Contents: Nicanor Parra—Ernesto Cardenal—Gonzalo Rojas—Jorge Eduardo Eielson
Juan L. Ortiz—Ana Enriqueta Terán—Raúl Zurita—Carmen Ollé.
1. Spanish American poetry—20th century—History and criticism. I. Title. II. Series.
PQ7082.P7 R69 2000   861'.640998—dc21   00–024196
ISBN 0–19–815892–0

1 3 5 7 9 10 8 6 4 2

Typeset in Baskerville by
Cambrian Typesetters, Frimley, Surrey

Printed in Great Britain
on acid-free paper by
Biddles Ltd,
Guildford and King's Lynn

To Nuri Gene-Cos

Oxford Hispanic Studies

General Editor: Paul Julian Smith

The last twenty years have seen a revolution in the humanities. On the one hand, there has been a massive influence on literary studies of other disciplines: philosophy, psychoanalysis, and anthropology. On the other, there has been a displacement of the boundaries of literary studies, an opening out on to other forms of expression: cinema, popular culture, and historical documentation.

The new *Oxford Hispanic Studies* series reflects the fact that Hispanic studies are particularly well placed to take advantage of this revolution. Unlike those working in French or English studies, Hispanists have little reason to genuflect to a canon of European culture which has tended to exclude them. Historically, moreover, Hispanic societies tend to exhibit plurality and difference: thus Medieval Spain was the product of the three cultures of Jew, Moslem, and Christian; modern Spain is a federation of discrete autonomous regions; and Spanish America is a continent in which cultural identity must always be brought into question, can never be taken for granted.

The incursion of new models of critical theory into Spanish-speaking countries has been uneven. And while cultural studies in other language areas have moved through post-structuralism (Lacan, Derrida, Foucault) to create new disciplines focusing on gender, ethnicity, and homosexuality, it is only recently that Hispanists have contributed to the latest fields of enquiry. Now, however, there is an upsurge of exciting new work in both Europe and the Americas. *Oxford Hispanic Studies* is intended to provide a medium for writing engaged in and taking account of these developments. It will serve both as a vehicle and a stimulus for innovative and challenging work in an important and rapidly changing field. The series aims to facilitate both the development of new approaches in Hispanic studies and the awareness of Hispanic studies in other subject areas. It will embrace discussions of literary and non-literary cultural forms, and focus on the publication of illuminating original research and theory.

Acknowledgements

I would like to thank the following people for their generosity in discussing various parts of this book with me: Hugo Gola, Jorge Eduardo Eielson, Tony Dunn, Gordon Brotherston, Chris Brookeman, Bill Griffiths, Gilbert Adair, Michael Hrebeniak, John Kraniauskas, Catherine Boyle, David Treece, Carmen Ollé, Liz Dore, Claudio Canaparo, Jordi Larrios, Dickon Hinchcliffe. I am also grateful to Paul Julian Smith, editor of this series, for his encouragement, and to Sophie Goldsworthy, commissioning editor at Oxford University Press, for her patience and help. For the most decisive advice, as well as the warmest support, I would like to thank Nuri Gene-Cos.

Antonio Miguel Sánchez, Cristina Pope, Anna Reid, and Alejandro Kaufmann have given substantial help with bibliographical matters and I would like to express my gratitude to them here. I am grateful also to Ben Bollig, for help with indexing.

Earlier versions of several chapters were published in the following journals and book, to whose editors I would like to express my thanks: *Indiana Journal of Hispanic Literatures, Poesía y poética, Tesserae, Gender Politics in Latin America* (ed. Liz Dore), *Journal of Latin American Cultural Studies (Travesia), Revista brasileira de literatura comparada*. My book *Hacia una poética radical: ensayos de hermenéutica cultural* (Rosario and Lima, Beatriz Viterbo and Mosca Azul) also includes earlier versions in Spanish of some of the material.

Part of this book was written during a two-year British Academy Research Readership: I am grateful to the British Academy for its support.

W.R.

Contents

Contents

Introduction

How terrible the mind
Is, open
To the world.
      (George Oppen)

WAYS OF READING

For poets writing in Latin America since the 1950s there have been two main inheritances to be used, modified, or abandoned: the work of the avant-gardes and the tradition of politicized poetry. But whereas the latter is widely known, and associated in particular with the name of Pablo Neruda, the general reader is less likely to have come across the contributions of Latin American poets to the avant-garde tradition of experiment with language and form. Avant-gardism is regarded as a European phenomenon, with Surrealism and Dada as the prime examples, and Latin American poetry is taken to be distinctive in its preoccupation with politics.[1] That view could be traced to a number of influences, such as the coloniality of established literary history and the populism of the Left, but the fact is that the way it divides up the territory is not accurate. Crucially, it diverts attention from the poetic imagination and its capacity to invent forms, which is a power that moves through all varieties of poetry. To perceive and respond to this is a prime condition for reading poetry.

A historical perspective can help to bring some clarity to the question of politics and poetic form. The debate about the political commitment of writers took hold in the 1930s. Increasing polarization of intellectuals between communism and anti-communism was intensified and dramatized by the

---

[1] The recent and otherwise useful reader V. Kolocotroni et al. (eds.), *Modernism: An Anthology of Sources and Documents* (Edinburgh, 1998) includes in its 618 pages of text only 2 by a Latin American.

Spanish Civil War. Pablo Neruda can serve as a marker of the process and example of the type of decision writers were confronted with. In the third book of his *Residencia en la tierra* [Residence on earth], published in 1939, he rejected the avant-garde language and form of the first two books (published 1933), declaring that his earlier poetry helped one to die and not to live.[2] He presents his decision for a new way of writing, which entails a different way of reading, in the long poem 'España en el corazón' [Spain in the heart] (1937), particularly in the section entitled 'Explico algunas cosas' [I explain a few things]:

> Preguntaréis por qué su poesía
> no nos habla del sueño, de las hojas,
> de los grandes volcanes de su país natal?
>
> Venid a ver la sangre por las calles,
> venid a ver
> la sangre por las calles,
> venid a ver la sangre
> por las calles![3]
>
> [You will ask, why doesn't his poetry
> speak to us of dreams, of leaves,
> of the great volcanoes of his native land?
>
> Come and see the blood in the streets,
> come and see
> the blood in the streets,
> come and see the blood
> in the streets!]

That is a clear declaration of a politics of poetry, consisting in the idea that responsibility to history takes priority over what one might call 'inner reverie'. The poet has to write as witness to what matters, or should matter, to 'millions of human beings'. The position is even clearer in the heroic realism of his 'Canto a Stalingrado' [Song to Stalingrad]. This response to what was probably the most terrible of all battles of the Second World War shows how Neruda was prepared to take the risk of reducing poetry to propaganda. A key difficulty for a reader of

---

[2] See Saúl Yurkievich, *Fundadores de la nueva poesía latinoamericana* (Barcelona 1971), 221–2.

[3] Pablo Neruda, *Tercera residencia* (Buenos Aires, 1961), 51.

this poem is that the figure of the author is completely identified with the expression of mass emotions. There are assumed to be no gaps or fissures between personal emotion and history, whether for the author or the combatants.

Later in life, Neruda himself pointed out the risks of political poetry: 'Political poetry is more deeply emotional than any other except love poetry, and it cannot be forced without becoming vulgar and unacceptable. [. . .] It seldom succeeds.'[4] The Chilean poet Nicanor Parra, who began writing in the 1950s, when Neruda's massively popular work was taken to be the defining model of poetry, found that trying to equate experience and history meant writing poems that excluded what was actually happening around him. His ambition had been to go beyond mere 'poemitas líricos' [little lyric poems],[5] as he calls them, towards a more epic type of poetry—he mentions Wagner and Whitman as models. But he came up against the difficulty of finding either a language or characters suitable for the Whitmanesque narrative poems he was attempting to write: the heroes kept turning into anti-heroes. The failure led to his 'antipoems', one of the most decisive inventions in recent Latin American poetics. Similar tensions run through the work of Ernesto Cardenal, another major poet of this period, whose long poem *Hora O* [Zero hour] (1960) is a twentieth-century epic which invents a poetics of popular history, by using the fullest resources of Latin American Spanish—in other words the language actually spoken—within Modernist techniques of collage: the result is an alternation of voices, both heroic and everyday.

The phrase *Hora O* was used as a name—and statement of position—by the most important grouping of Peruvian poets of the 1970s.[6] The Cuban Revolution (1959) and other subsequent national liberation struggles, such as those of Nicaragua, El Salvador, and Guatemala, were by then new urgencies that had entered any discussion of poetry as a public action. Indeed, the politically committed poet remains the most common image of Latin American poetry for European and American readers. But the idea of commitment in poetry can bring with it considerable confusion. The three conditions involved, which are the

---

4 Rita Guibert, *Seven Voices from Latin America* (New York, 1973), 75.
5 Leónidas Morales, *La poesía de Nicanor Parra* (Santiago, 1972), 194.
6 See the anthology J. M. Oviedo (ed.), *Estos 13* (Lima, 1973).

narrative of revolutionary struggle, the moral necessity to respond to injustice, and the question of the capabilities of poetry as an art, tend to collapse into each other. In the 1960s and 1970s in Latin America there was a widely shared attitude to poetry according to which poems that told the story of revolution were taken thereby to fulfil the other conditions.

There are several ways to attempt to unravel the confusion. One is to call attention to differences. There is for example a considerable distance between the work of Ernesto Cardenal, which combines popular and erudite poetic traditions extending back to the sixteenth century with Modernist procedures of composition, and the one-dimensional language of many of the poets included in the 1974 anthology *Latin American Revolutionary Poetry*.[7] Let the reader judge. Or contrast, say, the freshness of poems by the Guatemalan poet Otto René Castillo or the Peruvian Javier Heraud,[8] written in the 1960s, with the later committed or 'social' poetry, as it tended to be called in Latin America.[9] By the 1970s, the fashion for 'social' poetry often obscured a considerable gap between the reputation and the actual capability of a poet. In these cases, commitment functioned as an alibi, promoted by publishers, media, and university critics. In a poem published in 1972, Parra exposes the way that commitment—in this case to 'the peaceful road to socialism'—had become a requirement for submission to belief-structures:

> no creo en la vía pacífica
> me gustaría creer
> en algo—pero no creo
> creer es creer en Dios
> lo único que yo hago
> es encogerme de hombros
> perdónenme la franqueza
> no creo ni en la Vía Láctea.[10]

---

[7] Robert Márquez (ed.), *Latin American Revolutionary Poetry* (New York, 1974).

[8] Otto René Castillo, *Poemas* (Havana, 1971). Javier Heraud, P*oesías completas* (Lima, 1973). In English, see Gordon Brotherston and E. Dorn (eds.), *Our Word: Guerrilla Poems from Latin America* (London, 1968).

[9] The term 'poesía social' first became current in Spain in the early 1950s, in connection with the work of Gabriel Celaya and Blas de Otero.

[10] Published in *Emergency Poems* (1972), and included in *Chistes para desorientar a la poesía* (Madrid, 1989), 127. 'La vía pacífica' [the peaceful road] refers to the notion that the Allende government (elected in 1970 and ousted by Pinochet's coup in 1973) was achieving 'the peaceful road to socialism'.

[I do not believe in the peaceful road
I would like to believe
in something—but I don't believe
to believe is to believe in God
the only thing I do
is shrug my shoulders
excuse my frankness
I don't even believe in the Milky Way.]

Another way to cut through the confusion is to explore the capabilities of poetry in precisely those poets who have in specific and different ways expanded what a poem can do and therefore what it can offer to a reader. This has been a guiding principle of the present book. I have sought to make as clear as I possibly can how the work of these poets offers more than is generally suggested via the systems of interpretation currently promoted in the institutional field of literary studies. Their work shows how poetry can be a means of active discovery, and not simply a fulfilment, however well expressed, of what has been theorized already. I also argue that this sense of discovery is not a purely literary matter, but traverses other fields of human invention. One of the consequences of commitment to poetry as a movement outwards, away from packaged knowledge, is spelt out in a brief poem by Parra: 'TODO | ES POESÍA | menos la poesía' [EVERYTHING | IS POETRY | except poetry].[11]

A major problem with the reception of poetry in our epoch springs from available models of reading. A model of reading could be defined as the set of procedures one brings to the poem in hand in order to perform it to oneself and, potentially, to others. These procedures are trained but not necessarily conscious. They are transmitted, in different degrees according to time and place, by histories of literature, by literary and cultural criticism, by institutions, by media, by reputations. The problem is that they tend to confer stable meanings upon texts by fixing the ways they are read—everyone who has been taught literature will have come across this tendency to fence it in. The difficulty is that while the ability to read poetry is not 'natural' but learned, any given set of procedures, when it hardens into a model, starts to become an impediment to being open to work which is doing something

---

[11] *Chistes*, 133.

new.[12] One has to learn new ways of reading, then, from the poems themselves. This is as true of the past as it is of the present; poems which are not new in the chronological sense also require awareness of their capability to change and mean new things. Gonzalo Rojas's work, as I argue in Chapter 3, runs deeply against any idea that what was written has thereby become fixed. In fact the better the work the less this is the case; readers are invited to try this test on the poems discussed in this book.

The difficulty with models is that one needs them for guidance but they soon become impediments. One way to avoid getting trapped inside them is to check the models against the poems themselves. In what ways does the poem exceed the model or make holes in it? Does it even go so far as to demolish it? In addition, let the poems be arranged in particular relationships, such that these relationships embody the ideas put forward for the study of poetry. In this way study will extend into what the twentieth-century Greek poet George Seferis takes tradition to mean: 'In any human problem it is difficult to distinguish between the living and the dead; there are few who succeed in doing it. The paths of life and death are complex and dark, that is why we need all our attention. This is the problem of tradition.'[13]

Just as any notion of poetry as a public action includes the proposal of particular ways of reading, models of reading have to do with the place of the arts in society, which includes the cultural and educational policies adopted by political parties and governments. Currently fashionable in universities are notions of poetry as discourse, say in the idea that it should be analysed as a gendered use of language. But when it comes to reading work that is formally and linguistically innovative, the training tends to be lacking. The tendency is to put one's confidence in an interpretative system rather than to be guided by the poems. At the same time, in the media and schools, there has been a regression in the common notion of what a poem is: poetry is assumed to be rhymed autobiographical sentiment—

---

[12] See D. H. Lawrence, 'Chaos in Poetry', in *Selected Literary Criticism* (London, 1956).

[13] I am grateful to Professor Roderick Beaton of King's College London for advice on this translation.

which is not only to make it a reproduction of something already known, but to submit to the dubious assumption that biography has a privileged hold on the truth. The end result of these factors is a vacuum or blankness where poetry as a serious art is concerned. The need for conceiving the Word and the book in new ways drives the work of the poets included in this book, particularly Parra, Eielson, and Zurita. Readers may find it useful, for comparison, to look at the work of British or American poets with a similar concern, for example *Pearl*, by the contemporary northern English poet Barry MacSweeney, or *Pieces* by Robert Creeley, a senior American poet.[14]

To speak of models of reading is in the end an abstraction. What one is talking about are the ways a person's attention is engaged with the total environment. The act of reading is a particular training and focusing of that attention. That is why, although it is 'coded', that is, subject to repeatable procedures, reading can nevertheless be an entry into the outside—call it cosmos, chaos, ecstatic experience, or the not-known. Otherwise, in the end, poetry is not worth the effort. That, certainly, is what in different ways all the poets presented in this book suggest.

Ways of reading are not solely transmitted in the manners outlined above. They also adhere to texts, in the sense that once a particular reading of a book has been established by critics, media, and institutions it becomes a kind of coating around the words. Some cases are more blatant than others. In literature in English one could take Hemingway, say, as an example of how it happens. The writing is identified as 'misogynist' and the aura of misogyny sticks: a self-reinforcing selective reading encouraged by fashion. As a result, it becomes difficult to get to what that way of reading excludes, which is plenty. The name=the style=the reading. So the problem for a reader becomes how to cut through a layer of restrictive recognitions. Borges's extreme and anarchic remedy is to read all books as if they were by a single author—so much for biography!

It is also a problem for a writer. For example, once Parra was known as an 'antipoet', he became concerned with demolishing

---

[14] First published by Equipage in 1995, *Pearl* is included in *The Book of Demons* (Newcastle, 1997). *Pieces* is included in *The Collected Poems of Robert Creeley* (Berkeley, 1982).

the restrictive expectations that the term had come to imply, especially in the book *Artefactos* (1973), as argued below in Chapter 1. And much of Gonzalo Rojas's poetry attacks the restrictive force of recognition, in all senses of that word. Neruda also, when rejecting his earlier avant-garde style, was grappling with the problem of how a particular way of reading comes to adhere to a writer's name. In actual fact, rejection is not an accurate term for describing what he did in relation to the earlier books of *Residencia en la tierra* when he came to write *España en el corazón*. Take the image of bleeding oxen in the following two passages:

> De cada uno de estos días negros como viejos hierros,
> y abiertos por el sol como grandes bueyes rojos,
> y apenas sostenidos por el aire y por los sueños[15]
>
> De noche sueños negros
> abiertos por obuses, como sangrientos bueyes[16]

> [Of each one of these black days like old pieces of iron,
> and opened by the sun like great red oxen,
> and scarcely held up by the air and by dreams
>
> At night black dreams
> opened by howitzers, like bloody oxen]

In the first passage, the location of the oxen is uncertain: the medium in which they float is 'aire' [air] and 'sueños' [dreams], and thus is composed of inner reverie as well as of an external element. In the second, time and place are immediately and publicly recognizable, not just because this section of the poem is entitled 'Madrid 1937' but also because bombardment by artillery is referred to. Instead of simply avoiding his earlier style, Neruda actively recycles it in order to give it a different reading. 'Sueños' can be taken as an index of the change: 'negros', 'abiertos', 'bueyes', and 'sueños' all repeat but are now part of a narrative of the bombardment of Madrid by Franco, told in epic tone. As a result 'sueños', which before evoked a state of reverie, becomes, metaphorically, the nightmares of bombardment by artillery. A different, less subjective, model of reading is advanced, one of Neruda's intentions being to neutralize the avant-garde use of language, as he also does in

---

[15] 'Sistema sombrío', *Residencia en la tierra* (Buenos Aires, 1966), 41.
[16] 'Madrid 1937', *Tercera residencia*, 71.

the repeated statement about blood in the streets, quoted above.

The work of the Peruvian poet César Vallejo, also a key figure of the Latin American avant-gardes, can be used to locate and sharpen the issues under discussion here. In a book of essays which he began to write after his visits to the Soviet Union in 1928 and 1929, Vallejo struggles with the difficulties arising from the idea of a socialist art: on the one hand the political and ethical necessity for socialism, and on the other the problem of belief, of art having a system of beliefs imposed upon it[17]— hence the statement 'un artista puede ser revolucionario en política y no serlo [. . .] en el arte' [an artist can be a revolutionary in politics and not be one in art],[18] to which he adds that the reverse is also true. His insistence throughout the book is that to talk about socialist poetry means poetry that is written from 'una sensibilidad orgánica y tácitamente socialista' [a tacitly and organically socialist sensibility]. Thus,

en el poeta socialista, el poema no es, pues, un trance espectacular, provocado a voluntad y al servicio preconcebido de un credo o propaganda política, sino que es una función natural y simplemente humana de la sensibilidad.[19]

[in the socialist poet, the poem is not, then, a spectacular state of mind, produced wilfully and in the preconceived service of a creed or of political propaganda, it is a natural and straightforwardly human function of his sensibility.]

Further definition is given when he proposes that the test should be 'la verdadera vida interior del poeta' [the actual inner life of the poet] and 'la sinceridad afectiva y personal' [personal and emotional sincerity], as opposed to 'un arte basado en fórmulas' [an art based on formulae].[20] He extends his argument into the question of whether a poem is modern or not, which for him is not a matter of including topical words and references. His examples are cinema, aeroplane, jazz band, motor, and radio, but it is not difficult to find others for the end of the century. What matters is 'la poesía nueva a base

[17] For a discussion of how an avant-garde poet rejects belief structures, see William Rowe, 'E. A. Westphalen: The Poet's Intelligence and the Social Imaginary', *Travesía: Journal of Latin American Cultural Studies*, 4/1 (1995), 81–97.

[18] César Vallejo, *El arte y la revolución* (Lima, 1973), 34.

[19] Ibid. 28–9.   [20] Ibid. 108–9.

de sensibilidad nueva' [new poetry on the basis of new sensibility]:

En la poesía verdaderamente nueva pueden faltar imágenes nuevas—función ésta de ingenio y no de genio—pero el creador goza o padece en tal poema, una vida en que las neuvas relaciones y ritmos de las cosas y los hombres se han hecho sangre, célula, algo, en fin, que ha sido incorporado vital y orgánicamente en la sensibilidad.[21]

[In genuinely new poetry, topical images, which are a function of cleverness and not of genius, may be missing—but the poet enjoys or suffers in that poem a life in which the new relations and rhythms of things and human beings have become blood, cell, something in other words which has been vitally and organically incorporated into the sensibility.]

For Vallejo, a notion of 'vida interior' [inner life] is vital.[22] The metaphor *Sangre* belongs to common speech, while 'célula' and 'orgánicamente' are more complex terms which seek to define the notion at the level of the micro-structure of the body and of its processes of growth respectively. Clearly, though, the definitions are insufficient for the difficulty of the problem. One needs to go to Vallejo's own poetry for a fuller sense of his response: the poem *is* the place of inner life, it is its fullest expression. Consider some examples of the poems Vallejo was writing between the early 1930s (after his trips to Soviet Russia) and his death during the Spanish Civil War. Poems like 'Salutación angélica' [Angelic salutation], 'Parado en una piedra' [Stopped on a stone], and 'Solía escribir con su dedo grande en el aire' [He used to write with his thumb in the air] place what it means to be an individual human being, whose life and death are unsubstitutable and whose circumstances are unique, in the greatest possible tension with the necessity of mass struggles and collective identities. These poems have conventionally been read by critics as Marxist epics and/or as fulfilments of Christian love, where the individual and the collective are fused in heroic and/or sacrificial symbols.[23]

[21] Vallejo, *El arte y la revolución*, 101.

[22] See especially his essay 'El caso Maiakovski', which is included in *El arte y la revolución*.

[23] Jean Franco (*César Vallejo: The Dialectics of Poetry and Silence* (London, 1976)) and James Higgins (*Visión del hombre y de la vida en las últimas obras poéticas de César Vallejo* (Mexico City, 1970)) may be taken as examples: see César Vallejo, *Obras completas*, ed. R. González Vigil (Lima, 1991), 506–7.

Nevertheless, there is a problem about reading them in that way, which has to do precisely with the formation and functioning of symbols. In those three poems, and others similar to them, there are, alongside the powerful historical symbols of the Soviet Union, the unemployed in Europe, and the Republican combatant in the Spanish Civil War, certain things that resist becoming symbol: things that cannot be made permanent or resurrected. That is to say, there is a gap between things and symbols which occurs, precisely, where inner life and environment meet, and at a micro-level. Consider the difference between Vallejo's account of a dead Republican combatant:

> Y esta cuchara anduvo en su chaqueta,
> despierto o bien cuando dormía, siempre,
> cuchara muerta viva, ella y sus símbolos.[24]

> [And this spoon went in his jacket,
> awake or when he slept, always,
> alive dead spoon, it and its symbols.]

and Neruda's portrayal of the defence of Stalingrad:

> porque otras manos rojas, cuando las vuestras caigan,
> sembrarán por el mundo los huesos de tus héroes
> para que tu semilla llene toda la tierra.[25]

> [because other red hands, when yours fall,
> will sow throughout the world the bones of your heroes
> so that your seed may fill the whole earth.]

In Vallejo's poem a fissure is perceptible between the spoon as everyday object and spoon as symbol. In Neruda's lines, everyday life has disappeared and there is only the absolute continuity of a narrative and the complete spatial identity of symbol and human being. What one can do with each poem is therefore different. Neruda's incites to belief in a guaranteed permanence. Vallejo's can be used to probe all the ways in which the necessity to be part of a larger humanity may not fit one to one with the actual living of a life. His concern with the gap between symbols and what does not become symbol prevents an unquestioning acceptance of the symbols in which the social imagination is moulded.

---

[24] 'Solía escribir con el dedo grande en el aire', in *España, aparta de mí este cáliz*.
[25] 'Canto a Stalingrado', in *Tercera residencia*, 82.

The issue is crucial: if literature is still significant in society then it will have something to say about the realm of the symbolic. The usual approach, for example in criticism concerned with popular culture or gender, is to take this to be a question of whether a text proposes alternative symbols to the dominant ones, which is an argument about ideology. What matters, however, is the capacity of writing to intervene at the level of the formation of symbols, because where (or when) symbols are formed is the location of the poetic imagination's power. The work of Raúl Zurita, for example, may be taken as a very deliberate entry into this zone. Juan L. Ortiz, in a poem that responds to the song of a lark, writes of the uncertainty of that place where melodies—and, by extension, forms—come into being:

> Nada asegura que la melodía
> pasó a 'ser', allá, allá, donde las perlas se disolverían,
>   y de donde, a la vez,
> se desprenderían las perlas . . .[26]

> [Nothing can give certainty that the melody
> came to be there, where pearls disintegrate and where pearls
> also are formed]

The difficulty, however, in speaking of the place of symbol-formation is that one does not simply get there by having the right ideas, or theory, or even through procedures of analysis, however fine the distinctions made. It is the work of active imagination.

THE CRITICISM OF LANGUAGE

The questions under discussion involve two very large areas, history and form: history in the sense of a processing of experience, through particular operations of language, into a shared narrative; and form in the sense of poetic form, which is a specialized use of words that takes language to its limits of expression. The two uses of language may not coincide, especially in

---

[26] 'Canta la calandria . . .', *Obra completa* (Santa Fe, 1996), 816. My translation of this and other poems by Ortiz was published in *Poetry Review*, 67/1–2 (1977) 13–16.

their handling of the relationship between words and time. The poetry of the Latin American avant-garde, dating approximately from 1918 to 1940, has a particular concern with dismantling symbolism in poetic language. This occurs in three main ways: the sense that things in time never stop changing and do not fit with the stability produced by words;[27] the notion that only in a fixed and stable universe can one thing stand for another and thus that the mechanism of symbolism (which makes one thing stand for several) is dubious;[28] and the understanding, therefore, that social symbols cannot be used uncritically. The breakdown of confidence in symbols, which have a main role in constituting shared continuities, is specifically a province of the avant-garde, but it gathers together and brings to consciousness fissures that were occurring in the language as a whole, from 1918 onwards. The title poem of Vallejo's *Heraldos negros* (1918) with its repeated phrase 'Yo no sé' [I don't know], could be taken as a marker. With these words, the not-known starts to take the place of Rubén Darío's confidence in the harmony between inner life and the universe as a whole, a harmony which is formed through symbols. Darío (1867–1917), more than any other poet in Latin America, created a language for the expression of inner life, which he called 'el reino interior' [the inner realm]. The *vanguardista* poets, among them Huidobro, Vallejo, Neruda, and Girondo, undertook to dismantle that harmony,[29] in a thoroughgoing criticism of language. In the first poem of his book *Espantapájaros* [Scarecrows] (1932), Girondo builds the head and the belly of a typographical scarecrow out of the phrases 'Yo no sé nada' [I know nothing] and 'Creo que no creo' [I believe I don't believe], respectively.

The avant-garde criticism of language is the methodological basis of the present book, both in the sense that it offers a way to read poetry, and also because the experiments and discoveries of the avant-garde constitute a continuing challenge to poetics at the end of century, as Rothenberg and Joris make clear in

---

[27] This effect recurs throughout Vallejo's *Trilce* and Neruda's *Residencia en la tierra*, books I and II. *Trilce* II and 'Galope muerte' may be taken as specific examples, respectively.

[28] One of the best single examples would be Vallejo's *Trilce* LV.

[29] See the following in *Trilce* XXXVI: 'Rehusad, y vosotros, a posar las plantas | en la seguridad dupla de la Armonía. Rehusad la simetría a buen seguro.'

their exemplary anthology *Poems for the Millennium*.[30] In one of the best twentieth-century books on the subject, the *ABC of Reading*, Ezra Pound, a pioneer of Modernism in poetry, takes the break with the Middle Ages through the emergence of scientific method in the work of Francis Bacon and others as a key basis of the modern. Science is also his foundation where method is concerned: he proposes the experimental attitude as the way in which readers can find out for themselves. By testing the 'specimens' (i.e. the poems themselves), a reader can start from the particular 'evidence', and make comparisons, as opposed to having to start from abstractions which are themselves extrapolations from the evidence: 'an abstract or general statement is GOOD if it be ultimately found to correspond with the facts.' All of which is a matter of training oneself—in other words, of finding out what is good or bad.[31]

The emphasis on experiment is already there in Blake, who wrote at the beginning of industrial society, 'As the true method of knowledge is experiment, the true faculty of knowing must be the faculty which experiences.'[32] He then places alongside that assertion others which may appear somewhat incompatible: 'the Poetic Genius is the true Man [. . .] As none by travelling over known lands can find out the unknown, So, from already acquired knowledge, Man could not acquire more; therefore an universal Poetic Genius exists.'[33] How could experience include poetic imagination? That is the nub of it. The common sense of industrial societies, moulded by a narrow interpretation of scientific truth, regards imagination as something that comes after experience and elaborates upon it, and thus the reading of poetry tends to start from that assumption. In that case poetry takes its place simply as another form of discourse and representation—which is precisely what happens

[30] See Jerome Rothenberg and Pierre Joris, introduction, *Poems for the Millennium*, vol. i (Berkeley, 1995). See also Rothenberg's 'Pre-face' to his anthology of US avant-garde poetry (*Revolution of the Word: A New Gathering of American Avant Garde Poetry 1914–1945* (New York, 1974)).

[31] This rapid summary of Pound's method draws particularly on ch. 1 of *ABC of Reading* (London, 1961), esp. 17, 25, and 31.

[32] 'All Religions are One', in *Poems and Prophecies* (London, 1972), 5.

[33] Blake's claims are carefully worked out: 'If it were not for the Poetic or Prophetic Character, the Philosophic & Experimental would soon be at the ratio of all things & stand still, unable to do other than repeat the same dull round over again.' Ibid. 3.

in the types of criticism that predominate nowadays and that leave readers without adequate ways of reading poetry.

Jorge Eduardo Eielson, the subject of Chapter 3 of this book, adopts Blake's stance and finds an equal power of discovery in poetic imagination and in quantum physics. Such confidence in poetry is out of fashion nowadays. Nevertheless, it has been a common tenet of Modernist poetics, from William Carlos Williams to Haroldo de Campos to Gonzalo Rojas. Williams states the frontier condition when he says that a poem does not exist to express what has already been thought: 'The poet thinks with his poem, in that lies his thought, and that in itself is the profundity.'[34] The Argentinian poet Hugo Gola takes up some of the implications of such a radical stance when he states that thinking can interfere with the making of a poem:

El pensar implica una especie de imposición, de elección, de ordenamiento, que restringe la inmersión, la condiciona, la filtra, en fin, la vuelve incolora e insípida. Y es precisamente en el color y en el sabor que esa realidad tiene, donde reside la posibilidad de una experiencia que modifique la percepción de lo real y trastorne, en consecuencia, el funcionamiento normal de todos los mecanismos humanos.[35]

[Thinking implies a type of imposition, or choice, or ordering, that restricts one's immersion, conditions it, filters it, and ultimately makes it colourless and insipid. And it's precisely the colour and flavour of that reality which gives the possibility of an experience that might modify one's perception of the real and as a consequence change radically the normal functioning of all human mechanisms.]

This is not a call for there to be no ideas in the poem but for trust in what it does as poetry. Williams's answer to critics of his own work is useful as a corrective to those who would like to make poetry into a type of intellectual capital: 'the thinker tries to capture the poem for his purpose, using his "thought" as the net to put his thoughts into. Absurd. They are not profound enough to discover that by this they commit a philosophic solecism. They have jumped the track, slipped out of category.'[36] In one of the key books of twentieth-century philosophy, Deleuze and Guattari argue very carefully that art is as valid a mode of thinking as science or philosophy but that its 'route' is 'specific'

---

[34] *The Autobiography of William Carlos Williams* (New York, 1967), 390–1.
[35] Hugo Gola, 'Experiencia y lenguaje', *Nombres*, 3 (1993), 163.
[36] *The Autobiography of William Carlos Williams*, 391.

and that to look for a synthesis with the others is to diminish it.[37] The act of writing, Gola proposes, 'no intenta registrar un pensamiento previo al poema, sentido antes de que el poema sea escrito, sino que el pensamiento como la palabra se desplazan tanteando en la oscuridad. Movimientos en los cuales el poema adquiere una forma' [does not attempt to register a thought that is previous to the poem, felt before the poem is written, on the contrary, thought, just as much as the word, moves gropingly in the darkness. Movements in which the poem acquires a form].[38]

The terms in play, then, are thinking, 'darkness', and poetic form. Darkness is a name for the not-known, a better expression than the 'unknown', which can drag with it a whole train of ready-made Romantic imagery which becomes a substitute for what is needed. The not-known is precisely that and requires an active openness. As the American poet H.D. writes in her mid-twentieth-century book *Trilogy*, 'We know no rule | of procedure, | We are voyagers, discoverers | of the not-known, | the unrecorded; | we have no map.'[39] To speak of a necessary relationship between the poem and what is not known is to locate the writing—and reading—of poetry in some other place than those mapped by the analysis of ideology or of discourse. As always, the method of analysis creates its object, in these cases not an appropriate one. What poems can do is prior, that is, makes its own ground. A reading of Vallejo's *Poemas humanos* [Human poems] can show what that means in practice. Their probing of scientific, philosophical, and political languages amounts to a thoroughgoing critique of the whole Western archive.[40] These are poems which require a future to fulfil them, not a past to explain them. Apart from Paul Celan, is there any European poet who has taken this critique as far as Vallejo? That is not a rhetorical question but a challenge issued to Eurocentric literary criticism.

If we are talking about poetry as a capability for that degree of transformation, as opposed to an ordinary or conformist experience, then the language it works with will not be some

---

[37] G. Deleuze and F. Guattari, *What is Philosophy* (London, 1994), 198–9. See the whole of ch. 7. [38] Gola, 'Experiencia', 165.

[39] H.D., *Trilogy* (London, 1973), 59.

[40] See Introduction, César Vallejo, *Poemas escogidos*, ed. Julio Ortega (Caracas, 1991).

specialized jargon, preserving its meaning by sealing itself off from the unending flow of speech. There was no lack of that in the late Victorian and early Edwardian period and it is still some people's paradigm for what poetry is. An apparently opposite model predominates nowadays: that poetry should be 'conversational'. But this is no more radical than the other, which it reacts against, and in so doing preserves. Both need ditching. 'Conversational' means obey or ironize the moulding force of the ordinary, rather than attempt something more risky and far-reaching. Parra's poetry, for example, uses conversation not to replicate its dynamics but to criticize them, in a radical probing of the language. That is why 'conversational' is such an inadequate term for the poets who figure in this book, all of whom use the spoken Spanish of Latin America, not in some standardized form but from within its regional particularities of intonation and vocabulary.

Recognition of the independence of Latin American Spanish from that of Spain began with Rubén Darío, and was taken further by the poets of the avant-garde. Among the latter, Oliverio Girondo wrote in the key *Martín Fierro* Manifesto of 1924, ' "MARTÍN FIERRO", tiene fe en nuestra fonética, en nuestra visión, en nuestros modales, en muestro oído, en nuestra capacidad digestiva y de alimentación,' ['MARTÍN FIERRO' has faith in our phonetics, in our vision, in our manners, in our ear, in our digestion, and our food].[41] To place intonation and sound-structures alongside the whole range of sensibilities exercised in living indicates the total environment in which a poem breathes—if it is not to be cut off by some exercise of preciosity, social, academic, political, or religious. The poets of the 1950s and later, studied in this book, have taken up that challenge and developed it in varying ways. They mark a new stage in Latin American poetry, though as yet there is little recognition in scholarly publications of the range of new poetries and poetics.

The avant-garde was, as Eduardo Milán has pointed out, a hard act to follow.[42] In the poets who began to write in the 1950s, there is a concern with new starting-points. Parra's poem

---

[41] Nelson Osorio (ed.), *Manifestos, proclamas y polémicas de la vanguardia literaria latinoamericana* (Caracas, 1988), 135.

[42] Eduardo Milán, *Una cierta mirada* (Mexico City, 1989), 14.

as amoeba, Cardenal's use of collage, and Rojas's rejection of recognition structures are all crucial bases for a new poetics. Each chapter of this book seeks to explore the key lines of discovery in the work of a given poet and thus each is also introductory and designed to stand alone. And in relation to that principle, I have sought to follow another: there is no subordination of the work of each poet to a total interpretative scheme. To let the poems themselves say what they require of a reader is to respect each poet's work, not just as a guide to reading but as an opening of the field of poetry, unbounded by heritage or preconception. And if the not-known is inherent to a poetic action, then the limits of comprehension are also part of the process:

La relación con un poema es casi siempre incierta aunque nos deslumbre. Podemos aun ser deslumbrados sin que comprendamos lo que el poema significa. Y en el caso de que creamos comprender ¿qué es lo que comprendemos? Puede ser que comprendamos la luminosidad que encierra algo oscuro, pero esto no es comprender en el sentido corriente del término. En realidad lo que hacemos es *compartir*, experimentar nosotros también algo de lo que el poema encierra como misterio. Algún tipo de encantamiento, alguna iluminación, frente a la cual no hay explicación sino más bien silencio y temblor.[43]

[One's relationship with a poem is almost always uncertain even though it dazzles us. We can be dazzled without understanding what the poem means. And when we believe we understand, what is it we understand? It may be that we understand the luminosity that encloses something dark, but that is not understanding in the usual sense of the term. What we are doing in fact is to *share*, to sense ourselves something of what the poem encloses, its mystery. Some type of enchantment, some illumination, in the face of which there is no explanation just silence and trembling.]

Nevertheless, it may be useful, to conclude this Introduction, to say more about the similarities between the poets, in particular those which the terms history and inner life are intended to point to. Readers may prefer to skip this part of the Introduction altogether or else come back to it after having read one or two chapters. What follows, please note, is a delineation, not a discussion of issues, which is offered in the individual chapters, on the basis of analysis of the poems.

[43] Gola, 'Experiencia', 65–6.

INNER LIFE

Let us consider, in the first place, how all eight poets use the poem as a means of thinking. Gonzalo Rojas speaks of writing as 'navegación y número, carácter | y número, red en el abismo de las cosas | y número' [navigation and number, character | and number, net in the abyss of things | and number],[44] which is to delineate a risk: no ideas to hold on to, only the fact of letters and syllables—to trust that when entering 'the abyss' (i.e. the unknown). This is a very different action from the accumulation of information which the knowledge industry promotes, and which government, universities, and media tend to define as knowledge in the humanities, a principal cause of the diminution of poetry in recent years. The meanings of 'número' open out into the notion of measure: awareness of pattern and form in all senses. In his essay 'A sense of measure' (1964), Robert Creeley takes measure as basis of the ways in which a poem can make discoveries for writer and reader:

I am wary of any didactic programme for the arts and yet I cannot ignore the fact that poetry, in my own terms of experience, obtains to an unequivocal order. What I deny, then, is any assumption that that order can be either acknowledged or gained by intellectual assertion, or will, or some like intention to shape language to a purpose which the literal act of writing does not itself discover.[45]

The literal—in every sense—action of writing is what Rojas calls navigation: the power to move through time-space with some degree of accuracy. This is, then, a question or assertion of power, the power of the poem and not the poem as an agency of a power located somewhere else.[46]

Measure, which involves, in Creeley's words, 'much more than an academic sense of metric',[47] can be taken as all the ways

---

[44] *Oscuro* (Caracas, 1977), 13.

[45] *A Sense of Measure* (London, 1970), 31.

[46] See John Keats, Letter 32 (22 Dec. 1817): 'it struck me what quality went to form a Man of Achievement especially in Literature [. . .] I mean *Negative Capability*, that is when man is capable of being in uncertainties, Mysteries, doubts, without any irritable reaching after fact and reason.' See also Letter 31: 'I would call the top and head of those who have a proper self Men of Power.' *The Letters of John Keats*, ed. M. B. Forman (London, 1960), 71, 66.

[47] *A Sense of Measure*, 33.

in which a poem performs an action of discovery. In the work of Ernesto Cardenal, a poet for whom the sound of things and of words requires careful listening, the ear is central to any process of finding out. 'Oye el susurro de las cosas' [listen to the whisper of things][48] is a demand made upon reader and writer, and which requires silence. Silence is therefore inside the process as a necessity: something that arises within whatever initial frame was necessary in order to get started, and alters it. Hence the poems in which the writer is listening for sounds in the empty night of Gethsemany, Kentucky. If 'Dios [. . .] es [. . .] sin idea' [God is without idea] , the soul can only know God because the soul also exists without an idea of itself ('el ánima es sin idea de sí'). The notion of a place of unknowing within the soul or self has similarities with Christian mystical traditions, but it is placed, in Cardenal's work, within twentieth-century collage techniques. This permits a consistency to move across from inside to outside—'corazón adentro' [from the heart inwards] and 'corazón afuera' [from the heart outwards], as Enriqueta Terán calls them—and alter both.

   If uncertainty is an internal and external condition of expe-rience, it enters into reading, and, to be consistent, into criti-cism. Juan L. Ortiz's method of long, unfinished interrogations is exemplary in this respect. Often taking the form of extremely lengthy sentences, full of ellipses, they show how if entry into a field of uncertainties is to occur with any success, it requires an energy large enough to be sustained through a careful prepa-ration of the senses rather than short-circuited by conceptual programmes—frequently called 'theoretical frameworks'. Measure, at this level, becomes highly complex. Yet Ortiz's poems succeed in producing a trembling suspense which generates heightened attention.

   Eielson's work, for its part, suspends the frame or edge around the space of writing and in so doing opens it to an infi-nite outside, which includes the universe of twentieth-century quantum cosmology. The questions his verbal/visual poems raise have to do with the limits of poetry, and thus of literature as such. A line can be a line of sound, of visual space, of the shape of written characters, of clothes that wrap a body, of a

[48] *Cántico cósmico* (Madrid, 1992), 22.

subatomic particle that leaves a track, of the light of the stars, or of several of these at once.

For Rojas, knowledge intersects with the erotic, as when the name of a lover and 'la teoría del conocimiento' [the theory of knowledge] are taken to be the same thing. In the work of the two women poets included in this book, the relationship is more conflictive. Carmen Ollé, extricating her writing from a version of love which meant submission to an ideal, discovers 'lo desconocido' [the unknown] as crucial to the creative release achieved. The process includes uncovering a male Platonist inheritance which had invaded her writing and reading, and distancing herself from it. When Enriqueta Terán writes, 'En esta falta de conocimiento | arden el corazón y el pensamiento; arden los dos en este mismo fuego' [In this lack of knowledge | the heart and thought burn; both burn in this same fire],[49] the experience is of finding that what was thought to be known inwardly ('corazón adentro) is actually 'un no saber' [a not-knowing].

All relations of inside and outside, of inner and outer worlds, are embraced by Parra's poet or poem as amoeba, a conception which, as I elaborate in Chapter 1, is a convergence of his experiences as a poet and as a mathematical physicist. An amoeba does not have an inside, as in Darío's 'reino interior': it has no stable boundary between itself and the other. Parra's formulation is thus post-avant-garde, as is my use of the term inner life. In the poets of the Latin American avant-gardes, the self is multiple, broken up into changing images in the flow of time, in the rapidly changing scenes of urban life. Prime examples are Huidobro's *Poemas árticos*, Vallejo's *Trilce*, Neruda's *Residencia en la tierra* books I and II, Oliverio Girondo's *Espantapájaros*, Emilio Westphalen's *Las islas extrañas*.[50] These poets abandon any notion of single identity or ideal model of self. But, more than that, they abandon biography and confession as ways of giving legitimacy and thus power to a self. The speaker in Neruda's *Residencia I* and *II* is 'innecesario' [unnecessary], 'viéndome en los espejos' [seeing myself in mirrors], and is repulsed by 'un gusto a semanas, a biógrafos, a papeles'

---

[49]   *Casa de hablas* (Caracas, 1991), 95.
[50]   *Las ínsulas extrañas* was first published 1933 and included in *Otra imagen deleznable* (Mexico City, 1980).

[the taste of weeks, of biographers, of papers].[51] Girondo's poem '¡Azotadme!' [Whip me!] is a thoroughgoing anti-confession.[52]

The speaker in Parra's poems is not privileged: the word 'I' is not used as a value, and the characters in the poems are not exemplary but grotesque. The self-deprecating 'I' of much British poetry, normalized since the 1950s by poets like Philip Larkin, is the cause of some confusion: despite appearances, it is used to exalt the personality of the speaker. That makes for some particular difficulties when Parra is translated into English, since the place from which an 'I' speaks in Parra's poems is offered by the language and the culture, and Parra's gleeful satire is directed in the end to that platform and not to some idea of personality. When the speaker in one of his antipoems says, 'Era mi corazón ni más ni menos | Que el olvidado kiosko de una plaza' [My heart was no more or less | Than a forgotten kiosk in a town square],[53] the metaphor, far from giving a reassuring sense of inwardness, places inner feeling as an object in a specific environment (provincial town square), a thing seen from the outside—not any outside but one which makes for particular conditions of visibility (those of provincial life). Nevertheless, if Parra's antipoems did only that, they would not be exceptionally interesting. What is truly radical is his taking the idea of poem as container and turning it inside out: all enclosures of speaking, such as self, personality, confession, opinion, class, and knowledge, get blown apart. As a result, the antipoems are contained explosions. In some of his later work, such as *Artefactos*, he experiments with abandoning the container altogether and letting the poem turn into high-velocity fragments.

Parra's approach to actions of speaking from the outside of any notion of self-expression may be compared with Cardenal's notion of *exteriorismo*, the poetics of which have to do with building a poem out of precise, external details ('nombres propios y detalles precisos' [proper names and precise details]). One of his 'rules' for the poetry workshops set up in Nicaragua during and after the Sandinista Revolution is 'La poesía más que a base de ideas, debe ser a base de cosas que entran por los sentidos'

---

[51] 'Caballos de los sueños'.
[52] In *Persuasión de los diás, Obras*, i: *Poesía* (Buenos Aires, 1968).
[53] *Obra gruesa* (Santiago, 1969), 22.

[Rather than being based on ideas, poetry should be based on things that enter through the senses].[54] Participants in the workshops were encouraged to place their experiences of the war against Somoza alongside details of their personal lives: writing and reading poetry as a way of locating the self inside a larger space and time in a process of discovery. Examples of the workshop poems are given below, in the chapter on Cardenal.

An epic posits the individual and the collective as extensions of each other. The term individual can be taken in a purely operative sense, meaning component of a group. However, in the various traditions that make up the notion of modernity, the individual becomes a value, for example in the principle of individual rights. Socialist thought, in its critique of modernity, includes the proposition that the development of the individual is a condition for the development of society.[55] The difficulties of working that out have not been resolved, which is one reason why a modern epic is difficult to achieve. Cardenal's creation of an epic style has to do, among other things, with the fact that until the Revolution Nicaragua was an un-modernized country: traditional, rural forms of collectivity prevailed, and he uses their forms of verbal expression (the collective voice of the ballad, for example), but placing them alongside Modernist techniques. I outline below the tensions between the individual and history in Cardenal's poetry.

Raúl Zurita's work was produced in a very different situation. In the period following the Pinochet coup (1973), the terms of sociability in Chile broke down radically, yet the fissures in the language, the gaps that caused spoken idioms to be out of phase with the social power structures, had begun to appear before the coup. Zurita's poetry explores the breakdown of some of the basic terms of modernity, such as individual and nature. He exposes a vast chasm between the individual and the collective. At the same time, though, there is a completely opposite thrust in his work, particularly in his latest book (*La vida nueva*), as it moves into a remaking of collective spaces and representations.

---

54 *Barricada*, 10 Mar. 1980.
55 The idea is summarized at the end of ch. II of the *Communist Manifesto* ('an association, in which the free development of each is the condition for the free development of all') and discussed at more length , for example in the 'Chapter on Money', in Marx's *Grundrisse*.

In other poets or poems, the social may appear to be absent, but only as representations, not as the medium which one inhabits, as fish inhabit water. To say medium in this sense is to talk about environment, which includes technologies such as printed and electronic media which, as McLuhan has shown, extend the human body-mind. In the chapter on Gonzalo Rojas, I deliberately set up a confrontation between poems that may seem to be concerned only with inward realities, and a late twentieth-century environment in which electronic image dominates.

In Rojas's work, the individual does not emerge once and for all, whether from mother or childhood or historical past, but is constantly emerging or, to use Rojas's term, being born: 'vuelve a las entrañas I de millares de madres sucesivas' [returning to the bowels I of thousands after thousands of mothers].[56] And so what one is born into—childhood, adulthood, modernity, post-modernity—is not a finality but a condition of emergence. What does not change is the fact of emergence. Inner life, stripped of enclosure in the mother and of all subsequent enclosure, becomes part of the cosmos: human beings as 'Solos I con I la I velocidad I de la tierra' [alone I with I the I speed I of the Earth],[57] where *con* is a complex word, since it brings together, in constantly changing relationship, the speed of things as internal and external.

In Juan L. Ortiz, inner life is a listening, touching, and seeing which continually becomes more subtly refined as it enters Dionysian areas of experience. A relationship with an environment—in Ortiz's case a very particular provincial landscape—becomes ecstatic. World and self dissolve and are remade, and this happens without the support of symbolism, mythology, or religion. A comparison might be made, precisely there, with the work of Jorge Eduardo Eielson, who writes in a book whose title, *Noche oscura del cuerpo* [Dark night of the body], is a reversal of San Juan de la Cruz's night of the soul: 'No tengo límites I Mi piel es una puerta abierta I Y mi cerebro una casa vacía I La punta de mis dedos toca fácilmente I El firmamento y el piso de madera' [I have no limits I My skin is an open door I And my brain an empty house I The tips of my fingers easily touch I The

---

[56] Rojas, *Oscuro*, 59.   [57] Ibid. 44.

firmament and the wooden floor].[58] In Eielson's poems, the relation with environment, which is above all visual-tactile, does not take the form of self over against world, but of frontiers that dissolve and rematerialize, in unforeseen ways.

Inner and outer life become increasingly integrated in Enriqueta Terán's poetry, as one comes to her later books. But it is not a smooth process, not simply the application of an idea, or what Creeley calls 'intellectual assertion'. It requires reworking the sensual materials—among them language—that constitute self, society, and landscape, together with the fact that these materials are different for a woman, particularly in provincial Latin America. For Carmen Ollé, the inner is the repressed, and the breaking of moulds includes, particularly, the imposed definitions of the female in the Peruvian middle classes; the process is erotic and painful at the same time. In her later work, her sense of the forces brought into play by a woman who writes expands into the need to recuperate an inner life not only against invading noise, but against symbolism because it carries previous and now damaging moulds. The need is to make a place between noise and symbol, in other words, between the unformed and a tradition that imprisons.

What, finally, are the relationships between inner life and history in these poets' work? There is the problem of epic voice, already mentioned in connection with Cardenal. More widely, history, as a supposedly shared narrative, tends to offer itself as a kind of guaranteed continuity for the mortal self. Gonzalo Rojas is deeply against that use of the past as a type of salvation, and compares it with religion: 'Me hablan de Dios o me hablan de Historia. Me río | de ir a buscar tan lejos la explicación del hambre | que me devora' [People talk about God they talk about History. I laugh | at anyone who goes that far to find the explanation of the hunger | that devours me].[59] In Rojas's work, writing itself, in so far as it is an exercise of the necessity he calls *hambre*, is corrosive of any attempt to make history into transcendence.

Octavio Paz repeatedly asserted that poetry should not be taken as symmetrical with history, as 'the word of history or

---

[58] *Poesía escrita* (Bogotá, 1998), 228.
[59] Rojas, *Oscuro*, 156.

antihistory'.[60] But the difficulty with Paz's position is his tendency to make poetry itself into a type of transcending discourse, an attitude which runs through the work of those critics, like Guillermo Sucre, who have affinities with him.[61] Instead of the poet's political commitment becoming an alibi which takes the place of the poem itself (a problem mentioned earlier), Paz's followers have tended to carry out their own act of substitution. In their models of reading, the capacity of a poem to change the life of its readers is made into an intellectual construct, and thus a matter of will, or a religious statement, which entails accepting an apparatus of beliefs. At its most damaging, this attitude leads to poets becoming indebted to an institution—in Mexico, the State—for the achievement of prestige. Rojas, who calls himself an 'anarca'—anarch is the somewhat archaic English equivalent—rejects any guarantees of meaning in poetry, and they include social prestige, publishing success, literary prizes, literary criticism, and other forms of immortality.

Part of the issue is ownership over time. For Rojas, writing and reading take one to what he calls time inside the backbone, which cannot be turned into possession, meaning, or justification. If the decision is taken to immerse oneself in that time, then history is no one's property. It becomes instead the material traces left by human beings, made readable by an act of interpretation. Cardenal displays one such act of reading in the opening part of his long poem *Oráculo sobre Managua*, where the traces, which include palaeolithic footprints and Maya ceramics, are embedded in the various layers of soil and rock beside Lake Managua. On the top surface, children play in the sewage. The different surfaces or historical times can be read simultaneously in so far as the earlier ones become exposed by earthquake or human action. It is a method for finding out and as such has nothing to do with simply superimposing the present on to the past, a procedure which Parra satirizes in his poem 'Soliloquio del individuo' [The individual's soliloquy]. As

[60] Quoted by Mike Gonzalez and David Treece in *The Gathering of Voices: The Twentieth-Century Poetry of Latin America* (London, 1992), p. xi. Their introduction and ch. 8 include a discussion of poetry and history in Latin America.

[61] Sucre's book, *La máscara, la transparencia* (Caracas, 1975), is one of the most important studies of modern Latin American poetry.

a way of reading the past in the present, Cardenal's juxtapositions become a means of locating oneself and of thus having the power to act and make a future, which in his work includes social revolution.

History in this sense is a task to be fulfilled in the future, since the traces have been lost, suppressed, buried, appropriated by the various victorious groups since the Conquest, and the past demands justice. That concern runs through the major historical poems of Huidobro, Vallejo, Neruda, Juan L. Ortiz, Cardenal, Zurita, and others, and one of its principal manifestations is the unburied dead. There is also a question of method here. In order to become readable, the marks and traces have to be gathered together in a particular space and placed in specific relationships. That is achieved for example by a museum. Museums were founded across Latin America at the end of the last century in order to construct traditions that could be identified as a national heritage. But the space that Cardenal uses to gather together the tracks of the past has nothing to do with a museum or other institutional space. It is an assemblage of what the official image of the nation has excluded, and that may be taken as emblematic of the experience of the majority population of all Latin American countries. A satisfactory history has yet to be written. Its materials exist in memories which are not written or written in the wrong places, memories which are often precarious and scattered and at risk of being erased for good.

In Ana Enriqueta Terán's poems, attention is given to those materials (gestures, words, things touched, seen) which are prior to any writing of history: the traces and surfaces that become memory. These are selected according to place, time, and social relationships including gender, but also those inner necessities that are more obscure or mysterious. She calls her assembled materials scraps (*retazos*). The result is not a smooth surface or idealized story—as in the heritage industry—but a composition of fragments, particular to a locality and an experience, and thus unsubstitutable. What she does could be called post-history rather than history: she works with the humus that historiographers turn into narratives.

If the unburied, unmourned dead still haunt the present, that is because they have no place to go, in so far as their lives have not become a future but have been erased from record.

Neruda's *Alturas de Macchu Picchu* and Rulfo's *Pedro Páramo* are among the works that arise out of the necessity to mourn, bury, and restore the dead into lived time. Zurita's work too dramatizes that necessity in various ways. In one of his books, the whole American continent becomes a map of the disappeared, not only those who were executed and had their traces expunged in the Pinochet era, but those who throughout the Americas were removed from the record. As he expresses it, 'fuera de nuestros desaparecidos modernos, toda esta historia es de desaparecidos, de tipos que no han sido enterrados, de pueblos, de culturas que no han tenido ese derecho. Todos ellos penan permanentemente en el eje de la lengua' [apart from our modern disappeared, all this history is a history of disappeared people, human beings who have not been buried, peoples, cultures that have not had that right. They all permanently haunt the language at its foundations].[62] Those wounds have not disappeared. They leave their mark in the language, the very material of poetry.

[62] Interview in Juan Andrés Piña, *Conversaciones con la poesía chilena* (Santiago, 1990), 230.

Nicanor Parra: The Poem as Amoeba

> The vast majority of utterances occur as
> selections from a field of possibilities made
> relevant by some prior utterance, and in their
> turn project a range of possible 'nexts'.
> (J. Atkinson and J. Heritage)

THE METHOD OF ANTIPOETRY

The poetry of Nicanor Parra is a good deal more ambitious than most criticism suggests. Edith Grossman's statement, that Parra 'believes that only the ordinary spoken language, bare of poetic overtones and anachronisms, can communicate clearly and deeply enough',[1] may be taken as typical of the predominant response to *Poemas y antipoemas* [Poems and antipoems] in the forty years since it was first published. A sense of Parra's poetics as crucial to Latin American poetry of the later twentieth century requires both listening more radically to what he does to 'the ordinary spoken language' and entering into the ways of reading suggested in his propositions of poetry as an unboundaried action. Mathematics, cosmology, and the social analysis of language converge in this action, and it is the aim of this chapter to trace this multidimensionality, starting for the sake of clarity with its main component, which is language.

Poemas y antipoemas, Parra's first important book, assembles a major set of new procedures for Latin American poetry in the mid-twentieth century. It begins with a display of different verbal styles and rhetorical forms. The effect is parodic and the materials include neoclassical styles of pastoral and moral

---

[1] Edith Grossman, *The Antipoetry of Nicanor Parra* (New York, 1975), 92.

sententiousness, the lyrical language of *Modernismo*,[2] proverbs and clichés with an air of antiquity, and everyday colloquial statement. Social attitudes that correspond to these inherited languages are also displayed, for example the belief in the innocence of nature and children. The poems in the early part of the book offer a social diagnosis of different types of speaking and writing in terms of their prestige and function: a rapid inventory of some of the main forms of legitimacy in mid-century Chile. The first lines of 'Defensa del árbol' [In defence of the tree] exemplify many of these effects:

> Por qué te entregas a esa piedra
> Niño de ojos almendrados
> Con el impuro pensamiento
> De derramarla contra el árbol.
> Quien no hace nunca daño a nadie
> No se merece tan mal trato.
> Ya sea sauce pensativo
> Ya melancólico naranjo
> Debe ser siempre por el hombre
> Bien distinguido y respetado:
> Niño perverso que lo hiera
> Hiere a su padre y a su hermano.
> Yo no comprendo, francamente,
> Cómo es posible que un muchacho
> Tenga este gesto tan indigno
> Siendo tan rubio y delicado. (13)[3]

> [Why do you yield to that stone
> Almond-eyed child
> With the impure thought
> Of throwing it at the tree.
> Who has never hurt anyone
> Does not deserve such bad treatment.
> Whether pensive willow
> Or melancholy orange tree
> It should always be
> Properly distinguished and respected by man:
> Perverse child who would wound it
> Wounds his father and brother.
> I do not understand, frankly,

---

[2] *Modernismo* is used to refer to the Spanish American literary movement (approximately 1880–1910) associated with Rubén Darío.

[3] Textual references are to Nicanor Parra, *Obra gruesa* (Santiago, 1969).

How a boy can possibly do
Such an unworthy thing
Being so blonde and delicate.]

The general air of archaism, generated by inversions of word-order as well as by the vocabulary, is used to parody the notion that the archaic is worthy of respect. It also relates specifically to attempts in the nineteenth century to found an independent Latin American poetry on a neoclassical basis, as in Andrés Bello's pastoral poems. If the innocence of nature is undermined by its manipulative use for moralizing, the innocence of children—also a Romantic inheritance—collides with the speaker's unabashed adherence to the racial stereotype of the fair-haired (an elite minority in Chile) as pure. These attitudes may have been sedimented historically, but history is no excuse. Is the speaker perverse, for mixing delicacy and crudity so blatantly? Or is the language and rhetoric that can support and legitimize the values expressed perverse? Readers are given no direct help with these dilemmas and attempts to find interpretative security in some higher level such as tone or symbolism or reliable voice take away the particular pleasures of reading on offer. Which means, incidentally, that what were the predominant approaches of poetry criticism in the 1950s and 1960s, stylistics in the Spanish-speaking world and the New Criticism in the Anglo-Saxon, could not get very far with these poems.

The lack of any immanent guarantee of meaning, or of any original innocence, is part of a method whose prime strategy is to abandon any special language for poetry and assemble instead a variety of languages. What is offered is a diagnostic of the cultural functions of different languages and the possibility of moving among them without being possessed by any one of them. The assemblage makes it impossible to imagine a speaker (or poetic self) whose feelings are guaranteed authentic, though they may well be sincere, which is not the same thing. This is not a poetry without emotion, but one where feelings and their intensification are not the exclusive property of an admired self (offered for identification); in this sense it is a poetry without a personal voice. Which makes it difficult to read the poems as expressions of the poet's feelings, presumed to be significant because they are his. Although the idea and institution of the poet as an exceptional person expressing exceptional feelings (each guaranteeing the other) belongs historically to Romanticism, it still lingers on as a legitimization in the public reception of poetry, especially in classrooms.

Parra's poem 'Se canta al mar' [Singing to the sea] makes an ideal test case for these issues. It is a key poem in several ways: as an *ars poetica*, as an account of how the author became a poet, and as a negotiation of the inherited institution of poetry. It has the shape and atmosphere of an initiation. The father takes the son, still a young boy, to see the sea for the first time. The experience, which will mark the rest of his life and make him a poet, is like a revelation of something already obscurely known ('desde que existe el mundo, | La voz del mar en mi persona estaba' [since the world began, | The voice of the sea was inside me]; 23)—as in rites of initiation or in Cesare Pavese's account of how the personal symbols which touch us most deeply seem, when we discover them, to have been there already.[4] But there is a crucial sense in which a narrative exposition, like the one just offered, is a falsification, because in the poem itself there is no consistent voice that reserves itself the right to narrate, nor even a particular zone of the language marked out as a vehicle for narration. Interestingly, a similar questioning of the rights of single-voice narrative was occurring in the work of Latin American novelists in the 1950s (e.g. Juan Rulfo, Juan Carlos Onetti). Although Parra's poem retains an emotional aura of initiation, this is nevertheless placed inside a social and historical variability of language, at an extreme opposite for example to mythological language and its claims to authority. What is the need for such complication? Why not opt for a more simple method of presentation and just 'tell the story'? There are two reasons, one of them obvious and the other less so. Dead words, worn-out expressions, produce dead experiences: 'poesía es vida en palabras' [poetry is life in words], as Parra has said.[5] But also, to make the opposite possible requires the actuality of communicative action, and that involves the work of locating the speaker and the interlocutor.

'Se canta al mar' begins with several lines of archaic, non-

4 Cesare Pavese, 'Estado de gracia', in *El oficio de poeta* (Buenos Aires, 1970).

5 Mario Benedetti, 'Nicanor Parra, o el artefacto con laureles', in Alfonso Calderón (ed.), *Antología de la poesía chilena contemporánea* (Santiago, 1970).

spoken Spanish, marked by inverted word-order, and Romantic
types of expression such as 'aquella misteriosa lámpara':

> Nada podrá apartar de mi memoria
> La luz de aquella misteriosa lámpara,
> Ni el resultado que en mis ojos tuvo
> Ni la impresión que me dejó en el alma. (21)

> [Nothing can take from my memory
> The light of that mysterious lamp,
> Nor the effect it had on my eyes
> Nor the impression it left upon my soul.]

But there begin to intrude indications of a person anxious to
communicate his experience in a situation of actual speaking:

> Voy a explicarme aquí, si me permiten,
> Con el eco mejor de mi garganta. (21)

> [I am going to explain myself, with your permission,
> With the help of my throat's best echo.]

The act of listening, as well as the act of speaking, is brought
into the scene; instead of the authority of an archaic language
(for many people still a definition of poetry), the capacity to
convince in a conversation. The poem makes this transition
between languages several times, in both directions, in a kind
of alternation. A discourse includes instructions, albeit incomplete, on how it is to be received,[6] and to move rapidly between
two different types of communicative action is to invite a reader
to perceive the different rules for producing conviction in each
case. Not, however, as some dry exercise in critical superiority
but as a question of the aliveness of emotion in language, of the
ways it adheres to particular phrases but can be hijacked by
particular discourses. This is how Parra handles the moment of
first seeing the sea:

> Descendimos del tren entre banderas
> Y una solemne fiesta de campanas
> Cuando mi padre me cogió de un brazo
> Y volviendo los ojos a la blanca,
> Libre y eterna espuma que a lo lejos
> Hacia un país sin nombre navegaba,
> Como quien reza una oración me dijo

---

[6] See John Shotter, *Conversational Realities* (London, 1993), 2, 8, 89.

Con voz que tengo en el oído intacta:
'Este es, muchacho, el mar'. El mar sereno,
El mar que baña de cristal la patria. (22)

[We got down from the train amidst flags
And a solemn festival with bells ringing
When my father took my arm
And turning his eyes to the white,
Free, eternal foam travelling
away in the distance to a country without name,
Like someone praying said to me
In a voice still intact in my ear:
'This, son is the sea.' The serene sea,
the sea that bathes the fatherland in crystal waters.]

The first shift is from ordinary spoken Spanish to an archaic and literary register signalled obtrusively by no less than three adjectives placed before the noun 'espuma'. This figurative, anthropomorphic language is, depending on how you look at it, the result of strong feeling or a way of permitting it. But the shift that follows, to the father's actual (un-romantic) words, shows that the poem is not proposing to elicit feeling by using a time-worn Romantic tradition already out of phase with everyday life. The experience of seeing the sea is introduced as a gift of the father, but there is a curious distance between the father's words quoted in direct speech and the language that surrounds them. What the father turns to look at is a 'poetic' sea, product of an archaic written language, and his manner of speaking is described as like 'a prayer', another form of ritualized language. But the actual spoken words belong to a different register, that of ordinary 'unpoetic' speech. Thus the experience, despite its archetypal aura, occurs at an intersection between different languages. Rather than adhering to any one language, the aura adheres to an image. As Parra said of his work, 'es una poesía de raíces oníricas, y en el sueño lo que se hace fundamentalmente es ver' [it is a poetry with its roots in dream, and what one does fundamentally in a dream is see].[7]

The first parts of *Poemas y antipoemas* use the method of moving between literary and colloquial language, between 'poetry' and 'antipoetry'. But the terms are of course historical and not absolute. Poetry, in this particular case, means the pres-

---

[7] Leónidas Morales, *La poesía de Nicanor Parra* (Santiago, 1972), 219.

tigious inheritance of Romanticism and *Modernismo,* and antipoetry a practice of writing that takes ordinary speech as its material. By the final part of the book, Parra gives up this use of a double register and uses only materials that could occur in conversation. At the same time, the poems tend to become their own occasion, as dramatized speech actions, rather than memories or reproductions of other, previous occasions. Consequently, they are no longer concerned with nostalgic experiences.

But to call the poems 'conversational' would be an error if this is taken to mean that they produce maximum transparency.[8] What typically occurs in a conversation, as Harvey Sacks shows in his essay 'On Doing "Being Ordinary" ', is that the participants in order to be heard have to fashion what they say as something ordinary. If what you say falls outside the range of the ordinary, then it may be that you are 'venturing into making your life into an epic'—and the consequences might include losing your friends.[9] For the account of an experience to be received by the hearer as an experience—rather than, say, an occasion for showing off—the story has to sound ordinary. Or, as Sacks puts it, in order to have 'the experience you are entitled to [. . .] you have to form it up as the thing that ordinarily is, and then mesh your experience with that'.[10] The issue, therefore, is how conversations include the pressure to mould experiences so that they are ordinary, where ordinary means the whole range of legitimizations that make up a socially shared world. Or, to put it more directly, that conversation is a key place where what people think of as reality is shaped. The force operating here is a very powerful one, as Sacks notes: 'there is some immensely powerful kind of mechanism operating in handling your perceptions and thoughts, other than the known and immensely powerful things like chemistry of vision, and so on.'[11] What needs adding is that this mechanism is usually hidden by the trained belief that what is ordinary is natural.

---

[8] In this sense, Parra's poems call into question Grice's rules for conversational behaviour. See Paul Grice, *Logic and Conversation: William James Lectures,* reproduced in S*tudies in the Way of Words* (Cambridge, Mass., 1989).

[9] Harvey Sacks, 'On Doing "Being Ordinary" ', in J. Maxwell Atkinson and J. Heritage, *Structures of Social Action: Studies in Conversation Analysis* (Cambridge, 1984), 419.   [10] Ibid. 426–7.   [11] Ibid. 418.

Contrary to Grossman's assertion that Parra uses 'only the ordinary spoken language' as an instrument for communication, the poems are not modelled on conversation, they analyse it. And the analysis, the breaking into parts, involves confronting Sacks's 'immensely powerful [. . .] mechanism' and splitting it into its components. And this, to use Parra's analogy,[12] is like the action of splitting the atom and releasing very powerful forces. Parra's method is not to imitate conversation but to plunge into the forces that mould it. The possibilities of the method include the pleasure of risk and high speed. The freedom and pleasure gained help to make the work of analysis possible; it is no academic exercise.

Parra's investigation is simultaneously linguistic and cultural: the method of antipoetry is a poetics of cultural analysis. At one point, during a passage of colloquial language where the speaker is giving an account of himself as a boy ('No había escrito aún mi primer verso | Ni derramado mi primera lágrima' [I had not written my first line | Or shed my first tear]), he uses a metaphor, drawing attention to the fact that he is doing so: 'Era mi corazón ni más ni menos | Que el olvidado kiosko de una plaza' [My heart was no more or less | Than a forgotten kiosk in a town square] (22). A resort to figurative language, in the conventional separation of poetic and non-poetic styles, would normally indicate poetry. But though its style is poetic, the content of this metaphor is antipoetic: a forgotten kiosk in a town square does not allow any privilege or even intensity to inner feeling. It becomes one object among others in a landscape. Nevertheless this is a particular type of landscape. A kiosk in a provincial town square is visible in a way that one in a capital city is not. In the relative emptiness of a provincial city-scape, it is something. Just as the sea is, for someone who grew up in the Chilean central valley before the increased frequency of travel. These are conditions of visibility, in fact of perceptibility in its widest sense, since Parra includes the question of audibility in his investigation of cultural horizons. It is because of the circumstance that the father's otherwise unremarkable remark stands out. Parra handles a key event of inner life not as an expressive issue nor as a memory structure but in terms of a particular perceptual world and its

---

[12] Morales, *La poesía de Nicanor Parra*, 217.

horizons. The effect is not to eliminate the emotion but to place it, to probe the conditions for its occurrence, and thus to free it.

An alternative intensification effect to that of figurative language is a vocabulary of transcendence, as, for example, in words like *patria*, the possibility of a collective identity and purpose that reaches beyond individual lives into something more permanent. In the line 'El mar que baña de cristal la patria' [The sea that bathes the fatherland in crystal waters], the sea joins the fatherland as a transcendence, while the archaic metaphor of *cristal*=water adds its prestige to the force of the utterance: the whole line could belong to one of the patriotic songs that Parra's father, around the time of the journey to the sea, used to teach to military recruits.[13] In a subsequent line, the language enters the epic zone of war and lordship: 'en un instante memorable estuve I Frente a ese gran señor de las batallas' [For a memorable moment I stood I Before that great lord of battles]. The sea, which never entered into conversation at home, is granted this special vocabulary. The aim is not satirical: the feelings that adhere to those words are handled with respect. To place the epic and the ordinary alongside each other in this way is not to privilege one or other of them but to allow a reader the freedom to make out the shape of an affect by rendering perceptible the background (in other words, the discourse) it was embedded in.

Within the linguistic, socio-cultural, and existential variables that define the horizons of perception, the event itself remains a mystery. First seeing the sea was an early experience of something dream-like and ecstatic, and the process of the poem is not to take that away but to rescue its multiple resonance, that is its aliveness, from all types of dead language. Thus this poem, and Parra's work as a whole, does not dismiss what is usually called the sacred (the boy in the poem performs a ritual salutation to the sea), but that word is a problem because of the way it institutes an exclusive zone, controlled by a priesthood and religious language. In fact Parra frequently identifies the Church as having a prime responsibility for the deadness of the languages he inherited as a young man.

---

[13] Ibid. 170.

LANGUAGE AND CONTROL

Entry into conversation implies a risk of loss of control; listeners are likely to reject set-piece rhetoric, speech-making, and other conversation-stoppers. Many of Parra's poems dramatize a speaker's attempts, through rhetorical devices, to retain control. The listener is not present as a figure who speaks, but readers are placed in the position of virtual listeners, with the freedom to 'see through' the manœuvres of the speaker. In other words, these manœuvres are not hidden or otherwise given the power to be unquestionable. Speakers' attempts to retain communicative control are counteracted by the interpretative rights of listeners/readers. This is taken to an extreme of explosive ironies in the later poem 'Me retracto de todo lo dicho' [I withdraw everything I said], where the speaker insists on his right to have 'mi última palabra' [my last word]. But the phrase holds an irony that blows it apart. Do you really have the last word until you are dying? The speaker talks of 'un último deseo' [a last wish], a piece of self-dramatization that invokes a deathbed scene. And then don't the last words actually belong to other people? In other words, until you die, there is always something more to be said, and then there is an even larger conversation, extending beyond individual lives—in time, but also in space—into the vastness of the language itself. Words are not subject to ownership in the way the speaker would wish. The speaker's position in this sense verges on paranoia, as with the speaker in the poems 'La trampa' [The trap] and 'La víbora' [The viper].

The person who wants to have the last word is the one who is trying to keep control over the conversation. In this case, the speaker/writer is insisting on controlling the meanings of everything written in the book. He demands that the reader burn the book because 'No representa lo que quise decir | A pesar de que fue escrito con sangre | No representa lo que quise decir' [It does not represent what I wanted to say | Even though written in blood | It does not represent what I wanted to say] (195). The humorous spectacle of impotent obsession is supplemented by the (ironic) epic grandiosity of 'Las palabras se vengaron de mí' [Words took revenge on me]: the lone self, doing battle with language. The speaker oscillates between absurd grandiosity and morose pleading: 'Perdóname lector | Amistoso lector | Que no me pueda despedir de ti | Con un abrazo fiel: | Me despido de ti | Con una triste sonrisa forzada' [Forgive me reader | Friendly reader | I cannot say goodbye to you | With a faithful embrace: | I say goodbye | With a sad forced smile]. But if language has betrayed him, why should the speaker have any more control over the 'last word', the one he has just uttered and that now belongs to the hearer (a secondary and ironic meaning of 'última')? The instabilities and unpredictabilities of conversation enter the poem. There is no available position outside the situation of not being able to trust, given what words can do (take revenge). So that the speaker's confidence in the faithfulness of his own words is also grotesquely corroded. Neither speech nor writing nor the book stand up as forms of authority. Of course there is always the possibility of a reader not feeling comfortable with the multiple corrosions, but in that case he is not likely to have got beyond the first few poems of *Poemas y antipoemas*. The title and the final line are identical, 'Me retracto de todo lo dicho', which feeds into the various other ironies, since something that has been said cannot be withdrawn except in a highly formal situation, such as a court of law: to desire that degree of control over language is ridiculous—something that is not always obvious to critics who like to sit in judgement and have the last word.

Parra frequently sets up a particular irony with the titles of his poems. They appear to put a boundary round the poem's action by telling a reader what to expect and placing a limit around what the poem is 'about'. For example, 'Se canta al mar' appears to be a definition of the scene the poem describes, producing an expectation of a mimetic, naturalistic poem that sets out to convey an experience which occurred in the past. That is, the title appears to give a reassuring frame by saying that the poem is 'about' singing to the sea. But suppose the title describes not the 'subject' of the poem but the action of the poem: that the poem itself, rather than anything it refers to, can be considered a singing to the sea—a song subject to all the disjunctures of language that the poem displays. Which is not to say an impossible song or a failed song so much as that the singing arises inside divisions of time and society and their extensions in language. A singing that brings these divisions and the forces that accompany them into open play. *Poemas y antipoemas* presses the need for everything that was traditionally kept outside the poem (the non-poetic) to be allowed in. Which means that the poem is also 'about' these things. This extreme porousness of the poem is replicated in Parra's notion of the poet as an amoeba, capable of receiving substances from the environment through its membrane.

The title 'Preguntas a la hora del té' [Questions at teatime] (16) has a similar double function of being a boundary and an opening. As a traditional, naturalist frame—as in naturalist proscenium theatre—the title puts a border round a scene, the *preguntas* being (in this sense) the questions that the speaker articulates (for example, 'Qué vale más, ¿el oro o la belleza?' [What's more valuable, gold or beauty?]), questions whose proverbial character gives them an air of seriousness but which are revealed to be fatuous clichés, concordant with the down-at-heel lower middle-class *mise-en-scène* of tea and lace curtains with holes in them. If this were all that the poem does, then its irony would be like that of the English tradition associated with Philip Larkin, an irony that gives a reader a safe place outside those corrosions; that is, to put it bluntly, an alibi. At a particular moment the poem answers the questions and appears to offer readers a stance outside the scene presented: 'No se sabe, la gente se lo pasa | Construyendo castillos en la arena' [There's no knowing, people spend their time | Building castles in the sand]. The metaphor seems to offer a lifeline—to use another metaphor—in the sea of small-minded meaninglessness. Its content (the reference to fatuous speculation) is accurate to the scene; but its form is no less a cliché than the clichés it purports to stand outside of. The frame is just as much a function of the production of the ordinary as is the sense. How then to break out? But this might be just another false question. And both the title and the metaphor (which in Greek means to carry beyond) might be incapable of carrying us beyond what is occurring in the scene: an anxious business. Parra plays the same game in other poems with the sensation that ideas, because abstract, can somehow rescue one from situations that generate anxiety.

Formally, the questions in the poem offer false disjunctions, that is pseudo either/ors, offering the illusion that everything can be resolved one way or another. An illusion that by ordering things in this way it is possible to get outside. This is therefore a poem that interrogates itself—the other meaning of the title—without finding a place to do that from. It is misleading, therefore, to claim, as critics have done, that Parra's poems are a diatribe against the petty bourgeoisie. Although Parra was interested, early in his career, in the ironical tradition of English poetry in Eliot and Auden, he does not opt for their attitude of superiority. In that sense, this poem is more radical than Eliot's 'Prufrock' , which it clearly echoes. On the other hand, it does resort, near the end, to an Eliotesque voice: 'Lo que se vio una vez ya no se vuelve I A ver igual, dicen las hojas secas' [What was once seen cannot be seen I The same again, say the dry leaves]. The voice appears to come from a ritual or mythic area: there lies its authority. Although Parra later abandons this device, it points to his fascination with the idea of a sacred order.

'Recuerdos de juventud' [Memories of youth] enters the area of the awkwardness of youth, when diffuse anxieties and unrealized desires saturate the whole environment. This type of thematic material has, traditionally, been given various resolutions, from nostalgia for lost youth to the entry into (superior) adult awareness. Parra opts for neither, suggesting instead that the condition remains valid rather than being something that should—or even can—be overcome. The poem opens with a very careful avoidance of metaphor:

> Lo cierto es que yo iba de un lado a otro,
> A veces chocaba con los árboles,
> Chocaba con los mendigos,
> Me abría paso a través de un bosque de sillas y mesas,
> Con el alma en un hilo veía caer las grandes hojas. (39)

> [What's true is I used to go from one place to another,
> Sometimes I bumped into trees,
> Or I bumped into beggars,
> I made my way through a forest of chairs and tables,
> With my soul hanging on a thread I watched the big leaves fall.]

Instead of becoming part of something larger, of which the trees would be the obvious vehicle (for example, the cycle of birth and death), the protagonist is simply a thing among things, some of which he bumps into. In fact these lines include a parody of the opening of one Neruda's most famous works, *Alturas de Macchu Picchu*, where trees and their leaves become metaphors that convey a mythical-cyclical cosmology inside which Neruda's speaker is situated: 'Del aire al aire, como una red vacía, I iba yo entre las calles y la atmósfera, llegando y despidiendo, I en el advenimiento del otoño la moneda extendida I de las hojas' [From air to air, like an empty net, I I went between streets and atmosphere, arriving and dismissing, I in the coming of autumn the extended coinage I of the leaves].[14] Neruda uses metaphor to give an order into which things fit. In Parra's poem there is no higher or larger order. And where metaphors do occur ('un bosque de sillas y mesas' [a forest of chairs and tables]) they merely increase the awkwardness, the lack of harmony between self and things.

Therefore there is no transcendence. The place the speaker-protagonist goes to seek truth is the cemetery: 'Con una hoja de papel y un lápiz yo entraba en los cementerios I dispuesto a no dejarme engañar' [With a piece of paper and a pencil I went into cemeteries I prepared not to let myself be deceived] (39). In one sense, this is a piece of black humour, but in another it is simply a stoic procedure for reflecting on life. In traditional stoic doctrine, the world consists in bodies in movement, without transcendence.[15] The ending of the poem also moves along lines of stoic thought:

> ¡Adónde ir entonces!
> A esas horas el comercio estaba cerrado;
> Yo pensaba en un trozo de cebolla visto durante la cena
> Y en el abismo que nos separa de los otros abismos. (40)

> [So where to go!
> By then the shops were closed
> I thought of a piece of onion seen at supper
> And the abyss that separates us from other abysses.]

There is no higher reality, only objects surrounded by empty space, and thought, also surrounded by empty space. So that the pronoun 'nos' [us] brings no reassurance, only a vacuum. The awkwardness and anguish open out into a current condition, of things as they are, without either hope or despair, and which does not exclude joy.

There are further consequences to this empty space that clears the air of pastoral sentimentality and in fact of any

---

[14] Pablo Neruda, *Canto general* (Buenos Aires, 1963), 26.
[15] Bertrand Russell, *A History of Western Philosophy* (London, 1961), 260.

comforting familiarity. The ordinary, that powerful force of social modelling, starts to disappear because there is nothing for it to latch on to, nothing to make sense of; other possibilities are released. These are not easy to name, because they arise inside and against the everyday social use of the language. Parra gives us the language of the everyday but without the ideological, religious, and sentimental glue that makes it hang together and fill up whatever space there is.

'Palabras a Tomás Lago' [Words to Tomás Lago]—which is, incidentally, one of the great poems of the Spanish language— like the other poems in the third, final section of *Poemas y antipoemas*, does not use alternations of 'poetic' and 'antipoetic' styles. Its rhetoric, that is, its procedures of persuasion, is based on repetitions of phrase patterns and of types of speech act (for example, commands). Syntactically, it uses a great deal of logical sequencing—in terms of biographical time, and of connected propositions. But this display of social logic, of confidence in language as a guarantee of thought, is inherently punctured by the sensation of an abyss. This is most keenly expressed in the final section, which begins with the key word 'Piensa', followed by an expression of logical and temporal connection:

> Piensa, pues, un momento en estas cosas,
> En lo poco y nada que va quedando de nosotros,
> Si te parece, piensa en el más allá,
> Porque es justo pensar
> Y porque es útil creer que pensamos. (38)

> [Think, then, for a moment about these things,
> About the little or nothing that's left of us,
> If you like, think about the beyond,
> Because it's right to think
> And because it's useful to believe we think.]

The theme, a stoic meditation of what is left after we die, starts radically to undermine its form of expression. If thinking, as such, becomes an act of faith, this is because of an emptiness that comes after it (after death) but also, by the same token, before it. In other words, there is no prior basis of the real apart from living it, which includes speaking. To think of ideas as reaching beyond this ('más allá' being in Spanish a preposition capable of becoming a noun) is an invitation that the poem makes but also makes impossible to fulfil. The result is emptiness, but not an emptiness that causes horror or gloom:

> ¡Qué triste ha sido todo esto!
> ¡Qué triste! pero ¡qué alegre a la vez! (38)
>
> [How sad all of this has been!
> How sad! but how happy too!]

Part of the beauty—and joy—of this writing is how at the most minute level of words and their interactions—at a level 'beneath' that of ideas—an emptiness is knocking at the door. Consider the first four lines:

> Antes de entrar en materia,
> Antes, pero mucho antes de entrar en espíritu
> Piensa un poco en ti mismo, Tomás
> Lago, y considera lo que está por venir (37)
>
> [Before getting into matter,
> Before, but long before getting into spirit
> Think a little about yourself, Tomás
> Lago, and consider what is to come]

where the gap between the words 'Tomás' and 'Lago' cuts across all the logic of time (before, after), of categories (matter, spirit), of identity ('ti mismo'), and even of thinking.

The second section names some things that are left behind. But these things are not given definite articles, because they do not typify anything beyond them: 'Me refiero a una sombra, | A ese trozo de ser que tú arrastras | [. . .] a un objeto, | A esos muebles [. . .] | A esas coronas mortuorias [. . .] | (Me refiero a una luz)' [I refer to a shadow, | To that scrap of being that you drag along with you | to an object, | To that furniture | To those wreaths | (I refer to a light)]. There are no categories here, not even any classification, since, as things fail to add up to an order, in the emptiness of death those things are nothing. And nothing can take the place of anything else, since there are no equivalences; hence 'what is left of us' is not 'poco o nada' [little or nothing] (the usual form of expression) but 'poco y nada', both a little and nothing, alongside each other, without slipping from one to the other, the poem offering things and not ideas—that is what is mysterious in it, that it gives us things clearly, without ideas. Together with the mystery, there is a tremendous freeing of emotion (*desprendimiento*, in Spanish) from the confines of making sense of things.

Making sense requires concordance between rhetoric and belief. That is, the language of conviction needs to be backed by securities of belief; otherwise, the voice of authority mocks itself and belief-structures collapse through lack of any discourse capable of sustaining them. This is the effect of 'El peregrino' [The pilgrim]: it begins with the announcement of a matter of grave public concern. But the tone of public speech-making and the appeal to the higher realm of collective concern is emptied out by the content: what the speaker expresses is total isolation ('un alma que ha estado embotellada durante años I en una especie de abismo sexual e intelectual' [a soul bottled up for years I in a kind of sexual and intellectual abyss]; 36). The rhetoric of public concern is eroded from inside by the statements of a situation where the shared world or 'imaginary community' necessary for social communication does not exist. Just as the concordance of individual voice and the collective speech environment breaks down, so also what is spoken fails to find any echo in the visual environment: 'Mientras digo estas cosas veo una bicicleta apoyada en un muro, I Veo un puente I Y un automóvil que desaparece entre los edificios' [While I say these things I see a bicycle leaning on a wall, I I see a bridge I And a car disappearing between build-ings] (36). What the environment 'says' does not coincide with the voice: the things seen are random, they are not symbols or metaphors or even indices of any inner self or feeling.

Rather than represent, what this writing does is produce effects: in the first place, the effect of a gap between speech and social reality. This is a particular case of the gap between words and things that the Latin American poets of the early twentieth century avant-garde explored and used as a prime formal energy in their poetry. As Eduardo Milán has pointed out, there was a tendency in poets coming after the avant-garde to abandon the search for new forms of expression.[16] What has not been recognized is that Parra revives this major tradition and makes use of it in new ways. Despite its straight-forwardness of syntax and vocabulary, the result of his concern with language as speech, Parra's poetry renews the work of exploring the limits of expression. One of its key contributions is to shift the place of subversion from morphology and syntax

---

[16] Eduardo Milán, *Una cierta mirada* (Mexico City, 1989), 16, 40, 72.

(as in Vallejo and Neruda) to the social formulation of reality in speech.

This has a particular importance in the history of the Spanish language in Latin America. Writing was imposed, in and after the Conquest, as a key instrument of social control. The Spanish and Portuguese believed in the capacity of writing to justify and perpetuate a colonial hierarchy. The 'official' Latin American literature, written by Spanish and Creoles, was produced within this situation. Its 'degree zero', as Martín Lienhard puts it, was 'el testimonio del escribano Rodrigo d'Escobedo en la toma de posesión de la isla de Guanahaní [the testimony of the scribe Gregorio d'Escobedo on the occasion of the taking possession of the island of Guanahaní] on behalf of the Spanish crown.[17] That tradition of writing admits of no gaps between written statements and reality, and, given the continuation of colonial relationships inside the society, does not cease with independence from Spain. What Parra's poetry does is to exploit the distance between official written reality and the actual speaking through which flow the energies of life as lived. That distance echoes back to 1492 and becomes particularly tense at certain historical moments. One of these moments is the rapid modernization of Chile in the mid-twentieth century.

Speech is always heard against a background of values and broad assumptions (the ordinary again); once it begins to be prised apart from its usual background, which includes written authority, as happens in 'El peregrino' [The pilgrim], then it begins to be audible in new ways. The voice of the speaker in 'El peregrino', like that of the speaker in the poems of Neruda's avant-garde book *Residencia en la tierra*, lacks any social environment that would concord with and legitimize it. But in Neruda the speaker is presented as an embodiment of the poet, whose 'I' compensates the lack of any transcendent values in nature or the society by itself becoming transcendent, whereas the figure presented by the speaker in Parra's work is of someone trapped in overwork, obsession, or paranoia.[18] This immersion turns

---

[17] Martín Lienhard, *La voz y su huella* (Lima, 1992), 48.
[18] See Parra's statements in the interview with Mario Benedetti: 'Yo he ejercido siempre la poesía como una inmersión en las profundidades del yo. Este yo no es el yo individual, sino el yo colectivo, naturalmente. El yo de que se habla en *Obra gruesa* es un yo difuso, en último término el yo de la especie. [. . .] No es el yo lírico [. . .] es un yo psicológico, de varios pisos' (Benedetti, 'Nicanor Parra', 301).

loose an energy previously tied up in religion, patriotism, the family, politics, and other lesser schemes of permanence—a recurrent feature of late twentieth-century societies, which constantly seek new belief-structures, new fundamentalisms, in reponse to globalization.

Before writing *Poemas y antipoemas*, Parra thought he had found in Walt Whitman the model of a transcendent poetic self that he could use:

escribí un sinnúmero de poemas bajo la influencia de Whitman. Pero resulta una cómica: que mientras trataba yo de hacer esas imitaciones, esos ejercicios whitmanianos, algo fallaba por la base. Los poemas de Whitman eran poemas wagnerianos, y yo podía pescar a ratos esa onda, pero después como que se producían algunas pifias, los personajes empezaban a deshacerse y el héroe se transformaba imperceptiblemente en un antihéroe. Esto me causaba a mí en un comienzo una gran desazón, porque no podía yo estructurar un personaje heroico.[19]

[I wrote countless poems under the influence of Whitman. But something comic happened: when I tried to do those imitations, those Whitmanesque exercises, something basic was going wrong. Whitman's poems were Wagnerian, and I was able sometimes to catch that style, but afterwards it started to goof up, the characters began to fall apart and the hero turned imperceptibly into an anti-hero. This at first caused me great unease, because I wasn't able to construct a heroic character.]

But Parra, typically and brilliantly, turns the relationship of forces inside out. His acute sense of the topology of a poem is related to his experience as a physicist. If he cannot manage an epic, then what is interesting must be whatever is outside and cannot get in:

cuando me di cuenta de las limitaciones de Whitman,[20] algo que vi perfectamente a través de Kafka y tal vez de otros humoristas, solamente en ese momento me di cuenta que lo que podía haber de valioso en esos ejercicios era precisamente un personaje que pugnaba por entrar al poema, que era el antihéroe.[21]

[when I saw the limitations of Whitman, something I recognized clearly in Kafka and perhaps in other humorists, only then did I realize that

---

[19] Morales, *La poesía de Nicanor Parra*, 192–3.
[20] 'Se canta al mar' actually echoes Whitman's prose text 'Sea-Shore Fancies' (*Prose Works 1892*, i: *Specimen Days*, ed. Floyd Stovall (New York, 1963), 139), and his account of his initiation as a poet in 'Out of the Cradle Endlessly Rocking'.
[21] Morales, *La poesía de Nicaner Parra*, 193.

what might be valuable in those exercises of mine was precisely a character who was trying to get into the poem, and this was the anti-hero.]

Parra expresses here a key principle of antipoetry: that what is important is what is outside the poem and cannot get into it.

'La trampa' [The trap] is a good illustration of that decision and also shows how Parra is not merely a follower of Kafka but adds something particular of his own. The (anti-)hero of the poem begins by trying to keep anxiety at bay. He does this first by setting himself irrelevant problems: 'Prefería quedarme en casa dilucidando algunas cuestiones | Referentes a la reproducción de las arañas' [I preferred to stay at home elucidating certain problems | To do with the reproduction of spiders] (45). The sensation of clarity, of having ideas, obtained through the analysis of trivia, appears to keep away the force of the social, which is the source of anxiety. The goal is control: 'En la soledad poseía un dominio absoluto sobre mí mismo' [When alone I had absolute control over myself]. The next resort is vague occultism and dabbling in prediction through 'mi célebre método onírico' [my celebrated dream method]. But the occult in modern times, as Adorno has said, is the decomposition of monotheism 'into a second mythology'.[22] The goal is the same: a belief that will give security and take away anxiety. But such beliefs can also produce what they are supposed to keep away. Openness to the occult leaves Parra's protagonist open to other forces he cannot control: 'Comenzaba a deslizarme automáticamente por una especie de plano inclinado | [. . .] Caía fatalmente en la trampa del teléfono | Que como un abismo atrae a los objetos que lo rodean' [I began to slide uncontrollably down a kind of slope | I fell fatally into the trap of the telephone | Which like an abyss draws in the objects that surround it] (46).

Why is the 'abyss' a telephone and not some personal obsession like paranoid jealousy as, say, in Ernesto Sábato's *El túnel?* Through the telephone flows the voice of the Other, stripped of face and other background, and highly penetrative—the ringing sound, like a dentist's drill, carries over into the voice. It gives the illusion of total communication, producing a 'pseudo-erotic' aura. This is the trap: endless telephone conversations

---

[22] Theodor Adorno, *Minima moralia: Reflections from Damaged Life* (London, 1978), 230.

with a potential lover, leading nowhere but irresistible. On the one hand, there is the total transparency of the telephone, a voice heard inside, without exteriority; and on the other, what that does to the self, making it stutter, incapable of communication. In the face of the (apparent) absolute transparency of the telephone, Parra's protagonist cannot function. His tongue turns into a piece of meat:

> Mi lengua parecida a un beefsteak de ternera
> Se interponía entre mi ser y mi interlocutora
> Como esas cortinas negras que nos separan de los muertos. (46)
>
> [My tongue like a piece of steak
> Interposed itself between my being and my interlocutor
> Like those black curtains that separate us from the dead.]

The organ of speech regresses to an organ of eating; the body gets in the way of pure, disembodied communication: the body, with its capability of speech, but also of death. The 'cortinas negras', which are a fact not a metaphor, dramatize the multiple failures and residues in communication, in contrast with the communication with 'the beyond' desired by the protagonist and in contrast with the voice on the telephone becoming like the voice of a god or of madness—the black humour of the funeral scene offering a relief from paranoia.

There is a similarity between the situation here and the attitude of the speaker in 'Me retracto de todo lo dicho'. The latter seeks total control over meaning, while the protagonist of 'La trampa' seeks communication with the sacred and then is invaded by a voice, that is he submits to total control. But he is not happy with it: he suffers from it. This is the positive released in the experience of the anti-hero. The issue becomes one of survival, not of belief: how to survive the imposition of totalitarian and paranoid meanings. Parra's poetry is prophetic, in the sense that it uncovers forces in the language before they become generalized social realities. By taking the telephone as paranoid instrument, Parra dramatizes a reduction of communication—a reduction that many desire—to one single pole, that of the sole 'emitter' or speaker, who is the dictator and ultimately God. Parra's poetics are thus an investigation of a social pathology of communication.

The horrendous inner world of the speaker is traced to the environment that fosters it. The process we are considering

could perhaps be set out in four stages. (1) The heroic protagonist rules. (2) The anti-hero invades the poem. (3) The anti-
hero is invaded by paranoia. (4) The invasions can all be read
as effects of an outside, which is the communicative environment. If one imagines each stage as an enclosure, then, in
stages (2)–(4), in the same ratio that the enclosure is invaded,
the poem expands.

As Grossman rightly insists, in poems like 'La trampa' 'the
irony boomerangs and flies directly towards us', in the sense
that a reader is 'obliged to ask which of our attitudes or
postures confront the world more adequately', so that the
grotesque situation of Parra's protagonists is also 'no comic
matter'.[23] A reader of 'La trampa' is thus placed in a different
situation from a reader of T. S. Eliot's 'Prufrock': whereas Eliot
offers a reader some degree of superiority over his protagonist,
Parra allows no immunity from the forces his speaker is struggling with. And because there is no position, 'above' or outside,
to hear him from, his speech cannot be taken as a confession;
it is more of an implication.

The figure of a speaker concerned not with finding transcendent meanings to justify himself but with mere survival
recurs in 'Autorretrato', the title a pun with the double sense of
self-portrait and portrait of the author. The speaker is a
secondary schoolteacher, as Parra himself was for a time,
wrecked physically and mentally by grotesque overwork ('las
quinientas horas semanales' [five hundred hours a week]; 27).
As a dramatization of the poet, this figure ruins all the aura and
prestige of the romantic bard. Survival is extended in the poem
'Las tablas' [The tablets] to an extreme of the grotesque. The
precise social forces pushing the protagonist to the edge are
not depicted. But they are implied in his necessity to evade all
areas of value, law, and belief; that is, they are against him,
things to be survived. The narrative is presented as a dream,
that is a transposition of the real with a licence to distort it in
order to reveal what is not normally seen. The protagonist
begins by hitting a woman, who turns out to be his mother. A
stone then says, '¿Por qué maltratas a tu madre?' [Why do you
mistreat your mother] (51), parodying the biblical phrase in
which the stones cry out. The parody is of systems of guilt, and

[23] Grossman, *The Antipoetry of Nicanor Parra*, 156–7.

their use of law and religion—the speaker is being watched by his god. He then discovers 'las tablas de la ley' [the tablets of the law], and they repeat the same admonition and tell him he is being watched by the birds. His response is boredom: 'yo bostezaba, me aburría' [I yawned, I got bored]; he goes back to hitting the woman: 'Para mantenerse despierto había que hacer algo' [To keep awake something had to be done] (52).

The desire for survival, to which he is reduced, is extended into the handling of language. Instead of being a basis of identity, a way to express the self in the words with which one has been named by others, it is merely something to survive within. So that manners of speaking that lay claim to correctness and legitimacy, or forms of expression that sanction emotion, go by the wayside. It is a question of surviving inside language, not of making a mark on it. The flatness of expression in the poem is a means of escape; it permits sufficient velocity to escape being trapped: fast in relation to the insistence of the Law, slow in relation to religious leaps into transcendence (burning the bust of his god only gives a few seconds' warmth against the cold).

This language without style, whose rhetoric leads to no institution or platform of any kind but only to survival, is similar to that 'degree zero' of writing which Roland Barthes identified in certain French writers of the 1940s who sought through the use of non-literary, spoken languages to break the inherited mould of Literature. Crucial in Barthes's propositions is the link made between the existence of a specialized literary language and social division:

it is this stale language, closed by the immense pressure of all the men who do not speak it, which [the writer] must continue to use. Writing therefore is a blind alley, and it is because society itself is a blind alley. The writers of today feel this; for them, the search for a non-style or an oral style, for a zero level or a spoken level of writing, is, all things considered, the anticipation of a homogeneous social state.[24]

Parra's writing needs to be understood as an escape from the social hierarchies inscribed in the separateness and closedness of literature and a prefiguration of a society without castes or classes. The rapid growth of new social mobilities in Chilean cities in the mid-century made that possible to imagine. This

---

[24] Roland Barthes, *Writing Degree Zero* (London, 1967), 92–3.

projected future in Parra's poetry is his alternative to the para-noid and totalitarian controls he also dramatizes. Raúl Zurita has written that Parra more than any other Chilean writer came to represent confidence in the spoken language as means of communication:

La 'Antipoesía' representa precisamente la irrupción de la vida (según su autor) [. . .] frente al 'himno' retórico y pomposo. El comienzo vacilante de la aceptación de esta forma poética revela hasta qué grado lo dicho es cierto. Cuando aparece *Poemas y antipoemas* el consenso es del habla como lugar frágil, sujeto a desmentidos.²⁵

['Antipoetry' stands precisely for the irruption of life (according to its author) in the face of the pompous and rhetorical 'hymn'. The fact that this poetic form was at first given an uncertain reception shows to what extent that is true. When *Poems and antipoems* first appeared the consensus was that speech is a fragile place, subject to correction.]

If, as Zurita suggests, orality began to break out in Chilean liter-ature in Neruda's *Residencia en la tierra*, it is Parra who 'lleva hasta sus máximas consecuencias el discurso oral en la escrit-ura' [takes spoken discourse in writing to its furthest conse-quences].

AGAINST BELIEF-STRUCTURES

For Parra's marginal protagonist, the desire to survive tends to empty out whatever has been made symbolic in the environ-ment. The stones (=the Law), the birds (=sins), and the bust of the god in 'Las tablas' for example, become mere things—like the piece of onion in 'Recuerdos de juventud', or the urban environment in 'El peregrino'. This is particularly striking if 'Las tablas' is taken to be a dream (the protagonist says it is), since dreams, in the dominant interpretative system of the West in the twentieth century, are taken to be fundamentally symbolic. For Freud, a dream is the symbolic expression of a desire. But what if the desire is to survive (rather than to make a mark or be marked)? Parra subverts Freud's system of controls by turning it inside out: the symbolic is not inherent to the psyche—nor even to language—but a force of social control

---

²⁵ Raúl Zurita, *Literatura, lenguaje y sociedad (1973–1983)* (Santiago, 1983), 8.

to be evaded for the sake of survival in an authoritarian society.[26]

'Los vicios del mundo moderno' [The vices of the modern world], another of the three important long poems that *Poemas y antipoemas* ends with, continues Parra's investigation into the reduction of human beings. Around half of the poem consists in a long list of the said vices. Like a medieval homily on the world, the flesh, and the devil, the speaker seems to take pleasure in taking away just about everything that might be pleasurable or interesting, such as 'el automóvil y el cine sonoro [. . .] I Y la difusión de la radiomanía [the car and sound cinema I And the spread of radiomania] (48). But interspersed between these first and last items is a series that places genocide ('el exterminio de los pieles rojas' [the extermination of redskins]) on the same level as economics ('la fatídica danza de los dolares' [the fateful dance of dollars]), nature ('la locura del mar' [the madness of the sea]), death ('las pompas Fúnebres' [Funeral ceremonies]), and other kinds of solution ('la destrucción de los ídolos' [the destruction of idols] and 'la interpretación de los sueños' [the interpretation of dreams]). The latter two recall, not so incidentally, the titles of famous modern books (by Nietzsche and Freud), and their juxtaposition with the other 'vices' is in a sense summed up by 'El abuso de los estupefacientes y de la filosofía' [the abuse of narcotics and of philosophy]. The list is not linear: some parts of it include the whole of it. The whole thing, as the poem says, 'produce vértigo' [causes dizziness]. A reader is invited to recognize that all the items have become fetishes, and reductions of human beings. This clears the way not for submission to God (a higher form of magic) but for a world without magic: 'La poesía reside en las cosas o es simplemente un espejismo del espíritu' [Poetry resides in things or is simply a mirage of the spirit]. Free from seductions, from intensities that trap, abuse, and confuse, from symbols, a world of things becomes available.

Parra turns the form of the Christian homily inside out. Instead of offering a better belief (true God as opposed to false idols) as a solution, the speaker offers a possibility of getting

[26] On the symbolic as historical rather than inherent to language see Pierre Bourdieu, *The Field of Cultural Production* (Cambridge, 1993), 32.

free from belief. Against the reduction and diminution of life, the poem uses a de-transcendifying and de-sublimating effect. But it does so with an edge of anxiety, without seeking the moral high ground as it is currently called: if funerals are one of the vices of the modern world, then they may not be so easy to avoid. The speaker ends with a kind of stoic homily: 'Tratemos de ser felices, recomiendo yo, chupando la miserable costilla humana' [Let us try to be happy, I recommend, sucking the miserable human rib] (50), opposing flesh to spirit, and freeing one from the aura of high-sounding permanence that surrounds the 'vices' listed. To take away that aura is to engage in recouping the human energy that had fed it. But how far is that possible, given the main difficulty, which is where do you start from? Here Parra moves from politics to cosmogony, that is to reimagining origins: 'De sus axilas extrae el hombre la cera necesaria para forjar el rostro de sus ídolos. I Y del sexo de la mujer la paja y el barro de sus templos' [Man extracts from his armpits the wax for making the face of his idols. I And from woman's sexual organ the straw and mud for his temples] (51). As opposed to submission to (hidden) fetishes, the idea of returning to a non-sacrifical beginning.

The idea of a return to bases, as Parra says in an interview, became an obsession with him. He expresses it in various forms. One is the notion that human beings are the result of the explosion millions of years ago of an initial 'hombre gigante' [giant man], an obvious echo of the big bang theory of the origin of the universe. Another takes the form of the Egyptian and Greek myths of the scattered members of a figure coming together again (Osiris, for example):

Desde el comienzo de los antipoemas yo traté de reconstituir ese hombre por un método que podría llamarse método de regresión histórica. Lo que me pasaba a mí era más o menos lo siguiente: el pensamiento actual (el pensamiento del año 38) me parecía que olía a pescado podrido; algo no marchaba, estaba mal eso. Entonces había que retroceder para ver en qué momento estuvo fresco ese pescado.[27]

[From the beginning of the antipoems I tried to reconstitute that man through a method which could be called the method of historical regression. What was happening to me was more or less as follows: current thinking (that of 1938) seemed to me to smell of rotten fish;

---

[27] Morales, *La poesía de Nicanor Parra*, 211.

something was not working, there was something wrong. So the only thing was to go back and find out when the fish was fresh.]

Part of the process is a demolition of the false promises of modernity. Instead of replacing magical beliefs with a greater control over the environment, it has produced a world of new idols. No need, therefore, to seek a resacralization of life, as Paz proposed in his poems of the 1950s. But there are also consequences for language. 'Los vicios del mundo moderno' is a particularly strong example of something that is happening in the whole book: a becoming disintoxicated of language. In a sense this is Parra's only programme: a verbal detoxification programme. The result is not some ordinary matter-of-factness, but an abyss with nothing to hold on to—no justifications, no alibis. Instead of lusciously resonant phrases, overflowing with echoes and connotations (the prime example would be Neruda), a language stripped bare, a rib to suck on, and not in a spirit of misery and resentment but acceptance and happiness.

The full consequences of these moves emerge in Parra's subsequent books, by which time the cosmogony has become unnecessary. It is not a question of a mythic scheme to give the poems an overall meaning and coherence. A 'provisional mythology' would be a more accurate term. The crucial poem in this connection is 'Soliloquio del individuo' [The individual's soliloquy], which closes *Poemas y antipoemas*. In so far as it presents an essential History, that is a narrative of human existence in the world as something fixed, that always was and will be, 'Soliloquio' enters a mythological area. But by avoiding mythical language and refusing any idea that could give a meaning to existence, it empties out myth from inside.

Georges Bataille's critique of religion includes the notion that identifying 'with the entirety of the universe' keeps a person 'asleep' in the sense of believing they 'will never die'.[28] Parra's poem explores the realms of transcendent origins and universal goals—the usual religious dimension of cosmologies—in order to criticize them. Parra's speaker, though recognizably prehistoric man, instead of worshipping nature and turning it into symbols/gods, is occupied with survival:

[28] Georges Bataille, *Inner Experience* (New York, 1988), p. xxxii.

Primero viví en una roca
(Allí grabé algunas figuras).
Luego busqué un lugar más apropiado.
[. . .]
Primero tuve que procurarme alimentos,
Busquar peces, pájaros, buscar leña,
(Ya me preocuparía de los demás asuntos). (53)
[First I lived in a rock
(I drew a few figures there).
Then I looked for a more appropriate place.
First I had to gather provisions,
Look for fish, birds, look for firewood,
(I could worry about other things after that).]

Parra's 'hero' is someone who simply finds himself there. There is no creator, no cosmic scheme, no hidden meaning to make himself part of. Many cosmologies use the egg as symbol of the origin of the universe. Everything unfolds from there, in a drama of sacred prefigurations (and often also of malign, diabolical interferences with the divine plan). Borges, in his stories of the 1940s, plays with these motifs, among other things as a way of questioning Western faith in providential history. Parra's key device is to use an amoeba figure in the place of a stone or other idea of permanent origin. This occurs in the context of his concern with moving both backwards and forwards, imagining the before and the after of what currently exists, which includes language. In spite of the anti-epic stance of his poems, he shares this major concern of Chilean poetry with Huidobro, Neruda, and Zurita. As he stated in an interview, 'nosotros hemos sido expulsados del paraíso y queremos retornar a ese paraíso, y parece que la manera de retornar es precisamente reconstruyendo nuestra imagen inicial. El poeta anda buscando la casa para el hombre actual, que está a la intemperie' [we have been expelled from paradise and we want to return to it, and it looks like the way back is to reconstruct our initial image. The poet is looking for the home of contemporary man, who is out in the cold].[29]

The (anti-)hero of 'Soliloquio' is preoccupied with constructing a dwelling. But where does he get his ideas from? Is he indebted to something previous to him which he inherited?

---

[29] Morales, *La poesía de Nicanor Parra*, 213.

Parra's scheme, which draws on his training as a scientist, gets rid of the idea of indebtedness to anything previous:

llegué hasta el hombre de las cavernas, pero todavía no entendía bien la cosa. Y dije, bueno, hay que retroceder más aún, y en esta regresión llegué a la célula, a la célula viva. Me dije que más atrás no podía ir: si descompongo la célula, desaparece la vida. Me pareció que ese era el ladrillo fundamental de la vida. Me pregunté: ¿qué puedo decir yo realmente de lo que pueda responder? Bueno, que el hombre es una ameba que se nutre de lo que encuentra a su paso, y entonces hice esta formulación: el hombre es una ameba gigante que se nutre de lo que encuentra a su paso. Y me pareció que esa frase respiraba, que esa frase vibraba.[30]

[I got as far as the cave-man, but I still didn't understand. And I said, well, you have to go further back, and in that regression I got as far as the cell, the living cell. I said to myself you can't go further back: if I take the cell apart, life disappears. It looked like that was the fundamental building block of life. I asked myself: what can I say that I can really answer for? Well, that man is an amoeba that feeds on what it finds around it, and then I came up with this formulation: man is a giant amoeba that feeds on what it finds around it. And I felt yes, that phrase breathes and trembles.]

The key characteristics of the amoeba implicit here are its ability to draw in nutrients from outside through its membrane, without the use of specialized organs, and that it reproduces through endless division and so in a sense never dies. Thus as an analogy for human beings it has no essence to prefigure its destiny and no creator to obey or disobey: just an endless openness. Incompatible with schemes of cosmic purpose or its scientific surrogates (such as 'the survival of the fittest'), it is a device with a porous membrane, instead of fixed boundaries, capable of bringing all outside environments inside itself, which undermines all essential and unchanging definitions of 'Man' and 'human nature'.

The mathematics of this situation are of some relevance. The circle has been taken by mathematicians as a figure of perfect enclosure, of absolutely unleaky containment. As G. Spencer Brown writes, 'The skin of a living organism cuts off an outside from an inside. So does the circumference of a circle in a plane. By tracing the way we represent such a severance, we can begin

---

[30] Ibid. 212.

to reconstruct, with an accuracy and coverage that appear almost uncanny, the basic forms underlying linguistic, mathematical, physical, and biological science.'[31] This non-porous boundary becomes a mystical origin, prior to all experience: 'mathematics, in common with other art forms, can lead us beyond ordinary existence, and can show us something of the structure in which all creation hangs together.'[32] Meaning can arise only *after* the circle, according to Spencer Brown:

> a distinction is drawn by arranging a boundary with separate sides so that a point on one side cannot reach the other side without crossing the boundary. For example, in a plane space a circle draws a distinction. Once a distinction is drawn, the spaces, states, or contents on each side of the boundary, being distinct, can be indicated.[33]

But such use of the circle eliminates time and leaves no residue. Parra's amoeba has no such perfect inwardness. On the contrary, the outside is always getting inside it. Instead of the allure of perfect containment, which quickly translates into obsession, it offers a permanent and unpredictable interchange with the world. Equally, instead of putting a circle round a poem—as some critics do—by saying it is 'about' something, the amoeba-poem invites an appreciation of how limiting that boundary-making can be. As Parra puts it in a poem from a later collection, 'TODO | ES POESÍA | menos la poesía' [EVERYTHING | IS POETRY | except poetry].[34] There are some striking similarities with Jacques Derrida's later critique of structuralism, though Parra's method for a de-centred writing and reading is more down-to-earth without being less radical.

All of this has consequences for the poem's form of expression. It begins with the statement 'Yo soy el individuo' [I am the individual], a strong affirmation of identity, the utterance 'Yo soy' being an archetypal act of authority by kings, priests, dictators, and so on. The sentence is repeated eighteen times. But instead of a litany, a reiteration of belief that gives security, the repetition of the statement makes it leak, and instead of offering the safe boundaries of an identity it becomes increasingly empty—that is, porous to the outside. Instead of self as a value

---

[31] G. Spencer Brown, *Laws of Form* (London, 1969), p. v.
[32] Ibid.   [33] Ibid. 1.
[34] From *Artefactos,* in Nicanor Parra, *Chistes para desorientar a la poesía* (Madrid, 1989), 133.

or centre—a main strand of Western thought—the more the speaker repeats 'Yo soy el individuo' the less it explains or justifies anything.

If for liberals and neo-liberals the individual is the goal of social development, as in Lady Thatcher's famous declaration that there is no such thing as society, only individuals, Parra subverts their discourse by parodying the idea of all human beings as individuals. The image of the individual painting figures on the walls of caves not only makes individualism absurd, it also takes away the aura of caves as origins. The parody is double: of goals and of beginnings. And the idea that succession means purpose is overturned when, at the end, having exhausted the possibility of finding purpose in the new, the speaker thinks that going backwards, 'De atrás para adelante grabar I El mundo al revés' [To draw the world I In reverse, from back to forwards], might be better, only to conclude 'Pero no: la vida no tiene sentido' [But no; life has no meaning] (56). Instead of being a transcendent Subject of History, able to give meaning to everything through self-declaration, this 'individuo' has no higher motivations; the only thing to move him on, once the necessities for survival are attained, is boredom, the bottom line of desire.

The poem moves on, but as a narrative without process. There is no development, no accumulation. If 'before' and 'after' are the elementary bases of meaning in narrative as Roland Barthes suggests,[35] they fail to operate, producing as a result what could be called a degree zero of narrative, and of history, since history needs narrative. A lot happens, but there are no second-level meanings, only the immediate events and objects. The language is neutral, without rhetorical emphases, without making any moves towards a symbolic order. But if a zero inheritance is the ultimate consequence of Parra's anarchist cosmogony, it is of course impossible, not the least because a non-inherited language is impossible. The poem is an unravelling, unfolding, dismantling action against particular inheritances: for example, against authoritarian language, and against mythology, which is itself a sacralization of inheritance.

[35] Roland Barthes, 'Introduction to the Structural Analysis of Narratives', in *Image-Music-Text* (London, 1977), 94.

The purpose of this poem and of Parra's work as a whole could be defined as clearing writing and reading, speaking and hearing of the pre-formulated legitimizations which prevent perception of what is actually occurring in the language. Among these legitimizations is the basic one of cause and effect: the notion that without a prior assumption that speaker and hearer are inside a scheme of cause and effect it is impossible to make sense. Parra's anti-cosmogony invites a reader outside, to the outside even of 'La trampa' and 'Los vicios', ultimately to an outside of language. In this sense, it defies semiotics before it became a fashion, in that semiotics presumes that everything with meaning can be decoded, if only the right frame is found. There is an energy in Parra's writing that eludes any framing. That everything can get into the poem is a key to its transformations of writer and reader. *Poemas y antipoemas* performs intersections of mathematics, cosmology, and the social analysis of language with far-reaching results, results which have affected in crucial ways Latin American poetry in the second half of the century.

The early poem 'Desorden en el cielo' makes use of the type of humour, prevalent in medieval Europe and inherited by the subaltern classes in Latin America, which makes grotesque parodies of the Church's version of sacred order. The story in this poem is the common one of the priest turned away from the gates of heaven, because, as St Peter says, 'Mientras los demás mordían | Un mísero pan de afrecho | Tú te llenabas la panza | De carne y huevos frescos' [While the others chewed | A miserable piece of rough bread | You were filling your belly | With meat and fresh eggs] (24). Using God and the saints against the Church is a traditional tactic of popular anti-clericalism. Another popular resource against authority in Latin America is the devil. Historically, Christian notions of Satan were superimposed upon native magical beings that were not wholly evil but multiple, unpredictable, and often associated with the cult of the dead. In this sense, the devil is a convergence of two traditions: that of popular Christianity and that of native belief.[36]

But the issue of sacred order and its defence or destruction

---

[36] See William Rowe and Vivian Schelling, *Memory and Modernity: Popular Culture in Latin America* (London, 1991), 62–3, 66, 91–2.

reaches beyond religious scenarios into Parra's concern with other forms of order and authority, the language they use to legitimize themselves, and who (they think) their enemies are. The speaker in his poems changes from the passive, alienated victim of malign orders (in *Poemas y antipoemas*) to what Parra calls

un sujeto muy estrambótico, muy extravagante, que en la jerga teológica del abate Bergier podría llamarse 'energúmeno'. Recupera el dominio de sí mismo y se lanza contra el mundo [. . .] es un sujeto eminentemente activo, capaz de desarrollar grandes cantidades de energía.[37]

[a highly bizarre person, very extravagant, who in Abbot Bergier's theological jargon could be called an 'energumen'. He recuperates his self-control and hurls himself at the world. He is a highly active subject, capable of unleashing great quantities of energy.]

Etymologically, Parra explains, the term designates someone possessed by Lucifer, a demoniac; his name also includes the energy he radiates. As well as the devil of carnival traditions and the ambivalent native gods who slipped through Christian attempts to control them, Parra's energumen has links with the Greek figure Hermes, god of openings and bridges, disconnections and connections,[38] who makes boundaries or terms into doors that open. In 'Advertencia al lector' [Warning to the reader] he demolishes doctrine but is not responsible for the effects: the example given is of the theologian who demolished the dogma of the Holy Trinity:

Después de haber reducido a polvo el dogma de la
    Santísima Trinidad
¿Respondió acaso de su herejía?
Y si llegó a responder, ¡cómo lo hizo!
¡En qué forma descabellada!
¡Basándose en qué cúmulo de contradicciones! (30)

[After reducing the dogma of the Holy Trinity to dust
did he answer to his heresy?
And if he did answer, how did he do it!
In what a delirious way!
Based on what a pile of contradictions!]

37 Morales, *La poesía de Nicanor Parra*, 215–16.
38 See Michel Serres, *Hermes: Literature, Science, Philosophy* (Baltimore, 1982), 42.

That is, the author as energumen is not obliged to fill the hole left by collapsed belief, even if 'los doctores de la ley' [the legal experts] come along and say the book should be banned. The mercurial figure draws energy and speed from what he disrupts, a Promethean strand that combines with humorous and pleasurable disruption: 'el personaje', says Parra, 'se divierte como chino' [the character revels in it like a Chinaman].[39]

The collection *La camisa de fuerza* [The straitjacket], dated 1962–8, includes a sequence of four satires that expose the Christian religion as manufacturing guilt and offering alibis for selfishness. In 'Padre nuestro', a send-up of the Lord's Prayer, God the Father is let off the hook of absolute power and infallibility, and in the process collapses:

> Padre nuestro que estás donde estás
> Rodeado de ángeles desleales
> Sinceramente: no sufras más por nosotros
> Tienes que darte cuenta
> De que los dioses no son infalibles
> Y que nosotros perdonamos todo. (134)

> [Our father who are where you are
> Surrounded by disloyal angels
> In all sincerity, don't suffer any more for us
> You have got to realize
> That gods are not infallible
> And that we forgive everything.]

The devil is the main problem: 'Sabemos que el Demonio no te deja tranquilo | Desconstruyendo lo que tú construyes' [We realize that the Devil will not leave you in peace | Deconstructing what you construct]. The devil, therefore, is the ally, the producer of energy for the action of analysis, called here, in a prophetic parody of a later fashion in literary theory, deconstruction. In place of deconstruction as a laborious method for getting power over literature, Parra's action is vulgar, pleasurable, and releasing. 'Agnus dei' , another poem in the group, makes a series of calls for the devolution of energies tied up in the saviour figure:

> Cordero de dios que lavas los pecados del mundo
> Dame tu lana para hacerme un sweater.

[39] Morales, *La poesía de Nicanor Parra*, 217.

Cordero de dios que lavas los pecados del mundo
Déjanos fornicar tranquilamente:
No te inmiscuyas en ese momento sagrado. (134–5)

[Lamb of god who washes the sins of the world
Give me your wool to make myself a jumper.

Lamb of god who washes the sins of the world
Let us fornicate in peace:
Don't meddle in that sacred moment.]

The dizzy leaps between levels of reality and frames of reference are part of the disorganizing action, and a prime characteristic of Parra's books after *Poemas y antipoemas*.

The devil also comes in through that abyss which opens up when a person recognizes that they cannot control the meaning of words, even their last words. Just as the Church embodies control over meaning, so do inherited traditions of form and language in literature. But if the Church is the final instance of control over the sense of words, then it produces and uses paranoia, and all institutions of control, including those a reader considers legitimate, do the same. The devil in this situation offers a resource for eluding paranoia—by being multiple, not reductive, capable of levitation, invisibility, and communication with the dead,[40] instead of fixed in space-time; and without boundaries, as opposed to being nailed to a single, invadable self (it was he who tempted Jesus to use his powers to fly off the cross). The conditions for paranoia, in which everything that happens refers to a threatened and persecuted self, crumble. Parra's references correspond to a Catholic and highly codified society, but the techniques ally themselves with new, emerging social forces, unleashed by rapid modernization. These forces made possible the Popular Unity Government, which is not to say that that government necessarily represented them.

Parra's poetics parody faith in ideas. 'Se me ocurren ideas luminosas' [Luminous ideas come to me] has a mock-epic beginning, a Wagnerian backdrop to an encounter between the speaker and a woman who 'casi me vuelve loco' [almost drives me mad]. But the woman is a series of statements that do not add up, a bundle of unattractive attributes which will not resolve into an object of desire. The poem hangs on an edge

---

[40] Ibid. 216.

between sexual desire and a woman who will not respond; within that gap the speaker makes the statement which is the title:

> Se me ocurren ideas luminosas.
> Yo también digo cosas por decir.
> Cada cual teoriza por su lado
> ¿Nos metemos un rato en un hotel?
> —Dice que hay que esperar una semana. (89–90)

> [Luminous ideas come to me.
> I too say things just to keep talking.
> Each one theorizes on their own
> Shall we go into a hotel for a moment?
> —She says we've got to wait a week.]

Ideas are placed on the same level as the 'theory' of going to a hotel to make love, that is, as pseudo-resolution—the greater the frustration, the more 'luminous' the ideas. The disjunction is between the play of desire and ideas (including the idea of making love) as a control; which can be compared with Nietzsche's counterposing Apollonian clarity and a 'Dionysiaic substratum' of 'madness', where the boundaries of the individual are destroyed,[41] Dionysos being another devil-figure, in this case Greek, satanized by Christianity. For Nietzsche, the luminous images associated with Apollo are what makes it possible for the uncontrolled Dionysiac flow to 'enter an individual consciousness'; without the images, there would merely be an abyss (to use Parra's word). The poem 'La doncella y la muerte' [Death and the maiden] unveils precisely that kind of abyss. Instead of being in love with the maiden, death is bored and the maiden has to resort to all kinds of stratagems, increasingly unmaidenly, until finally she gets undressed in front of the mirror 'moviendo las caderas' [moving her hips]. The story explodes a favourite motif in the Christian and psychoanalytic imagination: death as a lover, a mythical fixing of desire. If death has to be worked on, then desire for its part has first to be produced and is not already moulded by inherited scenarios.[42] Sexual desire becomes dislodged from fixed representations, none more fixed than death.

---

[41] *The Birth of Tragedy and the Genealogy of Morals* (New York, 1956), 143, 145, 146.
[42] See Gilles Deleuze and Félix Guattari, *Anti-Oedipus* (Minneapolis, 1977), ch. I, s. 4.

Ideas are not the same as speech. Part of the poem's process is to prize the two apart, so that speech can be heard as action prior to its ordering and interpretation as ideas. There is an invitation to listen at precisely that edge where utterances emerge from undefined energies into the social—a place of laughter and high speeds. Depriving ideas of priority allows utterances—and thoughts, which are their prolongation[43]—to be perceived differently, as a dance of speech-actions, without plot. The difference is between having ideas (or representations) of the body, and being inside the body,[44] a difference that is not easy to convey, given that literary and cultural criticism tend to centre on representations as interpretative securities. Parra's poetry does the job by making evident the distance between verbal formulae and things, laughing at attempts to use ideas to fill that gap, and exploring the attractions of chaos:

> Un ojo blanco no me dice nada
> Hasta cuándo posar de inteligente
> Para qué completar un pensamiento.
> ¡Hay que lanzar al aire las ideas!
> El desorden también tiene su encanto
> Un murciélago lucha con el sol:
> La poesía no molesta a nadie
> Y la fucsia parece bailarina. (90)
>
> [A white eye tells me nothing
> How long to pose as intelligent
> Why finish a thought
> One has to throw ideas to the winds!
> Disorder also has its enchantment
> A bat struggles with the sun
> Poetry bothers nobody
> And fuchsia looks like a ballerina.]

These lines from 'Versos sueltos' [Loose lines], are utterances rather than thoughts. They interrupt each other before any one of them has time to be rounded into a thought or stabilized

---

43 See V. N. Volosinov, *Marxism and the Philosophy of Language* (New York, 1973), ch. 1, especially the following statement: 'all manifestations of ideological creativity [. . .] are bathed by, suspended in [. . .] the element of speech' (15).

44 See M. Merleau-Ponty, *Phenomenology of Perception* (London, 1962), ch. 6, especially the following: 'experience of one's own body runs counter to the reflective procedure which detaches subject and object from each other and which gives us only the thought about the body, or the body as an idea, and not the experience of the body or the body in reality' (198–9).

into an image. And when we seem to reach a point of climax ('un murciélago lucha con el sol') the materials refuse to gel and the climax cannot occur. And the last two lines, which gesture at a completion, offer only inanities, suggesting that all completion is fatuous—the inane being the ordinary in a grotesque form. The whole poem has a similar structure: seven verses of seven to nine lines which rise to apparent climax and completion, all ending with the same deflating line, 'Y la fucsia parece bailarina.' Every time one is given a complete thought or image, it collapses. The poem fails to build up into anything but in so doing displays the pressure inside language for rounded thoughts and completed images—and offers its reader a wild pleasure.

Parra's poetry resists Jakobson's famous definition of the poetic function: 'The poetic function projects the principle of equivalence from the axis of selection into the axis of combination.'[45] Jakobson explains selection as follows:

If 'child' is the topic of the message, the speaker selects one among the extant, more or less similar, nouns like child, kid, youngster, tot, all of them equivalent in a certain respect, and then, to comment on this topic, he may select one of the semantically cognate verbs—sleeps, dozes, nods, naps.

Combination occurs when the 'chosen words combine in the speech chain'. If the 'axis of combination' acts as a principle of equivalence, then sound, rhythm, and syntax all serve to shape and intensify the meaning of the particular words chosen. Such patterns are only a minor feature of ordinary speech: someone who starts to use a lot of alliteration, for example, is coming on. In Parra's poetry, selection has a primary role. The poems are assembled out of speech and they dramatize the selection of particular words and phrases out of the stock of available expressions. The poems also display this act of selection in such a way as to reveal what it operates inside of: the lines of force and the places of permission to speak within the language as a whole. Parra's technique is to make the poem continually return to the act of speaking by refusing to let it become a completed statement and thus a transferable meaning (sentiment, idea, image).

---

    45 Roman Jakobson, 'Linguistics and Poetics', in David Lodge (ed.), *Modern Criticism and Theory: A Reader* (London, 1988), 39.

In spatial terms, because the act of speaking does not become a completed meaning, it is not permitted to become a gestalt, a completed figure, and the result is two things: there is no meaning for a reader to identify with and the utterance does not stand out clearly—with the help of sound, image, and syntax—against an indistinct background of the language as a whole. On the contrary, statements collapse back into the language, and the language invades the foreground—the language as spoken and lived, not language as a set of abstract rules.[46]

'Versos sueltos' also exemplifies Parra's return to the ordinary after his excursion through cosmogony. The return is paradoxical because there is actually no longer an ordinary, just its components: that is, the poetic material consists in the things and statements which make up ordinary everyday life but they are not properly arranged, so that the sensation is of everyday life but with something missing. What is missing is not a thing or things, some key human feature as in science fiction (such as *The Invasion of the Bodysnatchers*),[47] but some force or principle that will put everything together (and prevent a reader feeling dizzy). The incoherence does not occur at the level of the juxtaposition of components of a tangible and visible world. Rather than a disordering of the senses, there is a disorder of rhetoric, or, to extend a suggestion of Parra's, a surrealism of rhetoric.[48] This can be defined as a disruption of the usual way the spoken is assembled to make up a world and its reassemblage in unexpected juxtapositions: a transfer of the surrealist method of juxtapositions to statements. Statements need to generate acceptance in order to produce a world that is felt to be normal, namely recognizable and legitimate. In order to persuade, they must both be spoken from a legitimate place and be consistent with each other. In fact the two conditions overlap: someone making inconsistent statements will provoke in a listener the question: where are they coming from? Parra's statements leap about—like an 'energumen'—between different positions. Consider the following lines from 'Versos sueltos':

---

[46] See Volosinov, *Marxism*, part 2, ch. 1.
[47] Film directed by Don Siegel, 1956. There have been two remakes: by Philip Kaufman in 1978 and Abel Ferrara in 1994.
[48] Morales, *La poesía de Nicanor Parra*, 199.

Se reparte jamón a domicilio
¿Puede verse la hora en una flor?
Véndese crucifijo de ocasión
La ancianidad también tiene su premio
Los funerales sólo dejan deudas:
Júpiter eyacula sobre Leda
Y la fucsia parece bailarina. (91)

[Ham delivered to your home
Can you see time in a flower?
Second-hand crucifix for sale
Old age also has its reward
Funerals only leave debts:
Jupiter ejaculates on Leda
And fuchsia looks like a ballerina.]

The place the statements are coming from shifts with great speed, producing a sensation of dislocation. The changes occur in tone, register, and content, and involve shifts between social groups, situation, purpose, and type of discourse. Syntactically the statements are very similar, consisting in subject, verb, and complement, and rhythmically they are all fairly close to the classical hendecasyllable. These similarities (on what Jakobson would call the axis of combination) serve to highlight the huge differences in who is speaking, how, and what for. For example, and the account is not exhaustive, the passage quoted moves from an advertisement to a romantic poetic expression, to another (this time hilarious) advertisement, to two proverbs, the second one blackly humorous, to a mythic discourse, and finally to a banal refrain; each case involves a different type of person speaking to different people in different situations.

All of this involves redefinition of the transaction of reading and writing against the tradition of the poet as a kind of god.[49] The poems that open *Versos de salón* serve as devices to dramatize and renegotiate that transaction. 'Cambios de nombre' [Name changes] begins by addressing 'los amantes de las bellas letras' [lovers of belles-lettres] but the address is ironical since what follows demolishes that sense of literature as exclusive object for the culturally refined:

---

[49] See Vicente Huidobro, 'Arte poética', in *El espejo de Agua* (Bueuos Aires, 1917).

A los amantes de las bellas letras
hago llegar mis mejores deseos
Voy a cambiar de nombre a algunas cosas.

Mi posición es ésta:
El poeta no cumple su palabra
Si no cambia los nombres de las cosas.

¿Con qué razón el sol
Ha de seguir llamándose sol?
¡Pido que se llame Micifuz
El de las botas de cuarenta leguas! (70–1)

[To lovers of belles-lettres
I send my compliments
I am going to change the names of a few things.

My position is this:
The poet does not stand by his word
If he does not change the names of things.

Why should the sun
Go on being called sun?
I propose he should be called Micifuz
The one with the seven league boots!

The naming is for real; it is not the biblical myth of Adam naming things taken as poetic metaphor. By giving actual new words for specific things, like the sun, the speaker disallows any metaphorical relationship between poetic language and reality. And so poetry ceases to be something set apart from the real, which it is for 'los amantes de las bellas letras'. Poetry as something set apart (from the culture as a whole) goes with readers set apart (from the society) and poetry as set apart (in a metaphoric realm).

But how is a reader to respond to a poet who starts renaming things? Does he have to submit to the poet as an authority? What is the authority to rename, in fact to name? How is it produced? In the myth, God gives Adam permission. Parra's poem turns the issue inside out, by giving its readers permission to name god: 'Que cada cual lo llame como quiera' [Let each one call him what he likes]. The conclusion therefore is anarchic: the speaker demolishes authority, instead of having a stake in it. Instead of Huidobro's option in *Altazor*, which was to set the whole of language adrift into endless metamorphosis, Parra's is to demolish all types of authority that anchor speech and its meanings, and this includes renouncing any such authority for his own practice as a poet.

In *Artefactos* (1973) Parra moves to a different type of poem, which is designed to have a powerful penetrative effect without making use of the device of a speaker. *Artefactos* is in many ways the most radical of Parra's experiments. The idea can be traced back to the 'Quebrantahuesos' [bonebreaker], a type of composition that Parra invented in the 1950s with Enrique Lihn and other associates. The texts were made from headlines and pictures cut out of newspapers and put together in a collage. Parra compares them with pop art:

por ejemplo, hay un texto que alguna vez va a haber que fotografiarlo y que dice lo siguiente: 'Muchas felicidades', con unas letras muy rococó y como con vidriecitos, así, que relumbran, tomadas de una tarjeta postal, y arriba de todo esto hay un gran corazón canceroso, lleno de grasa, cortado de una revista médica, y encima del corazón un par de noviecitos chicos recortados de 'El Mercurio'.[50]

[for example, there is a text that would be worth photographing sometime which says 'Congratulations', in very rococo letters which glitter like glass, taken from a postcard, and above that there is a large cancerous heart, full of fat, cut out of a medical journal, and above the heart there is a young engaged couple cut out of the 'Mercurio'.]

However, the later *Artefactos* do not use shocked subjectivity as a communicative device but instead seek to probe the communicative environment which moulds subjectivities.[51] There is no longer any similarity with surrealism. Take the following (see Fig. 1) where the words are printed inside an aura of dazzling light, as in popular religious images:

SILENCIO MIERDA!

QUE LEVANTEN LA MANO

LOS QUE QUIERAN RESUCITAR

UN PASO AL FRENTE

LOS QUE DESEEN

REJUVENECER[52]

---

[50] Morales, *La poesía de Nicanor Parra*, 202.

[51] The factor of shock suggests a similarity with Baudelaire. See Walter Benjamin, *Charles Baudelaire: A Lyric Poet in the Era of High Capitalism* (London, 1983), 113–16. However, with *Artefactos* Parra abandons the method of dramatizing subjectivity.

[52] *Poemas para combatir la calvicie* (Mexico City, 1993), 163.

Fig. 1 An *Artefacto,* as originally printed.

[SILENCE SHIT!
HANDS UP
ANYONE WANTING RESURRECTION
ONE PACE FORWARD
ANYONE FOR
REJUVENATION]

The effect of placing the voice of military authority beside religious promises is to expose the two main authority bases in the society.

These are in a sense found poems, but they deliberately select hyper-recognizable utterance in order to make use of its enhanced penetrative force. Thus they are like adverts seen as one comes into a city at night:

uno viene de la nada y los avisos luminosos como que lo llenan, como que de alguna manera lo hacen vibrar, lo hacen vivir, y uno va de un aviso a otro y cada aviso es una especie de pinchazo a la médula. [. . .] Se trata de tocar puntos sensibles del lector con la punta de una aguja, de galvanizarlo de manera que el lector mueva un pie, mueva un dedo o gire la cabeza.[53]

[you come from nothing and the neon adverts seem to fill you, somehow they make you vibrate and live, and you go from one advert to another and each one is a sort of jab in the flesh. The idea is to touch

---

[53] Morales, *La poesía de Nicanor Parra,* 209.

the reader's sensitive places with a needle, to galvanize him so that he will move a foot or a finger or turn his head.]

The Word becomes flesh, as it is wont to do with the invasive language of advertising, and the aim of these writings is to enter that process but with a different end in view. The function of an advert, as Parra points out, is to put you in touch with a need: 'A través de una configuración muy breve de palabras uno se pone en contacto con algo que está más allá. Por ejemplo, cuando se anuncia un departamento: a través de la configuración de palabras uno se puede imaginar ese departamento que necesita urgentemente' [Through a very brief configuration of words one is put in touch with something beyond. For example, when a flat is advertised, through the configuration of words one can imagine the flat one needs urgently]. An 'Artefact' seeks to do the same, but with a different type of need, as in the following example:

> Yo soy un hombre práctico
> no reconozco otra filosofía
> Que la de mi jefe
> por complacer a mis superiores
> Soy capaz de pararme patas arriba[54]

> [I am a practical man
> the only philosophy I recognize
> is my boss's
> to please my superiors
> I am capable of standing on my head]

The idea of submitting to the boss because it is the practical thing to do is normal enough in our societies, and in a normal conversation the first three lines would sound reasonable and pass without notice. The last two lines break the spell. Yet they do so merely by voicing what is thought internally but not said. What would be the reader's need in this case? Perhaps to disengage that voice from its reasonableness. There is a touch of Kafka in the final line, with its suggestion of a beetle—or maybe a dog—with its legs in the air.

The language of the 'Artefacts' is not created or invented but found in the environment. Parra's method was to select pieces of heard language that had the greatest quantity of energy.

---

[54] *Chistes*, 133.

There is a similarity with using the forms of popular poetry, something which Parra had done on a number of occasions, for example in *La cueca larga* [The long cueca] (1958),[55] where he uses a traditional Chilean song form. His interest in popular forms has to do with their ability to communicate, but he also recognizes that they had become museum pieces; the question therefore is how to find a modern equivalent: 'la poesía popular es una poesía ya de museo; no puede uno quedarse allí sin falsificarse a sí mismo. Lo que hay que hacer is seguir la línea de la poesía popular' [popular poetry nowadays belongs in the museum; one can't stay there without falsifying oneself. What has to be done is to follow the line of popular poetry].[56] This technique can be seen, for example, in those 'Artefacts' which use the language of political slogans, which of course has huge resonance and carries intense feeling.

> REVOLUCION
> REVOLUCION
> CUANTAS CONTRAREVOLUCIONES
> SE COMETEN EN TU NOMBRE[57]
>
> [REVOLUTION
> REVOLUTION
> HOW MANY COUNTER-REVOLUTIONS
> ARE MADE IN YOUR NAME]

Something breaks up here. It is not a question of inviting readers to go along with a sentiment expressed but of exposing them to fragments of discourses that have been detached from those discourses and their legitimizing functions. Parra compares it with an explosion: 'los fragmentos salen disparados a altas velocidades, o sea, están dotados de una gran cantidad de energía y pueden atravesar entonces la capa exterior del lector' [the fragments are shot out at high speed, in other words they possess high energy and can therefore penetrate the reader's outer layer].[58] The 'Artefacts' can be taken, Parra suggests, as the result of the explosion of the antipoem, or, more precisely, of the explosion of the world of the antipoem.

---

[55] The edition published in Santiago in 1958 includes a recording in which Parra performs this poem to music.

[56] Morales, *La poesía de Nicanor Parra*, 207.

[57] *Poemas para combatir la calvicie*, 161.

[58] Morales, *La poesía de Nicanor Parra*, 210.

The 'Artefacts' respond to the epoch of the Popular Unity government, but the last thing they show is real unity. On the contrary, they reveal severe cracks in the spoken language which signal the breakdown of a communicative pact.[59] The belief structures exposed in the antipoems, for example in 'La trampa', continue but they are no longer capable of holding together a society. Consider the following two 'Artefacts':

EL PADRE ETERNO

terminó fugándose con una colegiala[60]

[OUR ETERNAL FATHER

ended up running away with a schoolgirl]

L'ÉTAT C'EST MOI
LA REVOLUCIÓN
CUBANA
SOY YO[61]

[L'ÉTAT C'EST MOI
THE CUBAN
REVOLUTION
IS ME]

The juxtaposition shows briefly how the 'Artefacts' are designed not just to explode but to interact with each other. In each case, the precise form of statement is crucial: the unctuous language of the Church; the cheap voyeurism of the news; the absolutism of the bourgeois leader; and the unspoken thought of Fidel Castro (who visited Chile for Allende's inauguration) bang against each other so as to break down their legitimacy. Instead of a discursive formation, the function of which is to hold together in mutual legitimacy a range of different discourses, what we have is the disintegration of that mutual reinforcement.

It is not their content which allows these texts to accomplish that radical action, but the forms of expression which they display. This is shown at greater length in 'Como les iba

---

[59] More technically, the collapse of the discursive forms of the consensus politics that had characterized Chile since the 1920s. Jürgen Habermas defines communicative rationality, or a communicative pact, as what makes it possible 'to negotiate common definitions of the situation' such that the participants come 'to an agreement concerning the claimed validity of their utterances' (Jürgen Habermas, *The Theory of Communicative Action*, vol. i (London, 1984), 95, 99). The 'Artefactos' do not fulfil these conditions.　　[60] *Chistes*, 134.　　[61] Ibid. 135.

diciendo' [As I was telling you], a poem published in 1972, whose demolitional humour has to do not so much with the grotesque egotism of the speaker as with the fact that the language has degenerated so much that it actually allows him to speak the way he does:

> yo soy el descubridor de Gabriela Mistral
> antes de mí no se tenía idea de poesía
> soy deportista: recorro los cien metros planos
> en un abrir y cerrar de ojos
> [. . .]
> yo le dije al Che Guevara que Bolivia nó
> le expliqué con lujo de detalles
> y le advertía que arriesgaba su vida
>
> de haberme hecho caso
> no le hubiera ocurrido lo que le ocurrió
> ¿recuerdan ustedes lo que le ocurrió al Che Guevara
>   en Bolivia?[62]

> [I'm the one who discovered Gabriela Mistral
> before me no one had any idea of poetry
> I do sport: I can do a hundred metres
> in a blinking of the eyes
> I said to Che Guevara Bolivia no
> I explained it to him in plenty of detail
> and I warned him he was risking his life
>
> if he had listened to me
> what happened to him wouldn't have happened
> do you remember what happened to Che Guevara
>   in Bolivia?]

The traditional Chilean upper-class egomaniac lurches towards the insipid permissive egotism of a yuppie. But it is the language which allows it, the language is the permissive factor.

The ideas which are in play in the 'Artefacts' reveal the deep coherence of Parra's poetics. He goes back to his earlier idea—mentioned above—that human beings as they now are have come from the explosion millions of years ago of an original 'giant man'. Thus the poet is responding to expulsion from paradise, by reconstructing 'nuestra imagen inicial' [our initial image], which implies the future as much as the past: 'Tal vez el

---

[62] Ibid. 125–6.

concepto de tiempo tenga que revisarse también, porque esta imagen está atrás, pero a lo mejor también está adelante' [Perhaps the concept of time needs rethinking also, because this image is behind us but maybe also in front of us].[63] Thus the texts offer themselves not just as actions of exposure and demolition but also as restitutive of a happiness in and of the Word. When the modelling force of language, whose primary instance is discourse, is momentarily gone, there is a flash of paradise.

If the antipoems are designed to be read against an imaginary wholeness or continuity of self and environment, in that they show the breaking up of those ideals, the 'Artefacts' no longer imply any such presuppositions. Parra suggests a way of locating them in the story of his poetry: 'Lo que habría pasado sería lo siguiente: que el método antipoético habría fracasado. El poeta piensa ahora que existe otro método más radical, más drástico para reconstituir la imagen del hombre inicial' [What had happpened would be that the antipoetic method had failed. The poet now considers that there is a more radical and more drastic method for reconstituting the image of the initial man].[64] The method, as he sees it, is the discontinuous one of quantum physics:

La antipoesía fallaría porque se suponía todavía que era posible reconstituir en su totalidad esa imagen [. . .] En la imposibilidad de reconstituir efectivamente ese hombre inicial, renunciamos a esa empresa baladí y nos vamos a conformar exclusivamente con reconstituir ciertos puntos que pertenecieron a ese sujeto. En los artefactos las partículas que hemos encontrado las pondríamos sin rellenar con la imaginación aquello que falta, sino que nos quedaríamos con aquello que efectivamente es.[65]

[Antipoetry had failed because it assumed it was still possible to reconstitute that image in its totality. Given the impossibility of actually reconstituting that initial man, we have abandoned that trivial undertaking and we are going to be concerned exclusively with reconstituting certain points that belonged to that subject. In the artefacts the idea is not to fill in what's missing with the imagination, but simply to set out the particles we have found, so as to end up with what actually is.]

---

[63] Morales, *La poesía de Nicanor Parra*, 211, 213.
[64] Ibid. 212.   [65] Ibid. 213.

Thus if an 'Artefact' can be viewed as a compressed collage, into which vast discursive spaces have been compacted, it can also be seen as a micro-machine, navigating the discontinuities that were always there and in the process discovering and releasing sub-discursive particles.

EL MUNDO ES LO QUE ES

y no lo que un hijo de puta llamado Einstein
dice que es[66]

[THE WORLD IS WHAT IT IS

and not what a son-of-a-bitch called Einstein
says it is]

The method allows no preconception: there is always an outside to the amoeba-poem.

[66] *Chistes*, 136.

2

Ernesto Cardenal: Eros and Belief under Epic Necessity

Debemos contemplar todas las cosas como símbolos o figuras, como fotos de Dios. No como cosas que valen por sí mismas, para ser poseídas y gozadas por sí mismas.

(Ernesto Cardenal)

The words, in writing [. . .] transcend everything.

(William Carlos Williams)

Poetry is lines of sound drawn in the air.

(Basil Bunting)

ATTENTION AND THE POEM

Ernesto Cardenal, one of the most important Latin American poets of the later twentieth century, has written most of his poetry since entering the priesthood. To read his work as expression of the experience of conversion—and of other key biographical events, such as the decision to commit himself to the Sandinista Revolution—has been the chosen stance of most criticism.[1] What I propose here, without excluding biographical information where it is important to the process of writing, is to set up a sort of experiment in order to find out what types of reading Cardenal's various books invite. When I say reading, I do not mean interpretation, as when a sequence of ideas is extracted from a text and expounded. I mean the quality of attention which the poems solicit and exemplify, the controls they exercise upon a reader's ear, eye, and intellect. Because just as art requires a particular quality of attention, so also does

[1] See John Beverley and Mark Zimmerman, *Literature and Politics in the Central American Revolutions* (Austin, Tex., 1990).

religion, and similarly Cardenal's other main concerns, eros and politics. The aim is to explore Cardenal's poems as proposals of attention and therefore to avoid placing artistic decisions on a different plane from the religious, the erotic, and the political.[2] Otherwise art gets subordinated to other concerns, allowing religion, for example, to become a transcendence, for which the words are merely a vehicle. In plain language, the poetry uses the religion in order to get heard, which makes it less interesting as poetry.

The Latin word *attendere* means to bend towards, as in the phrase *animum attendere*, to give one's mind to something. What is it, in this sense, that requires one's attention? In Rilke's *Duino Elegies*, it is 'this Here and Now, so fleeting, [which] seems to require us and strangely | concerns us', and that includes speaking, in the sense of 'such saying as never the things themselves | hoped so intensely to be'.[3] That solicitude could be placed beside Heidegger's concept of 'care' as primary condition of being in the world.[4] Except that, in a poem, there is no concept that is not subject to the particular and mysterious movements of attention which the words elicit. In San Juan de la Cruz and in César Vallejo, the phrase 'no sé' speaks of a condition of not knowing:[5] all thinking becomes subject to that condition. 'No sé' speaks of a threshold between thought and poetry. The lines of movement made by a poem cannot be drawn in advance; as the Argentinian poet Hugo Gola writes: 'el poeta [. . .] no intenta registrar un pensamiento previo al poema, sentido antes de que el poema sea escrito, sino que el pensamiento como la palabra se desplazan tanteando en la oscuridad' [the poet does not attempt to register a thought that is previous to the poem, felt before the poem is written, on the contrary, thought, just as much as the word, moves gropingly in the darkness].[6]

The particular actions of Cardenal's poems—their movement, in all senses of the word—involve the deployment of a

---

[2] Julio Cortázar's short story 'Apocalipsis de Solentiname' (in *Nicaragua tan violentamente dulce* (Barcelona, 1984)), usefully points up the issues.

[3] Rainer Maria Rilke, Ninth Elegy, in *Duino Elegies*, trans. J. B. Leishman and Stephen Spender (New York, 1963), 73, 75.

[4] *Being and Time* (Oxford, 1962), I, 6.

[5] See *Cántico*, and 'Los heraldos negros', respectively.

[6] 'Experiencia y lenguaje', *Nombres*, 3 (1993), 165.

wide range of materials, political, historiographical, cosmological, ethnographical, theological, etc. The handling of these materials depends, as a poetics, on a variety of techniques of composition. The most important of these is, perhaps, the use of sound: sound is a crucial force or vector (directionality of force) throughout Cardenal's poetry. It is the penetration of matter or cosmos into the self and also the voicing of feeling. In an early poem, the howling of animals heard in the night becomes the force of the poem itself:

> ¿Has oído gritar de noche al oso-caballo
>
> 00-00-00-00
>
> o al coyote-solo en la noche de luna
>
> uuuuuuuuuuuuuú?
>
> Pues eso mismo son estos versos.[7]
>
> [Have you heard the horse-bear crying in the night
>
> 00-00-00-00
>
> or the lone coyote in the moonlight
>
> uuuuuuuuuuuuuu?
>
> That is exactly what these lines are.]

The penetration of a crude, non-human sound becomes meaning and poem in an exchange with an interlocutor (*tú*). The *yo/tú* relationship, as the series the poem belongs to makes clear, is an erotic one. In a later piece of writing, the monks of the Trappist Order, which Cardenal had joined, are praying at night; the sound of animals groaning in the night enters the chapel: that sound is heard as a prayer:

El coro de las ranas y los grillos cantando en la noche de luna, y las voces y cantos y quejas de todos los animales [. . .] son otros tantos oficios como el oficio de los monjes; son también salmos en otra lengua; son también oración.[8]

[The chorus of frogs and crickets singing in the moonlight, and the voices and songs of all the animals are other offices of worship like that of the monks; they are also psalms in another language; they are also prayer.]

In the second *Cantiga* of *Cántico cósmico* [Cosmic canticle], he writes:

---

[7] *Epigramas* (Buenos Aires, 1972), 64.
[8] *Vida en el amor* (Buenos Aires, 1970), 117.

Oye el susurro de las cosas . . .
                    Lo dicen, pero dicen en secreto.
Sólo a solas se revela.
        Sólo de noche en lugar secreto se desnuda. (*CC* 22)[9]
[Listen to the whisper of things . . .
                    They speak, but they speak in secret.
Revelation is only when you are alone.
        You undress only at night in a secret place.]

The scene assembles erotic contact, religious revelation, scientific cosmology, and sound-patterns, the sounding of the words echoing San Juan de la Cruz's poem:

> Y todos quantos vagan
> de ti me van mil gracias refiriendo,
> y todos más me llagan,
> y déxame muriendo
> un no sé qué que quedan balbuziendo.[10]

> [And all who come
> of you a thousand graces tell,
> and all increase my wound,
> and their whispers say
> I know not what but stay
> and leave me dying.]

SOUND AND LOVE'S BODY

Hora O, Cardenal's first major poem, uses variations of patterned sound to assemble and dramatize the secular narrative of César Augusto Sandino's uprising in the late 1920s. The march of Sandino and his men is told in a language that moves alternately towards and away from the ballad rhythm of the traditional Spanish *romance*. The *romance* or ballad has been the main form of narrative poetry in Spanish America, having served from the sixteenth century to the present day to shape popular speech and oral memory into memorable transmission:

Y no era ni militar ni político.
Y sus hombres:

---

[9] Textual references to *Cántico cósmico* (Madrid, 1992) are given as *CC*.
[10] *Cántico*, in *Poesía* (Madrid, 1989), 250.

muchos eran muchachos,
con sombreros de palma y con caites
o descalzos, con machetes, ancianos
de barba blanca, niños de doce años con sus rifles,
blancos, indios impenetrables, y rubios, y negros murrucos,
con los pantalones despedazados y sin provisiones,
los pantalones hechos jirones,
desfilando en fila india con la bandera adelante
—un harapo levantado en un palo de la montaña—
callados debajo de la lluvia, y cansados,
chapoteando los caites en los charcos del pueblo
                    ¡Viva Sandino!
y de la montaño venían, y a la montaña volvían,
marchando, chapoteando, con la bandera adelante.
Un ejército descalzo o con caites y casi sin armas
que no tenían ni disciplina ni desorden
y donde ni los jefes ni la tropa ganaban paga
pero no se obligaba a pelear a nadie:
y tenían jerarquía militar pero todos eran iguales.[11]

[And he was neither a military man nor a politician.
And as for his men:
    many of them were kids
wearing sombreros of palm leaves and sandals,
or they went barefoot and carried machetes, old men
with white beards, twelve-year-old boys with rifles,
Spanish, impenetrable Indians, blonds, curly-headed Negroes,
with their trousers in tatters, with no provisions,
with pennants they made from the rags of their trousers,
marching in Indian file with their banner in front
—a rag tied to a pole they had cut from the jungle—
marching silently under torrents of rain, worn-out,
their sandals splashing through the puddles in the villages
                    Viva Sandino!
and they came from the jungle and went back to the jungle,
splashing through puddles with the banner in front.
An army in sandals or barefoot with hardly any weapons
which had neither discipline nor disorder
and neither their leaders nor the troops had any pay
but no-one was compelled to fight;
and though they had a military hierarchy they were all equal.][12]

[11] *Poemas de Ernesto Cardenal* (Havana, 1967), 17–18.
[12] Trans. Donald Gardner, in Robert Márquez (ed.), *Latin American Revolutionary Poetry* (New York, 1974), 337–9.

When Cardenal reads this passage,[13] his voicing changes in the third line, where the sounds are enunciated more slowly and regularly, an entry into a zone of epic tension, similar in form to Homer's list of ships in the *Iliad*, after the previous more relaxed phrasing. The first line in the passage quoted is virtually hendecasyllabic, the classical metre of erudite Spanish poetry since the Renaissance. Up to this point (about a quarter of the way through the poem as a whole, which is a little less than 500 lines long) hendecasyllables and ballad-type rhythms (of seven and eight syllables) alternate. The hendecasyllabic lines are used for expository passages (on the economic history of Nicaragua, for example) or for fragments of conversation, and the *romance* pattern for presentation of scenario ('con lagunas y volcanes') or event ('Ubico está resfriado').[14] The *romance* rhythm of the third line quoted above, where Cardenal's tone of voice changes, includes the assonance of 'muchos' and 'muchachos', a thickening of sounds through repetition, but it is followed by two expository lines of lesser tension where the speaking moves away from the epic zone. The movement in and out of epic characterizes the whole poem, the epic mode generating here a counter-narrative and counter-memory to the shame of decades of dictatorship and economic and political dependency upon the USA: the voice of a people to come, sovereign and independent.

The epic list of Sandino's forces ends with 'negros murrucos' [curly-headed Negroes], making it a popular epic, in contrast to Homer's aristocratic one. After that the tone changes again and the rhythm moves back to that of the *romance*, though with some expository interpolations (the quasi-hendecasyllabic 'los pantalones hechos jirones', for example). The repetitions of semantic and acoustic elements (*pantalones; desfilando/fila*) make the scene presented stand out more vividly against its background of ordinary speech. But the irregularities of rhythm—a ballad interrupted by talk and vice versa—make this a non-standard epic, as also does the content, in several senses: the improvisation (the flag is 'a rag'), the unconventional organization (the troops are irregular, there is military hierarchy without inequality), and the sheer amount of pain in their

---

[13] For example in the Casa de las Américas recording (LD-CA-8).
[14] *Poemas de Ernesto Cardenal*, 9.

undertaking. The complex weaving of long slow *a* syllables with faster *i* sounds (e.g. 'desfilando en fila india con la bandera adelante') gathers together the irregularities just mentioned into an extraordinary play of sounds and movements, of emotional ambiences and ways of seeing: instead of the conventional heroes of the nineteenth-century Latin American republics, sung and admired in national anthems and recognized as statues in town squares, something more complex and difficult; instead of the prestige granted by the State to its founders, drawn from French and Prussian military iconography, a dignity that had to be invented in the act, without precedents: the organization of the verse repeats the organization of Sandino's army.

The difficulty of their movements is interrupted by the cry '¡Viva Sandino!', which is followed by a line (eight plus seven syllables, with caesura and rhyme) which would not sound out of place in a traditional *romance*: 'y de la montaña venían, y a la montaña volvían' [and they came from the jungle and went back to the jungle]. A ballad tells a collective story: the speaker here speaks for a collectivity not yet constituted, a nation not yet allowed to exist because of the indignity of the Somoza dictatorship. That future nation is summoned and heard, in the poem, as a rhythm of voices emerging out of popular speech, turned into collective memory through poetic phrases and narratives—the national-popular as a poetics.[15]

The six lines that follow this moment of epic intensification (and bring the passage quoted to a close) gradually reduce and disperse the tension into unemphatic spoken phrases, where the heightened rhythmic regularity breaks up into fragments of conversation. This other voice, closer to the accents of the ordinary, like a person addressing one in a conversation, without elevation or distance, opens the doors of hearing to a wider, less exclusive field of voices, closer to the infinite conversation that configures the everyday.[16] The emphatic language corresponds to a value area, an entry into transcendent meanings, where actions take on the quality of myth, whereas the unemphatic language takes the poem away from value-statements into the

---

[15] See Antonio Gramsci, *Selections from Cultural Writings* (Cambridge, Mass., 1991), 199–286.

[16] See the discussion of conversation and the ordinary in connection with Parra's poetry, in Ch. 1 (pp. 33–40).

drift of conversation, although the two are never entirely separate.

Their relationship occurs as an interweaving of two main
voices—more accurately, of two types of voicing, since it is not
a question of the natural expression of already-classified
persons/groups but of a speaking that emerges and as it does
so delineates the place it emerges from. On the one hand
there is the epic language of formalized collective enunciation,
marked by the ballad-type rhythms, and including quotations
from 'Si Adelita se fuera con otro', one of the most famous
ballads of the Mexican Revolution. At certain moments this
language occurs for sustained, uninterrupted stretches. More
usually, it is interrupted by the second type of voicing. The
interplay includes the use of quoted speech, as in the following, which follows immediately after four lines heard from 'Si
Adelita se fuera con otro':

> 'El abrazo es el saludo de todos nosotros',
> decía Sandino—y nadie ha abrazado como él.
> Y siempre que hablaban de ellos decían *todos*:
> 'Todos nosotros . . .' 'Todos somos iguales.'[17]

> ['All of us embrace each other instead of saluting,'
> Sandino said, and no one could embrace a man as he did.
> And whenever they spoke of themselves they said *all*:
> 'All of us . . .' 'We are all equals.'][18]

A contrasting communicative action enters the poem with the
forms of speech used by Somoza and the US ambassador in
conversation:

> 'He is a bandido', decía Somoza, 'a bandolero'.
> Y Sandino nunca tuvo propiedades.
> Que traducido al español quiere decir:
> Somoza le llamaba a Sandino bandolero.
> Y Sandino nunca tuvo propiedades.[19]

> ['He is a *bandido*,' Somoza said, 'a *bandolero*.'
> And Sandino never sold anyone's property.
> Which, being translated, means
> that Somoza called Sandino a gangster.
> And Sandino never stole anyone's property.][20]

---

[17] *Poemas de Ernesto Cardenal*, 18.   [18] Gardner's translation, 341.
[19] *Poemas de Ernesto Cardenal*, 19.   [20] Gardner's translation, 341.

The shift of language to English alters the way everything is heard. The repetition of 'Y Sandino nunca tuvo propiedades' dramatizes the change in meanings: on the first occasion it is heard in the aftermath of the switch to English, a switch that expresses the subordinate relation of Nicaragua to the USA and the indignity that goes with that, as well as the cynicism of President Somoza. The second time it is heard within the pact offered by the narrator of events in the poem to its readers. The two types of communication and the types of society they imply are worlds apart.

The narrative moves into the first person for the second event presented by the poem: the unsuccessful uprising of 1954, led by Adolfo Báez Bone, in which Cardenal himself took part. The event is placed between the the dry heat of April and the first rains of May:

> En mayo
> florecen los malinches en las calles de Managua.
> Pero abril en Nicaragua es el mes de la muerte.
> En abril los mataron.
>
> Yo estuve con ellos en la rebelión de abril
> y aprendí a manejar una ametralladora Rising.[21]

> [In May
> the malinche trees are in flower in the streets of Managua.
> But April is the month of death in Nicaragua.
> They killed them in April.
>
> I was with them in the April rebellion
> and I learned to use a Rising machine gun.][22]

Revolution as unavoidable violence in the achievement of nationhood is placed alongside rebirth as cosmic and political: 'cuando muere un héroe | no se muere: | sino que ese héroe renace | en una nación'[23] [when a hero dies | he is not dead | for the hero is reborn | in a Nation[24]]. The flow of sound (*muere | muere, nace | nación*) carries the flow of meaning into the future dreamed of. And within that vision of continuity beyond death (note the lovely pun on the name of the machine-gun), it is the land that sustains the epic continuity of meanings:

---

[21] *Poemas de Ernesto Cardenal*, 27.
[22] Gardner's translation, 353. I have added the final line of the quotation, which is missing in Gardner's version.
[23] *Poemas de Ernesto Cardenal*, 28.   [24] Gardner's translation, 355.

Porque a veces nace un hombre en una tierra
    que es esa tierra.
Y la tierra en que es enterrado ese hombre
    es ese hombre.
Y los hombres que después nacen en esa tierra
    son ese hombre.
Y Adolfo Báez Bone era ese hombre.[25]

[Because there are times when a man is born in a country
    who is that country.
And the country in which that man is buried
    is that man.
And the men who are born after him in that land
    are that man.
And Adolfo Báez Bone was that man.][26]

Near its ending, the poem recounts the results of the failure of the two rebellions: torture, persecution, poverty, exile—and a huge shipment of arms, all marked 'MADE IN USA', watched by the people in the streets, making a kind of anti-triumphal march:[27]

Yo vi pasar esas armas por la Avenida Roosevelt.
Y la gente callada en las calles las veía pasar:
el flaco, el descalzo, el de la bicicleta,
el negro, el trompudo, aquella la de amarillo,
el alto, el chele, el pelón, el bigotudo,
el ñato, el chirizo, el murruco, el requeneto.[28]

[And I saw these arms going down the Avenida Roosevelt.
And the people in the streets fell silent when they saw them
    passing:
the skinny fellow, the one with no shoes, the one with a
    bicycle,
the Negro, the one with a big nose, the one dressed in yellow,
the tall fellow, the blond one, the bald-head, the one with
    a moustache,

---

[25] *Poemas de Ernesto Cardenal*, 28.
[26] Gardner's translation, 353 (modified).
[27] See Walter Benjamin, 'Theses on the Philosophy of History', VII: 'Whoever has emerged victorious participates to this day in the triumphal procession in which the present rulers step over those who are lying prostrate. According to traditional practice, the spoils are carried along in the procession. They are called cultural treasures.' In *Illuminations* (London, 1973), 258.
[28] *Poemas de Ernesto Cardenal*, 28.

the flat-faced fellow, the scrawny one, the curly-head, the
one with straight hair.][29]

The sound thickens, with the particular music of the long *a*
sounds which Cardenal uses to enter the zone of pity. The
dignity of this music—so as not to say solemnity, a word
hijacked by Church and bourgeoisie—is not the music of a military band but of people in the streets watching silently a spectacle which could not be said then as spoken meaning but
which a poem, later, undertakes to speak. In the composition of
the poem, that music is interrupted by another music, the
sound of Somoza dancing mambo while the killings went on
and screams were heard in the night: 'mambo mambo I qué
rico el mambo I I cuando los estaban matando'[30] [mambo
mambo I qué rico el mambo I while they were killing them[31]].
The rhyme *mambo* I *matando* transmits a particular shameless
callousness.

But the final statement is of resurrection of the hero:

> Pero el héroe nace cuando muere
> y la hierba verde renace de los carbones.[32]

> [But the hero is born the moment that he dies
> and green grass springs again from the ashes.][33]

which includes the dream of a new land. To compose social
revolution, love, and cosmic order into an epic whole continues
to be the concern of Cardenal through his later poetry, though
the materials are reaccentuated in more complex ways. A key
change is that a tension arises between social love and erotic
love. Cardenal's later books handle the energy of that tension
in different ways, conserving it, extending it, or displacing it
towards resolution in religious belief-structures.

The *Epigramas* and the *Salmos* explore two ways of actively
using that tension, without resolution. Although the first are
without Christian belief-structures and the latter present themselves as translations or readings of the Old Testament Psalms,
there are interesting similarities in the handling of language
and affect. The epigrams have a classical tone, deploying the
type of voice used by certain Latin poets of the first century AD

---

[29] Gardner's translation, 355.　　[30] *Poemas de Ernesto Cardenal*, 29.
[31] Gardner's translation, 355–7.　[32] *Poemas de Ernesto Cardenal*, 33.
[33] Gardner's translation, 363.

such as Martial. This tone precludes any division between public and inner life, a division that later on Christianity systematically engendered through techniques such as the confessional.[34] Love and politics occur in the same space, without variation of the voice:

> Me contaron que estabas enamorada de otro
> y entonces me fui a mi cuarto
> y escribí ese artículo contra el Gobierno
> por el que estoy preso.[35]

> [They told me you were in love with someone else
> and I went to my room
> and wrote that article against the Government
> which is why I am here in jail.]

Energy is displaced from love to politics but there is also a sense of each being a continuation of the other. Consider the particular way an environment of sound is handled in the following epigram:

> De pronto suena en la noche una sirena
> de alarma, larga, larga,
> el aullido lúgubre de la sirena
> de incendio o de la ambulancia blanca de la muerte,
> como el grito de la yegua en la noche[36]

> [Suddenly in the night a siren goes off
> with a long long sound of alarm
> the lugubrious howl of the siren
> it is a fire or the white ambulance of death,
> like the cry of a mare in the night]

The various elements form an atmosphere of fear (night, siren, alarm, howl, fire, ambulance, death, cry, mare), becoming a sound-image ('la ambulancia blanca de la muerte') where whiteness in the visual imagination and whiteness of sound (the repeated open *a* sounds) converge in a softened rhythm as though the soul were being called, the tension held between the capacity for love and the proximity of death. At which point a European reader[37] might expect that particular scenario to be

---

[34] This is set out vividly and succinctly by Michel Foucault in *Technologies of the Self* (London, 1988), 40–3.
[35] *Epigramas* (Buenos Aires), 22.
[36] Ibid. 32.
[37] Less, a reader of US poets such as Paul Blackburn.

complete: the city at night has become like nature to an inner experience, each echoing the other. But the poem continues:

> como el grito de la yegua en la noche,
> que se acerca y se acerca sobre las calles
> y las casas y sube, sube, y baja
> y crece, crece, baja y se aleja
> creciendo y bajando. No es incendio ni muerte:
> Es Somoza que pasa.

> [like the cry of a mare in the night,
> that comes closer and closer along streets
> and houses and rises, rises, and falls
> and rises, rises, and falls into the distance
> rising and falling. It is not a fire or death:
> It is Somoza going by.]

The same *a* sound, fading now ('pasa'), invokes a different way of listening; instead of being heard by a self in isolation and solitude it convenes the population of a city. This tense public environment has been produced by the Somoza dynasty, dictators of Nicaragua since the defeat of Sandino. What enters here is the different history of Nicaragua, different in the sense that the conditions for a modern society, with enjoyment of individual rights, had not been achieved.

This begins to answer the question why transfer a Roman tone to twentieth-century Nicaragua? The absence of a sense of private self is caused by similarities of environment.

> Y otra vez te irritarás con mis yambos,
> mis inocentes yambos, Generalísimo.[38]

> [And once again you will be irritated by my iambics,
> my innocent iambics, Generalissimo.]

The poet's 'iambics' are the same verses that will make his lover immortal

> ... pero no te escaparás de mis yambos ...[39]

> [... but you will not escape from my iambics ...]

These are Cardenal's translations of Catullus, which also include:

[38] Translation of Catullus, lxxv, in *Epigramas* (Mexico City, 1961), 94.
[39] Ibid., liv, 73. The Latin text is: 'At non effugies meos iambos' (Catullus, *Fragmenta*, 1).

Pero me duele que los labios puros de una muchacha pura
hayas manchado ahora con tu inmunda saliva.
Pero no quedarás sin castigo: porque todos los siglos
te conocerán, y la Literatura Latina dirá quién fuiste.[40]

[But it hurts me that the pure lips of a pure girl
have been stained by your filthy saliva.
But you will not escape punishment: because you will be known
for all time, and Latin Literature will say who you were.]

The confidence in poetry as capable of sounding aloud in
public space is used by Cardenal in his own *Epigramas*:

Cuídate, Claudia, cuando estés conmigo,
porque el gesto más leve, cualquier palabra, un suspiro
de Claudia, el menor descuido,
tal vez un día lo examinen eruditos,
y este baile de Claudia se recuerde por siglos.
Claudia, ya te lo aviso. *(PE 7)*[41]

[Be careful, Claudia, when you are with me,
because the slightest gesture, word, or sigh
of Claudia, the smallest carelessness,
may one day be examined by scholars,
and this dance of Claudia's be remembered for centuries.
Claudia, I am warning you.]

But the relationship with the Roman poets is more an inversion
than a continuity. Catullus and Martial had confidence in love as
pleasure, a concern which made political power unimportant:

No me empeño demasiado en serte simpático, César,
y no he averiguado siquiera si eres moreno o rubio.[42]

[I am not trying too hard to be simpático to you, Caesar,
and I have not even found out if you are dark or blond.]

In Cardenal's own epigrams, however, politics invade with
violence and shame all areas of life, as when the title of one of
the poems states 'SOMOZA DESVELIZA LA ESTATUA DE SOMOZA EN EL
ESTADIO SOMOZA' [SOMOZA UNVEILS THE STATUE OF SOMOZA IN THE

---

[40] Ibid., lxxiii, 92.
[41] The textual reference *PE* refers to *Poesía escogida* (Barcelona, 1975). Clodia
was the real name of the woman Catullus was unhappily in love with, to whom he
gives the name Lesbia in his poems.
[42] Translations of Catullus, lxiv, *Epigramas*, 83. The Latin text is: 'Nil nimium
studeo, Caesar, tibi velle placere, | nec scire utrum sis albus an ater homo' (93).

SOMOZA STADIUM], the capital letters making it read as a headline. The very idea of a public sphere, in which social necessities can be made visible and debated, is lacking, and therefore has to be invented. Cardenal turns the relationship round: love enters the political sphere, and in so doing asserts an alternative politics:

> Yo no canto la defensa de Stalingrado
> ni la campaña de Egipto
> ni el desembarco de Sicilia
> ni la cruzada del Rhin del general Eisenhower:
> Yo sólo canto la conquista de una muchacha.[43]
>
> [I do not sing the defence of Stalingrad
> or the Egyptian campaign
> or the landings in Sicily
> or General Eisenhower's crossing the Rhine
> I only sing the conquest of a girl.]

That extension of love into the public sphere, so that what one cares about would stretch continuously from the individual to the realm of social and political life,[44] is an ideal which Cardenal later saw as fulfilled in the Sandinista struggle and which he expressed in his proposals for the poetry workshops set up during and after the Revolution.

The method adopted in the *Salmos* is different. The desire for justice, in Nicaragua and more widely, is articulated as a particular way of hearing the biblical Psalms, which is actually a way of rehearing them or retranslating them since they will—certainly for a Latin American ear—already have been heard in Latin and/or in the sixteenth-century Spanish translation. The key technique is not so much to modernize the biblical language as to interrupt or interpolate it with everyday speech. Compare the Spanish Bible with Cardenal's version of Psalm 36:

> No te impacientes a causa de los malignos,
> Ni tengas envidia de los que hacen iniquidad.
> Porque como hierba serán pronto cortados,
> Y como la hierba verde se secarán.[45]

---

43 *Poemas de Ernesto Cardenal,* 40.

44 Thus love in Cardenal's poetry is different from the Renaissance tradition of love as heightening perception. See Louis Zukovsky, *Bottom: On Shakespeare* (Berkeley, 1987), 17.

45 *La Santa Biblia,* Antigua Versión de Casiodoro de Reina (1569), rev. Cipriano de Valera (1602).

[Fret not thyself because of evildoers,
neither be thou envious against the workers of iniquity.
For they shall soon be cut down like the grass,
and wither as the green herb.][46]

No te impacientes si los ves hacer muchos millones
Sus acciones comerciales
                              son como el heno de los campos
No envidies a los millonarios ni a las estrellas de cine
a los que figuran a ocho columnas en los diarios
a los que viven en hoteles lujosos
y comen en lujosos restaurantes
porque pronto sus nombres no estarán en ningún diario
y ni los eruditos conocerán sus nombres
    Porque pronto serán segados como el heno de los campos.[47]

[Don't be impatient if you see them make millions
Their stocks and shares
                              are like the hay of the fields
Don't envy millionaires or movie stars
or the ones who get eight columns in the papers
or live in luxury hotels
and eat in luxury restaurants
because soon their names will not be in any paper
and not even scholars will know their names
    Because soon they will be cut down like the hay of the fields.]

The first difference one notices is that of vocabulary and reference, where realities of twentieth-century capitalist society are
substituted for the generic terms of the biblical text. This is
rather like the modernization of Catholicism that was happening in the 1960s, when liberal priests were substituting colloquial Spanish for the traditional Latin service and explaining
the Bible as a social message. Liberation theology was beginning to have an impact on everyday practices. But the poetics of
Cardenal's *Salmos* include a more radical intervention than that
of vocabulary. The phrases are of varied length and rhythm,
which has the effect of opening up the biblical text to the more
spontaneous flows of conversation. What remain formalized, in
the sense of creating a sense of heightened occasion, are the
repetitions of phrases or of syntactical patterns. The original
process of the biblical text, from non-written song to writing, is

[46] English: *Authorized Version.*   [47] *Salmos* (Buenos Aires, 1969), 39.

reopened by this influx of the spoken word, charged with immediate cares and energies, rather than enclosed by institutional ritual and exclusive interpretation by priests. Cardenal's intervention *vis-à-vis* the Bible is not different from his approach to the institution of Literature: to open it to the spoken world of the actual, wresting it from dead languages. His handling of the language of science and ethnography is similar, as will be shown below.

The book *Gethsemani Ky* (1960) gathers together meditational poems that date from the time spent training as a Trappist monk in Kentucky, under the direction of the American poet Thomas Merton. That decision came as a response to a sense of the failure both of love and of revolution. But whereas love is placed in the past ('no ha quedado nada de aquellos días, nada' [there is nothing left from those days, nothing][48]) or subsumed into a relationship with God, not so the terror of dictatorship in Nicaragua:

> Las luces del palacio de Somoza están prendidas.
> Es la hora en que se reúnen los Consejos de Guerra
> y los técnicos en torturas bajan a las prisiones.[49]

> [The lights of Somoza's palace are lit.
> It is the hour when the War Cabinet meets
> and the technicians of torture go down to the prisons.]

The poem these lines are quoted from begins:

> 2 a.m. Es la hora del Oficio Nocturno, y la iglesia
> en penumbra parece que está llena de demonios.

> [2 am. It is the hour of the Night Office, and the shadowy
> church seems to be full of devils.]

The mind, unprotected in this night vigil, in the discipline of listening in darkness, hears and sees all that would be irreconcilable to the socialized self, an impediment to its functioning.

Prayer is a listening also, the quality of its saying dependent upon the quality of hearing, and what is heard includes the activities of the secret police: 'un bulto cae al agua' [a bundle falls into the water], another disappeared corpse.

---

[48] *Poemas* (Barcelona, 1971), 48.   [49] Ibid. 47.

Y la iglesia está helada, como llena de demonios,
mientras seguimos en la noche recitando los salmos.[50]
[And the church is freezing, as if full of devils,
while we continue reciting the psalms in the night.]

That particular quietness when one can hear what is normally
occulted permits psychic integration of experiences that are difficult to reconcile, experiences that are normally survived by
reducing one's awareness. The long twelve- to sixteen-syllable
lines require long breaths and a slow speed, as in Gregorian
chant, and aid that integration, in an expansion of hearing, as in

> Un perro ladra lejos
> detrás del bosque negro
> Y le contesta otro perro
> detrás de otro bosque
> más lejos . . .[51]

> [A dog barks far away
> behind the black woods
> And another dog answers it
> behind another wood
> further away . . .]

where the shorter lines counterpoint the continuous extension
of sound. In gestalt terms, the figure becomes larger and larger,
integrating more and more of the background, towards a horizon of non-selection, of no cut-off point. In religion this would
be to open oneself to the infinity of God; in poetics it means
opening the poem to what inherited training of the senses and
moulding of the language have excluded.

Meditation, for Cardenal, does not mean turning away from
modernity, but hearing and seeing it differently. The glow of
adverts in the night sky, emblem of the birth of consumer society
in 1940s America—

> PEPSI-COLA
> PALMOLIVE CHRYSLER COLGATE CHESTERFIELD
> que se apagan y se encienden y se apagan y se encienden[52]

> [PEPSI-COLA
> PALMOLIVE CHRYSLER COLGATE CHESTERFIELD
> which go out and on again and out and on again]

---

[50] *Poemas* (Barcelona, 1971), 47.   [51] Ibid. 45.
[52] *Poemas de Ernesto Cardenal*, 54.

—is reinterpreted, by Cardenal, in the light of divine love: the adverts are seen as mass mediations of desires which can only be satisfied by God. In a later poem, 'MANAGUA 6:30 p.m.', written when Cardenal had left the monastery,

> TACA BUNGE KLM SINGER
> MENNEN HTM GÓMEZ NORGE
> RPM SAF ÓPTICA SELECTA
> proclaman la gloria de Dios! (*PE* 67)
>
> [TACA BUNGE KLM SINGER
> MENNEN HTM GÓMEZ NORGE
> RPM SAF ÓPTICA SELECTA
> proclaim the glory of God!]

To take adverts as mediations or vehicles for mass desires is one thing, but to interpret them as a desire for God is quite another, because this implies having at one's disposal another, more powerful vehicle and the problem then is that filling one's eyes and ears with this other model may diminish the quality of attention. To see God in adverts or as answer to Marilyn Monroe's anxiety (in 'Oración por Marilyn Monroe' [Prayer for Marilyn Monroe]) is to risk over-interpreting what actual people experience, and integration can become its opposite, that is, editing and filtering out awkward details and differences in order to find a higher, more powerful pattern. The devil is in the detail, as they say. These two tendencies, to integrate or to screen out, occur in varying measure through all the books that Cardenal wrote after *Gethsemani Ky.*

But in the *Gethsemani* poems themselves, instead of any dissolving, there is a sustained tension between three forms of love: erotic love, love of one's country, and divine love:

> Ha venido la primavera con su olor a Nicaragua:
> un olor a tierra recién llovida, y un olor a calor,
> a flores, a raíces desenterradas, y a hojas mojadas
> (y he oído el mugido de un ganado lejano . . .)
> ¿O es el olor del amor? Pero ese amor no es el tuyo.
> Y el amor a la patria fue el del dictador[53]
>
> [Spring has come with its smell of Nicaragua:
> a smell of earth fresh in rain, and a smell of heat,
> of flowers, of exposed roots, and of damp flowers
> (and I have heard the mooing of far-off cattle . . .)

[53] *Poemas de Ernesto Cardenal*, 51.

Or is it the smell of love? But that love is not yours.
And love of country belonged to the dictator.]

The rhymes carry the play of thought (*olor/ calor/ amor/dictador*)
and the tensions are held by the play of sound:

Y en su tierra amada está ahora el dictador embalsamado
mientras que a ti el Amor te ha llevado al destierro.

[And the dictator is now embalmed in his beloved land
while Love has taken you into exile.]

The sensual richness of internal rhymes and repetitions
conveyed by the first line has the dictator as its object; the barer
language of the second line carries to monastery and exile.
Cardenal's poetics of renunciation, at this time of his life, is
configured, not without humour, in these two lines. That
humour is a measure of acceptance, as in another poem of the
collection, which also begins with spring, season of lovers:

Ha llegado al cementerio trapense la primavera,
al cementerio verde de hierba recién rozada
con sus cruces de hierro en hilera como una siembra,
donde el cardenal llama a su amada y la amada
responde a la llamada de su rojo enamorado.[54]

[Spring has come to the Trappist cemetery,
the green cemetery with grass washed by rain
and iron crosses in a row like seedlings,
where the cardinal calls his beloved and the beloved
responds to the call of her red lover.]

Cardinal birds are red but so also are communists (Cardenal
called life in the Trappist monastery 'una vida comunista y de
amor' [a life of communism and love]),[55] the humorous
double meanings coming through in the sound play. The poem
contemplates resurrection as return of all that is lost, in a great
cycle of destruction and construction, of return to simple
elements and reconstitution of complexity:

Pero cuando el cosmos vuelve al hidrógeno original
—Porque hidrógeno somos y en hidrógeno nos hemos de
    convertir—

[54] Ibid. 49.
[55] Interview with Caupolicán Ovalles, cited in Paul Borgeson, Jr., *Hacia el hombre nuevo: poesía y pensamiento de E. Cardenal* (London, 1984), 51.

no resucitaréis solos, como fuisteis enterrados,
sino que en vuestro cuerpo resucitará toda la tierra:
la lluvia de anoche, y el nido del reyezuelo,
la vaca Holstein, blanca y negra, en la colina,
el amor del cardenal, y el tractor de mayo.

[But when the cosmos returns to its original hydrogen
—because we are hydrogen and hydrogen is what we will
     become—
you will not arise alone, as you were buried,
in your body the whole earth will resurrect:
last night's rain, the goldcrest's nest,
the black and white Holstein cow on the hill,
the cardinal bird's love, the tractor in May.]

The word *cardenal*, placed here in a more generic phrase, is
more easily heard as Cardenal, the poet, the word *amor* become
inclusive of life and death, human and natural, without strain
or dilution.[56] The later poetry extends that inclusiveness into
the vast cosmology of *Cántico cósmico*, but not always with that
same delicacy of hearing that senses the fissures between different types of desire.

'DEBEMOS HACER AQUÍ UN PAÍS': EPIC ASSEMBLAGE AND
THE PROBLEMS OF BELIEF

Cardenal's major achievement after the Trappist period
(1956–9) is a series of long poems which include historical,
political, ethnographical, and scientific concerns. *Canto
nacional* begins with three pages which articulate the song of
different Nicaraguan birds:

En las mañanas de mayo, cuando empiezan las lluvias
     canta el zenzontle
          en las tardes de julio, después del aguacero

---

[56] One could highlight the force of religion—always difficult to define—in
Cardenal's work at this stage through a comparison with William Carlos Williams's
poem 'Rain', where the tension between human love and nature does not allow
their religious or mythical integration: 'Unworldly love | that has no hope | of the
world | and that | cannot change the world | to its delight' (William Carlos
Williams, *Collected Earlier Poems* (New York, 1988), 76).

> canta su canto dulce el zenzontle
> canta libre en el norte. (*PE* 171)
>
> [On May mornings, when the rains begin
> the zenzontle sings
> on July afternoons, after light rain
> the zenzontle sings its sweet song
> sings free in the north.]

The birdsong is refrain in the repetitions of the bird and of the poem:

> el toledo de terciopelo negro y boina escarlata
> canta TO-LE-DO TO-LE-DO
>
> [the toledo in its black velvet and red beret
> sings TO-LE-DO TO-LE-DO]

By making the bird sounds approximately octosyllabic, Cardenal has them sing a *romance*, as in the famous Spanish ballad 'Canta la calandria', though not necessarily in Spanish:

> el pijul de plumaje de color de noche canta
> PIJUL PIJUL PIJUL
>
> [the pijul with its plumage the colour of night sings
> PIJUL PIJUL PIJUL

In the larger movement of the poem, the shorter ballad-type phrases enter a counterpoint with the longer lines (of up to eighteen syllables) which narrate the vicissitudes of Nicaraguan history. The birdsong refrains mark territories which are as yet not part of nation or history. Cardenal is not interested in the tradition of the troubadours, where birdsong is a territory of the mind and heart—a tradition that was crucial for twentieth-century poets of the other America such as Ezra Pound and Paul Blackburn—but in sound becoming place and vice versa, where place is a shared space in the arising of a sense of the land as a country.

The birdsong sounds are answered, in a form of dialogue, by the longer lines. The latter carry out a commentary or diegesis on the former, establishing the land as cultural landscape and time as the cycle of seasons, that is, cultural time. Consider, in the following, how song is countered by commentary:

                                                  Y el
zanate clarinero, *Cassidix nicaragüensis* (es un pájaro
nicaragüense) negroazulvioláceo vuela
en octubre o noviembre sobre los pueblos nicaragüenses
es un pájaro proletario—sin ningún adorno—anda siempre
entre pobres.
Y el pájaro-degollado (con mancha roja en el cuello)
    canta en los huertos

                                              [And the
bugler rook, *Cassidix nicaragüensis* (it is a Nicaraguan
bird) blackblueviolet flies
in October or November over Nicaraguan villages
it is a proletarian bird—without adornments—it always goes
among the poor.
And the beheaded-bird (with a red stain on its neck)
    sings in orchards]

We have the sonorous vernacular name (*zanate*), then the Latin,
then a humorous gloss on the Latin, then a sonorous and visually
vibrant phrase, then a statement of time and place, then a ballad-
type phrase ('pájaro proletario') which is expanded into a
commentary, followed by two ballad-phrases ('Y el pájaro degol-
lado | (con mancha roja en el cuello)'), followed by another state-
ment of place. The commentary includes interpretations and
evaluations (the notion of the proletariat) that do not depend
upon the senses but upon belief. But the two areas, sensation and
belief, are very carefully interwoven: for example, the phrase
'pájaro proletario' can be heard both as an onomatopoeic name
(like the toledo and the pijul) and as a value-statement. To call
this other language informational, so as to distinguish it from the
first, sensual language, is not in the end useful. The sensuality of
words is also information, of a different type.

   When, therefore, the poem moves into the economic history
of Nicaragua, one needs to take care not to allow the label
'political' to grant that language an exemption from careful
hearing, but to go on listening attentively, say, to how the birdsong cadences continue:

   (y los prestamistas han adquirido el Banco Nacional, y también
   los Ferrocarriles, comprando en un millón de dls el 51% de
   las acciones, y de lo que era la nación sólo ha quedado la
       bandera)
       Oscura la noche y sin kerosín en el rancho. (*PE* 176)

[(and the moneylenders have acquired the National Bank,
    and also
the Railways, buying 51% of the shares for a million
dls, and all that is left of the nation is the flag)
    Dark is the night and without paraffin at the farm.]

The fourth line echoes San Juan de la Cruz ('la noche oscura
del alma' [the dark night of the soul]) and introduces a
change of voice and sound-patterns. The poem takes up again
the sounds and rhythms of birdsong but for a different
purpose: to give the face of actual lives to economic data. And,
in the next two lines, to speak of the land as 'la patria', as love
of place made palpable:

> Un tecolote canta sobre la patria.
> Han callado el canto del pequeño pijul.
>
> [An owl sings over the fatherland.
> The song of the little pijul has been silenced.]

Song-like refrains of this type recur through the poem, and
produce alterations in the ways one receives the historical,
political, and economic information. They play a key role in the
way the latter is located in the larger composition which is the
poem's greatest accomplishment.

> Tierra Prometida dividida por los latifundistas!
>   Tierra a la que yo pertenezco, como
> la paloma tigüilotera y la paloma patacona.
>   Nindirí, Niquinohomo, Monimbó
>   Nandaime, Diriá, Diriomo
> Buey de nuestra niñez que Darío vio echando vaho
>   un día. (*PE* 180)
>
> [Promised land divided by landowners!
>   Land I belong to, like
> the tiguilote pigeon and the blotchy pigeon.
>   Nindirí, Niquinohomo, Monimbó
>   Nandaime, Diriá, Diriomo
> Childhood ox that Darío saw steaming one day.]

Darío, who had the finest ear of any poet of his time, though
born in Nicaragua spent most of his adulthood elsewhere, and
very rarely used anything seen or heard in Nicaragua in his

poems.[57] The sensual richness of Darío's poetry depends mainly upon exotic—for example, European—objects. Cardenal, around seventy years later, reverses the process and makes a rich texture of local sounds the fulcrum of his sense of place, sounds which include local, in other words native, place, and bird names.

To integrate a large field of varied information, that is the ambition of this and the later longer poems of Cardenal's. A central strategy used is collage: the placing together of objects, 'cut out' from the larger wholes they belong to, in multiple relationships. Multiplicity is crucial, since it is thus that the components of the composition remain undiminished and vigorous, which is the prime implication of the idea of integration, as opposed, say, to mere mixture. The best-known early twentieth-century collage actions are in cubist painting, and similar ideas of space were extended to literature by Pound and Gertrude Stein in the USA, Pierre Reverdy in France, and Huidobro in particular among avant-garde poets in Latin America. There are a number of long poems which use epic collage in the twentieth century: the best-known example is probably Pound's *Cantos.* Less well known are the Latin American epic poems: Vallejo's *España, aparta de mí este cáliz* [Spain, take this cup from me], Neruda's *Canto general,* Huidobro's *Altazor,* Zurita's *Anteparaíso,* and Juan L. Ortiz's 'El Gualeguay', to name just a few.

Cardenal's methods are various and involve three types of resource: sound-structures, voices, and time process. The sound-structures have been outlined above. Where voice is concerned, the poem is radically polyvocal: there are the voices of bankers, of Nicaraguan popular songs, of Darío, of Marx, the *Popol Vuh,* and the Bible, of Cardenal as author/speaker, to name just a few. The concomitant handling of language, which makes it polyvocal, capable of carrying different inflexions and accents, is well summed up by Alfredo Veiravé, who writes that Cardenal uses

recursos que rompen la univocidad de lo comunicado y convierten al texto en un gran cuadro polisémico que se bifurca en un collage de

---

[57] Cardenal's reference is to Darío's poem 'Allá lejos', published in *Cantos de vida y esperanza,* which begins as follows: 'Buey que vi en mi niñez echando vaho un día | bajo el nicaragüense sol de encendidos oros.'

formas, elaboradas con rupturas e interferencias. Cardenal utiliza abreviaturas, fechas, comillas, mayúsculas [. . .] imágenes visuales, onomatopeyas, nombres propios [. . .] exclamaciones, préstamos lingüísticos, interrogaciones, [. . .] coloquialismos, lengua arcáica, diálogos, documentos.[58]

[resources that break up univocal communication and make the text into a great polysemic canvas which is composed of a collage of forms that operate as cuts and interferences. Cardenal uses abbreviations, dates, quotations, capital letters, visual images, onomatopoeia, proper nouns, exclamations, borrowed words, questions, colloquialisms, archaic language, dialogues, documents.]

That is, techniques which allow one to move between different materials without reducing them to a single voice.

There are several important moments where the poem moves into the use of a *nosotros* (us) that proposes a shared identity. Two distinct, though overlapping, senses of plural identity occur. One works through shared personal experiences, located in the past of childhood or the distance of exile:

> Cuántas veces hemos dicho los nicaragüenses en el extranjero
> 'somos un país-de-mierda', en mesas de tragos, en pensiones
> donde se juntan los exiliados, pero
> hemos recordado los nacatamales, la sopa de mondongo con
> su culantro y su chile congo, los cantos
> de la 'Purísima' y el perfume de los madroños en Diciembre
> (*PE* 181)

> [How often have we Nicaraguans abroad said
> 'the country is pure shit', around a table with drinks, in
> pensions
> where exiles gather, but
> we have remembered the tamales, the tripe soup with
> its green coriander and congo chile, the songs
> about la Purísima and the perfume of arbutus in December]

—sensations which adhere to times and places and which, in the expanding field of echoes, include Sandino as another 'nicaragüense en el extranjero' (*Hora o*) alongside the sound of raindrops on a tiled roof ('tic tic tic tic tic tic tic tic').

The other *nosotros* is that of the nation, raided by foreign

---

[58] Alfredo Veiravé, 'Ernesto Cardenal: el exteriorismo: poesía del nuevo mundo'. in E. Calabrese (ed.), *Ernesto Cardenal: poeta de la liberación latinoamericana* (Buenos Aires, 1975), 79.

banks, like the US bankers Brown Brothers & Co. who in 1911
took over the issuing of currency in Nicaragua, leading to the
situation in which Sandino found the country:

>   con
>   una parte de su territorio enajenado,
>   la deuda exterior
>   acrecentada, la vida financiera sometida al
>   Sindicato de Banqueros de Nueva York

>   [with
>   part of the territory taken over [by the USA],
>   the foreign debt
>   increased, the financial system handed over to
>   the New York Bankers' Syndicate]

and the whole country

>   ya sólo una hilera
>   de chozas, con una única calle, y en ella, a dos metros del
>   mar
>   un zopilote y un perro disputándose una tripa de pescado.
>   (*PE* 178)

>   [just a line of huts
>   along a single street, and in it, two yards from the sea,
>   a vulture and a dog fighting over the guts of a fish.]

The voice of the nation finds two places from which it can
speak: the narrative of Sandino's earlier uprising and a vision of
the future. To exemplify each in turn:

>   y se oye una vitrola, también una guitarra, y afuera
>   a la luz de una fogata Sandino leyendo el Quijote
>   —el cuartel inaccesible como nido de quetzal—
>   Sandino está otra vez en el Chipote muchachos. (*PE* 198)

>   la visión
>   de una tierra con la explotación
>   abolida! (*PE* 199)

>   [and there's the sound of a gramophone, a guitar too,
>   and outside
>   in the firelight Sandino reading Don Quixote
>   —his headquarters as inaccessible as a quetzal's nest—
>   Sandino is in Chipote again, boys.

>   the vision
>   of a land with exploitation
>   abolished!]

Through the narrative of Sandino the two identities—the personal and the national—begin to be woven together, as also are the poet's voice and the birdsong refrains:

> Y canto como el pájaro león o cocoroca, un pájaro solitario
> que canta angustioso anunciando el puma
> [And I sing like the lion bird or cocoroca, a solitary bird
> that sings anxiously warning that a puma is around]

which is one of the long series of comparisons of poet and birdsong with which the poem ends.

Two questions arise with the idea of collage: the relation between the parts and the projection of a larger space by the arrangement of the parts within the frame. In other words, the materials inside the frame/the poem are extensions of and extend into a larger external environment. Thus, for example, the relationships of sounds and voices in the poem are extensions of the landscape and history of Nicaragua, and deployments of particular energies:

> La luna nueva como una leve garza.
> Oscurece en el Escondido y canta el cuaco.
>   Debemos hacer aquí un país.
> Estamos en la entrada de una Tierra Prometida
>   que mana leche y miel como una mujer
>   mel et lac sub lingua tua
> el beso llega a su tiempo y luego a su tiempo los besos
> 'en la tierra que te daré no mantengas analfabeta a tu hermano
> para que corte tu algodrón y recoja tu café. Habla Yavé.'
>   Una tierra prometida para la Revolución.
> Como las cosas en común
> 'como antes de la caída de nuestros Primeros Padres'
> He visto platanales verdes
>   y los cañaverales de otro verde. (*PE 187*)
> [The new moon like a light heron.
> It grows dark on the Escondido and the cuaco sings.
>   We have to create a country here.
> We are at the entrance of a Promised Land
>   that gives milk and honey like a woman
>   mel et lac sub lingua tua
> the kiss comes at its time and then kisses at their time
> 'in the land I will give you do not keep your brother illiterate
> so that he will cut your cotton and gather your coffee.
>   Thus speaks Yahweh.'

> A land promised for the Revolution.
> With things held in common
>   'as it was before the fall of our First Fathers'
> I have seen green banana groves
> and the sugar cane a different green.]

The first line gives a fine sense of sound and rhythm, comparable with Darío's mastery: the long syllables of 'luna nueva'
followed by the lightness of 'como una leve garza', the long *ar*
sound heightening the delicacy of 'como una leve': there are
five syllables, only one of them stressed [l*e*ve], echoing nu*e*va.
There follows the darker, harsher sound and image of the
earth, the new moon giving sparse light: Nicaragua is not a
country but a project to be achieved. Three types of material
make up the vision of the future: a utopian image of Nicaragua
attainable through social revolution; the erotic image of a lover;
and the voice of the Christian God heard, via a socialist reading
of the Bible, with a new accent.

The three types of discourse, political, erotic, and religious,
carry the three types of energy that make up the poem: social
love, erotic love, and spiritual love. The three energies
converge in this passage and in the poem as a whole; the
tensions of Cardenal's earlier poetry have diminished. But
there is a problem. If to integrate, in the full sense of the word,
implies unwoundedness and vigorousness, at the end of the
passage just quoted there is a diminution of the freshness of
perception: the green of banana trees and sugar cane is given
not as an excitement of the senses but as a kind of proof of the
validity of the social and religious statements that precede it.
Instead of love as refining the senses and the intellect, as in
Renaissance tradition,[59] the idea of beauty is a type of guarantee, directing attention elsewhere and diluting it.

Another type of integration occurs in the poem: a vast
process of destruction and creation that embraces all of matter,
where matter and spirit, as in the work of Teilhard de Chardin,
are understood as inseparable.[60] It first enters the poem
precisely at the point where Sandino appears, proposing a
larger dimension in which everything can be understood:

---

[59] See Louis Zukovsky, *Bottom: On Shakespeare*; Ezra Pound, 'Cavalcanti', in
Literary Essays (London, 1954).
[60] See *The Phenomenon of Man* (London, 1959).

Decía que desovan las iguanas . . . Es el proceso. Ellas
(o las ranas) en el silencioso carbonífero
emitieron el primer sonido
la primera canción de amor sobre la tierra
la primera canción de amor bajo la luna
es el proceso
El proceso viene desde los astros
Nuevas relaciones de producción: eso
también es el proceso. [. . .]
[. . .] Desde
el primer huevo de gas, al huevo de iguana, al hombre nuevo.
Sandino se gloriaba de haber nacido del 'vientre de los
oprimidos'
(el de una indita de Niquinohomo) (*PE* 178–9)

[I said the iguanas lay their eggs . . . It is the process. In the
silent carboniferous they (or frogs)
made the first sound
the first love song on the earth
the first love song beneath the moon
it is the process
The process comes from the stars
New relations of production: that
too is the process
From
the first gas egg, to the iguana egg, to the new man.
Sandino delighted in being born from 'the belly of the
oppressed'
(of an Indian woman from Niquinohomo)]

A cosmic time, vaster than any individual life or historical epic,
gathers together all the various voices and moments, and thus
the various energies, inside the collage and gives them an addi-
tional projection: the local place-name in cosmic time. But does
it—'the process'—dissolve the local? And does the new way of
overcoming tensions between the political, the erotic, and the
spiritual require something that would have to be called belief
in order for a person fully to enter into it?

Consider the overall shape of the narrative which this poem
deploys. Narrative, in verbal texts, is a prime form of process,
that is, of the interpretation of occurrence through time. The
sense of time-lapse and time sequence begins in Cardenal's
poem with the enumeration of the months of the year, marked
by the song of different birds. There follows the account of

Nicaragua invaded and despoiled, first by foreign bankers and then by domestic dictatorship. This narrative, like that of Sandino, which follows, is a version of the national popular: a story of the nation in which popular traditions and experiences offer a means of integrating a fragmented population into a sense of nation. Finally, there is the cosmic process, which includes all the others.

The movement, expressed schematically, is from cosmic to historical time, and then from historical to cosmic again. What interrupts the first section (the yearly cycle, marked by birdsong) is not just a different narrative (of foreign bankers, etc.) but also a different temporality, that created by international finance and modern technology. The first temporality is cyclical, without historical markings; the second is accumulative and usually called progress: an entry into history, signalled, as pointed out earlier, by the use of 'nosotros'. Here, for the first time, the railways—which already existed—are mentioned. So that the narrative of nation is based on the story of rural arcadia invaded: birdsong, the seasons, and agriculture signify values destroyed.[61] Rural arcadia invaded provides an evaluative basis from which modernity can be judged: the plot is similar to that of García Márquez's *Cien años de soledad*. Foreign bankers are wild boars or vultures (*PE* 176–7), the bases of the comparisons rural, evoking peasant culture as positive value.

At issue are the effects of twentieth-century capitalism and US domination upon a peripheral country. What does it mean to interpret this simply as colonial invasion? How much better would national banks be? How far is finance capital ever actually national? Actually occurring modernization, with the social divisions it causes, is treated as extraneous, and modernity, not yet achieved, becomes a 'promised land'—'comunismo o reino de Dios en la tierra que es lo mismo' (*PE* 202–3) [communism or the kingdom of God on earth which is the same]. So that we have not the modernization without modernity that characterizes the Latin American countries in the twentieth century,[62] but a utopian modernity. The consequences for poetry of a narrative that places value in a rural arcadia or a utopian

---

[61] See Andrés Bello's poem *La agricultura de la zona tórrida* (1826).
[62] See Néstor García Canclini, *Culturas híbridas: estrategias para entrar y salir de la modernidad* (Mexico City, 1989).

modernity can be that the lively interplay of intellect and senses
becomes diminished:

> Lago con luna.
> La luna sobre el lago y el agua color de luna.
> Tanta belleza, para la igualdad. (*PE* 185)

> [Lake with moon.
> The moon over the lake and the water moon-coloured.
> So much beauty, for equality.]

The beauty of the perceived, as sensation and understanding
embodied in proportion (rhythm and shape), is subsumed into
what is not so much information as belief. Compare Cardenal's
lines with Pound's Canto 45, or with Juan L. Ortiz's 'El
Gualeguay'. In both of the latter, what is received by ear and eye
as sensation, and what is discovered by the intellect as design,
are densely intertwined as form: the assertions of ethical values
are placed within that discovery of form and embodied by it.
Form is the test of value. In Cardenal, on occasions like the one
under discussion, value tends to depend ultimately upon an
assertion, which one believes or not.

To put it differently, the arcadia lost and the utopia desired
become, in Cardenal's poem, myths. But, as Georges Bataille
writes, in an essay on Blake, 'when poetry expresses the myths
which tradition proposes to it, it is not autonomous: it does
not contain sovereignty within itself. It humbly illustrates the
legend whose form and meaning can exist without it.'[63] What
Bataille calls 'legend', in Cardenal consists of belief-structures. But, as noted above, the dilution in Cardenal's poetry is
something that can sometimes occur: it does not always
happen. To take one example, consider one of the moments
when the narrative of Sandino is interrupted, as recitative in
opera by a song, by the smells of the land and the sound of
birds:

> En marzo el maíz está en elotes.
> La neblina sobre los cafetales y en la neblina
> el blanco olor de la flor del café (olor a azahar) con cantos
> de chichitote
> y de chiflador. (*PE* 189)

---

[63] Georges Bataille, *Literature and Evil* (London, 1985), 85.

[In March the maize has grown to cobs.
  Mist over the coffee shrubs and in the mist
  the white smell of the coffee flower (smell of citrus blossom)
      with the song
      of chichitotes
      and chifladors.]

The large order of a narrative of liberation is interrupted by the
particular play of sound, light, and smell: sensation and design
in balance. But at other times there is not so much balance as
conflict: a leakage between the senses themselves as the body of
love—as in the lines just quoted—and the beliefs they are
subordinated to. This conflict runs through all Cardenal's later
poetry.

FORM, EXPERIENCE, HISTORY

Cardenal was closely involved with the setting up of poetry
workshops (talleres de poesía) in Nicaragua. He was responsible for writing a set of guidelines for participants—who
included not just combatants in the revolutionary struggle but
members of the police and other institutions of the Sandinista
government. A central tenet of the whole undertaking was that
subjective experience, especially love, and the historical events
of revolutionary war should not be treated in different
languages: that the personal should not be taken as a separate
realm but placed alongside history. The guidelines, entitled
'Unas reglas para escribir poesía' [Some rules for writing
poetry] and distributed by the Ministry of Culture, which
Cardenal headed at the time, as a mimeographed sheet in
1980,[64] include the recommendation:

Hay que preferir lo más concreto a lo más vago. Decir árbol es más
vago o abstracto, que decir: guayacán, guásimo, malinche, que es más
concreto. [. . .] A la poesía le da mucha gracia la inclusión de nombres
propios: nombres de ríos, de ciudades, de caceríos. Y nombres de
personas. [. . .] La poesía más que a base de ideas, debe ser a base de
cosas que entran por los sentidos: que se sienten con el tacto, que se
gustan con el paladar, que se oyen, que se ven, que se huelen. [. . .]

---

[64] They were also published in *Barricada*, 10 Mar. 1980.

Hay que escribir como se habla. Con la naturalidad y llaneza del lenguaje hablado, no del lenguaje *escrito*.
[Choose the concrete detail rather than vague words. To say tree is more vague or abstract than to say guayacán, guásimo, malinche, which are more concrete. Poetry gains greatly by the inclusion of proper names: names of rivers, cities, farms. And names of people. Poetry, rather than based on ideas, should use things that enter through the senses: that are felt by touch, tasted by the palate, heard, seen, smelt. One has to write how one speaks. Not with the *written* language, but with the naturalness and straightforwardness of the spoken language.]

Here is a poem from one of the workshops, written by Comandante Hugo Torres and entitled 'Persona' [Person]:

> Estoy pensando en vos
> Hoy que es mi día de guardia
> Que tengo bajo mi mando unidades
> > > enteras, batallones,
> regiones, artillería, infantería,
> > > miles de hombres,
> armamento pesado, liviano, mediano
> un ejército entero
> (vuelvo la vista al teléfono)
> Si tan sólo me hablaras.[65]

> [I am thinking of you
> today which is my day on duty
> When I have under my command entire units, battalions,
> regions, artillery, infantry, thousands of men,
> heavy, light, medium armaments
> an entire army
> (I turn my eyes towards the telephone)
> If only you would talk to me.][66]

Cardenal's 'rules' draw on Pound's seminal essays, such as 'A Few Dont's',[67] but also on the practice of Nicaraguan poets: 'es preferible no usar el *tú* sino el *vos*, que es como hablamos en la vida diaria. La mayor parte de la poesía nueva nicaragüense

---

[65] In John Lyons (ed. and trans.), *Poems of Love and Revolution* (London, 1983), no page numbers. Also in *Poesía libre*, 2/7 (1982), 3.
[66] John Lyons's translation.
[67] First published in *Poetry*, 1/6 (1913), and included in 'A Retrospect', in *Literary Essays*, 4.

ahora está usando el *vos*' [It is preferable to use *vos* rather than *tú*, as that is how we speak in everyday life. Most Nicaraguan poetry is now using the *vos* form]. The initiators of that use of the rhythms and energies of the spoken language included in particular José Coronel Urtecho and Cardenal himself. Curiously, Octavio Paz, referring to that revolution in poetic language, deplores that Latin American poets should be 'repeating' Olson and Ginsberg, who he claims merely continue the line of Pound and Williams, when 'that poetic revolution *has already been made in the Spanish language*'.[68] His argument is that the early twentieth-century avant-garde in Mexican poetry (e.g. Tablada) had carried out a similar change. But that judgement can only be sustained if one ignores the gap between the spoken language and the language used by virtually all Mexican poets of this century.

Another poem from the *talleres* begins:

> Con tu pantalón azul
> una camisa a cuadros
> y tu UZI en el hombro
> así te conocí
> Euclides
> así me enamoré de vos.

> [With your blue trousers
> check shirt
> and your UZI on the shoulder
> that's how I met you
> Euclides
> that's how I fell in love with you.]

It is important to note that the *vos* form has been eliminated from the official written language, as it still is in Argentina, both in schools and in the work of many poets. The poem continues:

> Estabas organizando un CDC
> (los hoy Comité de Defensa Sandinista)
> y tenías un megáfono en la mano.
> Hoy después de tanto tiempo
> todavía no me acostumbro
> a tu nombre legal José David
> y es que yo sigo enamorada

---

[68] 'The Word as Foundation', *Times Literary Supplement*, 14 Nov. 1968, 1283–4.

de aquel muchacho clandestino
que conocí.[69]

[You were organizing a CDC
(today the Sandinist Defence Committees)
and you had a megaphone in your hand.
Today after so much time
I am still not used
to your real name José David
I am still in love
with that clandestine young man
I knew.]

The title is 'José David Zúñiga'. The affect is taken from particularities of time and place, as the 'rules' urge, over into the
poem. Love here becomes an adhesion of emotion to time and
place, which themselves have become history. That is the other
dimension of the workshops, which again draws on Cardenal's
own work: the use of poetry as the setting down of history. As
John Lyons points out in his introduction,

Taken on their own some of the poems might appear light-weight, yet
when placed in a collection they [. . .] gain strength from each other.
[. . .] The poetry from these *talleres* is the engaging voice of *that* generation which under Somoza's regime went unheard. These young
people meet in the workshop to articulate, to discuss and criticise each
other's work, highlighting the fact that poetry is a social event, that it
is not a record of being so much as an establishment of being.

Nearly all the workshop poems appearing in *Poesía libre*, the
journal published by the Ministry of Culture, reveal a heightened sense of occasion, as a history participated in and thereby
one's own. They can be read together, as Lyons suggests, as fragments of a larger public narrative, a recurrent feature of which
is the diminishing of intensity after the Revolution:

y comencé a enamorarme
cuando miré tus ojos color como de hierba.
Pero hoy ya no te amo
como en aquel noviembre.[70]

[and I began to fall in love
when I saw your eyes

---

[69] The original has 'me acostumbro y.', *Poesía libre*, 1/1 (1981), 11. The author is
Pastora Palacios.
[70] *Poesía libre*, 1/1 (1981), 14.

which had a colour like grass.
But I don't love you today
like I did that November.]

Detractors of the workshops have complained that the
poems coming out of them are written to a standard formula
and are poor in quality. That is to miss the point. The aim was
not to make everyone a poet but to alter people's relationship
with poetry and thereby also with the language. In this sense
the workshops served as training and preparation for a different relationship with literature. They took place in a particular
context: the rapid coming of age of a whole generation through
the experience of the Revolution, and the subsequent literacy
campaign which brought the majority of the population, for
the first time, into direct contact with the written language.
Some of the *alfabetizadores* were as young as 13, and the same was
true of the participants in the workshops. The following poem
was written by 'la niña' Irene Agudelo Builes and printed in
holograph in *Poesía libre.* [71]

Cuando te fuiste para la comuna a entrenarte
fue la ultima vez que te vi.
Recuerdo cuando me dijiste dame un beso Irene
yo te dije adios.
Alejandro y vos se subieron al bote
y fueron desapareciendo
y nos desiamos todos adios
mucho tiempo después pregunté por vos
me dijeron que estabas muerto
y el día que llevaron tus huesos a la plaza
estabas en nuestros corazones.

[When you went to the commune to train
it was the last time I saw you.
I remember when you said give me a kiss Irene
I said goodbye to you.
Alejandro and you got into the boat
and disappeared
and we all said goodbye
a long time later I asked about you
they said you were dead
and the day they took your bones to the square
you were in our hearts.]

[71] 1/3 (1981), back cover. I have kept the original spelling.

I have quoted poems from the workshops at some length in order to suggest several things: that the sense of participating in an epic story arose broadly throughout the population, that this was felt with particular intensity by the generation which fought in the Revolution, and that part of what made that generation new was a shift in the language. Cardenal's 'reglas para escribir poesía' extrapolate from that shift, rather than imposing a programme from outside. But also, crucially, the 'reglas' summarize Cardenal's own practice as a poet since *Hora o.* Which means that specific uses of the language in Cardenal's own poetry anticipate major shifts in the language which would only be fulfilled with the entry into history of a new generation.

It is time to consider more narrowly some of the key elements of the new poetics. In 1972, Cardenal edited a new anthology of Nicaraguan poetry for the Cuban publishing house Casa de las Américas. The principles he outlines in the prologue to *Poesía nicaragüense* follow the same line of thinking as those of the 'reglas para escribir poesía' but engage with a wider literary debate. He proposes the term *exteriorismo* in order to gather together a series of distinctions:

El exteriorismo es la poesía creada con las imágenes del mundo exterior, el mundo que vemos y palpamos, y que es, por lo general, el mundo específico de la poesía. El exteriorismo es la poesía objetiva: narrativa y anecdótica, hecha con los elementos de la vida real y con cosas concretas, con nombres propios y detalles precisos y datos exactos y cifras y hechos y dichos. En fin, es la poesía *impura*. Poesía que para algunos está más cerca de la prosa que de la poesía, equivocadamente la han llamado 'prosaísta', debido a que su temática es tan amplia como la de la prosa (y debido también a que, por decadencia de la poesía, en los últimos siglos la épica se escribía en prosa y no en verso).[72]

[Exteriorism is poetry created with images of the external world, the world we see and touch, which is, usually, the specific world of poetry. Exteriorism is objective poetry: narrative and anecdotic, made with elements of real life and with concrete things, with proper names and precise details and exact data and numbers and facts and statements. In a word, it is *impure* poetry. This poetry which for some people is closer to prose than to poetry has wrongly been called 'prosaic', because its themes are as wide as those of prose (and also because, given the decadence of poetry, in recent centuries epic has been written in prose and not in verse).]

[72] Ernesto Cardenal (ed.), *Poesía nicaragüense* (Havana, 1972), p. viii.

The word 'impura' was used by Pablo Neruda, in 1935, in order to distinguish from 'pure' poetry the necessity to include in the poem 'el contacto del hombre y de la tierra como una lección para el torturado poeta lírico' [contact with man and with the earth as a lesson for the tortured lyric poet].[73] 'Pure' poetry, at that time, meant the work of, say, Juan Ramón Jiménez, and Neruda's rejection of it is most clearly articulated in *España en el corazón*, the book he wrote during the Spanish Civil War. The epic urge there and in Cardenal's work, despite differences of circumstance, are similar in the need to gather together various energies into a narrative where the self is taken to be participant in a decisive collective experience. The imperative to tell that experience in poetry means claiming for poetry—more accurately, reclaiming, given that 'el exteriorismo [. . .] es tan antiguo como Homero' [exteriorism is as old as Homer][74]—the territory of epic. For Neruda, the change included a move towards the everyday language, in terms of vocabulary and syntax. But poetry, in *España en el corazón* and Neruda's later poetry also, is still an enclosure, in the sense of still being separated from the flows of speech, a factor which is most audible, perhaps, in the tone of voice he uses in readings that have been recorded. The change which is brought by removing the fence between poetry and speech occurs later in Chilean poetry, with the work of Parra in the 1950s.

The various energies and types of attention involved in epic assemblage are shown in Cardenal's prologue in a long paragraph of some thirty lines, which itself reads like a collage, or more accurately montage, since perceptions are linked by a filmic sequence:

Exteriorismo es cuando el poeta nos habla de un tractor Caterpillar D4; o de [. . .] un india atacada en el mercado con el estómago vacío, lleno de hambre; [. . .] o un pueblito en la ribera del río San Juan: y se oye el ruido de la picada de la carne cuando uno se acerca en bote, y la picada de la leña, y el del ruadal.[75]

[Exteriorism is when the poet talks to us about a Caterpillar D4 tractor; or an Indian woman attacked in the market with her stomach empty,

---

73 'Sobre una poesía sin pureza', in Pablo Neruda, *Antología esencial*, ed. Hernán Loyola (Buenos Aires, 1971), 313. First published in *Caballo verde para la poesía*, 1 (1935).
74 *Poesía nicaragüense*, p. vii.   75 Ibid., pp. viii–ix.

full of hunger; or a little village on the bank of the San Juan river: and you can hear the sound of meat cooking on the spit as you approach by boat, and the crackling of the wood, and the noise of the river.]

The US poet Charles Olson, in his seminal essay on poetics 'Projective Verse', published in 1950 and translated into Spanish by Cardenal and Coronel Urtecho, writes of the poet taking the energy from where he got it and transferring it into the poem. 'Form is never more than the extension of content', as Olson writes.[76] One of the consequences of that stance is that there is no mediation, by biographical self or other pre-given form, of the materials; if self is there, it is as part of the materials and not as a special zone of meaning.

Thus, in *exteriorismo*, which as Cardenal points out is not a school but an attitude to poetics, there is no 'reino interior', no sense of Darío's inner realm separated off from the outside: 'Poesía interiorista, en cambio, es una poesía subjetivista, hecha sólo con palabras abstractas o simbólicas como: rosa, piel, ceniza, labios, ausencia, amargo, sueño, tacto, espuma, deseo, sombra, tiempo, sangre, piedra, llanto, noche' [Interiorist poetry, by contrast, is a subjectivist poetry, made only with abstract or symbolic words like rose, skin, ash, lips, absence, bitter, dream, touch, foam, desire, shadow, time, blood, stone, tears, night].[77] The list fits pretty well with much of Neruda's poetry, which is perhaps what Cardenal had in mind. This is not to say that there is no outside in Neruda's poetry, but that—even in his most 'social' poetry—it tends to be figured as earth or cosmos and not as other voices and other intonations in a plural, polyphonic use of language.

Epic, for Bakhtin, 'accomplishes the task of cultural, national and political centralization of the verbal-ideological world',[78] whereas the novel is made of 'decentralizing, centrifugal forces', in other words is polyphonic in composition. The distinction fits Neruda as opposed, say, to Parra quite well. But it does not fit Cardenal, whose epic concerns, from *Hora O* onwards, include rather than exclude incompatible voices (e.g. Sandino and Somoza)—voices whose differences show up rifts

---

[76] *Collected Prose* (Berkeley, 1997), 240. Olson also coins the term 'Objectism' (247).
[77] *Poesía nicaragüense*, p. ix.
[78] *The Dialogical Imagination* (Austin, Tex., 1981), 273.

in the language and in the society. 'A poem is a society of words', as Robert Duncan put it, and where the society is cut through by vast differences of power, the epic poet has a choice: to project a utopian language spoken by all or to let the voices speak their differences. If the latter, then the difficulty is to find methods of composition which allow differences of intonation to be heard and understood as expressions of different historical forces. In that connection, a summary of the varieties of speech would include, in *Hora O*, Somoza, the American ambassador (including phrases in English), Sandino, the ballad form, the voice of the narrator in conversation mode; and, in *Canto nacional*, banks, mining companies, Darío, Nicaraguans in exile, a person under torture, a military torturer, Sandino, advertisements, press agencies.

The multiplicity of voices is organized by the compositional device of montage,[79] which is taken furthest in *Viaje a Nueva York*. Of those poems of Cardenal's with epic concerns this is also the one where self figures most extensively, which makes it a good test of the assertions made over the previous two pages about Cardenal's poetics. The journey of the title is by air, the distance between New York and Solentiname, the island where Cardenal lived alongside a community he had founded, so cut by speed that 'Me parecía estar esa tarde aún en mi isla de Solentiname | y no asomado a una ventanilla sobre la bahía de Nueva York' [It seemed I was still in my Solentiname island that afternoon | and not looking out of a window above the bay of New York] (253). The speed of modern technology alters the arrangement of memory, locating distant places alongside each other and permitting new compositions of the senses. This modernness of form is crucial in Cardenal's poems: it is an appropriation of technological modernity for other ends— other, that is, than those of consumer society.

The movement of the plane seems slow as it circles over New York, and at that moment attention shifts to a different form of rapid assemblage: that of the newspaper page,[80] with headlines

[79] See Robert Pring-Mill, 'Acciones paralelas y montaje acelerado en el segundo episodio de *Hora O*', *Revista iberoamericana*, 118–19 (1982), 217–40.

[80] See Marshall McLuhan's comment: 'To the alerted eye, the front page of a newspaper is a superficial chaos which can lead the mind to cosmic harmonies of a very high order.' *The Mechanical Bride: Folklore of Industrial Man* (New York, 1951), 4. The chapter is entitled 'Front Page Cubism'.

about Watergate, adverts about an island (not Solentiname!) for sports holidays, and a cartoon which plays with the visibility conferred upon a person by the press. At which point the plane begins its descent and a different visibility enters: 'fábricas, trenes, casitas suburbanas iguales, autos de juguete I y ya en la pista' [factories, trains, identical little suburban houses, toy cars I and we're on the runway] (253–4). The self is placed inside all of that, as name and visibility, and as speaking voice alongside other voices, forming the extended conversation—punctuated by shifts of scene—which the rest of the poem consists in:

'Es curioso: Ernesto Cardenal en Madison Avenue' Y miro
el hondo cañón, el produndo desfiladero de edificios
donde se esconden detrás de sus vidrios *the hidden persuaders*
    venden automóviles de Felicidad, Consuelo en lata (a 30 cts)
    The Coca Cola Company (*PE* 255)

['It's strange: Ernesto Cardenal in Madison Avenue' And I
    look down
the deep canyon, the steep ravine of buildings
with *the hidden persuaders* hidden behind their windows
    selling Happiness automobiles, tinned Consolation
    (@ 30 cents)
    The Coca Cola Company]

The speaker of the quoted statement, the first of those voices, is that of the American priest responsible for the invitation to New York. The name Ernesto Cardenal, in that environment and amid the directives by which it shapes attention, becomes a kind of advert, and the writing a making of counter-adverts: the poem itself as intervention in public spaces, using the same techniques for a different composition. That intervention includes Cardenal reading his own work: 'leo mi ORACULO SOBRE MANAGUA (lo del terremoto)' [I read my ORACLE ON MANAGUA (the earthquake poem)] (*PE* 257).

The field thus composed produces a high level of excitement through its intersections, because of the speed and range of possibilities opened, and because self is dramatized as convergence of the multiple and expansion of the single, through many connections. Given that, the propositional content of the conversations, which is radical liberation theology, does not require belief so much as willingness to hear and see the connections. The absence of emphasis upon inwardness is a strength. The poem is woven out of meetings, conversations, the networks of relationship and memory, in which readers are invited to become interlocutors, in a kind of public intimacy. In Cardenal's epic writing, Whitman's expanding self is no longer a model, as it had been for Neruda. Like Parra, Cardenal opens up the boundaries of the poem, to let in what was previously excluded, in this case mass culture and its informational environment.

The collection *Los ovnis de oro* [The golden UFOs], which brings together all of Cardenal's poems on American 'Indians', opens the boundaries in particular ways which have to do with non-Western societies and the question as to whether their traditions are valid not only as politics but also as knowledge. The earlier book, *El estrecho dudoso* [The uncertain strait], can be taken as preparatory for this, in the sense that it is a reading of early Spanish writings on Mesoamerica, where Cardenal's use of open verse form divests those writings of their rhetoric of legitimacy and explores them instead as attempts to construct an order out of the unknown. Cardenal uses colonial texts in order to explore how the Spanish language, when confronted by Latin American reality, starts to change and become local and to found a Latin American history.

The opening poem of *Los ovnis de oro*, which offers a frame to the book and has the same title, presents a meeting between Cardenal as trainee priest in Colombia and the Cuna ethnic group. The poem begins with a brilliance of perceptions, as sounds and images flash up:

> ¡Aquellas aldeas redondas rodeadas de mar!
>   Mulatupo:
> Toda la isla una compacta aldea de chozas
>   las chozas llegando hasta el agua,
>   Y aun sobre el agua,
> y pareció al llegar
>   una aldea flotando sobre el mar.
>   Chozas con cocoteros.
>   Y el mar color de cuello de pavo real.[81]

> [Those round villages surrounded by sea!
>   Mulatupo:
> The whole island a compact village of huts

---

[81] *Los ovnis de oro: Golden UFOs* [bilingual edition] (Bloomington, Ind., 1992), 2.

the huts going down to the water,
and even on top of the water,
and when you arrive it looks like
a village floating on the sea.
Huts with coconut palms.
And the sea the colour of a peacock's neck.]

The comparisons of sounds and of things occurs as delight and discovery. Sounds of syllables, words, and whole phrases are repeated at every level (word, phrase, line, paragraph) through the poem, making reprises through which the poem's movement circles back upon itself and gathers itself, shifting between the ordering of things and of words—for example in the repetition of the phrase 'de cuello de pavo real' (three pages later):

Agua color verde de arcoíris,
azul y violeta de arcoíris
iridiscente.
Cesta de peces de colores como un tesoro de pirata.
¡Isla Mulatupo!
Azul de cuello de pavo real.[82]

[Rainbow green the water
blue and violet of rainbow
iridescent.
Basket of coloured fish like a pirates' treasure.
Mulatupo island!
Blue of a peacock's neck.]

The iridescent quality of the colours is later found in the Cuna women's *molas*, the squares of brilliantly coloured cloth in varied pattern which they sew together to make their blouses.

But the poem also includes a discourse of evaluation, political and moral:

En la isla
'Todo es gratis'.
[. . .]
Yo sabía del sistema comunista
de esta desconocida nación centroamericana.
Me sentía como visitante en la URSS.[83]

[82] Ibid. 8.   [83] Ibid. 4.

[On the island
'Everything is free.'
I knew about the communist system
of this unknown Central American nation.
I felt like a visitor to the USSR.]

The phrase 'Todo es gratis' is actually spoken by the Cuna Chief, but its extensions into comparison with the USSR or into the later slogan-like phrase 'no circula dinero' [no money circulates] (4) are uttered without quotation marks, from somewhere else. Similarly the title phrase 'Los ovnis de oro' translates, without quotation marks, a Cuna myth about the gods' mode of travel (22). Because the tone and rhythm do not vary, the different places from which statements are uttered become, after a time, difficult to distinguish. The statement about money is immediately followed by 'Los cocos, como moneda para el trueque' [coconuts, like money for barter]. If one takes the latter as a cultural translation, then a non-Cuna concept is brought into play here, that of money as something which has a history. This thinking is a product of Western modernity. But the translation of Cuna culture by Western concepts is not particularly visible in the poem. What is made highly visible is the reverse process: the translation of Western culture by the Cuna. For example, their usual manner of greeting is given in their language and then translated as '—¿En qué piensas? | — Pienso en Dios' [What are you thinking about? | I am thinking about God] (20). Which concept of God is in play here? The poem urges a particular hermeneutic: 'Ahora Dios tiene teléfono. | Se habla de que para subir al cielo hay un ascensor' [Now God has a telephone. | They say that to get to heaven there is a lift] (20). One of the effects is that the Cuna translation of Western modernity is attractive, not to say seductive, because innocent or naive, which in practice means selective. The same method of selectivity innocence is used in order to make spontaneous perception (the flashing colours and sounds) seem to be evidence of moral values.

The method is frequently found in certain traditions of utopian writing—our civilization seen through the eyes of 'primitives'. But that is not the main issue. More important than that is the poetics of it, where poetics is responsibility in use of language. Take the following lines, where sound-patterns hold in place the moon and the village as visual concurrence:

El rielar en el mar
    de la luna
        y la aldea cuna.
Ya no creen que los albinos sean hijos de la luna.
Tener buena conducta
    para no ser detenido en el Muelle del Cielo.
    Todos unidos como un solo árbol.[84]

[Flashing in the sea
    the moon
        and the Cuna village.
They don't believe any longer that albinos are children
    of the moon.
Observe good conduct
    so as not to be detained at the Dock in the Sky.
    All united like a single tree.]

The shimmering of moonlight in the water rhymes with the peacock-tail iridescence from earlier on, just as the six-syllable phrases ('el rielar en el mar'; 'y la aldea cuna') echo the six-syllable phrases that recur from the beginning of the poem. And yet the unity of the scene (moonlight on the sea, the moral message) arises out of a seduction: the senses dance to capture and dull down judgement. Let us consider the detail. Iridescence of colour and flashing of moonlight in water ('agua [. . .] iridescente', 'cuello de pavo real', 'el rielar en el mar | de la luna'), these embody the fine, creative movement of perception as it destroys and remakes objects.[85] Yet this dance of the senses is made to serve a higher purpose, as happens, say, if the Song of Songs is read as religious allegory. One is opened up only to have the propaganda message laid upon one.

Moonlight and village occur in the same rhythms and vowel sounds (*luna/cuna*) and those equivalences are made to embrace Cuna beliefs and morality. Each of these elements is brought into a seamless whole, each upholding the other. The perceptions of the speaker and the beliefs of the Cuna, to whom he came at first as an outsider, become welded together in the same pronoun: 'Hablan en secreto del árbol de la vida, | el árbol *Palu-wala* (la madre que nos dio a luz a todos)' [They speak

---

[84] Ibid. 28.
[85] See M. Merleau-Ponty, *Phenomenology of Perception* (London, 1962), 30. See also his *The Primacy of Perception* (Chicago, 1989), 15: 'the object [. . .] is given as the infinite sum of an indefinite series of perspectival views.'

secretly of the tree of life, | the *Palu-wala* tree (the mother who gave birth to us all)] (28). In fact interpretation (the Cuna village and what it has been taken to signify morally and politically in the fifteen or so pages of the poem) is repeatedly being pushed inside perception (image of moonlight in water). It is as if you are seeing the beliefs, which means that the beliefs in question become part of nature—which they actually are in Cuna myth ('el árbol de la vida'). The method removes knowledge from Cuna tradition (Western modernity is the source of concepts in this poem) then uses the Cuna in order to create a naive gaze and so handle Western concepts (e.g. of money)[86] selectively, but without appearing to. These constraints upon how resemblance and difference are worked out receive validation from the patterns of sound and light.

Consider, by way of contrast, the following poem by George Oppen, one of the US Objectivist poets, a group with whom Cardenal has been compared:

> If 'Miss Moores's (birds) squeal, shuffle, lose their footing
> In the tree, in the mind, in the poem' as the critic
> Reproduces them, is not
> Something proven?—the bird
> With its hard
> Claws
> Clinging to the rough
> Tree, the small minds
> In the trees,
> The mind and the poem
> Proven? Or is that not
>
> What was in question? How terrible the mind
> Is, open
> To the world. The single mind
> Flinches, panics, would, from its distance,
> Its too large body and its irremediable
> Vision
> Crowd itself into the bird-life, but we observe
> The bird from safety,
> From the common culture.[87]

---

[86] See Cardenal's poem on the Inca system, 'Economía de Tahuantinsuyo', in *Los ovnis de oro*.

[87] George Oppen, 'Cultural Triumph', George Oppen Papers, University of California at San Diego, Box 27, folder 39.

The image of the mind crowding itself into the birds, out of panic at what it is to be open, is also an image of a particular way of reading and of writing—one that eliminates wildness, chaos, the Dionysian. It is a question of what Foucault calls 'the already "encoded" eye',[88] as the triumph of the cultural codes that shape perception and permit it to find order. The terror of openness that Oppen's poem speaks of is not a state of ordinary, everyday life but a place that poetry is capable of entering, with no other weapons than its own power, or sovereignty, as Bataille calls it.

Oppen's poem is also a reflection upon Objectivist poetry, several decades after the idea was first delineated by Luis Zukovsky in 1931.[89] The term itself is notoriously loose. There was no such thing, for example, as 'objectivism', only a group of poets who for a time were called Objectivists. Nevertheless there was a particular attention to objects and their locations in a poem. Zukovsky writes: 'Writing occurs which is the detail, not mirage, of seeing, of thinking with the things as they exist, and of directing them along a line of melody.'[90] The method implies that cultural codes can themselves be made conscious, rather than seeming to be part of things themselves. This is the case with William Carlos Williams, another poet associated with the Objectivist idea, who experiments with what happens when the coding of the eye—and ear—falls away, as in the well-known poem:

> So much depends
> upon
>
> a red wheel
> barrow
>
> glazed with rain
> water
>
> beside the white
> chickens.[91]

What remains is not realism, not imitation of objects—which, in Oppen's terms, would be 'cultural triumph'—but alertness of

---

[88] Michel Foucault, *The Order of Things* (London, 1974), p. xxi.
[89] Louis Zukovsky, 'Program "Objectivists" 1931', *Poetry: A Magazine of Verse*, 37/5 (1931), 268–72.   [90] Ibid. 272.
[91] Williams, *Collected Earlier Poems*, vol. i (New York, 1988), 277.

eye and ear as movement of intellect. There is no belief at all in Williams's poem—no belief required of a reader—but it is a spiritual exercise, as serious as any other. His slogan, 'no ideas except in things', does not mean naive perception, which is never anything other than perception trained in selectivities, but the work of the poem as revelation.[92]

The avoidance of interiority on the part of the Objectivist poets has to do with finding a method for handling perception so that prior schemata, which dull the movement of senses and intellect, are minimized. What I am suggesting about Cardenal's *Los ovnis de oro* and, by extension, his other 'Indian' poems is that there is a similarity with Objectivism and an important difference. To summarize briefly, Cardenal's technique is to allow objects, events, speech to establish their own articulations, without voice-over and without using the poet's inner feeling as frame. The movement of sound and visual shape, including colour, holds those articulations in a composition. At the same time, he uses the Cuna as innocent perceivers, to cut through the pretensions—schemata—of our culture. And although this permits a freshness of perception, there is also something else going on: through 'their' eyes, 'our' modernity looks different. They have no use for money, but they do for God and technology. 'Their' perception offers an alternative, utopian version of Western modernity. And in the process, 'their' perception, which includes the beauty of the environment, is made to fuse with ours (the readers', who are obviously non-Cuna), and to contain particular values such as communism and radical Christianity. This making of a fused 'us' is facilitated by the cultivation of naive vision, which, however, is not as innocent as it seems, since, for example, the idea that the Cuna do not use money depends on part of the 'us' knowing what money is historically. So part of the innocence is simply a restriction of knowledge, i.e. an ignorance, while the other part is the active imagination of an alternative modernity. The poems slip between the one and the other, between a closing down and an opening up of awareness, without acknowledgement, although the slipping can be felt in their use of sound.

---

[92] In 'Revelation', *Selected Essays* (New York, 1969), he writes of 'the necessity for revelation in order that we may achieve morality' (271).

Part of the difference no doubt has to do with the pressure of the need for national liberation, leading to large schemata of belief: the poet deciding to work inside those particular intensities of the social imagination and transferring them to the poem. The USA, by contrast, had already had that revolution. It was not, however, solely a Nicaraguan situation: the pressure on Latin American poets to adopt large-scale narratives of belief has been strong throughout the subcontinent since the 1960s. Poets have, variously, struggled with that difficulty, which has reappeared, since the 1980s, in other forms, such as feminism. Parra, to give one example, explodes those coagulations of energies—explodes them in the sense of de-energizing them, which has the effect of energizing the poem.

Cardenal resists diluting poetry into those narratives, in two main ways: by his fine attention to shapes of sound and vision and by his concern with techniques of assemblage through which a poem composes large extensions in time and space. There has already been some discussion, above, of both these areas. The analysis will now be taken further, into a consideration of the relationship between the two areas.

THE UTOPIA OF SOUND

In both the Objectivists (particularly Williams and Zukovsky) and Cardenal, sound is a training of the ear towards music, and the musical location of things brings them into revelation. For Cardenal, sound is both a thinking with things in their locations of space and time, and a relocation of things, a utopia. That tension carries through all of his later work. The long poem *Oráculo sobre Managua* (1973), a response to the obliteration of the city of Managua by a major earthquake on 22 December 1972, and to how it transformed the ongoing struggle against the Somoza clan, is Cardenal's most complex composition of different times and places, which are assembled here to be read as a history of the city and a narrative of heroic resistance. It begins with a series of very precise locations:

> Detrás de la fábrica de Hilados y Tejidos (si ha quedado
> la fábrica tras el terremoto) y junto al cauce de desagüe,
> cerca del lago, entre basuras, bacinillas rotas (*PE* 207)

[Behind the Spinning and Cloth mill (if there is anything
left of the factory after the earthquake) and beside the sewage
    channel,
near the lake, among rubbish, broken chamber pots]

The sense of precise position is given in the prepositions (*detrás,
junto, cerca, entre*). What follows is footprints, from palaeolithic
times but readable in the present, traced upon a stratum of
volcanic rock: 'están o estaban las huellas, impresas en estrato
volcánico' [the tracks are, or were, imprinted on volcanic
strata]. These earliest traces of the city are embedded, as a kind
of history because they are readable, upon the earliest of many
layers, the layers in turn superimposed on each other but sometimes exposed, as eruption followed eruption, over great spans
of time. The present thus figures as one of many strata, each
marked with its own tracks, readable if one cares to read them.
The result is a type of palimpsest, complex and multi-layered.
Here is part of Cardenal's careful reading of the palaeolithic
footmarks:

> huellas de gente en una misma dirección—hac el lago—
>   huellas huyendo del volcán
> unas hundidas más (indica que algunos llevaban cargas)
>   no corriendo (los pasos son cortos y regulares) (*PE* 207)
>
> [footprints of people going in the same direction—towards
>   the lake—
>   footprints escaping from the volcano
> some deeper (showing that some were carrying loads)
>   not running (the steps are short and regular)]

That reading—more accurately, voicing—of signs moves into
the territory of an epic narrative of origin:

> Sobre ellas cayó la lluvia negra.
> Después otra corriente de lodo, y otra ceniza negra.
> Luego espesas corrientes de lodo (varias) (*PE* 207)
>
> [Upon them fell the black rain.
> Afterwards another flow of mud, and another layer of black ash.
> Then thick flows of mud (several)]

The voice resonates with that of foundational epics like that of
certain Old Testament books or of Virgil telling the foundation
of Rome, or the Maya *Popol Vuh*. But there are two important
differences: the epic tone is interrupted by that of ordinary

speech, as in the comment ('varias'), and epic propriety is ruptured by the ugly, the vulgar, and the everyday,[93] in other words by those things that the high tone of epic excludes. After several other eruptions, passing through the Maya layer and the ceramics embedded in it, the poem comes back to the present one:

> En la costa del lago los niños juegan haciendo hoyitos
> con un palito a quién saca más moscas de su hoyito.
> En el agua, algodones, papel de inodoro, algún condón.
> (*PE* 209)
>
> [At the edge of the lake children play making holes
> with a stick to see who can get more flies out of his hole.
> In the water, cotton wool, toilet paper, the occasional
> condom.]

The poem's challenge is to include all of that, to hold all the layers, stories, and actions that make Nicaragua within a sharp, lucid whole.

However, when the children enter the poem, some of the sharpness of detail is lost: that list, for instance, of objects in the water does not ask for intelligence of perception—it is too much a commonplace for that.[94] The tone, in some of the lines, approximates to that of a sermon: 'Vi un papayo en una calle como un milagro en aquel horror' [I saw a papaya tree in a street like a miracle in that horror] (209). The papaya tree as a particularity of the senses gets washed away by 'milagro' and 'horror'. The play of sounds insists (*ayo/alle/agro/horror*) but what it insists upon has little clarity: the main rhythmic stress of the line falls upon mil*a*gro, a word that actually takes one into an elsewhere. Yet that lurch towards another place occurs alongside a very different use of sound-patterns. Consider, in the same section of the poem,

> Un arroyo de aguas-negras lechosas fluye hacia el lago
> a la derecha la envenenada laguna de Acahualinca verde-tierno

93 See Aldous Huxley's essay 'Tragedy and the Whole Truth', in *Music at Night and Other Essays* (London, 1949).

94 See T. S. Eliot's 'The Waste Land': 'The river bears no empty bottles, sandwich papers, | Silk handkerchiefs, cardboard boxes, cigarette ends | Or other testimony of summer nights' (*Collected Poems 1909–1962* (London, 1963), 70).

> [A black-water stream with milky waters flows towards the lake
> on the right the poisoned lake of Acahualinca tender-green]

or

> Allí desembocan otras cloacas
> sin llegar al lago   (la luna riela sobre la mierda) (*PE* 209)
> [There other sewers empty
> without reaching the lake   (the moon shimmers on the shit)]

There is precision of place ('hacia', 'a la derecha',
'Acahualinca', 'allí', 'sin llegar al lago'), then the soundless
gap—in which to imagine the effect of sewers that do not reach
the water—then a repetition of the earlier cadence ('laguna de
Acahualinca verde-tierno I la luna riela sobre la mierda'). The
recurrence, with variation, of that particular melodic pattern
situates and compares the two images, producing an effect of
shock. There is also an echo of 'El rielar en el mar I de la luna',
which is a recurrent cadence in *Los ovnis de oro*. Each image
configures contrastive shapes of filth and light: to be able to
see, alongside disgust, something else. The multi-layered
sounds embody the tensions in the seeing. Consider the difference between these lines and the message-conscious 'Vi un
papayo en una calle como un milagro en aquel horror'. 'La
luna riela sobre la mierda' places the horror and tenderness in
the seeing, which in fact brings one closer to the object than
the compassion expressed brings one to the children.

After the initial five pages, Cardenal adds a different procedure of assemblage. In addition to the layering of time, various
simultaneous narratives are set in motion: the torture of oppo-
nents by the Somoza clan; the evolution of the earth and the
universe; the life and heroic resistance of the Sandinist Leonel
Rugama; the ideas of Marxism and liberation theology; stories
of plagues in the Old Testament and of the Birth of Jesus in the
New. What is crucial is the particular relationship between
those various orderings of things in time. As a series of value-
statements their relationship is predictable enough, given
Cardenal's well-known position: they propose, in different ways,
a redemptive and utopian view of history. But they are not
handled sequentially: the poem cuts frequently from one to the
other, leaving the various expositions incomplete, and allowing
them to implicate each other. For example, the poem returns

various times to the story of Rugama, without following a linear order of biographical time. The technique, obviously enough, has been common in Latin American novels since the 1960s. But what is different, and not capable of achievement in a novel, is the combination of different speeds in the montage of materials and the musical weighting of phrases. Thus, in the space of a few lines, the poem places together

> Otros poetas se emborrachan o putean. Vos moriste.
>   MUERTE para dar VIDA
> [. . .]
> Y un día en 'La Prensa' a 8 columnas
> NIDO SANDINISTA DEMOLIDO A METRALLA Y CAÑONAZOS (*PE* 234–5)

> [Other poets get drunk or go whoring. You died.
>   DEATH to give LIFE
> And one day in 'La Prensa' an 8-column headline
> SANDINIST NEST DEMOLISHED BY MACHINE-GUNS AND CANNONS]

where the multiple resonances of *muerte* and *vida* (biological, epic, resurrectional) occur alongside the entirely different language of a newspaper headline and its simplifying order. There immediately follows a sequence of jump-cuts as the siege is presented, with 'cienes de espectadores viendo el combate como en un cine' [hundreds of spectators watching the combat like in a cinema]: cinema shapes the environment and trains the eye, it is part of the order of things. Its speed is a form of energy. And that speed and energy make the social revolution possible, a revolution that includes technological modernity; the poem places together the various accelarations brought about by the earthquake (geological, urban, social, political) as a shift from evolution to revolution:

> velocidad pasmosa de la evolución, esto es
> un preludio telúrico de la revolución

> [amazing speed of evolution, this is
> a telluric prelude to revolution]

the sight of the city destroyed giving a measure of the possible, facilitating utopian vision.

One becomes involved, therefore, as reader, in two types of ordering of materials: on the one hand the techniques of rapid montage, which engender mobile and constellatory relationships between the parts which are in constant rearrangement.

And on the other hand, the use of large, totalizing narratives: Darwin's theory of biological evolution, the Marxist[95] theory of social progress, the Christian story of redemption—the two great nineteenth-century schematizations of history, plus the most widely held Western belief in history as a transcendence. These narratives are made to interlock, or, more accurately, to implicate each other: thus the account of the devastation caused by the earthquake is interrupted by

—como la noche en que no hubo posada para ellos
todo Belén celebrando sus cenas de Navidad. (*PE* 244)

[—like the night when there was no room for them
all Bethlehem celebrating their Christmas dinners.]

A reader is expected to be able to work out who the 'ellos' are, and to read one narrative from inside the other and vice versa. Thus the universe is placed inside the cells of the human body ('dentro de las células órbitas del sistema solar' [inside the cells the orbits of the solar system]; *PE* 233), the cells are inside Darwinian evolution read from Marxism ('la revolución es semejante a una célula que se hace dos' [the revolution is like a cell dividing into two]; *PE* 215), and Marxism inside the utopian proposal of 'el hombre nuevo' as 'ley', 'nueva sociedad', 'progreso' [law, new society, progress]. A vocabulary of guarantees takes over the compositional excitement, using predictive statements that complete each other, with the result that a closed horizon is made: chaos, uncertainty, and the unknowable—of which an earthquake is a good enough example—are eliminated. Parra's poetry, by contrast, implodes those grand narratives of progress and redemption and transforms the energy thus released into anarchic glee and critical intelligence.

Yet the chaos of the earthquake, as the poem testifies, accelerated the social and political weakening of the Somoza regime. And the accelerated reordering of the city environment retrains the eye and releases passion in seeing, just as the cinematic projection of Rugama's extraordinarily courageous death changes the order of the possible. The poem's double commitment persists through to the end: on the one hand a

---

[95] Marxist rather than Marx's: see Cyril Smith, *Marx at the Millennium* (London, 1996).

scheme of utopian transcendence, on the other the actual, the human, incomplete and impermanent but capable of creating the new:

> No lloraremos por estos escombros sino por los hombres
> pero la muerte nace con el cuerpo y *muere* con él
>   la muerte es la del individuo
> 'un matiz' de dolor
> para resucitar hay que morir
>   (amaste el porvenir y moriste por él. Aceptaste
> antes que éstos este matiz, murió tu muerte compañero)
> [. . .]
> El pueblo se fue en camiones con sus trastes, sus roperos
> cogió las carreteras
> el pueblo nunca muere (*PE* 248–9)
>
> [We will not weep for this rubble only for the human beings
> but death is born with the body and *dies* with it
>   death is of the individual
> 'a touch' of pain
> to rise you have to die
>   (you loved the future and you died for it. You accepted
> that touch before these people, your death died compañero).
> The people got away in lorries with their kitchen things,
>   their cupboards
> they took to the roads
> the people never dies.]

To overcome pain, as a mere 'matiz', through sacrifice—the passage in brackets addresses the dead Rugama—is fed into the permanence of 'el pueblo', and that in turn is rolled up into the securities offered by the Bible and Marxism:

> A una clase salvaré
>   y a otra clase perderé. Oráculo de Yavé.
> Nadie sabe cuándo se realizará, dijo Lenin (el paraíso)
>   El pueblo está intacto. (*PE* 249)
>
> [I will save one class
>   and the other class I will destroy. Yahweh's oracle.
> Nobody knows when it will happen, said Lenin (paradise)
>   The people is intact.]

But there are also the details: 'trastes', 'roperos', or 'En la gasolinera Chevron I uno acariciaba la cara de su hija como si la durmiera' [In the Chevron garage I one was caressing his daughter's face as if to put her to sleep]: are these mere

residues, as pain ('un resto' [a remainder]) is supposed to be?
Do they resurrect as well? What kind of memory is being
proposed, inside the idea of resurrection? The question is not
asked, as it is in César Vallejo's *España aparta de mi este cáliz*—for
example of the dead soldier's spoon.[96] Vallejo's is an epic that
includes pain as the unresolved.

Consider the effect of the repeated six- and seven-syllable
cadences which run through the poem and become more
frequent towards the end:

> 'un matiz' de dolor [. . .]
> el pueblo nunca muere [. . .]
> el pueblo es inmortal [. . .]
> a una clase salvaré [. . .]
> Oráculo de Yavé [. . .]
> el pueblo está intacto[. . .]
> sólo los muertos resucitan [. . .]
> y esa es la esperanza [. . .]
> amaste el porvenir [. . .]

As their sounds echo each other, they wrap the details of times,
places, and objects into a grand continuity—but a grand continuity of discourse, which can be interrupted therefore by a
different language action:

> Sólo los muertos resucitan
> Otra vez hay otras huellas: no ha terminado la
> peregrinación (*PE* 250)
> [Only the dead rise
> once again there are other tracks: the pilgrimage has not
> finished]

There are none of those six- or seven-syllable cadences here:
the litany is broken. The two rhythmic units of the first line
('sólo los muertos | resucitan') are approximate inversions of
each other, with the result that the ear takes longer to work it
out and take it in, and with the ear the mind, to work out the
implications involved. The grand sacrificial continuity is
broken up with the fact of feet walking, the slow regular
rhythm of footsteps impinging on the ear ('otra vez hay otras

---

[96] The poem referred to, 'Solía escribir con el dedo grande en el aire', is
discussed in the Introduction, above. See also Charles Olson's poem 'The Chain of
Memory is Resurrection', in *Collected Poems* (Berkeley, 1987), 372–9.

huellas') and marking the ground, the action and its meaning incomplete and ongoing ('no ha terminado'). The marks left become memory that others will receive in another layering of time—a multiple text given to others, like the poem itself, which becomes a resuscitation, a making of forms capable of relative permanence, which is the sovereignty of poetry.

What, in those circumstances, does the poet do with the urgings of the social imagination, those other permanences and areas of belief, such as confidence in the efficacy of heroic sacrifice or, more widely still in Latin America, in the magical force of the Christian supernatural? Parra empties the energy out of them, by causing them to implode. Zurita, who considers himself an atheist, finds it impossible to ignore them when writing poems of epic scope. Let us consider William Blake's handling of the problem, which occurred in historical terms at the beginning of the cultural massification made possible by industrial technologies and finance.[97] In Blake's prophetic poems the personages of religion (gods, in conventional parlance) are born out of the energies of human beings, a situation not unlike the relationship between gods and human beings in the *Popol Vuh*, that compendium of Maya traditions sometimes known as the Maya Bible.[98] Blake's Urizen, a personage who configures the coming of the industrial epoch and the imprisonment of human beings in rigidities of reason, constructs religion out of his own pain:

> And he wept & he called it Pity,
> And his tears flowed down on the winds.
> [. . .]
> Till a Web, dark & cold, throughout all
> The tormented element stretch'd
> From the sorrows of Urizen's soul
> [. . .]
> And call'd it The Net of Religion.[99]

---

[97] I use 'massification' in Jesús Martín-Barbero's sense. See *Communication, Culture and Hegemony: From the Media to Mediations* (London, 1993).

[98] The best edition in English is Dennis Tedlock (ed.), *Popol Vuh* (New York, 1996).

[99] *Poems and Prophecies* (London, 1972), 90. See also Allen Ginsberg, *Your Reason and Blake's System* (New York, 1992).

Blake's critique of religion may be compared with Cardenal's reconfiguration of religion as projection of the social necessities of human beings and, more specifically, in the poem under discussion, with the notion of tracks made on the earth as foundation of meaning.

But one of Blake's preoccupations is why human beings are unaware of the imprisoning net of religion:

> The Senses inward rush'd shrinking
> Beneath the dark net of infection;
> Till the shrunken eyes, clouded over,
> Discern'd not the woven hipocrisy.[100]

His concern is to reinterpret religion as an action of human imagination. Thus when he proposes that the personages of religion envy human beings,[101] he shows how imagination has been captured by religion and, in doing so, turns the relationship inside out: to make the 'Net' of religion visible is to restore imagination to its powers. The gods become envious

> of the living Form, even of the Divine Vision,
> And of the sports of Wisdom in the Human Imagination,
> Which is the Divine Body of the Lord Jesus, blessed for ever.[102]

Sport here includes, as well as children's play, an idea of erotic play:[103] by contrast, in the poems Cardenal wrote after his entry into the priesthood, eros tends to be subsumed into the necessity of revolution, where revolution requires sacrifice. His scheme of values lines up sacrifice and revolution with celibacy, clandestinity, and catacombs: in other words, erotic desire sublimated, as in the official history of the Church, in order to ensure the fulfilment of a higher, more permanent purpose. And pain is not part of the permanence proposed:

> Dichosos los del dolor que es liberador
> 'un resto'
> [. . .] el pueblo nunca muere. (*PE* 249)

---

[100] Blake, *Poems and Prophecies*, 91.

[101] Note the similarity with the *Popol Vuh*, which sees the gods as a burden carried by human beings.

[102] Blake, *Poems and Prophecies*, 111.

[103] The *Oxford English Dictionary* gives the date 1796 to its meaning of amorous dalliance or intercourse. The Chilean avant-garde poet Vicente Huidobro, in canto III of *Altazor*, writes, 'Mientras vivamos juguemos | el simple sport de los vocablos | De la pura palabra y nada más.'

[Blessed they of the pain which liberates
'a remainder'
the people never dies.]

The proposal takes away the actual pain inside perception, which is there in the details in which time moves, and substitutes a blander permanence. Blake's Urizen had 'sought for a joy without pain, I For a solid without fluctuation',[104] an anodyne religion and a surface that does not move. Blake's 'sports of wisdom in the Human Imagination' allow the play of eros in the intellect and the senses. And yet in Cardenal's writing, that play never entirely goes away: it is there in the excitements of collage and montage and in the play of sound upon the aural imagination.

THE COSMOS: ORDER OR CHANCE?

Cántico cósmico may be taken as a recapitulation and expansion of Cardenal's major preoccupations. The figure of expansion is quantum cosmology, as in the title of the first *Cantiga*, 'El bigbang', but the materials include evolutionary biology, the New Man, imperialist economics, Nicaraguan history, the Gospels, the Sandinist struggle, and so on. One way of exemplifying the book as a whole, which totals over four hundred pages, is to look closely at the tenth *Cantiga*, the 'Cántico del sol' [Canticle of the sun]. There have been many hymns to the sun, the most famous in a European language being St Francis of Assisi's 'Canticle of the Sun', more pagan than Christian in its sense of the cosmos as sacred. Others include poems by John Donne, Vladimir Mayakovsky, and Frank O'Hara, all of which are deliberately modern in the way they juxtapose ancient sun-cults with modern, urban, secular life: Donne calls the sun 'Busie old foole', and O'Hara's title is 'The sun woke me this morning loud'.[105] In the Americas, there are, most famously, the Inca sacred songs to the sun, their principal deity. One of the distinguishing points of Cardenal's song to the sun is confidence in scientific knowledge and in the possibility of integrating it with one's perception of the world and behaviour in it. Far from

---

[104] Blake, *Poems and Prophecies*, 80.
[105] *Selected Poems* (New York, 1974), 138,

sitting uneasily with inherited conceptions of human feeling, scientific understanding is offered as a way of integrating inner consciousness with the place of human beings in the physical universe. This is the basis of the expansive and integrative movement of the book.

Three types of language or, more accurately, three types of saying lay the ground for expansive integration. Let us consider them in descending order of formality. In the first place, there is the hieratic diction of the first line,

> Lentamente el sol sale del mar (*CC* 71)
> [Slowly the sun rises from the sea]

where the movement of image and the speed of word-combination are slow, the tone solemn. The second type of language is intermediate: formalized in that the register is similar to that of expository prose and the measure approximately hendeca-syllabic:

> Clorofila verde y hemoglobina roja.
> Así a todos el sol nos alimenta. (*CC* 71)
>
> [Green chlorophyll and red haemoglobin.
> Thus the sun feeds all of us.]

The third type consists in the rhythms of informal speech, i.e. of speech which is not moulded by a special occasion but which flows with the movement of conversation:

> mejor dicho lentamente la tierra dando vueltas (*CC* 71)
> [in other words the earth slowly turning]

As in the example just given, with the third type the lines tend to be longer. In the composition of the poem, the different types of language are interwoven, as in the first five lines:

> Lentamente el sol sale del mar,
> mejor dicho lentamente la tierra dando vueltas . . .
> pareciéndonos que el sol sale del mar.
>   Sol sólo gas.
> Y sol que comemos. (*CC* 71)
>
> [Slowly the sun rises from the sea,
> in other words the earth slowly turning . . .
> seeming to us that the sun comes out of the sea.
>   Sun purely gas.
> And sun that we eat.]

The second line comes in as an interpolation, bringing us 'down' to the level of modern scientific common sense, and then with the fourth line the rhythm of utterance becomes slower, as in a ritual, while the content demands specialized scientific understanding beyond that of common sense. The placing of the most up-to-date understanding inside more ancient forms of song is one of the most interesting techniques of this work. What we have is not a progressive account of knowledge, as in nineteenth-century education (still prevalent!), but an unfolding of all earlier and/or 'unscientific' forms of understanding within late twentieth-century cosmology, so that they can all stand as forms of the same thing, just as everything can be dissolved into subatomic particles.

Two writers stand out among those who have expounded this profoundly twentieth-century vision of knowledge: Henry Adams and Pierre Teilhard de Chardin. Adams applies contemporary mathematics and cosmology to history, and proposes that just as all material substances can be dissolved, so history is finally dissolvable into thought:

This solvent, then,—this ultimate motion which absorbs all other forms of motion is an ultimate equilibrium,—this etherial current of Thought—is conceived as existing, like ice on a mountain range, and trickling from every pore of rock, in innumerable rills, uniting always into larger channels, and always dissolving whatever it meets, until at last it reaches equilibrium in the ocean of ultimate solution.[106]

Adams's ocean recalls the image of an alien sea in Stanislaw Lem's novel *Solaris*[107] and in the film of the same title, made by Tarkovsky. Teilhard de Chardin expresses a similar idea in his notion of the 'noosphere', meaning the sphere of thought, which is wrapped round the world, and the universe:

A glow ripples outward from the first spark of conscious reflection. The point of ignition grows larger. The fire spreads in ever widening circles till finally the whole planet is covered with incandescence. Only one interpretation, only one name can be found worthy of this grand phenomenon. [. . .] it is really a new layer, the 'thinking layer' [. . .] In other words, outside and above the biosphere there is the noosphere.[108]

[106] Henry Adams, 'The Rule of Phase Applied to History', in *A Henry Adams Reader*, ed. Elizabeth Stevenson (New York, 1958), 374.
[107] London, 1970.   [108] Teilhard de Chardin, *The Phenomenon*, 182.

That returning of the universe upon itself as thought is a prime concern that Cardenal shares with Teilhard; for both of them, love is at the core of that process of synthesis, which is, in Teilhard's words, 'the psychical convergence of the universe upon itself',[109] and, in Cardenal's, 'La fuerza de convergencia del universo hacia su centro | es el amor' [The convergent force of the universe towards its centre | is love] (*CC* 409).

What is the relationship between these ideas, which are a form of content, and the forms of expression in Cardenal's poem? Consider the question of speeds. The slow movement of hieratic language is interrupted by the quicker rhythm of everyday speech with its more rapid flow of word-associations. The rhythm also becomes more varied: there is less control. So there is an expansion here, into a contemporary environment of social communication. But where concepts are introduced, that is ideas which have to do with cosmology, another speed comes in, which is the speed of thought:

> (Ese montón de hilos
> que te cubren toda la cabeza
> y bajan enrollados hasta tu espalda
> ¿de qué mina sacaste o qué joyería?)
> Movimientos de las moléculas del ojo tocadas por la luz
> eso son los colores.
> Y nosotros sólo vemos el 30% de la luz. Los unicelulares
> la entera luz solar. ¡Ven el mundo como es!
> Como yo lo veré un día como es. (*CC* 71)
> [(That mass of threads
> that cover your whole head
> and coil down your back
> what mine did you take them from, what jeweller?)
> Movements of the molecules of the eye touched by light
> is what colours are.
> And we only see 30% of the light. Unicellular organisms
> the whole light of the sun. They see the world as it is!
> As I will see it one day as it is.]

Attention moves from sensual image of a woman's long hair—a Cuna woman, we later find out—to a question of origin: where does the richness of the seen come from? The answer offered takes us outside perception, into what can be known (empiri-

---

[109] Teilhard de Chardin, *The Phenomenon*, 265.

cally verifiable) but not seen: the molecular basis of human vision. A consequence of that knowledge is then derived: the difference, in terms of receptivity to light, between human beings and single-cell life forms—which were the beginning of life. Then we move from that knowledge to a radical ambiguity ('¡Ven el mundo como es!'), which is at once physical and spiritual: the spiritual sense, which echoes St Paul's famous chapter on love,[110] occurs inside the physical and the physical inside the spiritual. The double meaning embodies the possibility of a totality of knowledge which Cardenal, after Teilhard de Chardin, calls 'Omega', and which as speech is the many names or the namelessness of God ('sin nombre y con muchos nombres' [without a name and with many names]; *CC* 401).

Let us consider again the act of saying. When Cardenal moves from the physical to the spiritual, there is no shift into specialized language: '¡Ven el mundo como es!' has the rhythm and intonation of the everyday spoken language. In the space of two lines, we move from an intermediate, semi-formal register ('Y nosotros sólo vemos el 30% de la luz') to a formalized, slower rhythm ('la entera luz solar') to the faster rhythm of ordinary speech ('¡Ven el mundo como es!'). The interweaving of types of language occurs both between lines and within lines. In parallel with the shifts between different types of saying, one moves as reader from perception (a woman's hair) to knowledge (molecules) then back to perception (to see the world as it is), but a perception that has been altered by knowledge. I dwell on this point, because it is crucial to the overall form of the poem. To take another example:

> Luz sumergida.
>   El sol dentro del agua venida del sol.
> La luz líquida, el agua como sólida.
> La luz está hecha agua y el agua está hecha luz. (*CC* 74)
> [Submerged light.
>   The sun in the water which has come from the sun.
> Liquid light, the water as if solid.
> The light made water and the water made light.]

The first line and a half concerns perception, which then

---

[110] 1 Corinthians 13.

becomes knowledge (water, in the evolution of the planet, depending upon sunlight). Then in the fourth line cosmological knowledge and the phenomenal world (the world of perception) converge in the word 'agua'. Here there is more than one speed: the movement is very fast and very slow at the same time.

What that alteration of perception actually is, is perhaps the most difficult aspect of the poem to discuss. It certainly has nothing to do with the ways in which people's everyday consciousness has been altered by classical physics (as happened historically with, say, the Copernican revolution, or the technology of aviation, celebrated by Futurist poets). It has more to do with ways in which twentieth-century physics requires intuition and imagination. The poem also generates an interplay between the rhythms of the human body, where perception resides, and the infinite speed of thought. In Merleau-Ponty's phrase, 'I perceive with my body'.[111]

The realm of perception occurs as movement of water, light, and fish at the Cuna island of San Blas. The verse form changes, becoming less regular and more multiform:

> Esta agua de San Blas
> llena de luz.
>   Donde van y vienen los peces
> unos como anuncios de neón
>   o amarillo de semáforo.
> Fosforescentes,
>   o como pintados con pintura fluorescente,
>   iridescentes,
>   rutilantes,
>   otros como iluminados por dentro
>   —luz extraña en sus entrañas—. (*CC* 72)

> [This water of San Blas
> full of light.
>   Where fish come and go
> some like neon adverts,
>   or traffic light yellows.
> Phosphorescent,
>   or as if painted with fluorescent paint,
>   iridescent,

---

[111] Merleau-Ponty, *Phenomenology*, 326.

        glinting,
    and others as if lit from within
      —strange light in their entrails—.]

Among the effects is the way adjectives are freed from syntactic chains ('fosforescentes', 'iridescentes', 'rutilantes') to embody the dance of the senses, without beginning and never completed. Before, at the start of the *Cantiga*, syntax had served to carry the logic of biology: 'Pues las plantas comen energía solar | y los animales plantas o animales comedores de plantas' (*CC* 71). In the passage just quoted, there is unlimited movement, without the constraint of evolutionary thought. The movement is double: on the one hand that of light, water, the fish and on the other that of the seeing eye. In other words, we have both the phenomenology of the object, and the phenomenology of the gaze.[112]

This section of the text, which makes up the larger part of the *Cantiga* and is characteristic of a major proportion of the book, places a reader (willing to go there) inside the sport—Blake's word—of the senses, which is the dance of the body in time. The visible passes through unlimited metamorphoses, in the shape, for example, of aquatic creatures which endlessly become other in a 'bosque mágico' [magic forest]:

    Animales en forma de árboles
        y otros en forma de hierbas o de hongos
    y entre ellos otros corren y relumbran.
    [. . .]
    Colores sobre colores
        tras otros colores. (*CC* 73)

    [Animals in the form of trees
        and others in the form of grasses or fungi
    and among them others run and gleam.
    Colours upon colours
        behind other colours.]

[112] See Merleau-Ponty, *Primacy*, 16: 'The perceived thing is not an ideal unity in the possession of the intellect, like a geometrical notion, for example; it is rather a totality open to a horizon of an indefinite number of perspectival views which blend with one another.' See also *Phenomenology*, 325: 'If one tried, according to the realistic approach, to make perception into some coincidence with the thing, it would no longer be possible to understand what the perceptual event was.' Merleau-Ponty's sense of 'the perceptual event' as a process in time is useful for understanding how Cardenal's poem embodies in its slower rhythms the time-lapse of perception.

There is a multiplicity of forms and layers, without logic: a proliferation, in the sense of *proles+fer*, production of offspring, without the single controlling direction that classical theories of evolution impose. In that sense, the *Cántico del sol* counterposes uncontainable emergence with predictabilities of myth and nineteenth-century science. Prime examples of the latter are the myth of Persephone or the theory of evolution, both of which guarantee stability, the latter through the idea of a justi-fied, higher goal, a notion which Cardenal expands to include the universe: 'como se sabe, los ojos los creó la luz | para que hubiera seres que la vieran' [as is known, light created the eyes | so that there could be beings to see it] (*CC* 72).

That idea of a goal limits the play of the senses. The latter is embodied not just in the flashing of visual surfaces but in the ways in which light becomes sound. Light recurs as defining event through the poem, and the recurrence is carried by repeated sound-patterns: 'la luz difusa', 'llena de luz', 'la atmós-fera es turquesa', 'corren y relumbran' [diffuse light, full of light, the atmosphere is turquoise, run and gleam] (*CC* 72, 73), to give the main pattern, out of which variations are spun, such as líquida luz', 'atrapando la luz' [liquid light, trapping the light] (*CC* 73). Thus sound operates as pulsion, in the older sense of driving or pushing, but the poem always comes back to light. Light enters through the particular event but creates a theatre of multiple forms. Examples have already been given of colour and outline (the corals). The other forms include move-ment and stasis ('Pólipos inmóviles tentáculos' [Immobile polyps or with mobile tentacles]); of faces and masks ('Un pez pintarrajeado como payaso | —hocico rojo y negro con un parche blanco—y pasan otros con antifaces' [A fish painted like a clown | red and black snout with a white patch—and others go by with masks]); of textures ('Moluscos suaves como mucosas. | Lechugas pétreas' [Soft molluscs like mucus. | Stony lettuces]); of undulating, trembling, or shaking movements ('Abanicos morados moviéndose en el agua' [Purple fans moving in the water]); of the air or clothing surrounding bodies ('arrastrando la cola de traje de gala entre corales' [dragging the train of a gala dress between the corals]); of architecture and design ('Cabellos, cactus, candelabros' [Hair, cactus, candelabra]); and of art ('Pez Miró. Pez Paul Klee' (Miró fish. Paul Klee fish]) (*PE* 73). There is a sense of overflowing pleasure in the sheer bedazzlement, not to be contained in any scheme. If theory (θεῶρια) in early Greek culture meant moving away from the already-known in order to see the world (Hesiod), or else spectacle and theatre (Aeschylus), then Cardenal's poem recuperates that earlier meaning against Plato's use of the word as signifying reasoning.

To make visible the invisible is a major part of the desire that moves the poem. The invisible in this context includes both the preconscious and the non-conscious: both the innate human capacity for seeing change and complexity and that other light which is the environment that is invisible because we exist inside it, like the water for fish, 'invisible como anteojos' [invisible like spectacles] (*CC* 73). But in another, stronger, sense, that environment is not seen: light enters the body as subatomic particles/waves, which are the basic substance of the universe. Which takes us once again to Henry Adams's notion of Thought as ultimate solvent or Teilhard de Chardin's 'psychical convergence of the universe upon itself'. The image is of thought expanding infinitely, at infinite speed, to embrace the whole universe.

Yet alongside that major movement of the poem, and sometimes in tension with it—though the tension is not stated as such—is the fact of the time-bound human body. In the realm of perception as pulsion and pulsion as eros, who is to be king? Eros was a god in 'pre'-modern civilizations, a personage who configured the power of desire. Eros as Venus traps desire, but also can be trapped. In Cardenal's poetry after *Hora O* the force of the erotic and the power of belief vie with each other. But in *Cántico cósmico* a tendency which appeared earlier in a chronological sense[113] comes into its own: belief becomes dissolved into knowledge. Thus 'cosmic' convergence is also convergence of perception and knowledge: that they should become as one. Is there no resistance then to that possibility of infinite expansion of the human? Can we speak of 'átomos espirituales'? The question is Cardenal's: the questioning attitude, the continual returns to pragmatic, colloquial language keep the poem open. But there is also a contrary tendency, to find answers back in the old theology:

---

[113] For example, 'Condensaciones y visión de San José de Costa Rica', which is included in *Cántico cósmico*.

¿Átomos espirituales?
[. . .]
Ya todo confundido con el Todo, y las personas con la Persona
   en un Todo que es Persona
      y Persona que es Amor.
La materia era tan sólo un tenue velo de tu rostro. (*CC* 410)
   [Spiritual atoms?
All confused with the All, and persons with the Person
  in an All which is Person
     and Person which is Love.
Matter was only a tenuous veil over your face.]

The vehicle, i.e. the language, changes, the capital letters and
solemn tone registering a desire for a singular god and the final
line a theological commonplace: the god behind the veil, the
face as controlling presence.

   Hand in hand with the old theology, the old physics comes
back in:

Vemos rotación en toda dimensión, desde el protón
a la galaxia. Uno se pregunta,
con razón, si el cosmos entero estará también
en rotación.
      Y entonces: ¿alrededor de qué o de quién?
[. . .]
Y bien puedo decir:
      una creación con un plan.
[. . .]
¿O será sólo azar el universo?
   ¿Y lo más profundo de nuestro ser
      sólo azar?
O el Azar sólo otro nombre de él?
      ¿El Azar infinito? (*CC* 391)

[We see rotation in every dimension, from the proton
to the galaxy. One asks,
with reason, if the entire cosmos may also be
in rotation.
     And then, around what or whom?
And I can rightly say:
     a creation with a plan.
Or is the universe only chance?
   And the depth of our being
     only chance?
Or is Chance only another name for it?
     Infinite Chance?]

Having started with the spin of subatomic particles, realm of the uncertainty principle, we move to an idea which belongs to classical physics: rotation around a stable centre, which is used to support the idea of a creator with a plan.[114] Subsequently, however, the poem reopens the question: is the universe simply chance? And then, in the shift to the capital letter (*Azar*), we are back inside the transcendent, which is declared, in the *Cantiga* dedicated to Venus, to be the purpose of the poem:

> Esta mi épica astrofísica sólo tiene un sentido:
> proclamar que el universo tiene sentido. (*CC* 89)
>
> [My astrophysical epic has only one meaning:
> to proclaim that the universe has meaning.]

The birth of the goddess of love is told as the origin of life, the random movement of subatomic particles ('quarks sin los cuales no habría luz', 'una masa desordenada de cosas mal ligadas' [quarks without which there would be no light, a disordered mass of ill-linked things]) transposed into the order of a grand myth:

> Quién diría que de tal confusión
> surgiría un día tan bella y frágil filigrana,
> la vida.
> Salida del mar como Venus (*CC* 85)
>
> [Who could say that from such confusion
> would arise one day such beautiful and fragile filigree,
> life.
> Risen from the sea like Venus.]

Once again Cardenal renounces randomness and chance for seductive order. Venus as profusion and proliferation becomes Venus as selective order.

Uncertainty, as expounded most famously by Heisenberg, [115] is the prime characteristic of the subatomic realm: this is one of the—so far—inescapable bases of quantum physics. It is also crucial to twentieth-century poetics in the expansion of the poem—by Mallarmé, Vallejo, and other avant-garde poets—to

---

[114] Lest it seem I am castigating Cardenal for some theoretical incoherence, it perhaps needs saying that a good number of late 20th-century writers on cosmology (e.g. Stephen Hawking, to mention the most famous) show in their language a desire to enter what was traditionally the province of theology.

[115] *Physics and Philosophy* (London, 1989).

include that which formerly lay outside poetry. To embrace chance is an instrument of the transformation of poetry. And Cardenal does do that when the writing becomes immersed, as it does repeatedly, in the play of sound and light in the endless emergence of forms. But he also—and repeatedly—renounces chance, and with it the realm of the senses, for what, reputedly, lies behind the senses. And here there is the radical ambiguity.

The penultimate *Cantiga*, which is a rereading—or rewriting—of San Juan de la Cruz—takes what is behind the senses as both 'vacío' and 'Dios', 'nada' and 'todo', 'nada' and 'Nada':

> El ánima puede conocer todo mas no a sí misma
>   (esto es Meister Eckhart)
> pues no conoce sino por los sentidos
> y así no se conoce a sí misma, es sin idea de sí
> [. . .]
> y así se le puede unir Dios que es también puro y sin idea.
>   (*CC* 386)

> [The soul can know everything but not itself
>   (this is Meister Eckhart)
> since it only knows through the senses
> and thus does not know itself, is without idea of itself
> and so can be joined with God who is also pure and
>   without idea.]

To say there is nothing behind the world perceived is very different from saying there is Nothing. But the difference can disappear and does when a constant alternation absorbs the not-known into the Unknown. Openness and transcendence are not the same thing. And the danger to the artist, since that is what we are discussing, is that renunciation of the senses can become a diminution of the scope of the poem, of what it can actually do as event of language, as distinct from faith in belief-structures or in knowledge.

3

Gonzalo Rojas: Writing in the Wind

No explicar nunca el aire. Ni vamos a profanar
el cuerpo vivo de un poema

(Gonzalo Rojas)

[Never explain the air. Or profane
the living body of a poem.]

The bounded is loathed by its possessor.

(William Blake)

TIME AND MEANING

No amount of statements about the work of a poet can substitute for the work of reading, as propaganda can for thinking or advertisements for the enjoyment of things or pornography—easily enough—for the art of love. Do you then read in a closed room, where no such interferences can enter, in an atmosphere of high seriousness? Substitution is to do with making models, and training the receiver to relate to them and not to the things themselves, and in the case of literature its smell is familiar enough to any student with an examination coming up. The problem is the models become the currency of what can be said—or what gets heard, which is the same thing. The problem is particularly acute with Gonzalo Rojas, whose work, in a whole range of ways, refuses to seek power or take pleasure or refuge from fear in the already-known. Recognition is, as he puts it, an impoverishment of first discovery: 'Anagnórisis no es aleluya sino infinita | pérdida del hallazgo' [Anagnorisis is not alleluia but infinite loss of discovery] (*O* 68),[1] a deeply anti-Platonic statement since the word anagnorisis is used by Plato to express

---

[1] Textual references are to *Oscuro* (Caracas, 1977).

the idea of recovering knowledge possessed in an earlier state, before one was born.[2]

His work also runs deeply against the idea that what was written earlier is fixed and complete. This is a principle which includes his own writing and is expressed in the organization of his book *Oscuro*, which is the first time he gathered his work together for a larger public. The non-chronological ordering of the poems expresses the notion that it is a 'libro viejo y libro nuevo al mismo tiempo' [an old book and a new one at the same time] (*O* 213), a notion that carries with it a particular attitude to reading. Reading is a process that has no beginning and no end: since it is never complete it is always changing. The place of each poem changes: earlier ones can be read alongside later ones, and different groupings emerge which are themselves provisional, a 'metamorfosis de lo mismo' [metamorphosis of the same], as Rojas puts it.[3] This which is true to some extent of other poets is particularly so with Rojas. It is connected with particular ideas of time and of birth. For Rojas, one is being born all the time; there is no definitive birth just as there is no definitive age: 'uno tiene 10 años y simultáneamente tiene 20, y tiene 30, 40, 50, 60 y retrocede. Así, cuando tengo 70 también tengo 20 y tengo 30' [One's 10 years old and at the same time 20, and 30, 40, 50, 60 and going backwards. So when I'm 70 I'm also 20 and 30].[4]

The method of assembling *Oscuro* is to consider the poems not as fixed parts of a sequence but as fragments which can be moved around: 'Libro viejo y libro nuevo al mismo tiempo, jugado en el juego fragmentario que nada tiene que ver con la dispersión' [an old book and a new one at the same time, thrown into the play of fragments which has nothing to do with dispersal], where dispersal would be the abandonment of the poems to weak interaction, which amounts to leaving them open to the imposition of any framework that someone might care to impose. Rojas's test for a poem that needs to be written, i.e. become an object of public circulation which is not simply

[2] In Greek, 'anagnwrisis', see Plato, *Meno*, 74–81, especially 81c. (trans. W. K. C. Guthrie (Harmondsworth, 1956), 122–30).

[3] *Poesía y poética*, 30 (1998), 5–7. See also 'Discurso en Buenos Aires', *ibid.* 8–12.

[4] Faride Zeran, 'Gonzalo Rojas y la miseria del hombre', *La época*, 28 May 1995, 14.

the result of 'la tentación de la vitrina' [the temptation to be commercial], is rigorous:

> es que, como tantos otros aprendices, no creo gran cosa en la letra pública hasta que no se nos impone como palabra viva y necesaria, y parece exigirnos de veras la participación del oyente para poder seguir respirando, y respirándola.[5]

[the fact is, like so many other learners, I don't give much for publication until what one's writing imposes itself as living and necessary and seems to demand the participation of a listener so it can go on breathing while it is breathed.]

It sounds as if he is saying the test is whether a poem can come alive or not. But what then would be the standard of judgement? What would the judgement be modelled upon? Who would be the judge? The point is not that these questions are unanswerable—there is no lack of literary criticism—but that Rojas does not ask them because he is concerned with something prior: the test of necessity is does the poem need a reader's breath, in the sense of the energy which makes it possible to live?

That is where time comes in, since, for Rojas, writing and reading occur as necessities for the person who is open to the irreversible flow of time—for the person who is exposed to 'la intemperie' [bad weather],[6] to quote one of his insistent expressions—rather than the one who has built himself some sort of metaphysical or academic cocoon. Which means, among other things, that it has to compete with everything else—sex and religion are the main things for Rojas—that might penetrate and hold a person's attention. Vision occurs but is never completed, never perfected, because of

> la fragilidad, la caducidad de nuestra tan precaria existencia, [. . .] el no llegar, el no alcanzar. Dice San Juan de la Cruz: 'volé tan alto, tan alto que le di a la caza alcance', pero yo, como místico turbulento, no volé tan alto y no le di a la caza alcance.[7]

[the fragility, the brevity of our deeply precarious existence, the fact that we don't arrive, we don't reach our goal. Saint John of the Cross says: 'I flew so high, so high that I reached my prey', but I am a turbulent mystic, I didn't fly so high and I didn't reach the prey.]

---

[5] *Oscuro*, 214.
[6] *La intemperie* can also be translated as the elements.
[7] Zeran, 'Gonzalo Rojas', 24.

And thus there is no perfection of the eye: 'el ojo funciona en mí visionario y concupiscente' [In me the eye is visionary and lustful].

Rojas quotes and emends Blake to say not just that the readers of his poems are in eternity but that eternity is the act of reading itself: ' "—Mis lectores, dijo Blake una vez, se hallan en la eternidad". Pero la eternidad es esto mismo' ['My readers', as Blake once said, 'are in eternity.' But this itself is eternity].[8] What does it mean to say that a reader is in eternity and not God? Certainly, a prime implication in Blake's statement is that poetry exists to supplant priestly ownership of the word and its meaning—and philology took over that privilege from the priesthood, as George Eliot makes clear in *Middlemarch,* exposing the use of mythology as a nineteenth-century extension of religion. Between Blake and Rojas one would need to mention Mallarmé as index of the secularizing project of Modernism. If, as Mallarmé suggests, reading supplants God,[9] then the potential of the book is to take the place of Moses'—or any other priest's—tablets. And that is, among other things, to reverse the process of substitution of ideal models—which always turn out to be someone's property—for the actual.

To turn the written into a fixed, sacred inheritance is tied up with religion, and its model in the West has, obviously enough, been the Bible. In a poem addressed to the great Peruvian poet César Vallejo, Rojas sets out a contrary sense of reading, as unsubstitutable event in time:

Ya todo estaba escrito cuando Vallejo dijo:—Todavía.
[. . .]
     El tiempo es todavía,
la rosa es todavía y aunque pase el verano, y las estrellas
de todos los veranos, el hombre es todavía.
[. . .]
Cada cual su Vallejo doloroso y gozoso.
     No en París
donde lloré por su alma, no en la nube violenta
que me dio a diez mil metros la certeza terrestre de su rostro

---

[8] *Oscuro,* 24.

[9] 'Man's duty is to observe with the eyes of the divinity; for if his connection with that divinity is to be made clear, it can be expressed only by pages of the open book in front of him' (Stéphane Mallarmé, *Selected Poetry and Prose,* ed. Mary Ann Caws (New York, 1982), 80).

sobre la nieve libre, sino en esto
de respirar la espina mortal, estoy seguro
del que baja y me dice:—Todavía.[10] (*O* 149)

[Everything had been written when Vallejo said: Still.
   Time still is,
the rose still is and though summer passes, and the stars
of all summers, man still is.
Everyone their own Vallejo, painful and joyful.
   Not in Paris
where I cried for his soul, not in the violent cloud
at ten thousand metres that gave me the terrestrial certainty
of his face
upon the untouched snow, but in this thing
of breathing the mortal spine, I'm certain of it,
which he comes down from and says to me: Still.]

Rojas's Vallejo comes down from the vision—like Jesus from the sky (there is a note of parody here, immediate and familiar in a Catholic environment)—and speaks his Word, which is not Concept or Image or Fetish, and thus nothing to do with the logos or the idea of God or magic, but is an operative word that gets into everything because it is pure time. Another key word is *espina*, and one has to consider the phrase it comes in, 'esto | de respirar la espina mortal', which gives a location, here and this, as opposed to that and there: in other words, what one actually does in living. *Espina* is thorn, splinter, bone (of fish), backbone (*espinazo*), and 'pesar íntimo y duradero' [intimate and lasting suffering]. And that is not just what Vallejo's writing speaks of, but how it speaks, how, like anything else that is already written, it can come alive and still say something. *Todavía* is the irreversible and irredeemable force of time and the word that goes on speaking to one, both together in a single utterance. Rojas turns round the Romantic preoccupation: one does not read/write to overcome time (like Yeats, or early Darío), time is why one still needs to read—irreversible time, that is. And this time inside the backbone is not substitutable, no one can do it for you (Jesus, for example), there is no system of exchange, as money is, available. Money, in a poem of that title, is 'el río de la muerte' [the river of death], the great flow

---

[10] Note that, as would be obvious for Chilean or Peruvian readers, the vision of Vallejo's face in the snow occurs during a flight over the Andes.

of money charging us interest even while we sleep ('nos cobra
intereses por velar nuestra noche' [it charges us interest for
looking after us at night] (*O* 175).

Coming between the poem and the act of reading are 'los
letrados' [the educated][11]. The damage they do is set out in the
poem of that title:

> Lo prostituyen todo
> con su ánimo gastado en circunloquios.
> Lo explican todo. [. . .]
> Lo manchan todo con su baba metafísica. (*O* 165)

> [They prostitute everything,
> by wasting energy in circumlocution.
> They explain it all
> and slobber over everything with their metaphysical drivel.]

What they could not handle is the southern ocean, an environment where their packaged talk could not be exchanged for
prestige:

> Yo los quisiera ver en los mares del sur
> una noche de viento real, con la cabeza
> vaciada en frío, oliendo
> la soledad del mundo,
> sin luna,
> sin explicación posible

> [I'd like to see them in the southern ocean
> on a night of real wind, with their heads
> cold cast, smelling
> the vast solitude of the world,
> without moon,
> without possible explanation]

For the ocean, read time. Rojas recounts his response to the
condemnatory review his first book received from a famous
critic in Chile:

'Al paso que van, las letras nacionales no prometen nada bueno.' Y eso
me encantó. El dictamen oficial me puso de una vez frente a mí
mismo y asumí la intemperie que desde niño fue mi espacio, sin más
techo protector que las estrellas altas.[12]

---

[11] *Letrado* involves a specifically Latin American range of equivalences:
educated, learned, literate (as opposed to illiterate).
[12] Zeran, 'Gonzalo Rojas', 15.

'The way things are going, the future of our national literature does-
n't look too bright.' I loved that. The official judgement made me face
myself and I got back into the wild and open weather that had been
my space since childhood, with no roof but the high stars.]

In another poem, the sea once again is the element one can
only know by surviving inside it, a fact which makes institutional
knowledge useless:

> Dele con los estratos y la estructura
> cuando el mar se demuestra pero nadando.
> Siempre vendrán de vuelta sin haber ido
> nunca a ninguna parte los doctorados.
>
> Y eso que vuelan gratis: tanto prestigio,
> tanto arrogante junto, tanto congreso.
> Revistas y revistas y majestades
> cuando los eruditos ponen un huevo. (*O* 180)

> [Stuff your structures and strata,
> the sea can only be demonstrated by swimming.
> The academics are always coming back
> without ever having been anywhere.
>
> And their flights are paid: all that prestige,
> all those arrogant people together, all those conferences.
> Journals and journals and pomposities
> when the learned lay an egg.]

To take poetry as knowledge, as urgent and practical as knowing how to swim: what would be the consequences?

Vallejo is, in the poem quoted earlier, 'alguien que se llamaba César en peruano' [someone called César in Peruvian], not
the great universal poet, consecrated after death. Marginality,
for Rojas, is not something to be lamented, but a necessary
condition for the poet:

a los poetas que me oigan les digo: escriban en el viento, no transen.
No sean míseros escribas al servicio de la publicidad [. . .] Apuesten el
seso a las estrellas, aunque no los oiga nadie. ¿Quién oyó en su día
Hölderlin, a Baudelaire, a Vallejo? ¿A Celan, quién lo oyó? Sólo la
marginalidad nos hace libres.

[I tell any poets who can hear me: write in the wind, don't give in.
Don't be miserable scribes in the pay of the publicity[13] machine. Go
for the brain of the stars, even if no one listens to you. Who listened

---

[13] The meanings of *publicidad* include publicity, advertising, marketing.

to Hölderlin, or Baudelaire or Vallejo in their day? Who heard Celan? Only marginality can make us free.]

Rojas describes the necessary condition: 'soy y fui siempre un disidente y un anarca, es decir, uno que ve el mundo sin tener la adhesión total' [I am and have always been a dissident and an anarch, in other words someone who looks at the world without a total commitment].[14] That, for Rojas, is a necessity not only for a poet but for an intellectual also.

The poems which denounce the deadening activity of the Academy are placed in the third section of *Oscuro*, which is entitled 'Los días van tan rápidos' [The days go by so fast], a reference to time. These are poems which juxtapose metaphysical chatter with the pure flow of time. The section concerned with time is in turn placed alongside the other two, whose titles are '¿Qué se ama cuando se ama?' [What does one love when one loves?] and 'Entre el sentido y el sonido' [Between sense and sound]. Their concerns can be summarized as the erotic and language respectively. The three sections are presented not as discrete and separate but as 'vasos comunicantes' [communicating vessels], terms Rojas takes from alchemy via André Breton, the type of action envisaged being, as he describes it in an interview of 1981,

un ejercicio de vasos comunicantes donde lo numinoso [. . .] entra en lo erótico, lo erótico en lo tanático, esto a su vez en lo circunstancial de lo efímero, en lo histórico, como si urdido todo estubviera siempre confluyendo hacia lo Uno.[15]

[an exercise in communicating vessels where the numinous enters the erotic, the erotic the thanatic, and this into the circumstances of everyday life, into the historical, as if everything were woven together and flowing towards oneness.]

I propose to use these three divisions as lines of entry into the confluences which make up Rojas's work, referring in the main to poems which appear in *Oscuro*, since my aim is to show the ways in which Rojas establishes the principles of his poetics, but adding where it seems appropriate examples of poems published after 1976.

If the Academy dreams of a guaranteed reading system, an interpretation machine which will ensure prestige and success

---

[14] Zeran, 'Gonzalo Rojas', 14.
[15] Enrique Giordano, *Poesía y poética de Gonzalo Rojas* (Santiago, 1987), 98.

for its adherents, Rojas's poems confound that desire about as definitively as those of any poet writing in Spanish—or English, for that matter—in the twentieth century. One way of understanding the interpretation machine is, as I have suggested, to take it as a substitution machine. The poem 'Contra la muerte' [Against death] confronts time as a death sentence and refuses those substitutes with which human beings may try to escape from the condition: 'No quiero ver ¡no puedo! ver morir a los hombres cada día. I [. . .] Dios no me sirve. Nadie me sirve para nada' [I don't want to see—I can't!—human beings dying every day. I God is no use. No one is any use for anything] (*O* 155). God and History are transcendents that people use to evade that condition but Rojas takes us back to hunger for life, without those interpositions:

> Me hablan de Dios o me hablan de Historia. Me río
> de ir a buscar tan lejos la explicación del hambre
> que me devora, el hambre de vivir como el sol
> en la gracia del aire, eternamente. (*O* 156)

> [People talk about God they talk about History. I laugh
> at any one who goes that far to find the explanation of the
>   hunger
> that devours me, the hunger to live like the sun
> in the grace of the air, for ever.]

The beauty of these lines is that they embody that hunger, they give it a form which allows it to exist in the tension of its own necessity. The tremor and the agony in the voice disappear, not into quietude or resignation or belief but into an affirmation that becomes what it affirms, a cosmic force.

For the Word to become that it has to be stripped bare of metaphysical clutter and pretensions of permanence:

> Libros y libros, libros hasta las nubes,
> pero la poesía se escribe sola.
> Se escribe con los dientes, con el peligro,
> con la verdad terrible de cada cosa.

> No hay proceso que valga, ni teoría,
> para parar el tiempo que nos arrasa.
> Vuela y vuela el planeta, y el muerto inmóvil,
> ¡y únicamente el viento de la Palabra! (*O* 179)

> [Books, books, books piled up to the clouds,
> but poetry writes itself.

Written with teeth, with danger,
with the terrifying truth of each single thing.
There's no process, no theory
to stop time that wipes us out.
The planet flies and flies, and the immobile dead man,
and only the wind of the Word!]

When all the sterile weight of verbal pretension is gone
('páginas y más páginas de cemento' [pages and pages of
cement]), all that is left finally is the planet flying through
space and the word as cosmic wind. Because there is no
inside, 'todo está lleno de nada' [everything is full of noth-
ing], there is nothing to get inside of, neither one's skin nor
cities nor even poetry:

> no hay piel para esconderse, no hay,
> por mucho lujo que chille, por mucho cemento
> que ondee en la cresta del cielo, y esto se repite
> así en la tierra como en la estratósfera, así en las capitales
> gordas como en las flacas, esta estridencia
> con mito y todo, con *Inferno* y todo, con Baudelaire
> y todo, y Poesía. (*O* 190)

> [there's no skin to hide in, none,
> for all the screams of luxury, for all the cement
> waving on the crest of the sky, and this is repeated
> as on earth so also in the stratosphere, as in fat
> capitals so also in thin ones, this shrillness
> with myths and all, with *Inferno* and all, with Baudelaire
> and all, and Poetry.]

The parodic imitation of the Lord's Prayer ('así en la tierra
. . .'), and of pompous repetition, strengthens the point that
there is no refuge, though the area Rojas is entering has to do
not so much with the content of any statement, however
pointed it may be, as with the necessity that the act of saying be
as much without proxy as any person's death is, in this case the
death of a friend, addressed by name in the poem and its title
('Epístola explosiva para que la oiga Lefebvre [1917–1971]'
[Explosive epistle to be heard by Lefebvre]). Hence the disgust
for all the paraphernalia of millennium and angels which interpose themselves:

> Asco, Lefebvre libre cada día más joven, asco
> de Apocalipsis, arcangélico

milenarista,
  ¿todo estaba escrito?,
¿estaba escrito todo, como decías?
  Pero,
pero si reventamos,
si reventamos en la oscuridad, ¿dónde, entonces, quién
va a escribirte por escribirte, por
—pobrecillo ahi—
  llamarte? (*O* 191)

[Disgust, Lefebvre, free now and every day younger, disgust
with Apocalypse, archangelic
millenarian,
  was everything written?
was everything written, as you used to say?
  But,
if we explode,
if we break up in the darkness, where, then, or who
is going to write you so as to write you
—poor man, there—
  or call you?]

'El viento de la Palabra' [The wind of the Word] becomes, in the tremor of the voice, speaking as a breathing out, and to address the dead not a ghostly or sentimental act but a test of what needs to be said. It should be reasonably clear by now that Rojas's rejection of the idea that what is already written controls what can be said—or read—is somewhat more shaking than Harold Bloom's idea of the anxiety of influence, that is the writer's need to compete with great writers of the past in order to become immortal.[16] 'The issue is the mortality or immortality of literary works,' proclaims Bloom.[17] The issue is something else for César Vallejo, who writes '¡Y si después de tantas palabras, no sobrevive la palabra' [And what if after so many words | the word itself does not survive!],[18] and for Rojas, who calls such talk as Bloom's 'baba metafísica' [metaphysical drivel].

---

[16] For a summary see the preface, prelude, and ch. 1 of *The Western Canon* (London, 1995). For an example of Bloom used to interpret Latin American poetry, see Susana Zanetti, 'Rubén Darío y el legado posible', in Susana Zanetti et al., *Las cenizas de la huella: linajes y figuras en torno al modernismo* (Rosario, 1997), 15–38, esp. 25.

[17] Bloom, *The Western Canon*, 38.

[18] Vallejo's poem, whose title is its first line ('Y si después de tantas palabras'), was published in *Poemas humanos*.

Talking and writing are not the same thing. In writing, the relation between utterance and time becomes more open to fear, to 'la intemperie', more naked:

> Los días van tan rápidos en la corriente oscura que toda
>   salvación
> se me reduce apenas a respirar profundo para que el aire dure
>   en mis pulmones (*O* 211)

> [The days go by so fast in the dark river that any salvation
> is reduced for me just to breathing deeply so that the air lasts
>   in my lungs]

So what is to be done?

> Quedémonos desnudos
> con lo que somos, pero quememos, no pudramos
> lo que somos. Ardamos. Respiremos
> sin miedo. (*O* 212)

> [Let's stay naked
> with what we are, but let's burn what we are
> not let it go rotten. Let's burn. Let's breathe
> without fear.]

The sun also burns:

> mi fortuna es esa: quemarme como el sol,
> mi único rey, mi padre (*O* 189)

> [this is my luck: to burn up like the sun
> my only king, my father]

but in another poem the sun is not a vehicle of permanence that one can get into and be rescued by:

> A mi alrededor
> quema tu luz,
> pero
> yo te destruyo
> por dentro. (*O* 184)

> [Around me
> your light burns,
> but
> I destroy you
> from inside.]

The issue is that the sun is destroyed by writing, and that writing itself is a form of fire—'fuego eterno' [eternal fire] (*O* 187) as Rojas calls it[19]—corrosive of mythology, history, and meta-physics.

The self in Rojas's poems (indicated in the pronoun *yo* and/or in the first person of the verb) is not therefore a biographical actor but an embodiment of writing and its operative effects:

> Soy del aire
> y entro con él en toda la hermosura terrestre:
> en el fuego, en el vino, en las espléndidas
> muchachas. (*O* 189)
>
> [I am of the air
> and enter with it into all earthly beauty:
> into fire, and wine, and beautiful
> girls.]

The bottom line of mythology and history is story, 'la farsa del tiempo' [the farce of time] (*O* 191, 209) being the usual way time is packaged inside a story and thus held at bay (held inside transferable permanences): 'el gran público ríe I de la farsa, y yo río con ternura, I pues mi fortuna es esa: quemarme como el sol' [the public laugh I at the farce, and I laugh tenderly, I as this is my luck: to burn up like the sun] (*O* 189). In fact the self, as handled by Rojas, is strongly anti-biographical—biography also is story, as in the old joke where you ask what is the shortest novel ever written and the answer is 'Nació muerto' [He/she was born dead]—as when he proposes that being born is not something that happens once and for all but what one is always doing, right up to the last moment: 'Ardamos. Respiremos I sin miedo. Despertemos a la gran realidad I de estar naciendo ahora, y en la última hora' [Let's burn. Let's breathe I without fear. Let's wake up to the great reality I of being born now, and at the last hour] (*O* 212), which of course echoes and turns inside out the well-known Christian prayer 'now and in the hour of our death', since the option is not resurrection and 'rebirth' but being fully awake while it lasts. Being born is thus not just the only thing one can do but also the only thing one can be: an awake becoming equals a becoming awake. And there is no one to take one's place or stand in

---

[19] Echoing Heraclitus, Fragment 37, which speaks of the cosmos as 'everliving fire'.

for one: 'Vuelvo a mi origen, voy hacia mi origen, no me espera
nadie allá' [I return to my origin, I go towards my origin, no
one's waiting for me there] (*O* 211); 'no hay nadie, no hay
nadie, sino tú mismo en esto' [there's no one, there's no one
except yourself in this] (*O* 212).

In order to confront time like that, given there is no story or
system that can operate as a rescue vehicle, where does one
place oneself? Rojas does not say it, but the answer is clear
enough from his writing: the poem is that place—a
place/action that empties metaphysics out of word, statement,
image. The bottom line of metaphysics is meaning, that is some
type of inherent meaning, never mind whether it is good or bad
so long as one can wrap oneself inside it. Rojas rejects it: 'vivi-
mos tiempo que no se detiene, ni tropieza, ni vuelve' [we live
time that doesn't stop or stumble or return], he states in the
epigraph to part III of *Oscuro*. Against the anxiety of not achieving anything permanent, Rojas places the joy and necessity of
not being indebted to anything, either to things or to words:

> Que por qué, que hasta cuándo, que si voy a dormir noventa
>   meses,
> que moriré sin obra, que el mar se habrá perdido.
> Pero yo soy el mar, y no me llamo arruga
> ni volumen de nada. (*O* 158)

> [That why, that until when, that am I going to sleep for ninety
>   months,
> that I'll die without leaving an *œuvre* behind, that the sea
>   will have disappeared.
> But I am the sea, and I am not called wrinkle
> or volume of anything.]

If meaning is where there are folds and repetitions arising out
of mirror-effects, time is where there are none of these. Rojas
places himself, that is his writing, at that edge of non-meaning.
Volumen would be a container for something, a piece of the past
which has been turned into a framework of recognitions, a
packet of transferable (inheritable) permanence, call it Plato's
anagnorisis or Bloom's Western Canon. Packet and inheritance, word and thing, volume and substance: we are talking
about how any vehicle of permanence—a word is a minimal
one—becomes a magical container with nothing inside it.

What is left, then? Does Rojas's writing empty language of

any hold it may have upon how one lives? Bloom says aesthetic value is not an ethics but it can at bottom make a person a better citizen.[20] But a citizen of what? Inside what? In Rojas's poems there is no metaphysics but there is a morality and that morality begins with affect. Instead of the farce of time, tenderness, instead of 'everything has been written', a tone of deep tenderness: 'si reventamos en la oscuridad, ¿dónde, entonces, quién I va a escribirte por escribirte, por I —pobrecillo ahí— I llamarte?' [if we break up in the darkness, where, then, who, I then is going to write you so as to write you I —poor man, there— I or call you?] (*O* 191).

Affect becomes where one dwells, not the institutions of permanence, which include even the book: 'No hay libro I para escribir el sol' [there's no book I to write the sun] (*O* 158). The idea of some original light which has been lost is ditched as empty mythology:

> Me acuerdo, tú te acuerdas, todos nos acordamos
> de la galaxia ciega desde donde vinimos
> con esta luz tan pobre a ver el mundo.
> Vinimos, y eso es todo. (*O* 158)

> [I remember, you remember, we all remember
> the blind galaxy we came from
> to see the world with such poor light.
> We came, and that's all.]

The tone is flat, humorous, there is no tenderness there, the affect is in what is opened up in the negation, which is the possibility of building a place, a house as Rojas calls it, out of human feelings, with no other light than the light with which one sees ('El ojo no podría ver el sol I si él mismo no lo fuera' [The eye could not see the sun I if it were not itself that]). That is the size of the transformation desired. 'Uno escribe en el viento' [One writes in the wind], writes Rojas in the powerful poem of that title, 'con mi pueblo de pobres' [with my people the poor]: two statements which are incompatible with any notion of politics as ideology, of language as control. The issue is how one goes from being one to being numerous—to use George Oppen's phrase.[21]

---

[20] See Bloom, *The Western Canon*, ch. 1.
[21] George Oppen, *Of Being Numerous*, in *Collected Poems* (New York, 1975).

Una casa
para América hermosa. Una casa, una casa.
Todos somos obreros.

América es la casa: ¿dónde la nebulosa?
Me doy vueltas y vueltas en mi viejo individuo
para nacer. Ni estrella ni madre que me alumbre
lúgubremente solo. (*O* 159)

[A house
for beautiful America. A house, a house.
We are all workers.

America is the house: where the nebula?
I turn and turn in my old individual
so as to be born. No star no mother to give me light
sombrely alone.]

A vocabulary of darkness predominates, not relieved by light or birth (*alumbrar* is both to give light and to give birth; the root meaning of *lúgubre* is funereal). But what is interesting is that Rojas does not respond to the failure of the symbolism of Light (*nebulosa* as origin, for example) by reaching out for an alternative symbolic story, some other narrative that will protect meanings from time. On the contrary, the minimum stability required by State discourse, institutions, propaganda, control words, in fact by any embedding of social power in language, is abandoned. The issue is the stability of the surface of inscription, that is, where words are heard/produced:

Mortal, mortuorio río. Pasa y pasa el color,
sangra y sangra mi pueblo, corre y corre el sentido.
Pero el dinero pudre con su peste las aguas.
Cambiar, cambiar el mundo. (*O* 159)

[Mortal, funereal river. Colour passes by and passes by,
my people bleed and bleed, sense runs and runs.
But money poisons the waters with its plague.
Change, change the world.]

If the river is time—the ever-moving surface—meaning also flows by, and with it vision, and the blood of injustice: a recipe for quietism? On the contrary, to abandon any desire to anchor the Word in networks of guaranteed meaning (to desire, that is, to swallow the social injustice which keeps the discursive inheritance in place) is to confront the fact that the necessity of change includes language, that is, includes the need to transform the place or surface where sense occurs, which is the bottom line of language.[22] As Rojas said in a comment on this poem, he needed both Marx and Rimbaud.[23] And that, in turn, includes changing the nature of the book. To abandon inherited packets of permanence does not mean abandoning hope but starting with real change: that is what Rojas finds—or reads—in the story of birth, as given in the final line of the poem ('Hubo una vez un niño' [There was once a child]). Writing in the wind includes all of that.

BREATH AND FORM

Rojas's remarks on needing both Marx and Rimbaud ('cambiar el mundo dice el uno, y el otro dice cambiar la vida' [one says change the world, and the other change life]) are tied up with his vindication of the avant-garde in poetry. He associates himself in particular with the Chilean poet Pablo de Rokha (1894–1968).[24] In his own work, Rojas does not engage either in the fragmentation of syntax or in the fragmentation of image, these being—to simplify it a little—the two main forms of experimentalism in the Latin American avant-garde 1920–40. Does that mean he has abandoned the formal concerns of the avant-garde? The best way into an answer to that question is via a consideration of breath. In Rojas's poetry the basis both of rhythm and of thought is breath: that is, thought occurs in relation to breathing. Consider the following lines from a poem entitled 'Desocupado lector', which is organized around varying subjects of the repeated statement 'es herida', an idea which is clear and unclear at the same time:

[22] I prefer not to complicate the argument at this point with technicalities, since what Rojas writes, though difficult, is quite simple. However, I would like to indicate that what is at stake has its technical counterpart in a distinction between sense and meaning (see Gilles Deleuze, *The Logic of Sense* (New York, 1989)) and in the idea of historical change as change of semiotic regime (see Gilles Deleuze and Félix Guattari, *A Thousand Plateaus* (London, 1988), ch. 5). Note that there are parallels between Rojas's concern with changing the surface of inscription and the work of Terán, Eielson, and Zurita, all of whom are discussed in the present book, and with other key Latin American poets of recent years, such as Néstor Perlongher and David Maquieira.

[23] Zeran, 'Gonzalo Rojas', 15.

[24] See the poem 'Pablo de Rokha', *Antología del aire* (Mexico City, 1991), 185.

          el carrusel
pintarrajeado que fluye y fluye como otro río de polvo y otras
máscaras
que vi en Pekín colgando en la vieja calle Cha Ta-lá
cuya identidad comercial de 2.500 años de droga y ataúdes
     rientes
no se discute, es
herida; la cama en fin
que allí compré, con dos espejos para navegar, es herida,
                                                            la
perversión
de la palabra nadie que sopla desde las galaxias es herida
     (*A* 280)[25]

     [the roughly painted
roundabout which flows and flows like another river of dust
     and other
masks
which I saw in Peking hanging in old Cha Ta-la Street
whose 2,500 years of commerce in drugs and laughing coffins
is undeniable, is
a wound; the bed
I bought there, with its two mirrors for navigating, is a wound,
                                                            the
perversion
of the word nobody that blows from the galaxies is a wound]

Consider the typography. The first sentence runs from *el
carrusel* to *herida* in the seventh line. It is not possible to speak
it—without strain—in less that three out-breaths and four is
more comfortable. The lines, as arranged on the page, do not
coincide with out-breaths, as they would, approximately, in
nineteenth-century poetry. On the other hand, there is a relationship between breath and line. Sense is held up, not
completed in each out-breathing. And so we have two sets of
energies, in a kind of counterpoint: the completion of breath
and the completion of thought. If one does not catch this, Rojas
may seem a wordy poet: too many words to get to the point. But
the point is not just the completion of the sentence. The thrill
of discovery comes not when a recognized metrical pattern is
fulfilled, nor with the lining up of metre with syntactical and
semantic segments—as it does in poetry in Spanish until Vallejo

---

[25] The textual reference *A* refers to Rojas, *Antología del aire.*

and Neruda broke the pattern. Consider this other poem, entitled 'La Palabra' [The Word]:

> Un aire, un aire, un aire,
> un aire,
> un aire nuevo:
>
>> no para respirarlo
>> sino para vivirlo. (*A* 77)
>
> [An air, an air, an air,
> an air,
> a new air:
>
>> not to breathe it
>> but to live it.]

The poem moves semantically from *aire* as wind or the oxygen+nitrogen one breathes, to appearance, mode, figure. The feeling of discovery occurs in the form of a thought: to live the air (*vivirlo*) not to breathe it (*respirarlo*). The thought breaks the usual semantic division between air as physical substance and air as figure; the energy with which it does that is both of the body (the need to breathe) and of the soul or spirit. This is the core principle towards which Rojas's poetry moves: the physical and the semantic are the same. Which is actually a principle of so-called primitive thought, but also a characteristic of twentieth-century avant-garde experiment. The need to breathe—one's most immediate sense of life and death—is embodied in the typography of Rojas's poem, where the short phrase | short breath 'un aire' repeats, as if the person were struggling for breath: a common enough experience, and more acute if one has asthma, as Rojas has had since early childhood.

Breath is non-signifying and yet is a basis of meaning—think of all the ways in which speaking and breathing are inseparable and how they extend into the non-spoken—just as air is where words occur. Similarly, *herida* (damaging invasion of the body) is, Rojas proposes, the basis through which anything has sense, in other words is what it is. The term semantic is analytic. No utterance is purely semantic. No language-event, considered as event, allows something called the semantic to be cut surgically out of it. The cut destroys the event—removes it from time, which is breath. And if the physical *is* semantic, then semantics disappears. Every meaning in Rojas's writing arises in what does not signify: darkness, the sea, breath, wound, etc. Thus the fallacy of assuming that meaning in poetry can be derived from the terms of linguistics. The content of the thought that occurs in the poem entitled 'La Palabra' is *vivir*, which is an infinitive, an in-between, without beginning or termination, but the content of *vivir* is time. And this is not for Rojas time that repeats in mirror-effects but a pure flow: 'los días van tan rápidos I al invisible océano que ya no tengo sangre donde nadar seguro' [the days go by so fast I to the invisible ocean that I haven't blood any more to swim safely] (*O* 211). His concern is with the actual flow as where anything serious begins, not the conversion of that flow into symbols or epiphanies.

This 'tiempo que ni se detiene, ni tropieza, ni vuelve' [time which does not stop or stumble or return] is Nietzsche's imageless time, where time is pure becoming and being is the being of becoming.[26] In other words, no models, no original design; time open to randomness and chaos. What is the ability to think in those terms, that is, to grasp occurrence without gods or models? In Mallarmé's key poem *Un coup de dés*, syntax and typography produce the occurrence of space-time, in a new way of reading in which the smallest difference of spacing and timing of the materials on the page is an arising of time and space. The action is configured, echoing Nietzsche, as a throw of the dice. In Nietzsche the Gods throw dice and this produces time/space. In Mallarmé the question is how to imagine the future without recourse to gods or models. As there is no guide to subject oneself to, this requires the courage to take decisions, courage as one 'lives' the language, as the body-mind assembles sounds and signs together. Any sense of futurity has to pass through there, otherwise we are talking about the will to crass continuity, one variety of which is the wish to possess an inheritance.

The last few lines of Rojas's 'herida' poem include a meta-statement on its action and form: 'la hilera I de líneas sin ocurrencia de esta visión I sin resurrección es herida. Cumplo I

---

[26] See Gilles Deleuze, *Nietzsche and Philosophy* (London, 1983), 23–4; F. Nietzsche, *The Birth of Tragedy and the Genealogy of Morals* (New York, 1956), 140–3. In *The Will to Power*, Nietzsche makes this crucial statement: 'To impose upon becoming the character of being—that is the supreme will to power' (The *Will to Power* (New York, 1968), 330). Note that the idea of being as wound is also to be found in Nietzsche: 'the eternal wound of being' (*The Birth of Tragedy*, 108).

entonces con informar a usted que últimamente todo es herida' [the thread | of lines without occurrence of this vision | without resurrection is wound. I am therefore fulfilling | my duty to inform you that lately everything is wound] (*A* 280). If *líneas* refers to lines of thought and of sound/breath as the same thing, *hilera* would refer to the way those lines are assembled, the type of space-time produced. *Hilera* is an interesting word in this context: the dictionary gives 'orden o formación en línea de un número de personas o cosas; [. . .] hilo o hilaza fina' [the ordering or formation in a line of a number of persons or things; thin thread] and also 'hueca del huso, por ser donde se afianza la hebra para formarse' [the hollow part of the spindle, where the strands to be spun are fixed].[27] Thus within the connotations of *hilera* there is the notion of a point of anchorage, from which one starts spinning the thread. But 'sin ocurrencia' suggests an opposite effect: given that the range of meanings of *ocurrencia* includes happening, what one has, rather than the lining-up of word-events along an axis as finished meaning, is a sense of incompletion, that there is no vision in the sense of an idea of redemption but only a wound and/or that the incompleteness itself is a wound. Resurrection, presumably, would take the pain out of it. Thus the wound is of the content but also of the form. The phrase 'Cumplo con usted' makes a comic distance between those senses of wound and the language of public pronouncements, which relies upon a completely different rhetoric of the Word, as a representation that fits one to one with the thing. Since this is impossible, that means the Word in that kind of pronouncement is being used a model of the real,[28] a use which is entirely undermined by the notion that everything begins and ends in wound and by the relationship with language that arises from that notion. Asked '¿Hay que salvar al hombre?', Rojas replies:

No, el hombre se salva solo, se hace solo. Y esta es una postura del anarca, del que sabe que no alcanza a llegar y está cerca, se aproxima. En mí, la poesía se vio siempre como la aproximación y nada más. Un nadador que va entrando en las aguas, necesariamente entra en ellas,

---

[27] *Diccionario manual e ilustrado de la lengua española* (Madrid, 1958), 826.
[28] William Burroughs parodies that use of the Word by the media with his notion of 'Reality Studios' in *The Naked Lunch* (London, 1964).

lucha con ellas, pero no alcanza a llegar, está casi por llegar, y ese ejercicio respiratorio y todo ahogo es lo que lo hace totalmente fresco y lozano.[29]

[No, man saves himself alone, makes himself alone. And this is the position of the anarch, of someone who doesn't manage to arrive and is near, he's getting close. In me, poetry was always approximation and nothing else. If a swimmer goes into the water he has to enter it and struggle with it, but he doesn't manage to arrive, he's nearly there, and that exercise in breathing and struggling for breath is what makes him totally fresh and vigorous.]

The proposal then, is that the freshness and vigour of the poem arise from not arriving.

The primary question for Rojas is not that of identity—Who am I?—given that, in the flow of time and blood, 'ese yo es nadie' [that I is no one], but that of time—When? This is worked out at some length in a poem entitled 'Conjuro' [Spell], which is one of the densest and most exciting of his poems. The initial scenario consists in crossing a bridge by car over the River Lebu, a river which had become a memory/symbol of childhood for Rojas, as he writes on the first page of *Oscuro*, in a statement on poetics:

Voy corriendo en el viento de mi niñez en ese Lebu tormentoso, y oigo, tan claro, la palabra 'relámpago'.—'Relámpago, relámpago'—. Y voy volando en ella, y haste me enciendo en ella todavía. Las toco, las heulo, las beso a las palabras, las descubro y son mías desde los seis y los siete años (*O* 7)

[I run in the wind of my childhood in the stormy waters of the Lebu and I hear with complete clarity the word 'lightning'.—'Lightning, lightning'—. And I fly in it, and still, right now, I am on fire inside it. I touch, smell, and kiss words, I discover them and they're mine and it's been that way since I was six or seven years old.]

The flashing into consciousness of words and things is simultaneous: again, the physical and the semantic as one.

For the adult, what flashes up is the image of a bleeding horse. For the adult crossing the bridge again (scenario of the poem), there is no possession or belonging, the waters belong to no one:

---

[29] Zeran, 'Gonzalo Rojas', 14.

Espíritu del caballo que sangra es lo que oigo ahora entre el
    galope
del automóvil y el relincho, pasado el puente
de los tablones amenazantes: agua, agua,
lúgubre agua
de nadie: las tres
en lo alto de la torre de ninguna iglesia, y abajo
el río que me llama: Lebu, Lebu
muerto de mi muerte (*O* 21)

[Spirit of a horse that's bleeding is what I hear now between the
    car's
gallop and the neighing, the planks rattling
as I cross the bridge: water, water,
mournful water
nobody's: three o'clock
in the tower of no church, and below
the river calling me: Lebu, Lebu
dead of my death]

The horse, image in consciousness and image of consciousness, is complex in its time-space location. The loose planks of a wooden bridge jolted by a car's wheels sound like a horse's hooves—childhood, recurring, as sound-image (the child, presumably, would not have crossed the bridge in a car). The horse, displaced in time by the car (thus bleeding or dead), places the scene as happening after the wave of technological modernization that swept through Chile in the 1940s. But the bleeding, taken alongside the sense given to the flow of blood in other Rojas poems, is also to do with time as flow. Where are we then? Inside history or inside a flow of time which comes before there is anything that can be known as history? And what is dead in the phrase 'Lebu | muerto de mi muerte': the river or the self?

Multiple rifts in time and space give rise to the question:

    ¿y esto
    soy yo [. . .]?

    La pregunta es otra, la pregunta verde es otra
    de los árboles, no este ruido
    de cloaca hueca y capital, humo
    de pulmones venenosos, la pregunta es cuándo,
    la diastólica arteria, la urgentísima es cuándo y
    cuándo, alazán
    que sangras de mí, desprendido

del sonido
del límite
del Tiempo (*O* 21)

[and is
this me?
The question is something else, the green question
     is something else
of the trees, not that noise
of open sewer and capital, smoke
of poisonous lungs, the question is when,
the diastolic artery, the urgent question is when and
when, brown horse
bleeding in me, detached
from sound
from limit
from Time]

Two things are happening here, both to do with writing. The pure flow of time throws up an image which is not of time: the horse that bleeds, an image that stands over against the open sewer of money that time/the river has become since the mid-twentieth century. The horse is not a symbol of anything but an image over the abyss of time, an image of the process of writing, which Rojas treats as an interlocutor. Secondly, if the flow of time without meaning is where one is, there is nothing to rely upon except knowing where one is. Everything begins there. To know where one is, as the action of writing, is to affirm a responsibility and a morality: no substitutions, no feeble postmodern alibis about letting things flow and not taking decisions.[30]

The question When? is not just of the content but of the form. It has to do with the recurrent split-second decisions the poem turns upon, as the excitement migrates from the content to the form and vice versa. The decisions are where value is. And breath is where the actual occurs: the poem as timing. As Charles Olson writes in his seminal essay on twentieth-century poetics, 'Projective Verse', the line in a poem comes from breath and not from metrics and 'only [. . .] the man who writes can declare, at every moment [. . .] its [. . .] termination'.[31] The principle is that that action is non-transferable, though

---

[30] I am grateful to Chris Brookeman for pointing this out.
[31] Charles Olson, 'Projective Verse', in *Collected Prose* (Berkeley, 1997), 242.

shareable, as writing finds its pair in reading. To which can be added that breath is where body is spirit ('espíritu del caballo que sangra'), as in the etymology of the word spirit which brings together breathing, 'animating or vital principle', and what is not of time. Need and expression, physical necessity and the word, come together: one speaks with the same thing that one needs in order to survive. Breath is where the actual occurs in the unremitting flow of time.

Decisions, which are choices, only make sense if there are differences between which to choose. The question is nothing less than what you think, smell, hear—and, by implication, do with the other senses—as Rojas shows in the third and fourth sections of the 'Conjuro'. In other words, the differences have to be produced, actively. This is incompatible with passive submission to the world as it is, which Rojas calls 'parpadeante rito de semáforos aciagos para el sacrificio' [flickering ritual of fatal traffic lights for sacrifice], in a phrase that signals how submission reduces what can be thought and perceived to a single message. Not to ask the question, not to interrogate the world is the temptation of submission to what is, the temptation of renouncing morality, which is magnificently resisted by Pablo Neruda in section X of *Alturas de Macchu Picchu*, where he refuses the seductiveness of sacrifice. Decisions are made in a field of differences, and the denser the field, the greater the energy required to produce it: that is the dynamics Rojas is working with.

Hambre is the name Rojas gives to the necessities of the body/spirit, which include the necessity to interrogate the world:

> por hambre pregunta uno, por volver
> a volver, ¿a dónde?,
> > Tierra
> que vuelas en tu huso, ¿a dónde?,
> perdición y traslación, ciega serpiente, hija
> de las llamas, ¿a dónde? (*O* 23)

> [one asks the question out of hunger, to return
> to returning, Where to?
> > Earth
> flying on your spindle, Where to?
> perdition and passage, blind serpent, daughter
> of flames, Where to?]

Two images are given: the world flying around a spindle, figure
of anchorage and stability, and a blind snake born of fire, which
moves towards the imagelessness of eternal movement, where
place does not exist because there is merely 'perdición y
traslación', the poem at this point moving towards thought
without image,

> porque yendo-viniendo se aparta uno de todo,
> se aparta a su pensamiento de hambre
> como el silencio a su música
> tras las alambradas, no puede más con su suerte;
> como el cuchillo a su cuchillo se aparta (*O* 23)
>
> [because going-coming one moves away from everything,
> moves away from one's thought of hunger
> as silence from its music
> behind barbed wire, cannot take its luck any more;
> as the knife moves away from its knife]

Places, things, and thoughts in time become separate from
themselves, do not coincide with themselves, nothing *is*. So
nothing contains anything, stands for anything, or can be
substituted for anything: farewell semiotics! If the invention of
semiotics rests upon the substitutive delirium of capitalist
modernity, as the Chilean novelist José Donoso reveals in a
series of novels written in the 1950s and 1960s,[32] then once again
we have an index of the size of the transformation required by
Rojas's poems.

As 'Conjuro' moves from thought without image towards
non-space, non-thought, and non-thing, the response is
neither panic—the paralysis of feeling that nothing can be
done—nor permissiveness—everything is permitted because
nothing is true—but to write with that, 'como el cuchillo a su
cuchillo se aparta', with the knife that is not itself and with the
not-being-itself of the knife. The 'figure of Eternity' arises
precisely there, 'en la tormenta' [in the storm], which Rojas
elsewhere calls 'la intemperie', the same eternity that Blake
said his readers inhabit, as Rojas recalls. That eternity rests
upon a creative action and not upon inherited continuities. It
is not compatible with literary criticism used like a preserva-
tive. Beside Rojas's poem the sheer dullness and uselessness of

---

[32] See William Rowe, *Hacia una poética radical: ensayos de hermenéutica cultural*
(Rosario, 1996), introduction and part II, ch. 3.

much current criticism howls out what it is for: to possess the work, to compete with the artist, to be the priest of some new doctrine, or merely to bow to the new orthodoxy. Beside Rojas's storm of unknowing, the current fashion for over-knowing critical talk is cut down to size.

The first poem of the book, entitled 'Numinoso' [Numinous], includes the proposal that for the poet the sacred has nothing to do with priestliness: 'no | somos augures de nada, no abrimos | las vísceras de las aves para decir la suerte de nadie' [we | are not augurs of anything, we don't open | birds' innards to tell anyone's fate] (*O* 13). The sacred arises in the relation of time and the syllable:

> Míseros los errantes, eso son nuestras sílabas: tiempo, no
> encanto, no repetición
> por la repetición, que gira y gira
> sobre
> sus espejos (*O* 13)

> [poor wanderers, that's what our syllables are: time, not
> enchantment, not repetition
> for repetition's sake, turning and turning
> over
> its mirrors]

'Míseros', because for Rojas it is in poverty rather than priestly ritual, in precise relationships of time and timing rather than in sumptuous repetitions, that the numinous is found. The poet's trade is blind, cautious, and silent, without pompous display: 'Vamos sonámbulos | en el oficio ciego, cautelosos y silenciosos, no brilla | el orgullo en estas cuerdas' [We move like sleep-walk-ers | in the blind task, cautious and silent, pride | does not shine in these strings]. To write is to throw a net into the infinitely unknown, to navigate chance with nothing but the precisions of rhythm ('número') and graphic notation ('carácter'):

> no hay azar
> sino navegación y número, carácter
> y número, red en el abismo de las cosas
> y número. (*O* 13)

> [there is no chance
> except navigation and number, character
> and number, net in the abyss of things
> and number.]

Rojas's rejection of sumptuousness is directed in particular towards the handling of sound structures (*sílabas, cuerdas, silenciosos*). The title of this section of the book, 'Entre el sentido y el sonido' [Between sense and sound], suggests an in-between sound and sense, where the relationship between the two would have ceased to be automatic, that is where meaning and sound are no longer anchored in each other, but adrift, 'en la intemperie'. To keep faith with the unknown is also a question of the ear: sumptuousness would get in the way. It is not that there are no repetitions in Rojas's poems, but that what repeats throws us back into the not-known, which is the same as where we are, known with all the precision one is capable of. What repeat—more than anything else—in this poem are the words 'número' and 'tiempo', instances or placings of time which, precisely, take us, with all the capacity for knowing one is capable of, back into the not-known, which is where we are. And that is not repetition so much as recurrence, 'por hambre pregunta uno, por volver | a volver' [one asks the question out of hunger, to return to returning], and, in the lines from the Chilean poet Gabriela Mistral which serve as epigraph to the whole book, '¿Será esto la eternidad | que aun estamos como estábamos?' [Could this be eternity | that we are still how we were?]. 'Conjuro' gives a kind of response to that question:

> tiempo,
> paciencia de estrella, tiempo y más tiempo.
>   No
> somos de aquí pero lo somos;
>   Aire y Tiempo
> dicen santo, santo, santo. (*O* 14)
>   [time,
> the patience of a star, time and more time.
>   We
> are not from here but we are;
>   Air and Time
> say holy, holy, holy.]

What this requires of one, as reader, is both simple and difficult. Part of the difficulty is how to live without models, and, related to that, the fact that the shifts at infinite speed from content to form and vice versa have nothing to do with the speed of mental association, in fact nothing to do with the speed of intellect. At the same time, there is 'paciencia de estrella', which suggests an almost infinite slowness. The speeds the poem demands, in the recurrences of time and the word time, are infinitely fast and infinitely slow, both at once, in a coming together of the two.

The poem 'Latín y jazz' gives a further image of writing, as occurring in the combination of different speeds, which here are generated by reading Latin poetry and listening to jazz at the same time:

> vuelan los ángeles
> en el latín augusto de Roma con las trompetas libérrimas,
>   lentísimas,
> en un acorde ya sin tiempo, en un zumbido
> de arterias y de pétalos para irme en el torrente con las olas
> que salen de esta silla, de esta mesa de tabla, de esta materia
> que somos yo y mi cuerpo en el minuto de este azar
> en que amarro la ventolera de estas sílabas. (*O* 15)

>   [angels fly
> in the august Latin of Rome with the free, slow trumpets,
> in a chord without time, in a buzzing
> of arteries and petals as I go in the torrent with the waves
> that come out of this chair, this table made of wooden planks,
>   this material
> that I and my body are in the minute of this chance
> in which I tie down the blast of these syllables.]

Two things are happening: the wind of words—*ventolera* is a blast of wind—tied down in the indivisible moment of the unpredictable movement of time ('en el minuto de este azar'). And the material of the world, including one's body, becomes waves—not metaphorical waves suggesting a sea but actual waves.[33]

A poetics of the open would be a good definition of Rojas's way of working—that one lives in order to 'escribir en la cópula I el relámpago de seguir siendo' [write in the coupling I the lightning of continuing to be] and to 'jugar Ieste juego de respirar en el peligro' [play I this game of breathing in danger] (*O* 25). Or to 'poner I amor y más amor en la sábana I del huracán'

---

[33] D. H. Lawrence's 'man who died' in the story of that title (in *Love among the Haystacks and Other Stories* (Harmondsworth, 1960)), also sees the material world as waves. The last word of Rojas's poem is '¡Thánatos!', the Greek word for death.

[put | more and more love on the sheet | of the hurricane], the
condition Rojas elsewhere calls 'la intemperie', until one is
'desnacido' [unborn]. Art and morality come together in these
statements: to live without redemption is also to renounce any
use of form as a means of refuge or recognition. This is the
spirit of a poem entitled 'No le copien a Pound' which refers to
the fashion for imitating Ezra Pound which was prevalent in
Latin America in the late 1960s and early 1970s. Rojas uses the
occasion to talk about principles: that what one would need to
appreciate in Pound's work is the incompleteness, the blindness, which has nothing to do with any sense of Pound as an
'influence':

>   déjenlo suelto
> con su ceguera para ver, para ver otra vez, porque el verbo es
>   ése: ver,
> y ése el Espíritu, lo inacabado
> y lo ardiente, lo que de veras amamos
> y nos ama, si es que somos Hijo de Hombre
> y de Mujer, lo innumerable al fondo de lo innombrable (*O* 27)
>   [leave him free
> with his blindness to see, to see again, because the verb is that: to
>   see,
> and that is the Spirit, the incomplete
> and the burning, that which we truly love
> and loves us, if we are Son of Man
> and of Woman, the innumerable at the bottom of the unname
>   able]

What is the relationship between the human as not fully known
('lo innumerable al fondo de lo innombrable') and what one
truly loves? The latter repeats Pound's line(s) in the *Pisan
Cantos*: 'What thou lov'st well shall not be reft from thee.'[34] The
weak sense of the relationship has to do with the idea that if the
world is made up of uncertainties, then love is the only guide at
one's disposal. But the strong sense has to do with love as the
beginning of knowledge, and that its form is 'lo inacabado | y lo
ardiente'. This is not therefore the love that loves the already-
known, the recognized—already shaped in vision or formu-
lated in words. And it has nothing to do with Bloom's definition

---

[34] Ezra Pound, canto 81.

of influence. Influence here for Rojas has its basis in what affects one, what involves affect, what one loves.[35]

To be faithful to the open requires a 'lenguaje sin Logos' [language without Logos], language without any point of anchorage in pre-given meanings since there are no pre-given meanings: language without religion or mythology or meta-physics. To raise one's eyes and read the night-sky is an ancient human act of divination, of looking for the signs given by the gods. For Rojas the necessity remains but not the gods:

> Leo en la nebulosa mi suerte cuando pasan las estrellas veloces y
>   oscurísimas.
> Rueda: plazo: zarpazo. ¡Salud, oh tigre viejo
> del sol! Esta botella ¿nos dirá la verdad
> antes que el vino salga volando por el éter? O te quemas
> o te dejas cortar. (*O* 30)
> [I read my fate in the nebula as the swift and deeply dark stars pass.
> Wheel, time-limit, claw. Cheers, sun, you
> old tiger! Will this bottle tell the truth
> before the wine flies through the ether? You burn yourself up
> or you let yourself be cut.]

One writes with what cuts into one, which is the non-human cosmos, and the fact of having been born ('Mortal, mortal error | meter a nadie en esto de nacer: somos hambre' [Mortal, mortal error | to put anyone into this business of being born: we are hunger]). So writing is a cosmic action, but not in the sense of Patriarchs or astrologers transcribing gods' messages. Neither transcribing gods' writing nor supplanting God's writing, as Mallarmé proposes, but the book as the cosmos inside one. This is Rojas's relocation of the instrument and surface of writing (knife and tablets, as he calls them):

> Mortal, mortal error
> meter a nadie en esto de nacer: somos hambre.
> Pero el fuego está abajo con los muertos que crecen todavía.
> Somos hambre. Oigo voces y escribo sobre el viento sin hojas
>   de mi tabla
> de salvación. Ahí dejo temblando este cuchillo.
> No hay cielo sino sangre, y únicamente sangre de mujer
>   donde leen su [estrella los desnudos. (*O* 30)

[35] Note Pound's statement about influence, a few lines further on in the same canto: 'What thou lovest well is thy true heritage | What thou lov'st well shall not be reft from thee.'

[Mortal, mortal error
to put anyone into this business of being born: we are hunger.
But there is fire down below with the dead who still grow.

We are hunger. I hear voices and write on the leafless wind
   of my tablet
of salvation. I leave this knife there trembling.
There's no sky just blood and only woman's blood where the
   naked read their star.]

The phrase 'somos hambre' is not opinion (what is it an opinion of?) or representation (what does it represent?) but a
discovery of what the place of any act of representation would
need to be. That place is not the sky—traditional location of
visions—but what the eyes of erotic love can read. If that reading is where one writes, it is because hunger and the book come
together there.

   Discovery is also decision, in the sense of deciding to do
something: it changes one's life. Decision makes discovery
possible and decision arises in discovery. Decision means relocating oneself in relation to forces which are both cosmic and
inner. If to be born is to be cut from the mother and to enter
'la intemperie | del llanto' [the storm | of crying], it sounds, for
sure, like farce or melancholy—not very interesting, as we have
heard it before. What is interesting is Rojas's sense of needing
to abandon all of that:

            nos cortan de lo flexible
         de la doncellez de la madre, nos secan a la intemperie
         del llanto, y hay que subir, subir,
         para ser:
            perdernos,
                  perder
         el aire, la vida, las máscaras, el fuego:
                  irnos quedando
         solos
         con
         la
         velocidad
         de la Tierra. (O 44)

            [they cut us from the flexible,
         the mother's virginity, they dry us in the storm
         of crying, and one has to go up and up
         to be:

```
      lose oneself,
            lose
the air, life, masks, fire:
                become finally
alone
with
the
speed
of the Earth.]
```

To lose all of that, even fire, representation of what is ever-changing, that is the difficulty of the demand. Need become demand is decision, and the decision is the writing, in the sense of writing without relying upon any of that. Over to reader: read without relying upon any of that!

But is there any sense in reading in that way in the age of electronic culture? Is it not perhaps a little bookish, not to say irrelevant, when image rules and there is no 'abyss'? To spell it out, when image-durations are short but overlapping, so that memory though short cannot be punctuated by anything outside the electronic present, as one quick-fading image is overlaid by another image. When the speed of image-transmission (which is the speed of light) eliminates space and time, the time of events has become the time of their exposure. Paul Virilio attempts an initial investigation of the effects in his book *Open Sky*: 'the new conception of time [. . .] is no longer exclusively that time of classical chronological *succession*, but now a time of (chronoscopic) *exposure* of the duration of events at the speed of light.'[36] Among the consequences is that there is no longer such a thing as 'the vertigo of real space'—which Nietzsche, Mallarmé, and Juan L. Ortiz, among others, call 'the abyss' or 'the void'. We have already fallen upwards into instantaneous communications: the sky has vanished,[37] or become a brand-name for satellite TV. In place of the actual moment, 'electronic dazzlement' is taking over: 'the so-called "real" moment [. . .] suddenly detaches itself from the place where it happens, from its here and now, and opts for an electronic dazzlement.'[38]

The question posed is too vast to attempt anything like a full

---

[36] *Open Sky* (London, 1997), 3. William Burroughs works out similar issues in *Electronic Revolution* (Expanded Media Editions, n.d.).

[37] Virilio, *Open Sky*, 33, 3.

[38] Ibid. 14.

answer here. I will limit myself to two aspects: perception and
death. There is a sense in Rojas's work in which what exists
depends upon darkness. The poem 'Oscuridad hermosa'
[Beautiful darkness] is addressed to darkness:

> Corriste por mi casa de madera,
> sus ventanas abriste
> y te sentí latir la noche entera,
> hija de los abismos, silenciosa,
> guerrera, tan terrible, tan hermosa
> que todo cuanto existe,
> para mí, sin tu llama, no existiera. (*O* 39)

> [You ran through my wooden house,
> opened its windows
> and I felt you pulsing all night,
> daughter of abysses, silent,
> warrior, so terrible, so beautiful
> that everything that exists,
> would not, without your flame, for me exist.]

The idea is that things exist because touched by the flame of
darkness. What are the consequences for the senses? They
cease to be functions of the socially moulded body and become
organs of another body, the body of what Blake calls the poetic
imagination, which is capable of actively moulding the real.[39]
This constitutes a turning inside out of the senses in relation to
sensationalist/behaviourist models of consciousness, which
were imposed in industrial societies and are nowadays still the
basis of common sense. Common sense, however, lags behind
technology: electronic image nowadays moulds the real. If that
is the case, does not Rojas's proposition also become irrelevant?
Has not Blake's or Rojas's idea of imagination disappeared into
the infinite plasticity of electronic manipulation?

The most difficult part of the question has to do with light.
Darkness in Rojas—or in Henri Corbin's expositions of
Sufism—has to do with what occurs before perception, the
active basis of which is given in the interplay of light and darkness. But the nature of light changes in the condition outlined
by Virilio:

---

[39] There are similarities with Henri Corbin's term Active Imagination. See
Henri Corbin, *Creative Imagination in the Sufism of Ibn 'Arabi* (Princeton, 1981).

Since the turn of the century, the absolute limit of the speed of light has *lit up*, so to speak, both space and time. So it is not so much *light* that illuminates things (the object, the subject, the path); it is the constant nature of light's *limit speed* that conditions the perception of duration and of the world's expanse as phenomena.[40]

To put it succinctly, does the speed of light as ultimate solvent of everything also dissolve Rojas's use of light and darkness? The question boils down to whether there is any operative sense left in the notion of a light and darkness before perception (prior to perception but given in it).

Consider that the condition we are concerned with is based on the 'outering' or extension of the senses in electronic image, more precisely, in images which are 'at once optoelectronic, electroacoustic and electrotactile'.[41] This does not liquidate active imagination if one can get behind image. The question has still to be worked out.[42] One way of approaching the issue via Rojas's work is to compare the place of death in his poems with its non-place in the late twentieth-century city. In one of the early poems which set out the principles of his poetics, entitled 'El sol, el sol, la muerte' [The sun, the sun, death], Rojas writes:

> Como el ciego que llora contra un sol implacable
> me obstino en ver la luz por mis ojos vacíos
> quemados para siempre.
>
> De qué me sirve el rayo
> que escribe por mi mano, de qué el fuego,
>   lo
> hondo
> de lo hondo,
>   ¿de qué el Mundo? (*O* 50)
>
> [Like a blind man weeping against an implacable sun

---

[40] Virilio, *Open Sky*, 13. Virilio summarizes the context of this change as follows: '*Time* (duration) and *space* (extension) are now inconceivable without *light* (limit-speed), the cosmological constant of the *speed of light*, an absolute philosophical contingency that supersedes, in Einstein's wake, the absolute character till then accorded to space and to time by Newton and many others before him.'

[41] Ibid. 14.

[42] Burroughs's final trilogy is one such attempt, and the work of Don Delillo is also relevant. In Latin America, Reinaldo Arenas's narrative fictions would need mentioning and, among poets, Eielson, Zurita, Maquieira, Perlongher. Working out this issue has nothing to do with the use of film or TV images as such.

> I persist in seeing the light through my empty eyes
> burnt for ever.
>
> What use the ray
> that writes with my hand, what use fire,
> > the depth
> of depths,
> > what use the World?]

To be burnt by the sun means by its force, not by its image in the sense of a representation. And so the light seen through 'ojos vacíos' is neither physical light (emanating from the sun) nor a representation of light. Hence the blindness and the darkness in which the poem places itself as impulse are prior to any depth or expanse ('lo hondo', 'el Mundo' [depth, the World']), and are comparable, in the extent of the annihilation needed, to death.

Consider how death enters another early poem:

> Me consta que se guarda la fórmula, el cadáver
> de cada idea, lo ilusorio,
> el sudor, la saliva,
> mientras se arroja el semen al pantano
> por temor a que estalle la semilla:
> este es el mito aciago
> de la idea molida por el sol de la muerte. (*O* 59)

> [It's clear to me that what gets preserved is the formula, the
>   corpse
> of an idea, the illusory,
> the sweat, the spit,
> and the semen meanwhile is thrown into the swamp
> for fear that the seed will burst:
> that is the fatal myth
> of the idea crushed by the sun of death.]

The notion is that people are afraid that ideas can be destroyed by the force of death and therefore cling to the mere formula of an idea, which is its dead part. But that thinking can be turned inside out: only an idea which can occur at the same level as 'el sol de la muerte' is worth having. 'El sol de la muerte' can be paraphrased as the light which arises from the place of death, or the force of seeing things from the side of death. In the late twentieth-century city, death is the final taboo: the actual death of the individual cannot be seen or touched or heard, it is hidden behind taboos, even though—or because?—thousands of images of violence against the human body emanate from the media every day. There is no time for death: death is eliminated from time. Rojas addresses that condition:

> Por eso veo claro que Dios es cosa inútil,
> como el furor de las ideas
> que vagan en el aire haciendo un remolino
> de nacimientos, muertes, bodas y funerales,
> revoluciones, guerras, iglesias, dictaduras,
> infierno, esclavitud, felicidad (*O* 59)

> [That's why I can see clearly that God is useless
> like the fury of ideas
> that wander through the air in a whirlpool
> of births, deaths, weddings, and funerals,
> revolutions, wars, churches, dictatorships,
> hell, slavery, happiness]

This is the will to preserve, to have a time in which there is no death. Its means are ideas become formulae, models: in the modern age, ideology, media images. Which does not mean they are bland and harmless (see the list). The mention of God suggests that the air now occupied by mass media representations may have taken the place made by religion, and that so also may the timeless time of the mid- to late twentieth century which has nothing to do with biological time. Rojas's response is to re-enter a position of unknowing:

> Por eso estoy hundido,
> en esa posición de quien perdió su centro,
> la cabeza apoyada en mis rodillas,
> como una criatura que vuelve a las entrañas
> de millares de madres sucesivas,
> [. . .]
> nadando en la marea del instinto,
> buscando lo que soy, como un gusano
> doblado para verse. (*O* 59)

> [That is why I'm in this position,
> submerged and drifting without centre,
> head on my knees,
> like a child returning to the bowels
> of thousands after thousands of mothers
> swimming in tides of instinct,

looking for what I am, like a worm
bent over to see itself.]

The position is foetal—and this in Latin America also connotes death, because of native traditions of burial—and passes through thousands of births, in order to get behind representation (which ideas are, generically) so as to emerge, oneself, not once and for all but because emerging is all there is. That, obviously, is a paraphrase. One way of indicating what Rojas's writing is doing here is to place it beside a statement by Socrates in Plato's *Meno* (Rojas, who has a good knowledge of classical literature, would be familiar with the passage): 'Thus the soul, since it is immortal and has been born many times, and has seen all things both here and in the other world, has learned everything that is.'[43] This, in Plato's argument, solves the problem of how human beings apparently recognize (by *anagnorisis*) shapes and colours without previous experience of them. But Rojas's sense of the human is different. Instead of the unwobbling and eternal geometric ideas of Plato, there is no perfection of the idea, the only eternity is emergence, and emergence is of biological time and has to do with *hambre*.

There is another difference between Plato's metaphysics and Rojas's poetics. Plato's notion of successive births is an adaptation of an oral, pre-city-state belief. Plato builds on a transformation already begun by Pindar's writing, quoting a poem that relocates the 'folk' belief in souls returning from the dead in terms of 'noble kings' being returned souls.[44] In Rojas the dead also live, but not in State continuities. They continue to grow ('el fuego está abajo con los muertos que crecen todavía' [there is fire down below with the dead who still grow]; *O* 30). The word 'abajo' suggests the force here of a native popular belief, common to Peru and Chile, that the dead continue to grow under the ground. This converges in Rojas's writing with a particular sense of the time of death as a non-completed time, against the idea that when a person is dead their character is fixed for good, an attitude which he rejects in the poem to his dead friend Lefebvre, quoted above. In other words, Rojas's sense that the dead continue to grow includes the notion that they are not simply eliminated from the current frame or

---

[43] Plato, *Meno*, 81c (English translation, 129).   [44] Ibid. 81b.

turned into dead image: native belief becoming twentieth-century understanding.

That this is not the ordinary understanding of death is acknowledged in another poem, whose first phrase is its title:

> Al muerto lo bañaron, lo compusieron, lo cerraron
> y lo enterraron. Prohibida la nariz orgullosa
> que le dio el aire lúcido.
> >   Pero esto no se entiende sino abajo
> cuando la Oreja es tiempo y el sol brilla al revés
> y uno vuela en lo inmóvil. (*O* 63)

> [The dead man was washed, composed, shut in,
> and buried. Forbidden the proud nose
> that gave him an air of lucidity.
> >   But that can only be understood down below
> when the Ear is time and the sun shines in reverse
> and we fly inside the immobile.]

Two types of understanding are given here: the usual, common-sense narrative of someone dying and a different mode of understanding that has to do with 'abajo'. 'Abajo' is a region where the support of recognitions and of pre-given forms of memory-story is abandoned. Rojas is proposing the book as an instrument that can move in that way, into those areas, inside the actual of living in this epoch.

'La Oreja es tiempo' [The Ear is time] gives time as tempo or rhythm, to be found everywhere, in everything:

> Nace de nadie el ritmo, lo echan desnudo y llorando
> como el mar, lo mecen las estrellas, se adelgaza
> para pasar por el latido precioso
> de la sangre, fluye, fulgura
> en el mármol de las muchachas, sube
> en la majestad de los templos, arde en el número
> aciago de las agujas, dice noviembre
> detrás de las cortinas, parpadea
> en esta página. (*O* 64)

> [Rhythm is born of no one, thrown out naked and crying
> like the sea, rocked by the stars, gets small
> so as to pass through the precious pulse
> of the blood, flows, flashes
> in the marble of girls, rises
> in the majesty of temples, burns in clock hands
> with their fatal number, says November

behind the curtains, blinks
on this page.]

'Las agujas' make clock time, given as only one instance of the time/rhythm which is in everything, including words, which is the starting-point of a related poem, entitled 'Carta sobre lo mismo' [Letter on the same]:

> Palabras, cuerdas vivas de qué, pobre visible
> cuando tanto invisible nos amarra en su alambre sigiloso,
> urdimbre de ir volando pero amaneces piedra,
>   se
> va, se viene, se interminablemente las arañas,
> tela que tela el mundo: particípalo
> pero tómalo y cámbialo. (*O* 65)

> [Words, living strings of what poor visible
> when so much invisible binds us in its silent wire,
> warp for you to go flying but you wake up a stone,
>   going,
> coming, endlessly the spiders
> weaving and weaving the world: participate in it
> but take it and change it.]

This poem, quoted here in full, gives succinctly the movement of Rojas's poetics. The visible in/of words is 'poor' when set beside the invisible, the 'oscuro' which gives the whole book its title. The invisible, moreover, is where unpredictable transformations take place ('volando [. . .] piedra'). In one sense it escapes from words, but the poem's action is precisely to enter that zone. The darkness is in the sounds themselves, which tie us, through the ear, 'en su alambre sigiloso', that is the sounds of the words on the page as breathed-read, the poem shifting, at infinite speed, between sound and sense. But then the question is not to stop there, in the minute weaving that makes the world, but to change it.

LOVE AND SPACE

In the field of the erotic, the difference between the two types of light, that of life and that of death, becomes undecidable. Erotic desire moves across those and other boundaries:

¿Qué se ama cuando se ama, mi Dios: la luz terrible de la vida
o la luz de la muerte? ¿Qué se busca, qué se halla, qué
es eso: amor? ¿Quién es? ¿La mujer con su hondura, sus rosas,
   sus volcanes,
o este sol colorado que es mi sangre furiosa
cuando entro en ella hasta las últimas raíces? (*O* 89)

[When you love what do you love, my God: the terrible light
   of life
or the light of death? What do you seek, what find, what
is this thing: love? Who is it? Woman with her depth, roses,
   volcanoes,
or this red sun which is my furious blood
when I enter to the final roots?]

The first phrase gives the title of this middle section of *Oscuro*, and the question thus emphasized goes beyond the usual bounds of what is understood as the object of love. When the question is posed here in the first poem of the section, there is a suggestion that love might be an entry into a cosmic force like that of the sun, associated with 'la luz de la muerte'.

In several of the poems, the sheer repleteness of sensuality, its 'lujo y lujuria' (*O* 124), is given as a kind of death, for example:

> Todo es cosa de hundirse,
> de caer hacia el fondo, como un árbol
> parado en sus raíces, que cae, y nunca cesa
> de caer hacia el fondo. (*O* 110)

> [Everything is a question of submerging,
> falling to the bottom, like a tree
> standing on its roots that falls and never stops
> falling and falling.]

Handled like that, there are similarities with nineteenth-century erotic sensibility, say of Baudelaire or of the Spanish American *Modernistas* like Rubén Darío. But the movement suggested is something else. The tree goes down into but also out of itself. Consider the sense of movement in another poem, entitled 'El fornicio' [Fornication]:

> te fuera mordiendo hasta las últimas
> amapolas, mi posesa, te todavía
> enloqueciera allí, en el frescor
> ciego, te nadara

> en la inmensidad
> insaciable de la lascivia (*O* 106–7)
> [that I were to bite you to the final
> poppies, my possessed, that I drove
> you mad even there, in that blind
> freshness, swam you
> in the insatiable
> immensity of lasciviousness]

It is not a matter of death in satiety, a common motif since the Renaissance, but of what love does to a body in space, the alterations it brings about in both: for example, an effect of buoyancy, the body sustained or held up by the very force that would lose it, the space given here being the sea ('nadara [. . .] inmensidad'), which echoes 'la intemperie' of other poems, indicating the risk and danger entered. And this understanding can be extended to the air, location of writing for Rojas, not because of its inheritance of mythological associations, but, again, because the body buoyed up by air is buoyed by desire (just as dreams of flying can be taken not as imitations of flight but as what desire generates: the body floating in space).

And then there is the sun, a repeated presence in the poems of this section:

> permíteme juntar
> mi beso con tu beso, permíteme tocarte
> como el sol, y morirme. (*O* 118)
>
> [let me join
> my kiss with your kiss, let me touch you
> like the sun, and die.]

What is the sun doing there? Which is in fact part of a bigger question, what is present in love? Certainly, the sun here is more cosmological than mythological. That is, it is not part of a mythological narrative whose characters/gods shape whatever space is involved. John Donne's and Frank O'Hara's famous addresses to the sun play with the mythological star in order to collapse it into modern space,[45] and thereby relocate the body and its affect.

Rojas has the one who is loved speak as follows:

---

[45] John Donne, 'The Sunne Rising', in *Songs and Sonets*; Frank O'Hara, 'The sun woke me this morning loud,' in *Selected Poems* (New York, 1974), 138.

'Soy una parte
de ti, pero no soy
sino la emanación de tu locura,
la estrella del placer, nada más que el fulgor
de tu cuerpo en el mundo.' (*O* 110)

['I am part
of you, but I am nothing
but the emanation of your madness,
the star of pleasure, nothing but the blaze
of your body in the world.']

With 'estrella' and 'fulgor', the sun and the cosmos are found inside desire, and 'mundo' gives the space inhabited, that space a function of desire. But to say 'the cosmos' when the subject of discussion is literature sounds like an inflated—Romantic— analogy of desire, and/or a mythological arrangement. Part of the problem has to do with the envelopment of everything in discursive, representational space. The non-human, which, clearly, the cosmos is for a twentieth-century understanding, simply disappears.[46] Rojas's eroticism drives a wedge between that—inherited—space and what happens when a person moves (swims is his word) in the force of love. Clearly, in such a situation, desire will cease to be entangled in the stories and representations, the packagings of the past, in which it is usually held—and here is the charge of futurity carried by Rojas's writing. As a result of that disentanglement, desire and cosmos are not in a relationship of representation but of forces, in this case luminescent forces.

That is the proposition one would start with and come back to. To work it out is difficult because as a way of thinking it runs against the mainstream of current thought. The word desire— and this is the other part of the problem—as currently used, drags in a whole series of presuppositions which get in the way of the clarity of Rojas's erotic poems. The word desire has become the preferred word for talking about the erotic and the way it is used causes difficulty if one wants to get to the notion of desire investing a field, that is, energizing a field, without mediation. Freud and Jung, still taken to be the key inter-

---

[46] Charles Olson tackles the problem head-on in his mid-century essay 'Human Universe', which points out, among other things, that part of the problem is how to get rid of the sense of language as nothing but 'logos, or discourse' (Olson, *Collected Prose*, 155).

preters, 'share the belief that the libido cannot invest a social or a metaphysical field without some sort of mediation'.[47] And the Oedipus story is still taken to be the key mediation. Call it libido or desire, the problem is the mediations one calls in, which are not just associations of the words but instrumentations of a way of handling the body in space/environment: in the case of the Oedipus narrative, a way of subordinating it to inheritance as prediction.

Consider, by contrast, what Rojas's writing does, in a poem where the object of love is called María, which the poem allows one to take both as the name of an 18-year-old Scottish girl and as a generic word for a person desired. The location is the Chilean Andes, at 3,000 metres:

> y María era allí la cordillera
> de los Andes, y el aire era María.
>
> Y el sol era María, y el placer,
> la teoría del conocimiento,
> y los volcanes de la poesía.
>
> Mujer de fuego. Visible mujer.
> Siempre serás aquel paraje eterno.
> La cordillera y el mar, por nacer.
> La catástrofe viva del silencio. (*O* 111–12)

> [And María was there the chain
> of the Andes, and the air was María.
>
> And the sun was María, and pleasure,
> the theory of knowledge,
> and the volcanoes of poetry.
>
> Woman of fire. Visible woman.
> You will always be that eternal place.
> Mountain chain and sea, about to be born.
> The living catastrophe of silence.]

Reading habits, taught at school and university, will encourage a reader to assume that the poem is somehow dealing in equivalences ('María'='la cordillera', etc.), and that if one can explain them, by finding a third term that underlies the comparisons, then one can interpret the poem and fulfil the demands placed upon one as a student of literature. Finding a third term would presume some principle of knowledge to be

---

[47] Gilles Deleuze and Félix Guattari, *Anti-Oedipus* (Minneapolis, 1977), 46.

deployed by the reader in the explanation.[48] But if Rojas writes 'the theory of knowledge' also 'was María', then one can read it that the erotic also gets in there, into theory—that there is no place one can come from which it has not entered, which gives a rather different sense to 'María era la cordillera | de los Andes' and to the Andes and the Pacific Ocean as 'por nacer'. Consider further what Rojas writes in another poem, entitled simply 'El amor', where the relation between the erotic and knowledge is also taken as a particular relation with time:

> Pero los meses vuelan como vuelan los días, como vuelan
> en su vuelo sin fin las tempestades,
> pues nadie sabe nada de nada, y es confuso
> todo lo que elegimos hasta que nos quedamos
> solos, definitivos, completamente solos. (*O* 122)

> [But the months fly by like the days, like the storms
> fly in their endless flight,
> since no one knows anything about anything, and everything
> we choose is confused until we are
> alone, definitive, completely alone.]

If the erotic gets into everything, and that includes reading—'Si ha de triunfar el fuego sobre la forma fría, | descifraré a María' [If fire is to triumph over cold form, | I will decipher María], writes Rojas in the poem quoted just now—then the nature of reading changes. We are talking less about an all-catching interpretative grid than an entry into 'la intemperie': 'Hembras, hembras | en el oleaje ronco donde echamos las redes de los cinco sentidos | para sacar apenas el beso de la espuma' [Women, women | in the rough swell where we throw the nets of the five senses | and bring out no more than the kiss of the foam] (*O* 95). Reading is taken as territory of the senses and its action as concerned with what arises in the senses. Beautiful women 'germinan, germinan como plantas silvestres en la calle' [germinate, germinate like wild plants in the street] (*O* 95) Making, the act of *poiesis*, and the occurrence of things in time come together in Rojas's erotic writing. How does that happen?

---

[48] In the Hispanic academic world, the bottom line would be a dictionary of symbols, in the Anglo-Saxon one there are various, one of them still being Lacanian theory. I am not denying the force of knowledge, only suggesting that the action of a poem can be prior to the forms of knowledge, or is itself a form of knowledge.

It would be a tempting simplification to say that, for Rojas, love invests certain images and thus etches them upon the mind. It would be inaccurate because that is not what is happening, for example, in the following:

> tú
>
> cordillera, tú,
> crisálida
> sonámbula
> en el fulgor
> impalpable
> de tu corola:
>
> tú,
>
> nadie (*O* 93)
>
> [you
>
> mountain chain, you,
> chrysalis
> sleepwalker
> in the untouchable
> blaze
> of your corolla:
>
> you,
>
> nobody]

There is no mind waiting there for images to be traced upon it, there is no mind independent of the impulse of love. So where or what is it where the figure of love appears and is also nobody?

> tú,
>
> la que hila
> en la velocidad
> ciega
> del sol (*O* 90)
>
> [you,
>
> the one who spins
> in the blind
> speed
> of the sun]

The making of figure and image could not be placed more absolutely over the abyss of the non-human cosmos.

tú,

paraíso
o
nadie,
cuerda
para oír
el viento
sobre el abismo
sideral:

tú,
página
de piel más allá
del aire (*O* 91)

[you,

paradise
or
no one,
string
to hear
the wind
over the sidereal
abyss:

you,
page
of skin beyond
the air]

The skin is given as the place where the registering of things in the flow of time occurs. It is also the place of writing: the action of writing occurs as inscription upon the surface made by the senses. And that surface is the beloved as object of erotic desire, the body of love, and thus the becoming object or figure of the world. In that way, writing for Rojas is inextricably erotic. And when he locates writing in and upon the senses, we are not dealing with a framework that can be applied so as to produce guaranteed meanings: 'el oleaje ronco donde echamos las redes de los cinco sentidos' [the rough swell where we throw the nets of the five senses] and 'navegación y número, carácter I y número, red en el abismo de las cosas' [navigation and number, character I and number, net in the abyss of things] do not give a guaranteed ground, only the total act of writing/reading as the site of becoming.

Desire in Rojas's poems has the particularity of occurring without story. It is not therefore located inside interpretation but outside. This is not to say that there are no narratives, but that when a narrative begins to stake out territorial claims, Rojas then proceeds to dissolve it. The poem 'Pareja humana' [Human couple] places surfeit and orgasm ('hartazgo y orgasmo') inside two major Western narratives: orgasm as a form of death and sex as loss of paradise:

> Así el amor en el flujo espontáneo de unas venas
> encendidas por el hambre de no morir, así la muerte;
> la eternidad así del beso, el instante
> concupiscente, la puerta de los locos,
> así el así de todo después del paraíso:
> > —Dios,
> ábrenos de una vez. (*O* 105)

> [Thus love in the spontaneous flow of veins
> burning with the hunger not to die, thus death;
> thus the eternity of the kiss, the moment
> of lust, the gate of the mad,
> thus the thus of everything after paradise:
> > —God,
> come on and open the door.]

The story of original sin or of loss of a golden age, which implies a god or gods who threw us out, is sent up and short-circuited: desire produces the story, and not the story interprets desire, and all desires are connected as 'el hambre de no morir'. The use of 'así' as repetition of equivalences has a similar effect: 'así el así de todo' dissolves any theory of equivalence back into the force of equivalence (which Rojas here calls 'cuerpos deseosos') and any form of equivalence back into its erotic movement: desire as generative and not imitative. That is the horizon towards which or from which the poems do not cease to move.

'¿Qué se ama cuando se ama?' The question is almost what is 'behind' desire, except that if María *is* the cordillera and *is* 'nadie', then there is nothing behind desire, the surface of writing is *there*. Once again, we have the senses, with the force of desire, as giving the surface of writing, not the discursive inheritance. Thus this section of *Oscuro*, crucially, works out the question of the book and space. Another way of construing the question would be: what sense does desire make? This would make it clear that the question is not about the object of desire as socially classified. But the trouble with those ways of rephrasing Rojas's question is once you say desire you have an idea of lack (for Freud and Lacan, to do with the phallus) and a story (based on mythological controls) on your hands,[49] rather than the sun ('ese sol es ella, I ese sol que no habla' [that sun is her, I that sun that does not speak]; *O* 123), death ('todo era olor I nupcial, nupcial I a muerte' [everything was nuptial I nuptial smell I of death]; *O* 98), nothing ('después de gozarte y conocerte, I todavía eres tú, o eres la nada' [after enjoying you and knowing you, I you are still you, or you are nothing]; *O* 110), madness ('no soy I sino la emanación de tu locura' [I am nothing I but the emanation of your madness]; *O* 110), hunger ('el hambre de no morir' [the hunger not to die]; *O* 105), the sea ('adoras al mar que te arrebata con su espuma' [you adore the sea which drags you away in its foam]; *O* 126).

---

[49] Bloom's 'anxiety of influence' idea is based on envy of inheritance and thus Oedipal: once again a structure of lack.

4

Jorge Eduardo Eielson: The Boundaries of the Poem

Ciertas verdades, incluso las más altas, no se manifiestan
en ninguna teoría, sino siempre en la práctica.

(J. E. Eielson)

SPACE/WRITING

In *L'Espace littéraire* (1955), in a chapter on reading ('Lire'),
Maurice Blanchot suggests that a book may be compared with
a sculpture:

Rodin's *The Kiss* invites one to look at it and even takes pleasure in
being viewed. Balzac's work is unseeing, it is closed, dormant and self-
absorbed to the point of disappearing from sight [. . .] The statue
which is disinterred and placed before an admiring public expects
nothing from it and receives nothing from it. Instead, it looks as if it
has been uprooted. But the book which is exhumed, the manuscript
which is drawn from a receptacle and is read in full light, doesn't it
come alive again all of a sudden?[1]

Eielson's writings, particularly since 1950, explore what happens
when the visual space occupied by a text becomes an inherent
part of the work itself and the way it is read, rather than a material support of little importance. In this sense, it forms part of a
tradition whose leading exponent is Mallarmé. Nevertheless, as
will be seen, Eielson extends the role of the visual space in
poetry into new areas, radically redefining literary language
and establishing a link with the cosmology of the past seventy
years.

---

[1] Maurice Blanchot, *L'Espace littéraire* (Paris, 1955); 255–6. English translation
with an introduction by Ann Smock: *The Space of Literature* (Lincoln, 1989).

One work of his entitled *Papel* (1960) is twenty pages long, each page printed with words and sometimes inscribed with other marks. The words form only one part of the text, because what they describe the paper to be literally becomes visible:

>   papel blanco
>   papel rayado
>   papel con 4 palabras
>   papel y tinta
>   papel plegado
>   papel blanco con 5 palabras
>   papel agujereado
>   [. . .]
>   papel pisoteado
>   papel fotografiado[2]
>
>   [white paper
>   lined paper
>   paper with 4 words
>   paper and ink
>   folded paper
>   white paper with 5 words
>   paper with holes in it
>   paper that has been trodden on
>   paper that has been photographed]

What is the principle governing these words 'on' paper? They do not function solely as titles, nominations, or references, because they form part of what they are describing ('Paper with 4 words' *is* paper with 4 words on it). Nor are the effects they create purely visual: they form part of language. Furthermore, they create a conceptual framework: qualities are differentiated (white/lined) and they establish relationships, in other words, they establish an order. This order, however, resists becoming a series. For example, the fourth classification ('Paper and ink') includes all, or nearly all, the others. The words appear against a background (paper, language, space?) and disappear when they become part of the paper-language-space. That is, they become simultaneously accessible and inaccessible. The text produces a mysterious sense of inconstancy: the viewer cannot tell whether he is on

---

[2] J. E. Eielson, *Poesía escrita* (Lima, 1976), 291–301. This and the Mexican edition (Mexico City, 1989) are not the same in content. When a text appears in both, the Mexican edition is cited since it is more accessible.

the inside or the outside of it. It does not allow any knowledge, other than its actual happening.

The Peruvian writer of the prologue to the edition of *Poesía escrita* printed in Lima (1976) suggests that Eielson's work represents 'la destrución de la palabra' [the destruction of the word] and 'el fin de la palabra'[3] [the end of the word], and cites, significantly, the text 'Escultura horripilante' [Horrifying sculpture]. This text begins by listing the tasks necessary for the construction, over a period of '915 noches' [915 nights], of the sculpture which is situated underground, 'a 17 metros de la superficie' [17 metres below the surface]. The materials include '15000 metros de cinta grabada con los más importantes textos poéticos de todos los tiempos' [15,000 metres of tape recorded with the most important poetic texts of all time]. It ends with the words:

c) la escultura—que recitará continuamente, por boca de la muñeca, los más hermosos poemas concebidos por el hombre—se comportará igualmente como tal, es decir satisfará sus necesidades primordiales, repitiendo los mismos gestos humanos de la alimentación, procreación, defacación, etcétera, aungue tales necesidades, en este caso, no sean sino un artificio para mejor recitar los poemas. (Más que un repulsivo simulacro del ser humano, como podría pensarse, la escultura será el resultado de millares y millares de años de civilización);

d) sólo en muy raras ocasiones, a pesar de su inevitable contacto con el mundo exterior, empuñará la ametralladora o derramará una sola gota de su preciosa sangre humana en defensa de una causa justa;

e) poseedora de un alma lírica, la criatura surgirá muchas veces del seno de la tierra y con sus brazos peludos—indispensables en el arte de la recitación—eligirá una rosa o un lirio del campo;

f) la criatura explotará, con espantoso resultado, el mismo día que termine de recitar todos los poemas grabados en la cinta magnética. (328)[4]

[c] The sculpture, which will continually recite, through the mouth of the mannequin, the most beautiful poems conceived by man, will behave exactly like a puppet, that is, it will perform its primordial functions by repeating human actions such as eating, procreation,

---

[3]   *Poesía escrita* (Lima), 29, 30.
[4]   Textual references are to Jorge Eduardo Eielson, *Poesía escrita* (Bogotá, 1998). This edition does not include Eielson's visual poetry.

defecation, etcetera, although in this case these functions are simply an artifice for reciting the poems better. (Rather than being a repulsive simulacrum of a human being, as one might expect, the sculpture will be the product of millions and millions of years of civilization);

d) Only in exceptional circumstances, despite its inevitable contact with the outside world, will it take hold of a machine gun or shed a drop of its precious human blood in defence of a just cause;

e) Possessing a poetic soul, the creature will often rise up from the depths of the earth and with its hairy arms—indispensable for the art of reciting—will pick a rose or a wild iris;

f) The creature will explode, with terrifying results, the day it finishes reciting all the poems recorded on the magnetic tape.]

For the writer of the prologue just mentioned, the text deals with the 'aniquilación trágica' [tragic annihilation] of language. In my view, both these terms are erroneous, but it is worth mentioning them because they reveal what happens when Eielson's work is read from a conventional definition of literature. An alternative reading might suggest that the text represents a ritual death with grotesque apocalyptic dimensions. Also, that it has a humorous side, in many ways satirizing the relationship between body and poetry, in which the latter sublimates the former, clearing the way for a possible inversion in which the poem becomes an extension of the body and vice versa.

What would be 'annihilated'? The text is quite specific: '15,000 metres of tape recorded with the most important poetic texts of all time.' Regarding the object to be destroyed, there is no doubt whatsoever. Nevertheless, the interpretation of that object constitutes a cultural action on the part of the person who establishes a relation with the (imaginary) event. For some of course it means a destruction of the very best of Western tradition, the latter, for example, defined by T. S. Eliot in his well-known writings on literary tradition.

At the end of the text when it was first published, at the foot of the page, lie the words, in small print: *'esculturas para leer* 9 esculturas subterráneas colocadas por Jorge Eielson en diferentes lugares del planeta durante viajes realizados entre 1966 y 1969' [*sculptures to be read*, 9 underground sculptures placed by Jorge Eielson in different parts of the world during his travels between 1966 and 1969].[5] Obviously, these are not expressive objects which, like classical art, rise up into space and become eternalized through time. Instead of being sealed off and sublimated, they are left open to the cosmos. They assume the earth as the field of their action. Their actions radiate around the world and cut across the concepts which isolate us from it. One can assume that they continue their invisible work.

Eielson's poem-sculpture functions much like a rite of passage or a vast clearing of the ground which gives rise to a new situation, one of multiple and unpredictable interfaces between the word and the cosmos, between literature and what was traditionally excluded from it. Once the boundaries of the poem have been perforated, the poem is transformed. In the words of Nicanor Parra, in a poem from *Artefactos* written in the same decade as Eielson's *Escultura horripilante*: 'TODO | ES POESÍA | menos la poesía' [EVERYTHING | IS POETRY | except poetry].[6]

If one initially accedes to the nothingness and silence in Eielson's work, one can soon see how these begin to affirm themselves as necessary elements of the poetic text. This point will be returned to shortly. There is also an alteration of the internal realities of poet and poem. Finally, although the aim here is not to carry out a logical ordering, because there is no logical division between these issues, there is the question of the word becoming action. The latter will be tackled first, after a brief outline of Eielson's ideas on what he terms 'la literatura tridimensional' [three-dimensional literature].

Eielson uses the term 'three-dimensional' in relation to non-Euclidean geometry. This is where his interest in science, particularly in quantum physics, and cosmology is manifest:

El de nuestros días es un escenario casi apocalíptico, sobre todo en los países así dichos desarrollados, en los que la palabra creativa tiende a

---

[5] 'Escultura horripilante (homenaje a César Moro y S. Salazar Bondy', *Creación y crítica*, 12 (Feb. 1972). A note in the Bogatá edition of *Poesía escrita* (p. 324) states: 'las "esculturas" aquí presentes fueron reunidas en cinco libros-objeto, transcritas en cinco idiomas en cada uno de ellos. Cuatro de los libros fueron inaugurados el 16 de diciembre de 1969 simultáneamente en París, donde se encontraba el autor, en Roma, Eningen (Stuttgart) y Nueva York. El quinto libro (o "escultura para leer" [i.e. the "Escultura horripilante"]) estaba destinada a Lima, pero no pudo ser colocado al mismo tiempo que los otros, como era el proyecto inicial, sino más tarde. El trabajo completo se expuso en 1969 en la muestra "Plans and projects as art", realizada en la Kunsthalle de Berna.'

[6] *Chistes para desorientar a la poesía* (Madrid, 1989), 133.

desaparecer, sustituída por las imágenes y por los *media* electrónicos y computarizados. [. . .] Justamente por esto, para que la palabra escrita siga siendo un instrumento privilegiado de la comunicación interior, vehículo sin par del pensamiento y del sentir humanos, es necesario que abandone el *ghetto* literario, que se abra a una nueva forma de comunicación, asumiendo un rol en sintonía con los paradigmas ya operantes en campo filosófico, científico, artístico, religioso y hasta político y económico. De otra manera, la literatura habrá perdido su razón de ser, su capacidad de síntesis de las demás artes y disciplinas, su vocación crítica y testimonial, reduciéndose a un mero instrumento de poder en manos de políticos y mercaderes.[7]

[Today's situation is almost apocalyptic, above all in the so-called developed countries where the creative word tends to disappear and is replaced by images and by electronic or computer-generated media. Because of this, in order that the written word may continue to be a privileged instrument for communicating inwardness, an unrivalled vehicle of human thought and emotion, it must abandon the literary ghetto and open itself up to a new form of communication, assuming a role in harmony with the prevailing paradigms in philosophical, scientific, artistic, religious, and even political and economic fields. If not, literature will lose its *raison d'être*, its ability to synthesize other art forms and disciplines, and its critical and testimonial vocation, and it will be reduced to a mere instrument of power in the hands of politicians and businessmen.]

THE WORD AS ACTION

Ever since the mid-1960s, Eielson has created a series of 'actions' and installations in a number of places. In these, the boundaries between what one could call the textual and the non-textual are broken down. To cite an example, in Lima in 1978, Eielson gave a performance entitled 'Dormir es una obra maestra' [Sleep is a masterpiece],[8] in which a woman, wrapped in a white knotted sheet, lay asleep on a vertically suspended bed. Here, the concepts of action, word, and sculpture are extended by coming into contact with each other. If the act of

---

[7] J. E. Eielson, 'Defensa de la palabra: a propósito de "El diálogo infinito' ", unpublished manuscript, 3-4.

[8] *El diálogo infinito: una conversación con Martha L. Canfield* (Mexico City, 1995), 22, gives a photograph of the performance, wrongly stating, however, that it was given in the Venice Biennale of 1972. I am grateful to Sr. Eielson for this clarification.

considering means to trace shapes amidst the stars (*sidus* meaning star), the person who considers the piece just mentioned
finds that the link between the act of configuring and the figure
itself is constantly shifting, eliminating the possibility of a univocal and unilocal gaze. The plasticity of the scene, the colours,
the smooth texture of the sheet, the vertical position of the bed,
the concepts of sleep and masterpiece, the face of the sleeping
woman, all these elements function as vectors of energy-atten-
tion whose intersections cause endless reconfigurations of
space.

In the Venice Biennale of 1972, what Eielson calls an
'ephemeral action' took place:

en la Plaza San Marcos y con la ayuda de decenas de estudiantes de la
universidad veneciana que distribuyeron hojas de papel impreso en
cinco lenguas (italiano, español, inglés, alemán y francés), tuvo lugar
mi *acción* pública. Siguiendo las breves indicaciones impresas en el
papel, los espectadores-oyentes participaron activamente en el
concierto y fue muy emocionante ver la inmensa y suntuosa Plaza San
Marcos invadida por millares de hojas de papel blanco que se levanta-
ban, ondulaban, vibraban, agitadas por manos invisibles, desaparecían
y volvían a aparecer, hasta llegar gradualmente al final, cuando se
comenzaba a rasgar el papel, siguiendo el ritmo de los tambores y la
flauta para terminar en un frenesí de papeles rotos, convertidos en
confetis y arrojados al aire en medio de la euforia general. Todo eso
duró salamente siete minutos, pero fue de gran intensidad y
alborozo.[9]

[In St Mark's Square and with the help of dozens of students of the
University of Venice who distributed pieces of paper printed in five
languages (Italian, Spanish, English, German, and French), there
took place my public action. Following the brief instructions printed
on the pieces of paper, the spectator-listeners actively participated in
the concert. It was very moving to see the enormous, sumptuous St
Mark's Square invaded by millions of white pieces of paper which rose,
swayed and vibrated, shaken by invisible hands, disappeared and then
reappeared, until the end gradually came, when the pieces of paper
were slowly torn up, to the rhythm of drums and flute, culminating in
a whirlwind of papers turned into confetti and thrown into the air
amid the general euphoria. All this lasted only seven minutes, but it
was a very intense and joyful experience.]

The knot is a form-sign-action which has fascinated Eielson

[9] *El diálogo infinito: una conversación con Martha L. Canfield*, 41.

for more than three decades.[10] One of his installations consisted of forty knots, or knottings, made of cotton on which he had printed Leonardo da Vinci's manuscript-text *Codice sul volo degli uccelli e sugli annodamenti* [Codex on the flight of birds and their knottings]. The forty knotted objects were placed in the Le Stelline room of the palace in which Leonardo lived:

La instalación es auto-referencial y tautológica, puesto que los nudos descritos en el texto están hechos con el mismo texto, y se hallan suspendidos en el espacio, como los pájaros en vuelo a qu también se alude, por medio de cuarenta hilos de oro que evocan la sección áurea renacentista. También, evidentemente, hay en ese trabajo un irónico mestizaje espiritual entre el mundo clásico europeo y el mundo incaico americano.[11]

[The installation is self-referential and tautological, since the knots described in the text are made from the text itself and are suspended in space, like birds in flight, which are also referred to in the text, by forty gold threads representing the golden section of the Renaissance. Evidently, this work also represents an ironic spiritual miscegenation between classical Europe and the pre-Columbian world of the Incas.]

The mention of the Incas has to do with their use of knotted strings (Kipus) as a three-dimensional form of writing. This piece is an example of how working with words links up with other artistic practices in numerous ways. It does not, however, constitute an attempt to

amalgamar los diferentes lenguajes artísticos en una sola *obra total* [. . .] Mi tentativa es más bien ir más allá de los lenguajes, transgredir sus habituales límites convencionales, que tanto los empobrecen. Solamente entonces podrá ser posible el hallazgo de algo inédito, en un feliz encuentro que respete la esencia de cada uno de ellos.[12]

[amalgamate different artistic languages into one total work. My aim instead is to go beyond these languages, to transcend the conventional limits which impoverish them so direly. Only then will it be possible to make an entirely new discovery, to generate a harmonious meeting of elements where the essence of each is respected.]

---

[10] See Luciono Boi and Lorraine Verner, 'Bridging the Gap between Art, Science and Nature: The Visionary Work of Jorge Eielson on Knots', text presented at the Conference 'The Artistic and Literary Work of Jorge Eielson', King's College London and Institute of Latin American Studies University of London, Oct. 1997.

[11] *El diálogo infinito*, 49.

[12] Ibid. 40.

One of several examples would be the book *Canto visible* [Visible song] (Rome, 1960) which includes 'ESTATUA DE UN PENSAMIENTO CONVERTIDO EN ESFERA' [STATUTE OF A THOUGHT CONVERTED INTO A SPHERE] and 'ESTA VERTICAL DELESTE PROVIENE DE ALFA DE CANTAURO' [THIS CELESTIAL VERTICAL LINE COMES FROM ALPHA CENTAURI].[13] The first consists of a sphere placed in the middle of the page, and taking up about two-thirds of it, with the text lying beneath it, and the second comprises a vertical line, running down the centre of the page, also with the text beneath it. Obviously, mere description reduces the possibility of thought, sculpture, event, geometry, and writing coalescing. Thus, none of these is situated in a pre-given space, instead they are transformed in and by their convergence. As a result, the concept of the book also changes.

In the second case, the vertical line could be seen as the trace of a cosmic ray or the notation of the mark left by a quantum particle created in a scientific experiment. Trace, notation, and word could be seen to be related, as event, mathematics, and language are for Heisenberg, who disputes the adequacy of language in the context of quantum physics:

In theoretical physics we try to understand groups of phenomena by introducing mathematical symbols that can be correlated with facts, namely, with the results of measurements. For the symbols we use names that visualize their correlation with the measurement. Thus the symbols are attached to the language.[14]

In the case of the words 'vertical' and 'celestial', both terms are ambiguous: they suggest a number of possibilities, just as the word 'term' itself does. 'Vertical' evokes the position of man on the earth, in time (human time or cosmic time?), and the possibility or necessity for transcendence or for a vertical cut. 'Celestial' assembles colour (the word in Spanish also means sky blue), orientation, and sky (in all senses of the word). The intersection of both words creates a spatial effect.

If the elements used in this piece appear to be elementary, the effects they create are complex. Straightforward notations, when read as instructions for the *performance* of the reader, are capable of generating complicated results. The apparent

---

[13] *Poesía escrita* (Lima), 273, 276. *Canto visible* was first published in Rome in 1960.
[14] Werner Heisenberg, *Physics and Philosophy* (London, 1989), 160.

simplicity, partly due to the fact that referentiality has been abandoned, thus makes the effects radiate all the more.

INNER REALITY AND SURFACE

What happens to the internal reality of the poet, the poem, and of language? In Eielson's poems written between 1950 and 1970, there are repeated movements away from volumes and surfaces made by sound towards visual and/or physical spaces. Here is an example of the sensuous sound characteristic of the early poems:

> Nada impide ahora
> Que la onda de los aires resplandezca
> O que reviente el seno de la diosa
> En algún negro bosque. Nada
> Sino los puros aros naturales arden,
> Nada sino el suave heliotropo favorece
> La entrada lila de las bestias y el otoño
> En el planeta. (67)

> [Nothing now prevents
> The sway of breezes from shining
> Or the goddess's breast from bursting
> In some dark wood. Nothing
> But the pure rings of nature burn,
> Nothing but the soft heliotrope favours
> The lilac entry of beasts and autumn
> Into the planet.]

There is a certain equilibrium here between the sound of these verses and the visual images they conjure up. We have the circular movement of the sound, in short repetitions which end within the ten seconds or so of automatic aural memory, and which give shape and volume to it. At the visual level, there are sudden dilations and conflagrations, temporarily contained in the image of the 'soft heliotrope'. The visual manifests itself in the traditional literary sense, that is, the visual imagination is situated within the traditional parameters of literature. The image does not exceed the word, it is rooted entirely within it, as is shown by the repetition of the word *refer* in the following definition:

in literary usage, *imagery* refers to images produced in the mind by language, whose words and statements may refer either to experiences which could produce physical perception were the reader actually to have those experiences, or to the sense-impressions themselves.[15]

In other words, there is an internal space which is never breached down: the internal reality of language, of the image (the poem), and the mind (the poet) are held in a symmetrical relationship. Each of these internal realities includes the others. In the lines cited above, however, a contrary movement can be traced: that which contains ('seno', 'aros') breaks up ('reviente', 'arden') and is extended into the cosmos ('planeta').

Other poems reveal an opening of the volume of the poem and the body-locus of the senses towards external spaces and forces:

> escucho
> Los silenciosos pasos de la luna
> Entre el boscaje, lejanas y altas
> Velocidades, ruidos que adivino,
> Diamantes en marcha y lineales
> Vientos en perpetua rotación. (119)

> [I hear
> The silent steps of the moon
> In the forest, distant and high
> Velocities, noises which I guess at,
> Diamonds set in motion and linear
> Winds in perpetual rotation.]

'Volume', from the Latin *volvere*, meaning to roll up, signified book before its meaning was extended to include the notion of material mass, and the word brings together or combines the different functions that a book may perform. The book *Noche oscura del cuerpo* [Dark night of the body], published in Rome in 1955, inverts the title of San Juan de la Cruz's book and pours the body (inner life) outwards. Thus, in 'Cuerpo multiplicado' [Multiplied body]:

> No tengo límites
> Mi piel es una puerta abierta

---

[15] *Princeton Encyclopedia of Poetry and Poetics* (Princeton, 1990), 363. The author of the entry on imagery is Northrop Frye.

Y mi cerebro una casa vacía
La punta de mis dedos toca fácilmente
El firmamento y el piso de madera (228)

[I have no limits
My skin is an open door
And my brain an empty house
The tips of my fingers easily touch
The firmament and the wooden floor]

Rather than a project to conquer new spaces, which would ultimately only lead to existing limitations being replaced with new ones, Eielson's is an attitude, or better said an action, of experimentation which rejects the boundaries that make the human soul an inner reality. In some of his other texts, the coinciding of the internal realities of poem, poet, and language is dispelled through a particular use of reference and speech acts, which one could call incitement to disruption. *Cuatro estaciones* [Four seasons] (Rome, 1960) starts with:

> tome este rectángulo de papel en primavera con
> una temperatura de 17 grados sobre cero y léalo
> tranquilamente

> [take this rectangle of paper in spring under
> a temperature of 17 degrees above zero and read it
> calmly]

and it ends like this:

> tome este rectángulo de papel en el invierno con
> una temperatura de 7 grados bajo cero y quémelo
> en la chimenea[16]

> [take this rectangle of paper in the winter under
> a temperature of 7 degrees below zero and burn it
> in the fireplace]

When the text-paper itself becomes a referent, the dichotomy between inside–outside is removed. And if one is provoked to burn the paper, rather than to keep it within a 'literary' sphere, the emotion no longer originates from an intensity internal to the text, but from a sensation of pure externality. Using literature for combustion challenges one to question the relationship between material and cultural worlds. The

---

[16] *Poesía escrita* (Lima), 263, 266.

notion of the text as an autonomous entity, celebrated in European capitals towards the end of the nineteenth century, no longer elicits an excited response.

THE WORK, A SPIRITUAL EVENT

Reducing every volume to nothingness is for Eielson also part of the process of writing. The ninth poem of the book *Mutatis mutandis* (Rome, 1954) reads:

> nada
> sino una masa clara
> de millones y millones de kilos
> de plomo de plata de nada
> vacío y peso y vacío nuevamente
> nada de plomo   plomo en la nada
> nada de plata   plata en la nada
> nada de nada   nada en la nada
> nada
> sino la luna   la nada
> y la nada nuevamente (213)
>
> [nothing
> but a clear mass
> millions and millions of kilos
> of lead of silver of nothing
> emptiness and weight and emptiness again
> nothing of lead   lead in nothing
> nothing of silver   silver in nothing
> nothing of nothing   nothing in nothing
> nothing
> but the moon   nothing
> and nothing again]

The text constitutes a spatial rather than an ethical or existential reality, or more accurately, it presents a textual topology uniting dimensions on a single surface, disallowing any reality beneath that surface. The nothingness is prevalent both inside and outside, behind and in front. Thus, image, poem, and book-volume ultimately become pure exteriority.

In *El diálogo infinito*, the interlocutor says: 'quisiera insistir en la presencia del vacío que me parece constante en tu obra. Y no sólo a partir de la década del 50, cuando descubres el budismo, sino desde antes' [I would like to emphasize that the theme of nothingness is prevalent in your work, not only since the 1950s, when you discovered Buddhism, but before that]. Eielson replies: 'Sí, es verdad. Probablemente, como me dijo Deshimaru, yo era budista desde que nací, sólo que no lo sabía' [Yes, it's true. As Deshimaru told me, I have probably been a Buddhist since I was born, only I didn't know it].[17] In another poem he writes:

> escribo algo
> algo todavía
> algo más aún
> añado palabras   pájaros
> hojas secas   viento
> borro palabras nuevamente
> borro pájaros   hojas secas   viento
> escribo algo todavía
> vuelvo a añadir palabras
> palabras otra vez
> palabras aún
> además pájaros   hojas secas   viento
> borro palabras nuevamente
> borro pájaros   hojas secas   viento
> borro todo por fin
> no escribo nada (214)
>
> [I write something
> still something
> something more
> I add words   birds
> dry leaves   wind
> I erase words again
> I erase birds   dry leaves   wind
> I still write something
> I add words once more
> words again
> words still
> also birds   dry leaves   wind
> I erase words again
> I erase birds   dry leaves   wind
> I erase everything finally
> I write nothing]

---

[17] *El diálogo infinito*, 31.

212 *Jorge Eduardo Eielson*

The writer of the prologue of the edition published in Lima reads this text as a tragic commentary on time: 'Este es el fin de la palabra, de la palabra asida, en su extinción, a los últimos objetos y seres naturales [. . .] La acción de la escritura del poema es su tema mismo en un trágico y estremecedor balbuceo' [This is the end of the word, of the word attached, as it becomes extinct, to the last natural objects and creatures. The act of writing the poem becomes the theme of the poem, it represents a tragic and alarming stammer].[18] This reading, however, ignores the fact that the text also represents an alternative temporal framework: an ecstatic time of detachment and release. This suggests a time that expands in the way that space does. Commenting on the difficulty of thinking about eternity, Charles Olson writes that Islamic philosophers describe: 'a time which extends into exterior time (*outertime*), in the same way that we conceive (more easily) space extending or expanding.'[19] The internal time of Eielson's text does not progress, it is not a historical time, it does not travel towards an end, since the end of the word is a release.

In this sense, all context becomes text and the text becomes purely external. Two routes into and out of Eielson's work may be established: one through cultural history and another through the topology of reading. The first brings in the *quipu*, the Inca form of the book, and, amongst other things, the fact that for social reasons literature in Peru never achieved full autonomy. The second concerns the discovery of astral constellations, as in Mallarmé's *Un coup de dés*, a poem which inaugurates the twentieth century by locating on the same plain the pattern of stars in the sky and the arrangement of letters on the page, allowing the unknown to reveal itself through the 'virtual' reality of the text. This mirrors much of what Eielson is doing in a work that dates from 1965, to which he gives the title *Firmamento*. It sets up a dialogue with Mallarmé's statement: 'one does not write luminously on a dark field; the alphabet of stars alone, is thus indicated, sketched out or interrupted; man pursues black on white.'[20] The idea of the book is radically

[18] *Poesía escrita* (Lima), 29.
[19] *Muthologos*, I: 61. Olson is referring to Henri Corbin's essay 'Le Temps cyclique dans le Mazdéisme et dans l'Ismaélisme', *Eranos-Jahrbuch XX* (1951; Zurich, 1952). English translation: *Cyclical Time and Ismaili Gnosis* (London, 1983).
[20] Stéphane Mallarmé, *Selected Poetry and Prose*, ed. Mary Ann Caws (New York, 1982), 77. The statement is from *Quant au livre* (1895).

reformulated by Eielson's work, which comprises a black background covered in small white marks. As one approaches, one sees that these traces make up letters and the letters, words which read 'stars'. At the end of the page there are five lines which say:

> No escribo nada
> Que no esté escrito en el cielo
> La noche entera palpita
> De incandescentes palabras
> Llamadas estrellas[21]
>
> [I write nothing
> Which is not written in the sky
> The whole night pulsates
> In incandescent words
> Called stars]

THE BOOK AND SPACE

Works like the one just discussed are an inversion of literary space, or, to coin a word, an exvolution, in the sense of an unrolling of what made the book into a volume with interiority. Mallarmé's famous statement, that the world exists in order to end up in a book,[22] can be interpreted as meaning that the book is the place for the becoming of everything. The human universe changes as new discoveries are made. And this, for Eielson, produces the necessity to change the space of the book. To say book, in this sense, is to refer to a space or territory shared by writers and readers, and consequently to the book as a device that permits these conjunctions: the book as a physical-mental space, both physical and imaginary at the same time. The physical book in front of a reader and the spiritual book that arises in the act of reading are each prolonged in the other.

Since the 1950s, Eielson's written work has been concerned with the handling of physical space or, more accurately, with the

---

[21] J. E. Eielson, *Il linguaggio magico dei nodi* (Milan, 1993), 63, gives the text in Italian: 'Non scrivo niente | Che no sia scritto nel cielo | La notte intera pulsa | Nelle incandescenti parole | Chiamate stelle.'

[22] A more precise translation might be 'all earthly existence must ultimately be contained in a book' (Mallarmé, *Selected Poetry and Prose*, 80).

physicality of space. In the poems of that decade, the topologies of everyday life, of amorous affect, and of urban space all touch and extend each other. In the book *Habitación en Roma* [Room in Rome] (1952), 'habitación is to be taken both as the room one lives inside and also as the fact of inhabiting a larger space, as is indicated in the titles of the poems, such as 'Poema para leer de pie en el autobús entre la puerta Flaminia y el Tritone' [Poem to be read standing up in the bus between the Flaminia gate and the Tritone]. There is in this and the other poems of the book a rejection of any way of writing which hollows out its space in the notion of desire as lack. For example,

> de nada sirve
> de nada sirve escribir
> siempre sobre sí mismo
> o de lo que no se tiene
> o se recuerda solamente
> o se desea solamente
> yo no tengo nada
> nada repito
> nada que ofreceros. (167)

> [there is no use
> nothing of use in writing
> always about yourself
> or what you do not have
> or you only remember
> or you only desire
> I have nothing
> I repeat nothing
> nothing to offer.]

That 'nothing' is an abandonment of certain traditional flows of communication and, at the same time, a jubilant affirmation of affect:

> nada en la mirada
> nada en la garganta
> nada entre los brazos
> nada en los bolsillos
> ni en el pensamiento
> sino mi corazón sonando alto alto
> entre las nubes
> como un cañonazo (168)

[nothing in my eyes
nothing in my throat
nothing in my arms
nothing in my pockets
nothing in my thought
only my heart beating loud loud
among the clouds
like a cannon shot]

All physical and metaphysical productions of enclosure, called self, desire, good, evil, disappear in the ecstatic force of that nothing.

It could be said that these poems display an innocent gaze, but in the old sense of the word innocent: a person who does no injury or evil. And it is a pure gaze, also in the radical sense: unmixed with anything that defiles, corrupts, or impairs. Hence the act of undressing and the gaze that falls upon it are recurrent. Undressing (*desvestirse*) becomes a divesting oneself, in all senses of the word, as in the poem entitled 'Via Veneto':

me pregunto
si verdaderamente
tengo manos
si realmente poseo
una cabeza
y dos pies
y no tan sólo guantes
y zapatos y sombrero
y por qué me siento
tan puro
más puro todavía
y más próximo a la muerte
cuando me quito los guantes
el sombrero y los zapatos
como si me quitara las manos
la cabeza y los pies (175)

[I ask myself
if I actually
have hands
if I really possess
a head
and two feet
and not just gloves
and shoes and hat

and why I feel so pure
even purer
and closer to death
when I take off my gloves
hat and shoes
as if I were taking off my hands
my head and my feet]

That gaze extends into Eielson's visual artwork of the 1960s, for instance in the compositions which use clothing, such as shirts and blue jeans. In *Habitación en Roma*, seeing, touching, and kissing are equivalent: their object is the surfaces or wrappings that the body inhabits: among them are cities, and also words. The poems produce a mysterious movement at the edge of things, which is not a play of surfaces inside an already given frame, but a process of discovery—in all senses—in which the primary hermeneutic act of being in what we call world, of framing the real so that there can be world,[23] becomes joyful and sometimes dizzy movement. The mystery is the visibility and invisibility of what surrounds us: landscapes, cities, rooms, gestures, clothing, body.

The way this book works implies an alteration in the topology of reading. Consider how Rilke presents the relationship between reading and surrounding spaces in his poem 'The Reader' from *The Book of Images*:

I have been reading for a long time. Since this afternoon,
with its smell of rain against the window.
I heard nothing of the wind outside:
my book was dense.
I saw it in the leaves, as if in faces
becoming dark with pondering,
and around my reading time was dammed up.[24]

Rilke's image of reading is that of a room, separated from the outside by windows. The outside becomes perceptible through and in the inner world of reading. In Proust's essay *Sur la lecture*, reading is similarly pictured as an interiority:

---

[23] See Ludwig Wittgenstein, *Tractatus logico-philosophicus* (London, 1963), s. 1.
[24] Rainer Maria Rilke, *Das Buch der Bilder* (Leipzig, 1913), 163. The German goes as follows: 'Ich las schon lang. Seit dieser Nachmittag | mit Regen rauschend, an den Fenstern lag. | Vom Winde draussen hörte ich nichts mehr: | mein Buch war schwer. | Ich sah ihm die Blätter wie in Mienen, | die dunkel werden von Nachdenklichkeit, | und um mein Lesen staute sich sie die Zeit.'

my only companions, very respectful of my reading, used to be the painted plates on the wall, the calendar with yesterday's page freshly torn off, the clock's pendulum and the fire, things which speak without requiring an answer.[25]

Or in a later passage, the image of reading melts into that of being alone in one's room in a provincial hotel, which holds a faint perfume of thoughts and memories which fascinate the imagination and give an acute sense of a 'secret life'.[26]

Eielson profoundly alters the way Rilke and Proust had configured the relationship of the inside and outside of reading/writing in the early twentieth century. His poem 'Poema para destruir de inmediato sobre la poesía la infancia y otras metamorfosis' [Poem to be destroyed immediately on poetry childhood and other metamorphosis] takes one through a dissolution of boundaries and doors:

> damas y caballeros
> las ventanas abiertas
> ya no dan al cielo
> como hace tanto tiempo
> ni la pálida luna
> que todos conocimos
> alumbra el corazón
> de los pastores
> una pared muy alta
> de cemento ciertamente
> y una columna de humo
> ocupan el lugar
> que antes ocupaban
> la pálida luna
> leopardina
> y la retama
> los burgueses dicen
> es horrible
> la municipalidad
> no defiende nuestra luna
> nuestro cielo
> nuestras nubes
> pero yo no comprendo
> no comprendo francamente
> cuántas veces

[25] Marcel Proust, *Sur la lecture* (Arles, 1988), 10.   [26] Ibid. 20–1.

me despierto a medianoche
con los bolsillos llenos
de centellas
y es tan grande mi alegría
que se despiertan los vecinos
con un balde de agua fría
considerando un peligro
el mismo cielo encendido
y mi alegría (185–6)

[ladies and gentlemen
windows
no longer open on to the sky
as it used to be so many years ago
nor does the pale moon
we all knew
give light to the heart
of shepherds
a very high wall
of concrete for sure
and a column of smoke
have taken the place
that the pale
Leopardine moon
and broom flowers
used to occupy
the bourgeois say
it is horrible
the council
does not defend our moon
or our sky
our clouds
but I do not understand
frankly I do not understand
how often
I wake up at midnight
with my pockets full
of sparks
and my joy is so great
that the neighbours wake up
with a bucket of cold water
considering the bright sky itself
and my joy
a danger]

The joy of this poem is the break with bourgeois possessiveness, which identifies both self and property in the word private. Taken as a proposition, it repeats one of the main trajectories of the avant-garde: to destroy bourgeois conceptions of art.[27] But this poem is more than a proposition. The visual radiates, its surfaces are capable of becoming windows of a different consciousness, which is what H. D. calls Leonardo da Vinci's paintings,[28] and also part of Eielson's own fascination with Leonardo. His most recent installation is a response to Leonardo's *Last Supper*, about which he writes:

In daily life we consider shadow and light as opposites; our own existence seems oriented towards the light, imbued as we are in the old
rhetoric of good and evil. But in other cultures—in the orient, for
example—the borders of the mind, in the widest meaning of the term,
coincide wonderfully with the double nature of reality, made of
shadows and light. And it is on this borderline that almost escapes our
perception, it is in this spiritual awareness that the mystery of sight is
to be found. [. . .] Leonardo's chiaroscuro [. . .] is the most beautiful
homage that Western genius has made to the ancient Orient.[29]

This statement refers to the work of Eielson the visual artist, yet he does not consider the different areas of his art as separate but as parts of a single concern. The poems of the 1950s play exuber-antly with the appearance and dissolving of frames, worked out in a city-scape, which is a place of memory, invention, and love. They are preparatory to the major series of canvases he under-took in the 1960s. He is, it should be added, important interna-tionally as a visual artist, with work in the Museum of Modern Art in New York, among other major collections.

The movement of these poems is composed of acts of seeing which are physical and tactile as well as affective. They change the space of habitation, by not basing themselves, finally, on any other set of affirmations than themselves: there is nothing 'behind' them. They are capable of carrying us away and returning us to primary and hidden dimensions of things—all

---

[27] *Veinte poemas para ser leídos en el tranvía* (1922), by the Argentinian avant-garde poet Oliverio Girondo, may be taken as an example of that trajectory and its refor-mulation of the space of writing/reading.

[28] See H. D., *Notes on Thought and Vision* (London, 1988), 18: '*The Madonna of the Rocks* is not a picture. It is a window.'

[29] Text published on the occasion of the inauguration of the installation 'The Last Supper 1998' at Fattoria di Celle, Santomato di Pistoia, Italy, June 1998.

that is occulted by wrappings, clothing, and voices of a society spellbound by consumerism. They are poems which cause horizons to drift, and their effects extend into the series of canvases called 'paisaje infinito' [infinite landscape] begun at the start of the 1960s, which includes the series 'Paisaje infinito de la costa del Perú' [Infinite landscape of the Peruvian coast]. In relation to the word *infinite*, Eielson has commented that the idea was to 'llevar adelante este tema al infinito y no sólo como una secuencia de telas, sino como un todo orgánico que involucrara la narrativa, la poesía, las instalaciones, la fotografía y los performances' [to take this theme towards the infinite and not just as a sequence of canvases but as an organic whole which would involve narrative, poetry, installations, photography, and performances].[30]

Among his books of the 1950s, two in particular explore the relationship between words and the visual. These are *Mutatis mutandis* and *De materia verbalis*. They generate an apprehension of what is at the edge of and in between words and things. And that is a question of what surrounds them, which is something lived but not expressed, precisely because expression consigns that surrounding environment to the unspoken and unseen background against which expression becomes perceptible. By returning us to what is between and around words, Eielson's writing proposes a break with inherited literary space.

His visual poetry is part of that break. The physical page and the gaze meet and produce a movement not mediated by the voice. Voicing may be added to the event but it does not define it. To give an example, one of the poems of *Canto visible* consists in the phrase TE AMO [I LOVE YOU] repeated twenty-four times. The page is divided by a horizontal line, with twelve of the phrases below it, printed upside down.[31] Despite the simplicity of the verbal material, the effects are complex, due to the constantly varying effect of spatial location and orientation upon the words. Emotion in the traditional form of an inner scene or voice of the phrase is replaced by the affect of the moving gaze.

[30] Interview published in the Eielson Exhibition Catalogue, Milan, Galleria Silvano Lodi, 1998.

[31] *Poesía escrita* (Lima), 272. *Canto visible* is included in this edition but not in the 1998 (Bogotá) edition of *Poesía escrita*.

Another aspect of the break is the invitation to sense the space that surrounds words as the same space that surrounds things and exists between them. This simple enough proposition runs directly against the predominant training in reading, which is to take text as expression of voice and voice as expression of inner mind. Thus the invitation turns out to be radical in its implications. It is also capable of infinite extension, as what is in between can only be known in the endless experiment of finding out. In a recent text, written in Italian to accompany an exhibition entitled 'La scala infinita' [The infinite stairs/scale] held in Milan in 1998, Eielson writes:

In my personal idea of art, to say is not necessarily to communicate. That is why I have above all had recourse to written poetry—which surrounds the silence of saying, of writing, and of reading itself more closely—and to abstract images, which do not explicitly communicate anything, but something which is there in all language and which for that reason, though in a subdued way, is saying a great deal.[32]

And he adds, 'it is because of all this [. . .] that I have come close to Zen Buddhism and at the same time to the history and philosophy of science'. The way of working proposed has its similarities with the practice of Paul Feyerabend in the philosophy of science and with that of the French philospher Gilles Deleuze, who spoke of the unpredictable relationships between things as the necessary starting place for a way of thinking adequate to our epoch, which he called 'radical empiricism'.[33] The practice delineated by Eielson in 'La scala infinita' also entails the inclusion of non-signifying signs in writing: perception-signs, object-signs, signs which are events.[34] These are increasingly important in his poetry from the late 1950s.

A particular aspect of the range of practices under discussion

---

[32] Jorge Eielson, *La scala infinita* (Milan, 1998), 11.

[33] Feyerabend is the author of *Against Method* (London, 1988). For a sample of his work, see his entry on the 'History of the Philosophy of Science' in *The Oxford Companion to Philosophy* (Oxford, 1995). On 'radical empiricism', see Gilles Deleuze and Félix Guattari, *What is Philosophy* (London, 1994), 47. Deleuze also discusses empiricism in *Dialogues* (London, 1987), 54–9.

[34] For the idea of non-signifying signs in literature, see William Rowe, *Hacia una poética radical: ensayos de hermenéutica cultural* (Rosario, 1996), s. II, ch. 2. Perceptual signs are a term used by Merleau-Ponty. See *Phenomenology of Perception* (London, 1962), introduction and chs. 1–3.

here is summed up in the introit to *De materia verbalis*, a book
which Eielson dates 1957–8:

> La oscuridad de este poema
> Es sólo un reflejo
> De la indecible claridad
> Del universo. *(232)*
>
> *[The darkness of this poem*
> *Is only a reflection*
> *Of the unspeakable clarity*
> *Of the universe.]*

The book therefore becomes a place in which the cosmos is
registered. Art and science are gathered together as necessary
imagination, in fulfilment of Blake's observation that 'if it were
not for the Poetic or Prophetic Character', science and philosophy would soon 'stand still, unable to do other than repeat the
same dull round over again'.[35]

Eielson's attitude to verbal art allows comparison between
the work of the poem and that of a shaman, not as an evolution
of one from the other but in a relationship of total contemporaneity. The shaman's table, which is the earth itself, on which
he places with great care a series of magical objects, is revealed
as a book, a book before writing. And Eielson's writing can be
seen as a revelation of the multiple connections which make up
human existence. In both cases, that of the shaman and the
poet, we have an active and practical multiplying of connections. What would be the opposite case? The extraction and
emission of isolated blocs of information, in the forms of
commodification, propaganda, and the malign use of the electronic image as a form of control.[36] Or using the book as
subject of academic routines and packages of knowledge which
give power to their agent but cut the poem off from the many
worlds it is capable of touching. Because the book touches the
space that surrounds it and whoever takes over the exclusive
function of arbiter of meanings finishes by walling it up, instead
of allowing it to receive and radiate freely.

Eielson speaks of 'el infinito tejido de interconexiones que
nos rodea y del cual formamos parte nosotros mismos' [the

---

[35] William Blake, *Poems and Prophecies* (London, 1972), 3.
[36] See William Burroughs, *Electronic Revolution* (Expanded Media Editions,
n.d.).

infinite weaving of interconnections that surrounds us and of which we ourselves form part], and adds:

entre los años 20 y 30 un grupo de físicos iluminados se encontraron ante una realidad subnuclear tan absurda e imprevisible que no pudo no causar en ellos un terremoto espiritual y un acercamiento a la fe religiosa. Esto confirma que ciertas verdades, incluso las más altas, no se manifiestan en ninguna teoría, sino siempre en la práctica.[37]

[between 1920 and 1930 a group of inspired physicists found themselves faced by a subnuclear reality that was so absurd and unforeseen that it caused a spiritual earthquake in them and brought them close to religious faith. This confirms that certain truths, including the highest ones, are not manifest in any theory but are always revealed in practice.]

The main theme of his recent work as a visual artist has been knots and knottings. He uses the notion of the knot in all its senses, from classical physics to super-string theory. He conceives space as 'un vacío repleto de energía, la del nudo, que a lo mejor comunica algo de la armonía del mundo, justamente porque no pretende comunicar nada' [a void full of energy, that of the knot, which perhaps communicates something of the harmony of the world, precisely because it does not claim to communicate anything at all].[38] In this, though it may appear contradictory to say so, there is an ethics: 'toda nuestra existencia es la historia de una estructura que, para sobrevivir, debe continuamente inventarse una red infinita de información y de respuestas interactivas que alargan su horizonte vital' [all of our existence is the history of a structure which, in order to survive, must continually invent an infinite net of information and of interactive responses which expand its living horizon].[39] The practice of multiplicity becomes, then, a definition of the human as a constant redefinition of itself, and Eielson's writing a privileged site of that.

---

[37] *El diálogo infinito,* 70   [38] Ibid. 37.   [39] *La scala infinita,* 12.

5

Juan L. Ortiz: Verticality from the Margins

Este paisaje es mi alma y será siempre mi alma.
(Juan L. Ortiz)

DOUBTS AND UNCERTAINTIES

The introduction of doubts, vacillations, and uncertainties at the most intense moments of a poem is a prime characteristic of Juan L. Ortiz's writing and it makes the act of reading approximative. Instead of giving definite contours to inner experience, making it distinct from public space, Ortiz's poems move into ecstatic areas which cause such classifications to dissolve and a different sense of time and space to emerge. Let us begin by considering some specific features of their movement.

What is the effect when Ortiz interrupts the syntactic order of language and even the construction of images with expressions like 'si me lo permitieras, diría' [if you allow me, I would say] (872)[1] or 'si se prefiere' [better, perhaps, to say] (873)? It is customary to think that someone who is too tentative is not going anywhere. However, with Ortiz, these expressions of uncertainty do not paralyse, they are approximations to a state of ecstasy: approximations in the sense of movements towards, but without the word 'towards' implying linear movement, since there is no goal to be desired or even conceived in advance. The poetic process questions any sure delineation:

[1] All page references are to *Obra completa* (Santa Fe, 1996).

Y éso que, del imposible
casi, de su secreto, se deshace y se deshace, y por el sueño,
        aún, de una bruma
    de vidrio. . .?
—Los pájaros, en efecto, dan en cernirlo
        por ahí
    pero no dividen
no, la palidez de desmemoria, ésa que enciela,
    y ubicuamente, todavía,
        una ausencia como de lino. . . (872)

[And what of that which, out of the impossible,
almost, out of its secret, dissolves and dissolves, and with the dream,
        even, of a fog
    of glass. . .?
—In fact the birds manage to sift it
        over there
    but they don't divide
the pallidness of unremembering, that which makes
        sky everywhere, still,
    an absence like that of linen. . .

Any appearance of romantic mistiness is banished by the rigorous combination of abstraction with particular textures of space. The abstract becomes tangible: the birds refine but do not divide the space of 'desmemoria' [unremembering], pale like unbleached linen. One imagines their movement: concrete and airy at the same time. Instead of a logical progression, which would mean that what is possible is determined by the initial terms, one space arises after another, altering each other, without contradiction.

There is no content, in the sense of completed image or narrative, yet everything is at stake. To read this writing is to find oneself at the edge of a figure (in the sense of a completed perception) which is postponed, questioned, and kept unresolved. John Keats defined his notion of 'negative capability' as 'when man is capable of being in uncertainties, Mysteries, doubts, without any irritable reaching after fact and reason'.[2] Ortiz's uncertainties are comparable in that they offer an alternative mode of comprehending the world, as consistent as the

---

    [2] John Keats, Letter 32, in *The Letters of John Keats*, ed. M. B. Forman (Oxford, 1960).

conventional one, but more open. Where they have a twentieth-century quality is in their sense of intellect finding itself precisely in the absence of certainty. The main form this takes in Ortiz's poetry is the dissolving of substantiality—though not its replacement with a world of unsubstantial spirits. Unlike some writers who have turned magical realism into a genre, he does not opt for a restoration of the idols which Bacon, at the beginning of modernity, had called on us to abandon. His frequent interrogatives, which cause the poems to be strewn with question marks and which sometimes continue unbroken for several pages or for the length of a whole poem, are the activity of an intellect which operates without imposing conceptual controls. Words move towards the not-known, the not yet thematized.

Another frequent form of punctuation in these poems is the ellipsis (. . .). Ortiz's ellipses are not devices for delaying the completion of a sentence in order to increase the pleasure when it comes. They are ways of causing sentences to dissolve and risk nothingness. They make emptinesses which are not filled, only replaced with other emptinesses when other sentences arise, as things also arise on the incomplete horizon of perception.

Let us look more closely at the workings of Ortiz's sentences. The poem 'Preguntas al cielo' [Questioning the sky/heaven] submits this traditional symbol of transcendence to sustained interrogation. The manner of questioning is not that of Socratic dialogue: it is not an activity in search of its own conceptual ground. Nor is it done in the manner of a catechism or other probe into correctness of belief. The intensity occurs not in those parts of the sentence where logical relationships are affirmed (if A, then B), but in its least heavy parts, where it branches sideways:

> Qué relación la tuya, oh cielo que extasías
> un aura de hojillas
> en nimbo
> de primaveras de éter con el cual, acaso, un elegido
> te quisiera redimir
> del destino de abajo y del destino
> de arriba. . . (863)

> [What is your relation, sky, ecstatic
> with aura of little leaves

```
          in a cloud
   of ether-springs with which, perhaps, a chosen person
          would wish to redeem you
       from the destiny of below and the destiny
          of above. . .]
```

There is no movement towards a goal of any kind, not even a sense of a path, but only an arising of things such as a 'suspiro | hacia no sé qué halo en no sé qué equilibrio' [sigh | towards I don't know what halo in I don't know what equilibrium] (865) or 'una ausencia que fuera, a la vez, un dios en devenir' [an absence which was, at the same time, the becoming of a god] (866), and which includes 'the cat's' eyes, at which point the poet writes 'reíos' [laugh] for those who associate literature with decorum.

All the suspensions and ramifications bring about something like an incessantly extending surface, without frontiers or points of anchorage, a surface which expands so much as to become lighter than air. That surface has the consistency of time, that 'tejido | de la millonésima de segundo que tú mueres al vivirte. . .' [cloth | of the millionth of a second which you die as you live yourself] (870). And with the entry into the micro-spaces of time, 'hasta el minuto | que bajo los párpados se nos iba | en un nada de gris' [into the moment | that beneath our eyelids was lost | in a nothing of greyness] (874), the continuity of personal being ceases, along with the conceptual schemes that shore it up. Instead of concept controlling whatever perception is capable of, something else is allowed to arise: 'el tiempo de todos, sobre todos los relojes, habrá al fin | de acceder en niño | al desplegar y etéreamente consumar la eternidad' [the time of everyone upon all clocks, will finally | accede as a child | to the unfolding and ethereal consummation of eternity] (875).

Paradisal is a word that suggests itself in response to Ortiz's un-making of conventional time, yet even that conception is dissolved by his writing. This happens at the moment when the sky speaks and answers the questions:

```
     yo no tengo nombre, al fin. . .
   y aunque todo está en todo y el envés y el revés
        te rezara para mi
 rostro si él no fuese, por una eternidad, su propia huida,
```

> tu no podrías referir
> las series de una pasión que, ocidentalmente, se ensangrienta
> aún por
> firmarlas,
> desde siglos. . .
> referirlas
> a lo anónimo que deslíe
> las noches y los días,
> con antelación a ellos, si tu me lo permites. . .
> y con antelación, entonces, al paraíso
> de ustedes (868–9)

> [in the end I have no name. . .
> and although everything is in everything and the reverse
> and hidden side
> would speak for my
> face if it were not, for an eternity, its own flowing away,
> you could not recount
> the series of a passion which is occidentally bloodied still by
> signing it,
> from centuries back. . .
> recount them
> to the nameless thing that unties
> nights and days,
> before them, if you allow me. . .
> and, in that case, before your
> paradise]

Here even the formulations of Western mysticism (that everything is inside everything, for example) fall down in the face of
what has no face or name. But to say that of the poem is to put
it back into a language of paradoxes, a language which
expresses 'your paradise' but not Ortiz's method.

Without imposition of will, and with utmost delicacy, he takes
one into a zone of the Word—'lo desconocido' [the unknown],
'ausencia' [absence], 'vacío' [emptiness], 'nada' [nothing],
'abismo' [abyss], etc.—that removes any sense of reliable knowledge. One has to put one's confidence in something else. This is
not a poetry either of certainty or of cynicism, attitudes which are
more soporific and less demanding. Ortiz's method is to enter
into the zone of greatest risk and trust in one's capacity to stay
afloat: instead of salvation through 'una religiosidad de oro' [a
golden religiosity] (863), the question is to take up 'esa vía | cuya
aventura es sólo vía' [that way | whose adventure is only way]

(867). The difficulties are stated in the poem 'El Gualeguay' [The Gualeguay], where history, stripped of transcendent goals, is characterized as apparently endless destruction—'Por qué sólo el horror detendrá, eternamente, el horror?' [Why would only horror, eternally, put an end to horror?] (668)—and the moment of happiness is followed by a 'recaída | en no sabemos qué exilio' [fall back | into we don't know what exile] (874).

The action undertaken requires a maximum of freedom. The suspensions and interrogations of sense are characteristics of a language which does not fear the risks that occur when religious and ideological guarantees are abandoned and responsibilities increase. The ear has to become finer, so as to hear the tiniest movements, touch become lighter, so as to be capable of the most delicate contact, and vision, finally, become more subtle. All of this is worked out in an extremely intimate dialogue with a reader, who is treated, literally, like a friend and invited to take part in a mutual adventure. The tentative approximations articulate that dialogue: they ask a reader to move with them and yet they respect his freedom:

> Está por florecer el Jacarandá. . . amigo. . .
>   Es cierto que está por florecer. . . lo has acaso sentido?
>
> Pero dónde ese por anhelo de morado, dónde, podrías
>   decírmelo? (858)
>
> [The jacaranda is nearly in flower. . . friend. . .
>   It's true it's nearly in flower. . . haven't you felt it?
>
> But where that desire of purple, where, can you
>   tell me?]

The events of perception in these poems occur in a real and specific landscape, which is that of Entre Ríos in the north of Argentina. At the same time the landscape, as perception, enters the poems: the embedding is double. The region where Ortiz lived is characterized by wide rivers with sandy banks and a multitude of islands. The same details can be found in the work of Juan José Saer, such as the novel *Nada, nadie, nunca*.[3]

Ortiz's poem 'Pueblo costero' [Coastal village] may be taken as an example of how he handles the social dimension of that landscape. It begins with images of children:

---

[3] Mexico City, 1980.

Ved ese niño oscuro que mira como desde otro mundo,
el blanco de los ojos más blanco, medio amarillo, mejor.
Oh, la niñita y de anteojos que lo guía o lo alza,
barro leve ella misma sobre palillos aún más leves.
Ved aquella en un carrito, tan frágil,
con esa flor monstruosa de las rodillas casi terminales,
conducida por los suyos, más pequeños, hacia la orilla de qué
        esterella? (451)

[See that dark-skinned boy who seems to gaze from another
        world,
the white of his eyes whiter, or maybe yellowish.
Ah, the little girl already wearing glasses, leading him or
        carrying him,
the lightest clay herself upon even lighter willow-sticks.
See the other girl in a little cart, so fragile,
the monstrous flower of her knees almost terminal,
led by brothers and sisters, smaller than her, to the edge of what
        star?]

The fact that the boy is dark-skinned is not used ideologically to
signal oppression: the poem requires one to look more closely
and to see how in a black-skinned person the white of the eyes
looks yellowish. One has to be near a person to see that: the
poem's gaze is close to the people seen, close enough to be
almost intimate. The 'palillos' refer to the first girl's thin legs:
the word means little sticks but as the trees on the river banks
of the Litoral region are willows, I have used 'willow-sticks' to
translate it. The second girl is a cripple, and the metaphor of
'flower' again moves in close, with a sense of shock, as with this
other one that follows it:

Ved esa cabeza pálida, de diez años, de pescado imposible,
que por poco os fijará desde los mismos oídos. . . (451)

[See, a ten-year-old, with the pale head of an impossible fish
which all but transfixes you through the very ears. . .]

'Pescado', as opposed to 'pez', is a dead fish, out of the water,
and the image has to do with the look of a fish's head when
dead. There is not an ideological project here but rather a
sensibility in action, and a sensation of being wounded. The
poem is a *poiesis*, in the sense of a making that will stand
autonomously, by its own architecture. But it projects another
world than the one conveyed by narratives and icons of the

nation, of that version of modernity which from the 1880s in Argentina became the official one:[4] Ortiz makes visible the invisible of the nation. A main part of that something else is poverty. But Ortiz does not present poverty in a narrative of pity, since there is no place—his poem does not allow any such place—from which pity can be proposed. Nor is there any logic of guilt in the poem, as will be seen in the following account of how some people in the village made it rich:

> Ved esa rama vieja, sobreviviente de 'las canteras',
> doblada sobre otra rama corta que se hinca
> con una cadencia cada vez más seguida:
> sobre ella y sus iguales, anónima ceniza, allá,
> más bien que sobre las piedras,
> se elevaron algunas casas aladas y algunas pilas de billetes. . .
> y con su sangre, ay, tan roja, alquimia 'misteriosa',
> se azularon algunos apellidos que luego dieron chapas por
>   ahí . . . (451)

> [See that old branch that survived 'the quarries',
> bent back over another short branch stuck in the ground
> with a cadence that quickens:
> upon it and others like it, turned to anonymous ash, there,
> and not upon stones,
> a few winged houses sprang up and a few piles of
>   banknotes. . .
> and with their blood, ah, so red, a 'mysterious' alchemy:
> a few names were polished and in time became brass
>   plates. . .]

The fact that a few people made a quick buck and polished their names is told, once again, from close in to the poverty of the others, but without any populist robbery of their voice.[5] The words ' "mysterious" alchemy' are not theirs, though the irony depends upon the way things look to a people who are poor. There is empathy with them, and thus a morality, but not a use of their voice in order to articulate an idea of the popular. The writing mobilizes the full intelligence of poetic invention, which populism and its derivative, *Testimonio*, cannot stomach.

4 See David Viñas, *Indios, ejército y frontera* (Mexico City, 1984), and Nicholas Shumway, *The Invention of Argentina* (Berkeley, 1991).

5 Josefina Ludmer, *El género gauchesco: un tratado sobre la patria* (Buenos Aires, 1988), 3, defines gauchesque literature, which includes *Martín Fierro*, as the use of the gaucho's 'oral register (his voice) by literate culture'.

Let us consider further Ortiz's use of metaphors. After beginning with the children, the poem moves into a 'list' of the inhabitants and their trades (*oficios*). Among them is a fisherman:

> Y este pescador de silencio que llega de una fiebre de silencio,
> y aún demora, nocturno, sobre los nácares grasos y la leña,
> para abrir su sueño, al fin, al primer contacto, igual que un
> irupé. . . (452)

> [And this fisherman, silent, back from a fever of silence
> still loitering, nocturnal, over fatty mother-of-pearl and embers,
> then sleeping, finally, at first contact, like a water-lily bloom . . .]

The mother-of-pearl metaphor takes its sensuous detail from the actual feel of fish-scales when the fresh catch is cooked over a wood fire, the fat released by the cooking making them glint. It is a sumptuous image in the midst of poverty: a flash of forms of beauty inside an everyday action.

Shortly after the appearance of the fisherman, an old washerwoman is presented:

> Y esta 'abuela' toda envuelta que busca todavía los velos de la
> hora
> para destocar su plata y diluirla entre lirios de jabón, en
> cuclillas. . . (452)

> [And this 'granny' wrapped all over still looking for the veils of
> the instant
> so as to bare its silver and dilute it into soap lilies, squatting. . .]

The word 'silver' is used to convey the sense of a fine substance inside moments of time, something other than the mere succession of hours. But the glimpse of a paradisal time is given inside the most ordinary and non-prestigious activity: the 'silver' becomes dissolved in the soap bubbles of the washtub, a transformation which is beautiful but not precious. Ortiz's handling of language involves a key issue in modern poetics: the things that words can be made to do through the power of suggestion—or alchemy or magic, to use the words current in the avant-gardes. And that leads to the question of what to do with the verbal alchemy invented by Rimbaud and others, given that it allowed unlimited metaphorical transformations. Ortiz opts for placing poetic invention inside the local, using local words, actions, and sensations. But his method for including the local is not that of irony, which was developed by T. S. Eliot out of

Jules Laforgue and which became the dominant mode of English poetry, from Auden onwards.

Ortiz also had to confront the question of universality: to use a vocabulary of words with universal acceptance or to adhere to the speech and the perceptions of a particular place, however 'out of the way' it might seem in relation to literature that circulates internationally. But what does 'universal' mean when set out like this? It means, in the first place, the capital city, and the language and literature which has gained acceptance there, which in turn is influenced by the prestige of what is taken to be the best European literature.[6] On the other hand, there is what José María Arguedas calls 'el peligro del regionalismo que contamina la obra y la cerca' [the danger of regionalism which contaminates and closes off the work of literature]:[7] regional expression which calls attention to itself as a value is a ghetto, because it makes difference as such into a value. Arguedas's struggle with these difficulties was more dramatic than Ortiz's, given the particular history of Peru, but the principles are the same. The necessity is to achieve a language which 'deja ver el profundo corazón humano, [. . .] nos tramite la historia de su paso sobre la tierra' [reveals the profound human heart, transmits the history of its passage over the earth], and then 'la universalidad podrá tardar quizá mucho; sin embargo vendrá' [universality may take a long time to come; nevertheless it will come].

The crippled girl's knees, or the glinting fish-scales, or time dissolved in the washerwoman's soap bubbles are images which take us to the revelation of another time, arising out of ordinary time. Time in writing is both image and composition. Ortiz's poem is assembled in ways that bear some similarity with Walt Whitman's poetry: the use of 'lists' of names, objects, and people, the spatial juxtaposition of materials through repetitions of the word 'and', or the repetition of the word 'see' as invitation to look empathetically. But Whitman's materials stretch outwards from his birthplace across the whole of the USA, as in section XVIII of 'Starting from Paumanok':

---

[6] Here I am merely sketching an argument which has been thoroughly set out by Ángel Rama in *Transculturación narrativa en América Latina* (Mexico City, 1982), but which has not been properly worked out in relation to Latin American poetry. In what senses, for example, does Paz opt for the international-universal?

[7] José María Arguedas, *Obra completa* (Lima, 1983), 196.

See, steamers steaming through my poems,
See, in my poem immigrants continually coming and landing,
See, in arriere, the wigwam, the trail, the hunter's hut, the
     flat-boat, the maize-leaf, the claim, the rude fence, and the
     backwoods village,
See, on the one side the Western Sea and on the other the
     Eastern Sea, how they advance and retreat upon my poems as
     upon their own shores

There is a homogeneity of place, brought about by a whole
range of journeys and means of travel, which are modes of
social expansion towards a united territory. And that politics of
space goes with a particular politics of time: stretching behind
the present ('in arriere') but experienced inside it are all the
previous modes of settlement and travel across the land. Time
in Whitman is continuous, unbroken, carried from past into
future by technologies of movement ('the strong and quick
locomotive') and of information ('the many-cylinder'd steam
printing-press'), making the poet a 'uniter of here and hereafter'.[8] Those homogeneities of place and time are synthesized
in section II of 'Starting from Paumanok':

> Victory, union, faith, identity, time,
> The indissoluble compacts, riches, mystery,
> Eternal progress, the kosmos, and the modern reports.

The differences from Ortiz are various. The nation is not a
union, either socially, or politically or technologically. The
provinces are marginalized by a continuing coloniality of power.
Space does not for Ortiz stretch continuously across a national
territory but exists only as particular intensities at particular
moments, and there is nowhere that those particular moments
can be gathered together into a continuity. The crippled girl is
pulled by her younger brothers and sisters in a fragile little cart:
'to the edge of what star?', the poem asks. Instead of Whitman's
expansive movement across the continent and into the future,
Ortiz's poetry moves vertically, from the margins.

One of the best texts for appreciating the character of this
movement is his epic poem 'El Gualeguay'.[9] The title comes

---

[8]   The latter quotation is from 'Out of the Cradle Endlessly Rocking'.
[9]   A small part of 'El Gualeguay' was published in translation (by William
Rowe) in *Poetry Review*, 67/1 (1977), 13–14.

from the name of a local river, and the poem is full of the names of local places, flora, and fauna, many of them regional and many of these derived from native languages such as Guaraní, like the word 'irupé', for water-lily, quoted earlier. What Tamara Kamenszain says of his work as a whole is particularly true of 'El Gualeguay': a 'verdadero tratado de botánico, zoología, hidrografía' [a real botanical, zoological, and hydrographical treatise].[10] This poem, which is one of the least known and yet one of the greatest Latin American epics, is a lyrical narrative, to use Saer's term,[11] which combines history, geography, and politics with ontology in the space of 110 pages.

The river itself defines the inner movement of being, entering, like pre-Socratic philosophy, a zone where animism and physics are not separate:

Sí, era también todo el don, todo. . .
en el oro y en la plata de su seno
con todos los estremecimientos del amanecer y del véspero
y una ternura pálida. . .
Pero por qué la vida o lo que se llamaba la vida, siempre
    tragándose a sí
misma para ser o subsistir,
en la unidad de un monstruo que no parecía tener ojos
sino para los 'finales equilibrios'?
Por qué todo, todo para un altar terrible,
o en la terrible jerarquía de una deidad toda de dientes? (667)

[Yes, he was also the whole gift, the totality. . .
in the gold and in the silver of his chest
with all the trembling of dawn and evening
and pale tenderness. . .
But why life or what was called life,
always swallowing itself to be or subsist,
in the unity of a monster that did not seem to have eyes
except for some 'final equilibrium'?
Why everything, everything for a terrible altar,
or in the ghastly hierarchy of a god entirely of teeth?]

[10] Tamara Kamenszain, *El texto silencioso: tradición y vanguardia en la poesía sudamericana* (Mexico City, 1983), 33.
[11] Juan José Saer, 'Juan', in Ortiz, *Obra completa*, 11. There are many other, shorter, poems by Ortiz which would fall under this heading, such as 'La casa de los pájaros' and 'El doctor Larcho'.

These reflections on being are preparatory to Ortiz's treatment
of history: 'Por qué sólo el horror dentría, eternamente, el
horror?' [Why would only horror, eternally, put an end to
horror?] (*A20*). Before history, there is the coming of the first
human beings:

> Eran esas las criaturas que secretamente esperaba
> para abrir las 'leyes' del sacrificio?

> Sí, eran una sola cosa con los follajes, y las ramas, y las hierbas,
> y lo que latía debajo de las hierbas. . . (669)

> [Were these the creatures he was secretly waiting for
> to open the 'laws' of sacrifice?

> Yes, they were a single thing with the foliage, branches, grasses,
> and what pulsated under the grasses. . .]

Previous to this there have been several pages of names of trees,
birds, and fauna. The birds are introduced as follows:

> Pero el cielo ya goteara, arriba,
> con los envíos del norte o con los envíos de las islas
> los llamados más puros
> de la herida de septiembre:
> cuándo el zorzal y la calandria,
> y el jilguero y el cardenal,
> se hallaran por primera vez, ahí, en una sangre invisible? (663)

> [But was the sky dripping, above, already,
> with the sendings of the north or the sendings of the islands
> the purest calls
> of September's wound:
> when the thrush and the lark,
> the goldfinch and the cardinal,
> first found themselves, there, in an invisible blood?]

The delicate, questioning approximations make the substances
extremely fine, as the ear enters into the smallest intervals: this
is the lyrical verticality.

Then the native groups enter the poem, with the particular
sounds of their speech, still audible in surviving words:
' "Yaguarí", primero, en el espanto del jaguar' ['Yaguarí', first,
in the terror of the jaguar] (669). Then, with the Spanish
Conquest, another language enters: Spanish, and behind it
Latin, and in them the ideology of colonialism: 'y los hombres
oscuros sólo debían 'sostener', pues, 'el amor', I bajo el rocío

de los latines?' [and did the dark-skinned men only have to
'bear', therefore, 'love', I beneath the dew of Latin?] (673).
Then the *encomenderos* are named, who, as we know—the poem
does not need to say it—used their right to Indian labour in
exchange for evangelization, as a right to enslave. That wound
raises a question about time and memory:

> Y dónde, la herida, dónde, si él era irreversible?
> Pero si él era, al mismo tiempo, otro sentimiento del aire,
> y en el aire nada se perdía? (674)

> [And where, the wound, where, if he also was irreversible?
> But if he was, at the same time, another sensibility of the air,
> and in the air nothing was lost?]

The 'he' is the river, constant interlocutor of the poem, and
once again another, vertical time intervenes.[12] Note the word
'other' in Ortiz's lament for the victims of the *encomenderos*:

> Ay, las cenizas únicas de los Caxas y Mepenes,
> bajo las hierbas de 'arriba'
> o en esos gemidos, de qué aves? sobre las lunas del Guayquiraró.
> Ay, las cenizas únicas de los mismos hijos de Charrúas y
>   Minuanes,
> perdidas bajo los musgos y los helechos
> o en esas luces, de qué llantos? sobre unos dobladillos de la
>   noche
> que se hundían en otras lágrimas . . . (678)

> [Ay, the unique ashes of the Caxas and the Mepenes,
> under the grasses of 'above'
> or in those groans, of what birds? above the moons of the
>   Guayquiraró
> Ay, the unique ashes of the sons of Charrúas and Minuanes,
> lost beneath mosses and ferns
> or in those lights, of what weeping? upon hems of the night
> folded into other tears. . .]

All through the poem, which moves into modern times, with
precise dates and places of events of local history, the sense of
another dimension periodically interrupts and calls to another
way of hearing and feeling.

---

[12] There is a similarity with Juan José Saer's handling of the question of
memory and the disappeared in his novel *Nadie, nada, nunca*. English translation:
Nobody nothing never (London, 1993).

SOUNDS AND VOICES

The voice is one of the most subtle factors in Ortiz's poems. Perhaps it is the most important of all, if one takes voice in its widest sense, as breath and accent, and therefore the mode in which being becomes sound and vice versa. That definition would also imply intonation, given that accent, which is the component of song audible in the speech of anyone, is the material of which intonation is made. Intonation, in turn, links what is said with the boundaries that shape the social environment. It also transmits emotion. But all this can only be prefatory to the question: where does the voice in Ortiz's poems come from? And that, in the end, might be a question without an answer, as one can only actually talk about the qualities of the voice, how it acts and how that action affects the environment—an environment which obviously includes the listener and the language he is immersed in. The starting-point would then be the fact that the language one finds in Ortiz's poetry is composed of the spoken language of his region, with the addition of other terms, sometimes unusual and/or erudite: he is no populist. The spoken language gives the intonation, the sense of active engagement with other speakers and listeners, while the other sources of his diction allow the possibility of exploring spiritual and intellectual concerns.

I have for convenience used the word voice in the singular. In fact there is always a plurality of voices in Ortiz's poems, heard either directly or indirectly: the highly characteristic voice is actually a multiplicity. To begin to read one of the poems is to enter into a dialogue in more than one sense: there is a voice which speaks to itself (which folds over on to itself) and a speaker who speaks to other speakers, and both of these processes involve an interplay between speaking and listening. The result, if we follow the drift of the metaphors used by Ortiz himself, is a process of weaving. But where does the weaving occur, in what time or space? If one can speak of a voice which folds over on to itself, where does that folding happen?

A large proportion of the poems in the book *La orilla que se abisma* [The bank, the abyss] which first appeared inside the 1970 edition of the collected works (*En el aura del saúce* [In the aura of willow]), carry titles which imply one or more interlocutors, such as 'Sabéis, amigos' [You know, friends] or 'Me dijiste' [You said to me]. In the latter poem, the dialogue begins as a response to a sound:

> —Escucha, es un latido,
>   solamente un latido, o qué? de la ranita, no? (809)
> Listen, that beat,
>   it's only the sound—or what?—of a frog, isn't it?

The sound of a frog croaking—though that is an approximation—is a non-human sound, heard at the edge of awareness. Ortiz avoids personifying it, which would be to give it a meaning by making it express something already thought. Instead, it is an event, accompanied by questions, doubts, uncertainties:

> En el pulso de las hierbezuelas
>   o de la lunilla,
>   él?. . .
>
>   o dónde, o dónde,
>   si la circulación del silencio, melodiosamente, nos anega, sí,
>   también a nosotros. . .
>   y no tenemos, de pronto, orillas . . . (809)
>
> [In the pulsing of small grasses
>   or the moon
>   . . .?
>
>   Or where, where,
>   if the circulation of silence
>   drowns us also in melody. . .
>   and suddenly we are without limits. . .]

The questions themselves are events through which the dialogue moves and changes direction. They are not the acts of a will to prove something but tenuous penetrations into something unknown, something which any imposition of will would simply destroy. There is nothing in them of the police station or court of law or parliament—or even the classroom—as there is no fixed list of possible answers, from which the listener has to select.

What is unusual in the questions is the tone, the lightness and delicacy of voicing. If one looks for an equivalent in English poetry, one would have to start by finding a similar freshness and sweetness of diction, capable of moving between sensations and ideas without difficulty. There is plenty of that in the work say of Spenser and Sidney, but not the teasing out of the smallest, lightest movements of sound. From a different angle, the attitude of enquiry into the emotions that rhythms carry can be found in Gerard Manley Hopkins, but not the lightness of touch. What gives the tone of the questions is the sensing of the lightest sounds, making them a particular act of attention—to that edge of awareness where things both appear and disappear.

Ortiz's use of questions is compositional: they distend the making of the poem by suspending any conclusion: they attenuate tension without resolving it. The result is an extensive plateau rather than a pattern of climax and catharsis. And this is achieved through radically non-repetitive structures of rhythm and sound. That particular use of distension as a compositional device can be compared with Mallarmé's experimental poem *Un coup de dés*, where the main sentence is stretched out over a number of pages. Typographically, Mallarmé abandons the idea of the verse as a return of eye and ear to left margin (etymologically, verse is that) and instead distributes shorter or longer groupings of words over the whole space of the page. These techniques (parataxis and typographical plasticity) are crucial to twentieth-century poetry. What is particular to Ortiz's use of them, and makes his poetry comparable to Mallarmé's experiments, is the extent to which he suspends continuities of syntax, image, and idea. Here another comparison suggests itself: with D. H. Lawrence's proposal for a 'poetry of the present',[13] which would consist in a 'nakedly passing radiance', without orientation towards a past or a future. For Lawrence, this meant using a line with variable length and variable cadence. In that way, the sense of the actual could expand in whatever direction it needed, without being bound to an orientation forwards or backwards in time. Ortiz adds something else: the interstice. He suspends indefinitely any arrival at a goal—fixed object, fixed meaning—and instead discovers interstices in the world, and these interstices, in turn, are opened by other interstices. And there is no way they can be contained inside any conception, since they are themselves the condition of any thinking or feeling. So the poem uses no grid

[13] D. H. Lawrence, 'Poetry of the Present', in *The Complete Poems* (Harmondsworth, 1977), 184.

or frame of time and space other than the one it traces by its own action:

> Y no sería, en su nivel, esta cañita que, líquidamente, vocaliza
>   las acentuaciones sin fondo,
>   una emisión en que suspira, entre las briznas,
>   el himeneo, ése,
>   el mismo
>   del espacio y el tiempo,
>   aunque en una dimensión que únicamente, únicamente,
>   canta
>   en el pasaje del ser? (812)

> [And wouldn't it be, in its particular mode, this small reed that
>   voices, liquidly,
>   accents without bottom
>   an emission in which, between blades of grass,
>   hymen breathes, this one,
>   the one
>   of space and time,
>   though in a dimension that sings
>   only, only
>   in the passage of being?]

The continuing enquiry into sound, as well as breaking up 'continuity itself' ['trizar [. . .] | la continuidad misma'], also takes us—more subtly than the rather wilful word 'enquiry' tends to suggest—towards the zone of ecstasy, which demands a surrender of will:

> no podemos menos de mirarnos al trizar, aún, con los filos, ya,
>   del hálito,
>   la continuidad misma,
>   y responder, lívidamente, a los dioses. . . (811)

> [we can only look at ourselves as we shatter continuity itself
>   with each filament of breath
>   and respond, bruised, to the gods. . .]

That first sound, made by a frog—though in the poem this is never a statement, only a question—unleashes threads of sound, which are felt, sensed, spoken, wrapped in a dialogue of voices, and thence woven together. And the voices are bathed in the environment of sounds which in turn become music as word, word as music: the terms are 'acento' [accent], 'acentuación' [accentuation], 'tonillo' [tune], 'modo' [mode], 'notas' [notes], 'cadencia' [cadence], 'tintineo' [tinkling], 'escala' [scale], etc. So one can hear the poem as a becoming music of the environment ('los armónicos de este mar' [this sea's harmonics]) but at the same time as an extremely subtle act of listening, refined by doubt:

> En qué escala, pues, el oído
> para la campanilla de ese sentimiento que se olvida a menudo
>   de sí
>   en una suerte de eternidad
>   que duda? (809)

> [So in what scale the ear
> to hear the small bell
>   of feelings often lost
>   to memory
>   in a kind of eternity
>   of doubt?]

This listening breaks down any frontier between inner self and outer world since the voices heard do not emanate from anything that could be called person or character. Voice and hearing occur simultaneously: hearing the voice is equivalent to giving voice to hearing. And in both there is a breathing, which is also aspiration, that permeates body and surroundings.

The condition has similarities with pantheism. But the work of the poem is concerned more with where sound occurs. And that is a question that has in the end to do with Ortiz's conception of the book as place of inscription. There are various images of the place where sounds happen: 'sobre los tejidos de octubre' [upon the woven threads of October] (809); 'sobre la sabanilla sin fin | que espuma para las celebraciones, | el "navío de Isis"' [upon the endless fabric of foam made, for these celebrations, | by 'Isis's boat'] (810). Upon the same surfaces the visible world is revealed also: 'la noche, por encima de esas fibras, pálidamente se vacía | más allá de su límite . . .' [the night, above those fibres, palely empties itself | beyond its limit] (810).The space where sound and image are registered—the space of the book—is not given in advance, either by tradition or by modernization: 'qué imposible, por otra parte, el de una vida que debemos remitir | a un laberinto de espejos | por sobre tapices de mataderos, y ésos, desde luego, | de la evasión | en una dicha de gasolina. . .' [how impossible, too, a life deferred | to a labyrinth of mirrors | upon abattoir clothes, | evasion—of course—inside a gasoline happiness] (811). If the abattoir signals the rural bases of Argentinian society (as it does in Echeverría's nineteenth-century text *El matadero*), gasoline enters as index of the twentieth century. But the territory of the poem cannot be made in those terms; it has to be invented over an abyss: 'canta también, y a su modo, lo terrible de jugar al azar | de una chispa sobre los abismos. . .' [something else is singing, in its particular way, | the terrible play of chance, | of a spark over abysses] (812). If these phrases recall Mallarmé's language, there is also something else in Ortiz's poems: a late twentieth-century sense that sensations and symbols have become separated:

> Canta
> y no confía su tonillo, no, a las afinaciones de los ángeles,
>   ni menos al ajuste
>   de los hilos que alguien trama
>   debajo, no:
>   le llega de su relación con la corriente sin sonido
>   de la raíz de los números (812)
>
> [It sings
> and does not entrust its tone, no, to the tuning of angels,
>   still less to the adjustment
>   of strings that someone weaves
>   below, no:
>   it comes from the silent current
>   that floods the root of numbers]

The sound, which has here become a voice that sings, cannot be heard in its peculiar and specific tone unless one leaves behind both the ideal symbols of the angelic realm and the approximations of human music. Leaves them behind for what? Ortiz takes us to the emergence of number as such, before language, music, or even sound: his work is that radical.

In a sense, the action is like an initiation, an action of rebirth as in the Greek Eleusinian mysteries, or shamanic rituals. But all divinities, or what Ortiz calls 'las "superioridades" del éter' ['higher powers' of the ether], are suspended by being placed in inverted commas: 'sílfides', 'devas', 'el navío de Isis' [sylphs, divas, Isis's boat], to mention a few. One passes through the gods, in a return through beginnings, in order to bathe oneself in them again and emerge. The gods in Ortiz do not turn upon themselves, as in religion, but dissolve into a more radical action of enquiry, which permits one to emerge into late modernity. For that, a supremely free movement of breath, voice, and thus of words on the page is needed.

But it is not an abstract freedom, as would be the idea of a freedom from all limits. Ortiz's poems enter particular relationships of place and particular moments of time and create their woven dialogue out of those particulars. Yet at the same time their phrases, freed from the hierarchies of syntactic or logical subordination, sing each in their manner. That freedom would be impossible without the techniques of French Symbolism. But Ortiz goes on to do something else, entirely his own. Consider these two lines from Valéry's *Le Cimetière marin*:

> Quel pur travail de fins éclairs consume
> Maint diamant d'imperceptible écume[14]

The ungraspable foam becomes diamond, the ever-moving Heraclitan fire held inside that hard fixity, the latter held in place by regularities of rhyme and metre. What makes the comparison interesting is that Ortiz's diction is similar. The difference is in the relationship between free movement or flow and figuration. Ortiz's questioning of sound, intonation, and image is unending. The result is a major invention of poetic form, major in the sense that it alters one's relationship with language.

To reach that point required a process of learning:

> —Aunque de los 'aprendices', es verdad, el movimiento salta
> 　　a la 'vía de la leche' [. . .]
> 　　y abre una manera de ofrenda, al fosforecer el camino. . .
> 　　　un apuro, acaso, de trepadoras
> en emulación con las otras, por florecer, también, el vértigo?
> 　　　　O el desplegamiento,
> luego de la concentración, ésta, que hace todavía, todavía
> 　　　nuestra 'verdad' o nuestra facilidad,
> en el deshora de los junios que no terminan de mirarse,
> 　　　curvados sobre el ombligo,
> o en este Octubre que quisiera sellar, hasta 'a la letra', así,
> 　　　　'trasnochadamente'

---

[14] The rest of the verse is as follows: 'Et quelle paix semble se concevoir! | Quand sur l'abîme un soleil se repose, | Ouvrages purs d'une éternelle cause, | Le Temps scintille et le Songe est savoir.'

los labios de la vigilia en abandono de espaldas,
        en gracia, sólo a unas sílabas? (811)

[Although an 'apprentice', it's true, leaps
        into the 'milky way' [. . .]
    and initiates a kind of offering, a luminous path . . .
        the haste, possibly, of climbers
who emulate others, to make vertigo flower too?
            Or the unfolding,
after concentration, which still, still is the thing that makes
        our 'truth' or our capability,
in the non-time of June which does not stop gazing at itself
        bent over the navel
or in this October with desire to seal, 'literally' even, in this way,
        'awake the whole night',
    the lips of vigil when defence is abandoned
        in the grace alone of certain syllables?]

The apprenticeship suggested follows the pattern of Ortiz's
books: in the earlier ones a more symbolic use of angelic figures
together with a more concrete presentation of the landscape.
His earliest published book, *El agua y la noche*, was written
between 1924 and 1932. It is not until 1957, when he began to
write *El junco y la corriente* [The reed and the current], that the
characteristic language of his later and finest work emerges,
with its question marks, ellipses, quotation marks, and the
phrasing extended irregularly across the whole page. The
movement of the later poems is both more abstract and more
attuned to micro-perception in the sense that the words themselves yield to the gaps and uncertainties that emerge as one
moves closer in to the real. These poems are thus both more
abstract and more physical, an effect which includes the physicality of the words. 'Fosforecer' [phosphoresce], 'trepadoras'
[climbing plants], 'florecer' [flower], 'vértigo' [vertigo] can be
read in a metaphoric key, but what would happen if one took
them at the same level as 'el desplegamiento' [unfolding] and
'la concentración' [concentration], that is to say 'literally', as
Ortiz puts it? If, as Ortiz suggests, concentration and unfolding
are always there, since they are part of 'our "truth" ', then they
are palpable abstractions that permeate everything. And it will
follow that words which suggest tangible objects are equally
part of that underlying process of gathering together and
unfolding, of tension and distension.

The technique is radically different from the common tendency in poetry of the 1950s to present a series of metaphors as a type of story by highlighting their figurative aspect. Octavio Paz's *La estación violenta* [The violent season] and Juan Sánchez Peláez's *Elena y los elementos* [Helen and the elements] would be two well-known examples. Take these lines from Paz's 'Himno entre ruinas' [Hymn among the ruins]:

> ¡oh mediodía, espiga henchida de minutos,
> copa de eternidad![15]

> [Midday, ear of wheat swollen with minutes,
> cup of eternity!]

The two metaphors (ear of wheat and cup) propose themes for development rather than holding one's attention to physical senses of time. Similarly, in contrast once again with Valéry, for whom foam becomes 'diamond', Ortiz does not filter the physicality of things. What is extraordinary is the immersion— brought about by his poems—in the world of phenomena, without selection, without filtering 'the seethe of phenomena', as D. H. Lawrence calls it,[16] into themes to be developed.

Consider again a few of the lines quoted earlier:

> O el desplegamiento,
> luego de la concentración, ésta, que hace todavía, todavía
> nuestra 'verdad' o nuestra facilidad,
> en el deshora de los junios que no terminan de mirarse

> [Or the unfolding,
> after concentration, which still, still is the thing that makes
> our 'truth' or our capability,
> in the non-time of June which does not stop gazing at itself]

That 'todavía, todavía' pulls one into time not as a theme accomplished but as unceasing interstices. To go again through that beginning is the awareness that we never finish looking. The apprenticeship, then, is to learn the difference between a haste for transcendent, phosphorescent images and a willingness to enter perception which is never finished: on the one hand the dazzling results of sacrifice ('ofrenda') and on the other writing which chooses to stay unresolved, and by its own

---

[15] *Libertad bajo palabra* (Mexico City, 1968), 213.
[16] 'The Man Who Died', in *Love among the Haystacks* (Harmondsworth, 1960), 144.

movement alone takes us into a state of grace. Thus the choice is for a writing which, through the letter and the syllable and by no other power, becomes a graphy of the spirit—to listen to the becoming of a sound in which is inscribed all our capability.

Reimmersion in beginnings is a main concern of Henry Miller's in *The Colossus of Maroussi*, a book that is also deeply opposed to sacrifice in all its manifestations. For Miller the emergence of the voice is seminal to human capabilities:

What an astounding thing is the voice! By what miracle is the hot magma of the earth transformed into that which we call speech? If out of clay such an abstract medium as words can be shaped, what is to hinder us from leaving our bodies at will and taking up our abode on other planets or between the planets? [. . .] Who or what is powerful enough to eradicate this miraculous leaven which we bear within us like a seed and which, after we have embraced in our mind all the universe, is nothing more than a seed—since to say universe is as easy as to say seed, and we have yet to say greater things.[17]

In Ortiz, similarly, a voice arises, out of the earth, but it is accompanied by doubt, by 'una suerte de eternidad I que duda' [a kind of eternity I of doubt]. The voice of doubt and uncertainty turns towards the first voice and opens up interstices in it, but out of that 'wound' comes sweetness:

> Ah, pero esa eternidad, sin explicárnoslo, la hiere,
>   mas de la herida
>   sangra, un sí no es, de dulzura
> que titila, anónimamente, o que apenas se deja adivinar,
>   sobre los tejidos
>   de Octubre. . . (809)

> [Ah, but that eternity wounds, without explanation,
>   yet from the wound
>   bleeds a thing of sweetness[18]
> that trembles, without name, or can barely be guessed at
>   in the woven threads
>   of October. . .]

The movement is deeply contrary to religious faith, where doubt is a threat to belief-structures. Grace comes, for Ortiz, in abandoning certainties.

---

[17] Henry Miller, *The Colossus of Maroussi* (Harmondsworth, 1963), 77.
[18] Literally, 'un sí no es' means 'not a yes'.

If Lawrence's proposal for a poetry of the present requires the avoidance of regular metrical forms—those which produce the smoothness of continuity—in Ortiz's poetry there is in particular an endless emerging which cannot be consumed by any scheme that feeds on it or fixed by any transcendence that requires sacrifice. The only scheme is the book, the book of a whole lifetime.

6

Ana Enriqueta Terán: In the Midst of Things

I am a tree planted by the rivers of water.
(H.D.)

Ana Enriqueta Terán often compares herself with a tree, not with any allegorical intention, but as a way of exploring the physicality of standing in the world. The weight, spread, and growth of a tree are forms in which to discover the forms of her imagination. Crucial among these is the rising of sap as unceasing process:

> Oh! savias transitorias,
> alondras ascendentes del nocturno
> fuego de las memorias (69)[1]
>
> [Oh transitory saps,
> larks rising from the night
> fire of memories]

Sap rises into visible shapes from the darkness of memory. If memory is a place of fire, then, equally, oblivion is part of the process:

> ¿estuvo el fuego
> en la raíz profunda del olvido? (75)
>
> [was there fire
> in the deep root of memory?]

That way lies freedom, not in the repetition of the past or celebration of inheritance, and solitude is a necessary part of the condition of creativity:

---

[1] Textual references are to Ana Enriqueta Terán, *Casa de hablas* (Caracas, 1991).

Libertada me entrego
al clamor presentido
que a tanta soledad fue concedido. (75)

[Freed I yield
to the voices I sense
a gift to so much solitude.]

But that decision does not, for Terán, mean freedom from
limits; she does not choose to occlude pain and death:

O estuvo la ceniza
desde entonces en llena curvatura
de labio, o la sonrisa
entre savias madura
reclamó para sí la faz obscura? (75–6)

[Or were ashes
thence in the full curve
of a lip, or did the smile
that grew in sap
reclaim its dark face?]

Sap rises eventually of course to flower and fruit, but these
are not taken as the end of the process. When forms come into
existence this is part of what Terán calls a changing story or
history:

A través de mi llanto
pude mirar tu flor invulnerable
y mis ojos levanto
en pos de la mudable
historia de tu linfa perdurable. (72)

[Through my tears
I could see your invulnerable flower
and I raise my eyes
seeking the changeable
history of your everlasting lymph.]

The rhyme *mudable/perdurable* gives fixity and change as terms
that occur inside each other and define the action of imagination. What flows inside the tree also does so inside the body
(*linfa* can apply to blood as well), giving an image not of disembodied thought but of what grows inside self and world. Terán's
tree is not the logos but, like Parra's amoeba, in the midst of
things, assimilating. The tree as connection with the world was
given to her at birth, as she tells in a taped interview:

Yo nazco en una hacienda de caña en una noche de tempestad, oía decir. Mi gente no era una gente común: se sembraba un árbol cuando nacía un niño, y el mío fue un samán [. . .] Y también había la creencia de que si el árbol crecía robusto, el niño crecía robusto y que si se moría el árbol, el niño disminuía también.[2]

[I was born in a sugar hacienda on a stormy night, that's what I was told. My people were not ordinary people: they used to plant a tree when a child was born, and mine was a saman.[3] There was also the belief that if the tree grew strong, so did the child and if the tree started to die, the child would lose strength also.]

The sugar cane becomes, in the poem, cane-syrup, and supplies one of the images of what flows through the tree/body, simultaneously contained and overflowing:

> Por el llanto y el fuego
> supe de tu melaza conmovida
> y tiernamente llego
> a tu desconocida
> vertiente derramada y contenida. (72)

> [Through tears and fire
> I knew your syrup had been moved
> and tenderly I come
> to your unknown
> flow contained and overflowing.]

The aura of ritual carried by the tree comes across strongly in an anecdote she told on the same occasion:

Yo tenía con mi samán una comunicación muy extraña. Yo recuerdo que me quejaba si yo creía que habían cometido una injusticia conmigo. Una vez perdí la identidad: estaba sentada a los pies del samán y perdí la identidad y salí corriendo desesperada y le pregunté a yaya: 'yaya, ¿quién soy yo?' Ahí fue cuando ella me dijo, pues usté es la hija—tan inteligente—me dijo, 'usté es la hija de Don Manuel María Terán y de doña Rosa Madrid de Terán, y usté se llama Ana Enriqueta.' Y volví de esa sensación tan espantosa.[4]

---

[2] Unpublished transcription of interview by Yolanda Salas, May 1991, 11. I am very grateful to Yolanda Salas for making this material available to me.

[3] The botanical name is *Calliandra saman*.

[4] Salas, interview, 11. I am very grateful to Marcel Smith and to Ana Enriqueta Terán's daughter for corrections to the transcription and translation of this interview.

[I had a very strange relationship with my saman. I remember that I
used to complain if I thought anyone had been unfair to me. There
was an occasion when I lost my identity: I was sitting at the foot of the
saman and I lost my identity and I ran desperately and asked yaya:
'aunty, who am I?' That's when she said to me, 'well you are the
daughter', she said—she was so intelligent—'you're the daughter of
Don Manuel María Terán and of doña Rosa María de Terán, and you
are called Ana Enriqueta.' And I came back from that terrible sensation.]

The story implies a set of hidden links, between receiving
injustice from the world, losing her identity, and finding an
alternative place in the world through the tree. The only way
to be brought back is to be given one's name, to become a
person in the world of speaking and naming. But that is an act
of others not of the poet, not poetry but biography. In a much
later poem, 'El nombre' [The name], Terán speaks of 'la
aceptación del nombre. I No la firma, sino el nombre
completo en los calveros de poema' [the acceptance of the
name. I Not the signature, but the complete name in the clear
spaces of the poem] (205). *Calveros* means clearings in the
midst of vegetation, spaces made by writing but not by one's
signature, which is different because it functions as an autho-
rization within the realm of already-given social identities.
The poem involves a self-making, not in a vacuum but within
an environment which in Terán's later books becomes more
and more actual, specific places with specific histories, located
between the Andes and the coast in north-western Venezuela.
The twenty-page poem entitled 'Verdor secreto' [Secret
greenness], which is the one I have been quoting, occupies a
middle place: not only between the world of vegetable existence and the world of speech but also between her earlier
and later poems. *Verdor secreto* was published as a book in 1949
and her next book was not published until 1970. What it shares
with the earlier poems is the play of light and darkness as a
relationship between inner and outer worlds where the working of creative energy occurs. Where it points to the later work
is the way it moves towards a sense of inner and outer worlds
as one, without division. I will come back later to how that
integration is achieved. Before that, let us consider how, in
Terán's earlier books, the poem is made into a place of
creative action.

POSSESSION AND DISPOSSESSION, LIGHT AND DARKNESS

The relationship between light and darkness, in Terán's earlier poems, is crucial to renewing creative energy as opposed to allowing it to be wasted and exhausted. Thus she writes, in the opening poem of her first book,

> para vivir como he vivido
> no basta la pasión, no basta el fiero
> amor que mi esperanza ha consumido. (33)

> [to live as I have lived
> passion is not enough, the fierce love
> that has consumed my hope is not enough.]

In poem XX of the same sequence, which carries the title 'Sonetos del amor perenne y del amor fugitivo' [Sonnets of perennial love and passing love], the danger of loss and being lost is amplified in metaphors of a boat lost at sea or a bitter cup or a flower destroyed:

> Bajel perdido en mares de dulzura
> y en mi pasión de toda luz dejada;
> cáliz de pesadumbre deshojada,
> penumbra que me llena de amargura. (44)

> [Small boat lost in seas of sweetness
> and in my passion abandoned by all light;
> cup of heavy grief stripped of petals,
> shadow that fills me with bitterness.]

Light and darkness ('luz' | 'penumbra') enter to make mere sweetness not enough. If there is only endless sweetness, then the possibility contemplated at the beginning of Shakespeare's *Twelfth Night* can occur: 'If music be the food of love, play on; | Give me excess of it, that, surfeiting, | The appetite may sicken, and so die.'[5] Something more is needed, which could be called intelligence or spiritual discipline, except that the first, nowadays, has come to mean abstraction as power and the second religion. Though love is 'the seed of the writing',[6] light and shadow enter as knowledge of something else.

---

[5] I. i. 1–2.
[6] As Louis Zukovsky says of Shakespeare (*Bottom: On Shakespeare* (Berkeley, 1987), 19).

For Terán, as a woman, for whom the problem is more acute, a major part of the difficulty has to do with the necessity for *entrega* [yielding] in love and the equal and often opposite necessity to protect one's own energies and gifts. Sonnet no. VI envisions loss occurring when the heart is carried away:

> Por donde vas, el aire va vencido
> y vencido mi llanto y prisionero
> mi corazón, tan fiel y tan lucero
> que de sus dones fue desposeído. (36)

> [Wherever you go, the air is defeated
> and my grief defeated and my heart,
> so faithful and shining bright, a prisoner
> dispossessed of its gifts.]

'Lucero', as bright star or lustre, gives what can be lost by falling in love. Light and darkness are not taken by Terán as fixed opposites but as interfused in complex fashion. Light can arise inside the zone of darkness ('aquella lumbre [. . .] en mi propia sangre relucía' [that light shone in my own blood]; 33) and darkness inside the region of light ('ciego pensamiento' [blind thought]; 34). Thus light and darkness, in their play, are terms through which experience can be transformed into knowledge. Knowledge is not to be confused with that 'vana ciencia' which merely seeks to dominate and kills joy (Sonnet IV), nor is it simply to be identified, in some symbolic fixity, with light. Sonnet III speaks of a 'saber oscuro' [dark knowledge] whose nature is that of a tree:

> Hoy te recuerdo puro y acerado,
> ardido en tus ocultas agonías,
> laurel de llanto, dulce te me hacías
> por tu saber oscuro y arbolado. (34)

> [Today I remember you pure and steeled,
> burnt in your hidden agonies,
> laurel of tears, sweet you became for me
> in your dark wooded knowledge.]

There is here a subtle shift, not marked grammatically, from an image of the lover towards a form of the imagination, from what one loves to the shape of one's imagination, which is a contrary movement to being dispossessed of one's capabilities. Yet in the same poem, because the lover cannot trust in 'alegría', the woman's passion falls on dead ground. I say 'woman's', because like many of the sonnets, this one marks the ground of love with signs of femaleness and maleness, as socially made, so that melancholy, for example, emerges as a male mode, in a line that echoes Neruda's famous 'Canción desesperada' [Song of despair]: 'Oh! soñador de sal y zumo triste' [Oh dreamer of salt and sad juices]. A difference emerges between her darkness and his, she who sought in love an eternal and unbreachable form:

> yo que busqué la eterna siempreviva
> del amor y su fuego defendido

> [I who sought the eternal immortelle
> of love and its unbreached fire]

and in the past ('lo ya vivido'), a model:

> Yo que en el cauce de lo ya vivido
> puse a gemir mi carne pensativa;
> yo que ignoro la causa primitiva
> de mi vivir y mi naciente olvido,

> alabo el soplo de la primavera,
> la incierta lumbre que en secreto admira
> el despojado corazón que espera.

> Alabo mi vivir humilde y denso,
> mi corazón de tintes indefensos,
> que es más oscuro cuanto más se mira. (39)

> [I who in the path of life lived
> gave my thinking flesh to suffer;
> I who do not know the first cause
> of my living or my growing oblivion,

> I praise the breath of spring,
> the uncertain light that in secret
> the empty waiting heart admires.

> I praise my humble dense life,
> the unprotected shades of my heart,
> which the more you look the darker it is seen.]

For Terán, where one lives is not a place of light, but humble, dense, and vulnerable ('dense' rhyming, in the Spanish, with 'unprotected'), nor is 'carne pensativa' the usual abstract subject of knowledge. And 'incierta lumbre' cannot be confused with the idea of divine light. 'Lumbre' is defined in the dictionary as 'materia encendida' [material set alight] or 'luz de los cuerpos en combustión [light of materials in combustion]. In various Latin American countries *lumbre* was until recently common parlance when asking for a light for a cigarette.

Lumbre can be lost with giving birth, in 'Canto a la madre en la paz' [Song to the mother in peace], which plays on the words 'alumbrar' (=illuminate, give birth) and 'deslumbrar' (=dazzle):

> Nada, nada consuela
> su deslumbrada entraña misteriosa;
> en el hijo desvela,
> lastimada y umbrosa,
> como el derrumbe de la blanca rosa. (50)

> [Nothing, nothing consoles
> her darkened and mysterious womb;
> unsleeping in her child,
> hurt and shaded,
> like the collapse of a white rose.]

'Deslumbrada' carries a deep ambiguity: giving birth is both to receive light and to have the light-giving substance taken away from one. That sense of loss and destruction (in another line, 'se desangra la rosa' [the rose bleeds]) of course runs against the customary Catholic mythology of the Mother, whose losses are occulted in her idealization as giver of life. The mother in Terán's poem rebels, in the last verse, against that:

> Que mi voz la acompañe
> y no ceda a la boca que consuela;
> que mi lengua no dañe
> el círculo que hiela:
> allí donde la madre se rebela. (51)

> [Let my voice accompany her
> and not yield to the mouth that consoles;
> let my tongue not damage
> the circle of ice:
> there where the mother rebels.]

'Se rebela' and 'se revela' have the same sound in Spanish: the mother, it is suggested, is revealed in her rebellion. Terán does not take childbirth as a metaphor for artistic creation but as a reality of the dense and vulnerable body, which endures pain and loss, without consolation. This poem was published in 1946 and Terán herself did not become a mother until 1957, at the age of 39. Nevertheless the poem is prophetic of the later experience: 'No sé porque yo fui una madre a los 39 años de edad, pero para mí la maternidad fue un deslumbramiento' [I don't know why I became a mother at the age of 39, but for me motherhood was a revelation.] She again uses the word 'deslumbramiento', but in a positive sense. However, asked '¿No le has escrito un poema a la maternidad?' [Haven't you written a poem to motherhood?], she replies,

Yo pensaba que cuando yo tuviera un hijo iba a escribir montones de canciones infantiles, pensando también en Gabriela Mistral, pues no escribí ni una sola canción infantil. Yo me dediqué única y exclusivamente a gozar la maternidad, a mí no me quedó tiempo de más nada, por eso es que la mujer no se ha distinguido como se han distinguido los hombres en las artes. La maternidad en sí es una hartura total de todo, llena absolutamente todo; yo creo que es uno de los grandes privilegios que tiene la mujer y también una de las cosas más negativas.[7]

[I used to think that when I had a child I would write masses of children's songs, I was thinking about Gabriela Mistral too, but I didn't write a single children's song. I spent the whole time just enjoying motherhood, there was no time left for anything else, that's why women have not become as famous as men in the arts. Motherhood in itself is a completely saturating experience, it fills absolutely everything; I believe that it is one of the great privileges of women as well as one of the most negative things.]

The poem also suggests a potential strength in that role ('el círculo que hiela | [. . .] donde la madre se rebela'); the space inside that circle remains unspoken in the poem—except as a coldness that paralyses the usual language of praise for motherhood—but is filled out in the later poetry with Terán's sense of the woman poet as maker, through her many roles, of a whole environment.

That the loss of *lumbre* by dispossession, in the form of negative attachment and loss of creative energy, can occur in love and in childbirth, causes Terán's poetry to be out of phase with the usual language of love and motherhood—with the inherited baggage of idealities which surrounds those roles in society.

[7] Salas, interview, 11–12.

Terán is not the first Latin American poet to break with them.
Alfonsina Storni, the Argentinian poet, had explored in the
1920s and 1930s her sense of herself as woman and mother
against the prevalent legal and religious models, and in the
process had needed to construct a language against the inherited language of *Modernismo*. But whereas Storni drew upon
urban popular culture and the poetics of the avant-garde in
order to accomplish that,[8] Terán in her first books does
neither. She uses the poetic language of sixteenth- and seven-
teenth century Spanish poets, such as Garcilaso, and with that
as her main resource creates her own path, which makes her
example extraordinary.

Her chosen path is *gozo*, in the sense of joyful pleasure:

> Certeza que me guía
> por la extendida lumbre de mi gozo;
> oscura sangre mía,
> golpear amoroso
> de mi pulso salobre y melodioso. (55)

> [Certitude that guides me
> through the extended light of my pleasure;
> dark blood of mine,
> amorous beat
> of my salty, melodious pulse.]

Joy taken as a form of light ('lumbre') and knowledge
('certeza') brings the darkness of the blood into music. But
lumbre can also destroy one who follows the 'senda de sangre'
[pathway of blood], as in Sonnet XIII:

> Ya sin dulzor la cálida figura
> y de profunda noche enarbolada,
> la oscura ramazón que finge airada
> mariposas de sombra y espesura.

> Alguna lumbre hiéreme los ojos;
> algún mar, en la noche marinera
> de mi sueño, se yergue y me destroza. (40)

> [Now without sweetness the warm figure
> and raised up from deep night,
> the dark shaking branches which
> fake butterflies of shadow and density.

---

[8]   As shown in Nathalie Teitler, 'The Reconstruction of the Body in the Poetry
of Alfonsina Storni', Ph.D. thesis, University of London, 1999.

Some light wounds my eyes;
some sea, in the marine night
of my dream, rises up and destroys me.]

The 'pathway of blood' leads into regions of darkness, but this
is not, as I said before, a symbolic darkness, meaning evil, in
opposition to light, meaning good. Darkness is a region where
figures and shapes appear and multiply (*mariposas*), as in the
passivity of dreams, but held in that passivity the person is in
danger: the dark sea, the light denied can rise up and destroy
them. The issue is submission to fantasy as opposed to fostering
active imagination, and the danger is of being smashed to
pieces in a collision of forces. As Henri Corbin writes, 'The
notion that the Imagination has a noetic value, that it is an
organ of knowledge because it "creates" being, is not readily
compatible with our habits,'9 habits which cause active imagination to be 'confounded with fantasy'.

There is also a discovery, in these early poems, that an equilibrium of states might be possible. In Sonnet IX, limitless light
and sweetness are imagined abolishing darkness and pain:

> si en videntes jazmines naufragara
> toda mi sombra cruel y desatara
> mi llanto por dulcísima pradera. (38)

> [if all my cruel shadow sank
> in jasmine vision and unbound
> my tears in sweet meadow.]

But the conclusion is that that condition would be one of blindness ('ciega vida' [blind life]), since it excludes what the body
knows:

> Si en ciega vida todo se me fuera
> [. . .]
> siempre mi boca de color seguro
> tu inseguro color reconociera:
> oh! sombra de mi sombra prisionera.

> [If in blind life all that's mine were lost
> my mouth with its sure colour
> would always recognize your unsure colour:
> oh shadow prisoner of my shadow.]

---

9 Henri Corbin, *Creative Imagination in the Sufism of Ibn 'Arabi* (Princeton, 1981),
180.

The condition of imprisonment, in the beautifully complex final line, is balanced by the movement of active understanding which is able to see how darkness occurs: *sombra* is both shadow and darkness, and 'shadow of a shadow', Plato's description of the darkness of human knowledge cut off from absolute idealities—which are no place for the dense and vulnerable body.

The equilibrium of states made possible by active intellect permits the creation of forms:

> Oh! caballero de mi sangre oscura,
> sombra viviente de sabor ardido,
> el sentido del aire y tu sentido
> abarcan mi sutil arquitectura. (45)

> [Oh sire of my dark blood,
> living shadow of burnt savour,
> the sense of the air and your sense
> encompass my subtle architecture.]

The poem is addressed to Garcilaso, but 'caballero' can also be read as the lover: passion becomes artistic form. And this occurs alongside all the difficulty of objectifying love, not just in the conventional sense of the couple but in terms of subtle inward energy, the 'delicate flame', which is so easily lost in customary representations or in currently fashionable philosophies of desire which only succeed in cutting it off from active imagination. The body of love is not the human body of anatomy or the mechanical body of predictable sexuality but a 'sutil arquitectura'.

The 'subtle architecture' can also be taken as that of the poems, with their marvellous suppleness, which is the movement and form of what Terán calls her blood:

> Te me doy sangre mía,
> huida mineral para mi boca,
> cera de poesía,
> [. . .]
> Líquida y diestra huyes
> cuando la muerte iza sus banderas.
> Te me doy y rehuyes
> vidas perecederas
> para abarcar mis horas verdaderas. (56)

> [I give myself to you blood of mine,
> mineral flow for my mouth,
> wax of poetry,

Liquid and deft you flee
when death raises its flags.
I give myself to you and you shy away from
dying lives
to encompass my true hours.]

Although Terán's language in this book has not been affected
by the experiments of the avant-garde of 1920–40, it does not,
on the other hand, show the *Modernista* attraction to static
figures which freeze the movement of the senses. Despite superficial appearances, her attitude to poetics is not classical—or
neoclassical. Consider the following:

En este día, en esta misma llama,
en este día, en este mismo fuego,
en este corazón que tierno clama,

en esta falta de conocimiento,
arden el corazón y el pensamiento;
arden los dos en este mismo fuego. (95)

[In this day, in this same flame,
in this day, in this same fire,
in this heart that tenderly calls,

in this lack of knowing,
heart and thought burn;
both burn in this same fire.]

The not-known enters the actual of the poem and of time, as a
zone of fire, a word with multiple senses, which include the
creation/destruction of memory and of forms. Similarly, in
another poem,

Existo por mi muerte, para mi muerte y amo
libremente mi vida, libremente mi muerte
con su silencio en alas de ardientes mariposas
escucho, me detengo en sus frágiles sienes.

Y recuerdo la mar, siempre la mar echada
a la orilla de un árbol limpio como la vida (94)

[I exist through my death, for my death and I freely
love my life, freely my death
with its silence in wings of burning butterflies
I listen, I pause at its fragile temples.

And I remember the sea, always the sea lying
at the edge of a tree clean like life]

These lines are from the book *Presencia terrena* [Earthly presence] published in the same year as *Verdor secreto* (1949). The poems in this book have begun to draw in region, as known rivers, coast, sea, place names, in a sense of locality which includes domestic space—tablecloth, oil, salt, water—as 'presencias humildes':

> Quiero llevarme todas las presencias humildes:
> la tamizada luz del aceite;—la gracia
> de los manteles blancos y sus blancos jardines .
> —albos alemaniscos para la sal y el agua—(101)

> [I want to take all humble presences with me:
> the sifted light of oil; the grace
> of white tablecloths and their white gardens
> —fine white linen for salt and water—]

Here a whole environment has entered, and *sangre*, the inner life, has turned outwards:

> Quiero dejar constancia de mi sangre, mi sangre
> que ama las tierras altas y las tierras dormidas;
> quiero dejar constancia de mi cuerpo en las sales
> de los futuros cuerpos erguidos en la brisa. (100)

> [I want to leave a record of my blood, my blood
> that loves the high lands and the sleeping lands;
> I want to leave a record of my body in the salts
> of future bodies standing up in the breeze.]

But the only permanence claimed is that which the trembling body can effectuate:

> Nada es como esto, nada como saberse toda
> a flor de labios, toda en las mansas rodillas;
> como escucharse tibia y vital en la sombra
> o en el rendido tinte del verano en la espiga.

> Lanzo a todos mi nombre, me lo digo a mí misma
> para saberlo bien, el nombre de mi cuerpo (101)

> [Nothing is like this, like knowing oneself
> wholly on the lips, wholly in the gentle knees;
> like hearing oneself warm and alive in the shadow
> or in the exhausted colour of summer in the ear of wheat.

> I throw out my name to everyone, I say it to myself
> to know it well, the name of my body]

The difference she opens up is between the name as a record of social permanence and the name as a bodily substance.

To know through or with the body means to be without reliance on pre-given schemes or formulae, and that, in terms of language, means abandoning or working against the way in which language gives us the world as something already defined. That effect is there, to cite the prime example, in the predicative force of the less than innocent word *is*: to say a thing 'is' something else does not involve simply making a link (copula) but also asserting (predicating) that it exists.[10] The predicative force runs through the language and is particularly evident in closed systems such as propaganda. Robert Creeley draws attention to it in what is possibly the shortest poem in the English language:[11]

—it

it—

Creeley's poem carefully stays at the edge of any predication. A piece of writing by Borges, entitled 'El idioma analítico de John Wilkins',[12] fiercely parodies the desire to use words as ready-made models of reality. To reject that attitude to language can be taken as a particularly Latin American necessity, if one bears in mind that the language brought to that America carried with it a baggage of definitions elaborated elsewhere for a different world and, moreover, that the process continues with the continuing imposition of European and US intellectual fashions upon Latin American culture.

PHYSICAL AND CULTURAL PLACE

In many of Terán's poems, the way the body becomes an organ of knowledge is explored in terms of the vegetable existence of a tree, as when 'mis vegetales labios inexpertos | van pulsando lo oscuro' [my inexpert vegetable lips | probe the darkness]

---

[10] See the discussion of the same issue in Ch. 7 (pp. 311–12).

[11] From *The Finger: Poems 1966–1969*, in Robert Creeley, *The Collected Poems* (Berkeley, 1982), 391. This poem was first published in 1968.

[12] *Otras inquisiciones* (1960). It is worth mentioning that one of the objects of the parody is the dictionary of the Spanish Royal Academy of the Language, and that the satirical effect spreads more widely to include confidence in any dictionary.

(122), where the focus is on physical sensation inside a physical environment. Entering the not-known means giving up thinking in models, which one is supposed to apply to things— including literature. As the Cuban poet Lezama Lima writes, a model is 'un objeto realizado en el espacio y liberado de las corrosiones del devenir' [an object made in space and freed from the corrosions of becoming].[13] To enter the not-known is, for the American poet H.D., a question of voyaging without procedures or maps: 'We are voyagers, discoverers | of the not-known, | the unrecorded; | we have no map.'[14] If knowledge is of the body, this makes the senses the site where world and self are in a state of becoming:

> Mis vegetales labios inexpertos
> van pulsando lo oscuro, conmovido
> lugar del tiempo y páramos inciertos. (122)
>
> [My inexpert vegetable lips
> probe the darkness, the shaken
> place of time and uncertain moors.]

The sense of the uncertain and the un-formed is there in at least five of the words: 'inexpertos', 'pulsando' (=tanteando), 'oscuro', 'páramos' (=empty lands), 'inciertos'. We are in the territory of Keats's 'negative capability', which, as Charles Olson puts it, was able 'to wreck Hegel, if anything could'.[15] The larger process is given in detail in a later section of the same poem:

> Es el mar, es el fuego, es el caballo
> turbio de la gran noche; es el latido
> de aquella flor juzgada donde callo
>
> oscuramente, allí donde convido
> esculturas moradas y desiertos
> para lanzar el signo convenido;
>
> lo que me indica rostros entreabiertos,
> citas de minerales; migraciones
> de máscaras y el pan, el vino y ciertos
>
> espejos contra el ángel y canciones
> con los brazos en alto. Lo que implora
> desde alguien las dolidas extensiones

---

[13] José Lezama Lima, *El reino de la imagen* (Caracas, 1981), 221.
[14] *Trilogy* (London, 1973), 59.
[15] Charles Olson, *Collected Prose* (Berkeley, 1997), 120.

del tiempo-girasol que me devora. (123–4)

[It is the sea, it is fire, it is the turbulent
horse of the great night, it is the beating
of that judged flower where I am

darkly silent, where I invite
purple sculptures and deserts
to launch the agreed sign;

which indicates to me half-open faces,
meetings with minerals; migrations
of masks and bread, wine and certain

mirrors against the angel and songs
with arms stretched upwards. Which implores
from someone the pained extensions

of the time-sunflower that devours me.]

It starts with *is*, but none of the logical predicates ('mar', 'fuego', 'caballo', 'latido') actually orders or classifies or defines: we are not being given a foreknown, or a place of memory, a store of archetypes, a collection of stories. That darkness is attributed to this not-knowing is of course a device to dismantle the religious or rationalistic symbolism of light used by Christianity and the Enlightenment, and the figure of the horse, frequently used by Terán in this middle period,[16] a revaluation of Plato's figuration of the irrational part of the soul as a horse.

What is very interesting in this poem is that, against any slipping into symbols—Terán could easily have let the aliveness of the darkness leak into symbolic figures—darkness is the place and the force that produces signs and perceptions ('allí [. . .] el signo convenido', 'lo que me indica rostros'. That is, darkness has the aliveness of the actual, of becoming. This is, in Merleau-Ponty's words, 'the ante-predicative life of consciousness. In the silence of primary consciousness can be seen appearing not only what words mean, but also what things mean.'[17] Thus Terán's flower arises not as an image in the usual sense—it has no shape or outline—but as a *latido*, heard in silence, against pre-judgement ('juzgada'). As she states in a lecture given in 1989,

---

[16] See 'abajo el gran caballo taciturno' (113); 'el caballo nocturno' (131); Plato, *The Republic*, 8–9.

[17] M. Merleau-Ponty, *Phenomenology of Perception* (London, 1962), p. xv.

Ni antes ni ahora he sabido de artes poéticas. No conozco nada de lo que se ha dicho sobre esto. En mí hablan intuición y 'conocimiento' ante lo hechopoema. Idea y lenguaje forman una misma esencia para ocasionar lo inmediato del verso. Una misma transparencia mezcla tiniebla y luz en latidos de lenguaje. (272)

[I have never known about 'the art of poetry', neither before nor now. I don't know any of what has been said about that. In my work, it is intuition and 'knowledge' that speak to the poem-event. Idea and language form a single essence so as to bring about the immediacy of the line. The same transparency mixes darkness and light in the throbbing of language.]

To use Merleau-Ponty again, 'It is necessary that meaning and signs, the form and matter of perception be related from the beginning and that, as we say, the matter of perception be "pregnant with its form." '[18] Terán places her confidence in the 'matter of perception' and not in models, whether of knowledge or of poetic form. There is also, somewhere in this, an experience she had as a child:

palabra—objeto repetida muchas, muchas veces, hasta desaparecer. Por ejemplo, silla, y quedarme solamente con una especie de vacío (digo ahora metafísico), que me producía gozo y terror al mismo tiempo. [. . .] Mi primer juguete es pues la palabra. (269)

[word—object repeated many, many times, until it disappears. For example, chair, and to be left only with a sort of emptiness (which I now call metaphysical), which gave me pleasure and terror at the same time. My first toy is the word.]

Immersion in the matter of the senses, figured as darkness and silence, is a source of refreshment and renewal, against tired preconceptions. Things come into being precisely there ('rostros [. . .] vino'), things that include local beliefs and cultural expressions ('espejos contra el ángel y canciones'). Time as becoming also destroys ('me devora') and is included in the process of the poem, not as schema or symbol but as the material of feeling arising in another human being, in mutual response. Once again, Terán chooses to stay immersed in the uncertainty of becoming. She opts for the forms that arise,

---

[18] M. Merleau-Ponty, *The Primacy of Perception* (Chicago, 1989), 15. Eric Mottram puts it perhaps more succinctly: 'a language might be made of anything; the body makes and uses systems out of anything' (*Towards Design in Poetry* (London, 1977), 5).

whatever they are, and not for submission to schemes of permanence.

The poem just quoted belongs to the 1970 book *De bosque a bosque* [From wood to wood], a collection that displays the poetics of the transition to the later poetry. The key principle, that words and things are given simultaneously, recurs in various statements, such as 'a veces la palabra incorpora persigue | otras la luz persigue incorpora' [sometimes the word incorporates pursues | others the light pursues incorporates] (195). 'Poema instantáneo' [Instantaneous poem] explores the process in fuller extension:

Recordaré la frase espléndida ajustada a la táctil hondura
que retiene
   acosa
      verifica anillos secretos
supremas constancias de hociquillos morados;
innumerables, sedientos pulsos para tu goce
y enrarecidas mieles para hacer el vacío
la culebra acumulada y humilde
   que habrá de erguirse entre los astros. (191)

[I will remember the splendid phrase adjusted to the tactile
   depth
which holds
   pursues
      verifies secret rings
supreme constancies of little purple snouts;
innumerable, thirsty pulses for your pleasure
and rarefied honeys to make the void
the humble accumulated snake
   that will rise among the stars.]

There has been a shift away from the vocabulary of interiority (the word *sangre*, for example) towards a single plane where not only words and things but also depth and surface (as with 'táctil hondura') are given at the same time. The phrase heard holds, seeks, and tests so that the geometrical and the animate, the very small and the very large, the humble and the cosmic all become available through the work of the poem.

That sense that place, in the poem and of the poem, needs to be what is *humilde* (ordinary) extends into a critique of the male, feudal discourse which still attaches itself to family histories ('Caballero para qué devolverse girar sobre documentos |

de haciendas perdidas, encuadernaciones, y lujosos signos'
[Sir why go back to turn around documents | of lost estates,
bindings, and luxurious signs]; 194), as Terán settles accounts
with her experience of Andean Venezuela, where she had
grown up. The history of the area and her ancestors becomes
important to her: 'Gentes que fundaron pueblos acá, gentes
que los apellidos son muy antiguos: de madre y padre'
[people who founded towns here, people with very old
surnames, on both sides of the family]. But she then adds,
with her characteristic refusal of passive submission to tradition and her concern with becoming individual, 'pero gentes
que de pronto se desgajaron de lo convencional, de lo
convencional importante, y empezaron a ser protagonistas de
vidas propias y distintas' [but people who suddenly broke away
from convention, of conventions of importance, and began to
be protagonists of their own distinctive lives].[19] This includes,
in a statement addressed to her daughter, a need to move
outwards from 'palacios' [palaces] and 'catedrales' [cathe-
drals] (194), and a need to resist the 'relato sagrado' [sacred
story]:

> gritos de hombre, vigilias de hombre
> en la ciudad de sobresello púrpura
> que recibe órdenes, que empuña colgajos de banderas
> mientras avanza hacia el relato sagrado. (202)
>
> [a man's shouts, a man's vigils
> in the city of purple seals
> that receives orders, holds up rags of flags
> while advancing towards the sacred story.]

—icons of war inside a language of orders and obedience. Once
again, there is the difficulty of objectifying the non-male, but
here placed within specific histories and localities.

Locality in the *Libro de los oficios* [Book of trades] written at
the same time and published in 1967, has to do with physical
place and with the human actions that make it cultural place,
actions or 'oficios' which are inextricable from what Terán calls
the domain of woman. This book, which is the most important
constellation of her work, is ambitious enough to propose an
alternative geography and historiography of Venezuela, written

---

[19] Salas, interview, 8.

from the physical and cultural particularities of a region. The notion of 'oficios' includes any significant action in the making of environment but in particular those carried out by women, which are traditionally invisible and which involve the arrangement of things, places, gestures, clothes, and thus also of the senses in the making of a human world. All this is in the poem 'Escena de comienzo' [First scene]:

Bien estuvo señalar oficio, salud y situación de la torre
sedera y trapos para brillo y pulir objetos macizos.
Que se reciban las llaves de este dominio de hembra
acrecentado por la cercanía de las lluvias. También islas.
También rescatar, prender hilo a sedas de fondo
siguiendo contornos y libertad en lo escrito. Palpando
de rodillas el dibujo a seguir. Adentrarse en la escena de
   comienzo:
Místico Tráfico: acercar el ave a la sombra del corazón. (201)

[It was right to signal office, health, and situation of the silk
tower and cloths to shine and polish solid objects.
Let the keys be received for this female domain
increased by nearness of the rains. Islands also.
Rescue also, attach thread to background silks
following contours and freedom in the written. Touching
the design to be followed, kneeling. Enter into the first scene:
Mystical Traffic: bring the bird into proximity with the shadow
   of the heart.]

If the tower and the keys recall a feudal/romantic imagination, 'cloths' and 'polish' interpret the domain of women as the ordinary work of caring for things, and this is taken as a composition, in Gertrude Stein's sense: 'the composition is the thing seen by every one living in the living they are doing, they are the composing of the composition that at the time they are living is the composition of the time in which they are living. It is that that makes living a thing they are doing.'[20] Terán's composition includes 'rains' and 'islands' in the key action of 'acercar el ave a la sombra del corazón'. The word 'corazón', used so frequently in the earlier poetry as region of shadow never fully rendered, is here placed in active commerce with the physical thing ('ave'), permitting the integration, in a single composition, of inner and outer worlds, which she had

---

[20] Gertrude Stein, *Selected Writings* (New York, 1972), 515.

previously called 'corazón adentro' [from the heart inwards] and 'corazón afuera' [from the heart outwards].

STONES

The composition which brings heart and bird into proximity involves writing as a palpable, physical action, occurring between freedom and the contours of things, configured in this poem as grasping threads of silk and kneeling down to feel a pattern with the hands. Surfaces felt and patterns traced with the senses include in particular stone and cloth. The poem 'Piedra de habla' [Speech stone] centres on stone, in multiple senses, as the place of speaking-writing—not speaking in a general or abstract sense (that would be 'piedra *del* habla'), but speech as local action, in the sense of an environment of things and of locally used words, such as 'peladeros' and 'guacamaya' in the following:

> La poetisa ofrece sus águilas. Resplandece en sus aves de nube profunda.
> Se hace dueña de las estaciones, las cuatro perras del buen y mal tiempo.
> Se hace dueña de rocallas y peladeros escogidos con toda intención.
> Clava una guacamaya donde ha de arrodillarse.
> La poetisa cumple medida y riesgo de la piedra de habla. (200)
> [The poet offers her eagles. Shines in her birds of deep cloud.
> Becomes owner of the seasons, the four bitches of good and bad weather.
> Becomes owner of rock scree and clearings chosen with full intention.
> Places a macaw where she will kneel.
> The poet fulfils measure and risk of the speech stone.]

The word 'poetisa' in Latin America, unlike 'poetess' in English, can express the dignity of an *oficio*, which here includes taking possession of one's chosen environment ('dueña' is repeated twice) and choosing, in adulthood, one's own emblems. Asked whether the stone which figures in the *Libro de los oficios* is universal or else simply a stone found on the ground, Terán replies,

Es la piedra universal, es la piedra de la ruinas de Grecia cuando estuvimos allá, y es la piedra de aquí que se mueve: 'la piedra que crece', y es la piedra corriente, y es la piedra preciosa, porque me han encantado las joyas: el diamante, la esmeralda, el topacio, el crisoberilo, que me encanta la palabra. Pero no desde el punto de vista del valor específico de esas piedras. Con decirte que si las piedras preciosas estuvieran en las calles, yo estaría recogiendo piedras eternamente. Es la piedra también de la profecía, de la poesía; es la piedra que es un núcleo de fuerza. Es la piedra en el sentido americano, en el sentido de los aztecas.[21]

[It's stone in a universal sense, the stone of the Greek ruins when we were there, and it's the stone from here that moves: 'the stone that grows', and it's ordinary stone, and precious stone, because I have loved jewels: diamond, emerald, topaz, chrysoberyl, I love that word. But not because of the specific value of those stones. If there were precious stones in the streets, I would be for ever gathering them. It's also the stone of prophecy, and of poetry; it's the stone that is a gathering of force. It's stone in the American sense, in the Aztec sense.]

To appropriate stone as all and each one of those things, that is the measure of Terán's ambition, which is not an ambition to compete—who but the dominant institutions would decide the outcome, who but they would be the ultimate victor?—but to make out of the local a work of art as serious as any other, without sentimental alibis of localism [regionalism]. Asked whether the stone is 'la piedra sobre la cual escribe el poeta' [the stone the poet writes upon], she replies,

Bueno eso sería el gran deseo: que el poema estuviera escrito en piedra, que estuviera esculpido en piedra. Pero yo digo que para mí es la piedra corriente, la piedra de todos los días. Además la piedra que se talla. Entonces, ya esa es la Gran Piedra, con un sentido plástico o un sentido de la creatividad del hombre.

[Well, that would be my great desire: for the poem to be written on stone, sculpted in stone. But as I say, for me it's ordinary stone, the stone you find every day. And also the stone you carve. And so that is the Great Stone, in a plastic sense or in the sense of the creativity of human beings.]

Cloth is another material that frequently recurs in the book, as 'sedas', 'sábanas', 'traje', the latter embodying the process of writing: 'Traje por solo presencia en mano que fluye, atornilla

---

signos sobre página no escrita' [Dress on its own presence in hand that flows, tightens signs on unwritten page] (213). In a poem that clearly refers to the making of her own sensibility,

> La joven construye su casa
> [. . .] nombrando renglones dulces, experiencias de hilo muy
>   fino
> torcido sobre el muslo, hilo y mano, figura entera en el umbral,
> figura que recuerda cuanto esperó, cuantas lluvias, techos de
>   lluvia sobre el desamparo.
> Nombrando piedras (211)
>
> [The young woman builds her house
> naming sweet lines, experiences of very fine thread
> twisted over the thigh, thread and hand, whole figure in the
>   threshold,
> figure that recalls how much she waited, how many rains, roofs
>   of rain over abandonment.
> Naming stones]

where cloth and rain become surfaces of memory, and house, name, and the sensation of cloth on the skin all make the history of the person who writes. The last two examples given are from a later book, but one which is a continuation of the *Libro de los oficios* with regard to the materials and their handling. The feeling of cloth, upon the skin of hands or eyes, is a composition of the senses and Terán speaks of the acuteness of her own senses as something she inherited:

> yo he sido una persona que he dependido mucho de los sentidos. Yo tuve un olfato extraordinario, yo descubría, por ejemplo, un grupo de jabillos que no tienen ni perfume ni flor, y sin embargo yo sabía por el olfato que había un grupo de jabillos en tal parte. Huele a samán, decía yo, huele a jabillo. ¡Son árboles, no son flores! Tuve por herencia sentidos muy aguzados.
>
> Sentido del tacto: [. . .] las telas han sido para mí un placer. Mi madre [. . .] una vez nos llamó y estrujó un pedazo de seda cruda natural. Dijo: 'Vengan acá, oigan como suena la seda cruda.' Nunca me olvido. Puedo descubrir una textura por el sonido. Cuando voy a comprar telas es difícil que a mí me engañen porque sé exactamente lo que toco, si tiene mezcla.[22]
>
> [I have been a person who depended very much on my senses. I had an extraordinary sense of smell, for example I could discover a clump

---

[22] Salas, interview, 6.

of jabillos[23] which have no perfume and no flower, and yet I knew by smelling that there was a clump of jabillos in such and such a place. It smells of saman, it smells of jabillo, I used to say. They're trees, not flowers! I inherited very sharp senses.

Sense of touch: cloths have been a pleasure to me. My mother once called us and crumpled a piece of crude silk. She said: 'Come here, listen to how crude silk sounds.' I never forget that. I can discover a texture through sound. When I go to buy cloth it's difficult for them to cheat me because I know exactly what I'm touching, whether it's been mixed with something inferior.]

Writing, as she puts it in the poem 'Piedrecillas de adivinación' [Little stones for divination], gets its 'medida' [measure] from a 'paladeo total' (total tasting or savouring).

Cloth in the poems embraces the whole range, from 'retazos' [scraps] to 'tejidos preciosos' [precious cloths] (213), but always for their feel and their active use.[24] It might be tempting, talking of cloth, to speak of Terán's assemblage of materials as a patchwork. However, that image would not be accurate, because her action of assemblage is composite not singular, consisting in a multitude of distinct learned abilities which include the work of the senses. Along with that, the materials themselves are heterogeneous, as stone and cloth are.

If Terán is concerned with stones, cloth, and other worked surfaces, including those made by the senses—here gathering up the earlier poetry into a new integration—one needs to know, in order to understand the particularity of her work, what it is written against as well as what it moves towards. In other words, one needs a sense of the larger field, both of poetry and of the social imagination. In terms of the traditions of Venezuelan and Latin American poetry, the most crucial fact is perhaps her refusal of neoclassicism, though she does not herself use that term. In a poem entitled 'Hablas como desgastes', she draws attention to certain specific features of her own language in contrast to that of a younger Venezuelan poet, exemplified in an epigraph:

> *Abrimos la ventana para que el día pase en su barco.*
> Eugenio Montejo.

---

[23] Trees whose Latin name is *Hura crepitans.*
[24] In 1980 Terán founded 'un taller de costura y bordado, en el cual trabaja y enseña a las jóvenes moradoras' (266).

Se establecen fuegos, pañuelos y ribazones que atestigüen la
  abundancia,
hablas como desgastes sobre galanuras y desenfados de pícaros,
de bellas acomodadas dulce, castamente en su precio,
ceñidas de falso oscuro en tejidos que remedan la dicha,
también copias rebasando imagen, telones crudos donde
  forcejean trapos de hechura breve.
Sinembargo un joven dice: 'Abrimos la ventana para que el día
  pase en su barco'. (215)

[*We opened the window for the day to go by in its boat.*
                                        Eugenio Montejo.

Fires, handkerchiefs, and shoals are established which bear
  witness to abundance,
speakings like wastage upon gallantries and forwardness of
  villains,
of beautiful women sweetly and chastely accommodated in their
  price,
wrapped tightly with false darkness in cloths which mimic
  happiness,
also copies that exceed image, crude curtains where brief cheap
  rags struggle.
Nevertheless a young man says: 'We opened the window for the
  day to go by in its boat.']

The easy flow of Montejo's metaphor speaks of a confidence in
the sublime and of a cultivation of universality that sustains
that confidence. There is an unproblematic commerce
between the real and the metaphoric, the world and the poem,
based upon the poet's location within a particular economy of
things and words. But in Terán's writing cost and value do not
coincide, they do not share the same measure or vocabulary.
The economy of 'precio' is given in male and female posturing
('pícaros' and 'bellas') but it is not the same as value—if one
takes 'dicha' as value and 'remedan' as the action of modelling
or imitating, whether in actions or in writing. The economy of
value is a different one, and is given in the words 'abundancia'
and 'desgastes' as well as 'dicha'. Cost is one thing and value
another, and for Terán acts of speaking ('hablas') occur inside
that difference or, more accurately, are charged with it and
thus also is the poem, which is an assemblage of those acts or
utterances. The poem shows that if one chooses the abundance of the local as spoken words and things (*ribazones*, for

example, are shoals of fish), the result is one's speaking becomes a 'desgaste' [wastage] in relation to the world of price. But the relationship can be turned round, as happens later in the poem, and 'desgaste' can become excess in a good sense, i.e. that which breaks out of the mould because it has chosen different measure. What is at stake is nothing less than the entire referential function of language. Speaking-writing is shown to be a waste upon/about ('sobre') 'galanuras' [gallantries] and other facilities of image, as opposed to a gathering up of everything inside a metaphor that guarantees permanence because it is adjusted to the law of the sublime, which covers over the actual making of the scene in which things are seen, the actual crude cloth (*telón* meaning cloth backdrop in a theatre) forced together out of brief pieces. If one has come that far, then Montejo's line—heard again at the end of the poem—sounds different from the way it would do to someone used only to a neoclassical manner, where there is no fissure between the work of the senses and the social circulation of images.

Day and its boat in Montejo's poem are almost a mythology, they partake of the lustre and naturalness of myth—in Egyptian mythology, the sun passes through the sky in a boat. When Terán makes the local into the imaginary, constructing it out of utterances and perceptions, this could also be taken as a proto-mythology—'magic' is the term used by José Napoleón Oropeza in the prologue to her collected poetry. However, her poems are, more accurately, a replacement of mythology, precisely because their action of construction takes us back into the humus of things felt and words said. The imaginary is not the same as imagination: what we have, in the work of the poems, is imagination probing, assembling these shapes, using them in varying design.

A poem like 'Nuestros signos' [Our signs] sets out examples of the signs which enter into the design and reveals that particular design as what makes a place and a time:

> Aprenderemos a conocer nuestros signos: aves de plumaje
>   encarnado,
> semillas sombrías que deposita el mar en nuestra vigilia,
> tablas lavadas, las bellas del entresueño que se apoderan de lo
>   escrito.
> Aprenderemos a despertar el año echado al pie de la casas.

Ocuparemos piedras mayores y de consolación. Piedras
mayores.
Oh vencimiento: ubrecillas de niebla amamantando días
futuros. (207)
[We will learn to know our signs; bird of red plumage,
dark seeds the sea deposits in our waking,
washed planks, the beautiful objects of daydream which take
over writing.
We will learn to wake up the year that lies at the foot of houses.
We will occupy greater stones, stones of consolation. Greater
stones.
Oh supersession: little teats of mist feeding future days.]

Let us consider 'tablas' as sign. Like the seeds, the wooden
planks have been brought in by the sea. There is a memory
here which is recounted in the biographical note written in
collaboration with Terán's husband, 'su compañero y amigo
durante treinta y cinco años' [her friend and companion for
thirty-five years]: in Morrocoy, Terán

descubrió de nuevo el paisaje soleado de su pubertad en Puerto
Cabello, las noches de alta marea, cuando el océano se introducía en
alguna humilde vivienda y arrastraba muñecas y zapatos. Dejaba en su
lugar un guijarro, un caracol. (266)
[discovered again the sunny landscape of her puberty in Puerto
Cabello, the nights of high tides, when the ocean entered some
humble habitation and took dolls and shoes with it. And left in their
place a pebble, a shell.]

If the seeds are dark things placed by the sea in waking awareness, the planks, 'lavadas' and 'bellas', are a kind of inversion of
that chiaroscuro: their brightness exists in 'entresueño'
[daydream]. In what sense do they have power ('se apoderan')
over the act of writing? They enter as early memories, as forms
striking the visual imagination, as materials, like the pieces of
cloth ('retazos') which make up a larger surface. Thus we are
dealing both with signs and with the surface on which they are
perceived. Here the multiple semantic field, generated by the
various uses of 'tabla(s)', comes in: plank, tablet (for writing),
flat piece of cloth as in a skirt, table (as in index), flat piece of
earth for planting, counter in shop, surface for painting, stage
in theatre. The various materials are composed in such a way
that the place constructed shapes the flow of time. If 'casas' and

'piedras' carry the past as memory traces, then 'ubrecillas' take one into the small, half-visible places in which the future is nourished, in which the pure, image-less flow of time is given shape out of one's own energy, something which Terán places in the sphere of the feminine and takes as a necessity (hence 'vencimiento' [defeat, expiry, supersession] and its emotional charge).

The signs which carry memory constitute a historical humus, in the sense of the stuff out of which history is written. More precisely, they are the stuff out of which memory, which when written becomes history, is made. In this sense Terán's work sets out very seriously the necessity for an alternative writing of history (historiography). This is clear, for example, in her differential use of the word 'patria'. Instead of the name for the centralized state, imposed by the authoritarian liberalism of the creole elite,[25] with its heroes and its epic history, 'patria' in Terán is placed alongside a series of icons of place such as 'banderas', 'reino', 'ídolos', 'palacios', 'oro', 'mitos', and these are folded in with the physical and cultural particularities of the region of Morrocoy and the latter include rituals of death and renewal—of social reproduction—such as those carried out by old ladies, called 'Las culebras del reino' [Snakes of the kingdom] in the title of the poem, who say, 'Queremos agujas, hilo, tela blanca. Cenizas para el despido y la luz' [We want needles, thread, white cloth. Ashes for farewell and light] (206). These are not the 'colgajos de banderas' [tatters of flags] (202) carried by the men who take orders, but the 'resplandor de MITOS' [splendour of MYTHS] tied back into an environment of 'pan, sal [. . .] manteles blancos [. . .] cubiertos que alguna vez fueron de plata' [bread, salt, white tablecloths, cutlery that was once silver] (205). And these, in a poem entitled 'Cena' [Supper], make a place where the memory of a past marked by 'los gestos de quien anduvo entre montañas oprimido por la lealtad' [the gestures of someone who walked among the mountains oppressed by loyalty]—in the guerrilla wars of the 1960s—and held in a photo where the frozen figure of the horse conveys what was 'terrible y solo' [terrible and solitary] about that time. In that context, where the things and gestures of a

[25] See William Rowe and Vivian Schelling, *Memory and Modernity* (London, 1991), ch. I.

social and domestic ritual are laid out before one, the splendour of history is rescued from the State and re-enfolded into the splendour of collective desires.

To speak of history is also to raise the question of the history of Terán's own work. The way one handles history extends into decisions about literary history, and the latter proposes models of reading literature just as the former proposes particular ways of reading traces of the past. It would be tempting to read the history of Terán's poetry as a progression, in the sense of a move 'forwards' from her earlier use of Garcilasian language towards the Modernist free verse of the later work. As she herself points out, in the lecture previously quoted, it was after spending some time in Paris that she began to write in free verse. However, there are two large problems about looking at the question in this way, one factual and one methodological. The factual one is that Terán has continued to write sonnets of Garcilasian form alongside free verse. Methodologically, the issue is that one would be missing the point: the 'pre'-modern, in Venezuela and in Terán's writing, exists alongside and simultaneously with the aesthetics of modernity. There is not a progression. This is, as Néstor García Canclini and others have shown, a key condition of the twentieth century in Latin America,[26] and it includes the fact that the non-modern tends to be associated with regional or subaltern social formations.

If one considers, specifically, the issue of Terán's move from a sixteenth-century to a modern diction, the temptation would be to assume that she had 'modernized' her language. What is misleading in that type of assumption is the fact that sixteenth-century diction, which has mainly disappeared from speech in Spain, is related to particular characteristics of creole speech that persisted, particularly in regional Latin America, at least until the 1980s. And for the poet, the issue is that creole sensibility was tied up with that language, as is demonstrated by many twentieth-century poets, among them Lezama Lima, Martín Adán, and Carlos Germán Belli.[27] This is not to say that Terán's later language does not reveal limitations in her earlier

---

[26] See Néstor García Canclini, *Culturas híbridas: estrategias para entrar y salir de la modernidad* (Mexico City, 1989), ch. 2.

[27] Martín Adán asserts for example that 'la literatura peruana y, extensamente, la hispanoamericana es sustantivamente la barroca española delongada e influida,' (*De lo barroco en el Perú* (Lima, 1968), 376–7).

work. The most important of these have to do with the materials and the types of speech a poem is capable of handling. The question of materials should be clear enough by now. In terms of speech, a comparison between *Al norte de la sangre* [In the direction of the blood] and *El libro de los oficios* shows that there is a fairly severe restriction of types of intonation in the earlier work. The later work explores a variety of speech energies, in a similar move to that of Parra and Cardenal.

But perhaps the most interesting difference in the later work has to do with design. The phrases tend to be laid out without connectives and their verbs tend to be infinitives or present participles. Instead of finite verbs, there are unfinished actions which give doing as what is happening, as what is making the composition. Interestingly also, there is a different attitude to 'lumbre', to the effect of intensity upon the visual imagination. In the poem 'EL NOMBRE', already quoted, words and things come into appearance in 'los calveros del poema' [the clearings of the poem], which link up with the multiple senses of where one writes as 'tablas'. Consider the first three lines:

> Como quien escribe una oración y pide en la oración mucha
> humildad
> y un extenso aliento para resistir brillo y cercanía de la PALABRA.
> Es mi oficio y la frase resulta de arena negra con pespuntes de
> oro. (205)
> [Like someone writing a prayer and they ask in the prayer for
> much humility
> and a long breath so as to resist shine and nearness of the WORD.
> That is my trade and the phrase comes from black sand with
> gold stitches.]

Instead of 'brillo y cercanía de la PALABRA', the decision is for the phase constructed out of the light and darkness of sand and stitches. Thus the locality of the action alters the terms of its visibility: instead of the Garcilasian mode of intensive luminosity, a decision for extensive construction.

But let the poet have the last word, with the 'oficio' that touches all the others:

> Cuánta dulzura para adrizar la noche, y este ramo de actinias
> hacia piedras lamidas, de consolación;
> piedras, fondeaderos de tiempo sur.
> De mujer que atestigua vaivén de cefeidas

por entre relampagueos de mangles.
De mujer que ofrece cimófanas, clemátides
sólo para restablecer, Islas, el compromiso con la alegría. (201)

[How much sweetness to raise the night, and this bunch of
    sea-anemones
towards licked stones, of consolation;
stones, anchorages of southern time.
Of woman who bears witness to swinging of variable stars
between lightning flashes of mangroves.
Of woman who offers cymophane,[28] clematis
only to restore, Islands, the commitment to joy.]

[28]   A form of green chrysoberyl.

7

Raúl Zurita and American Space

Many are the forms of the sacred [. . .]
the god finds the path of the unexpected.
(Euripides, *The Bacchae*)

The creation of a different society, as a great work of art.
(CADA)

As though art were not enough for any of us to behave to!
(Charles Olson)

The perception of what is possible is the most important
constant of the social imagination.
(J. J. Brunner)

THE PLACE OF MEMORY

According to the transitologists, the transition to democracy in
Chile under the arrangements set up by Pinochet after sixteen
years in power does not include as an issue the torture and
disappearance of human beings during those sixteen years.
This, in their view, is because those violations of human rights
affected only a small minority of the population. There is logic
in their stance, and let us define it as clearly as possible: if
violence does not need to be kept in mind, this is because it
only continues to affect those few it touched; it did not penetrate the whole society; it is not part of the long-term structures
of the society as a whole, its history, and its culture; it is not and
does not need to be generally remembered. Transitology, a new
specialism in the business of social control, exemplifies in these
respects the unprecedentedly sterile social thought of late twentieth-century capitalism. For Raúl Zurita, the pain of recent
Chilean experience is something that needs to be purged, if any
regeneration is to occur. The pain, and the sense of history as

including the intolerable violation of human beings, did not
begin in 1973 and does not affect just a small proportion of the
population:

fuera de nuestros desaparecidos modernos, toda esta historia es de
desaparecidos, de tipos que no han sido enterrados, de pueblos, de
culturas que no han tenido ese derecho. Todos ellos penan permanentemente en el eje de la lengua.[1]

[apart from our modern disappeared, all this history is a history of
disappeared people, human beings who have not been buried,
peoples, cultures who have not had that right. They all permanently
haunt the language at its foundations.]

The statement serves to point to the vastness and necessity of
what Zurita himself attempts. The common and popular senses
of *penar* as haunting and pain open out the Catholic notion of
the torment of souls in purgatory to include any exclusion from
paradise, if the latter is understood in its widest possible projection as counteraction to unacknowledged and unnecessary
suffering, wastage, and death. The area thus defined, which
includes the necessity for rites of burial and reconciliation,
continues to be a seminal—though often ignored—tradition in
Latin American literature, from Nahuatl, Maya, and Quechua
responses to the Conquest in poetry and drama to the work of
Rulfo, Neruda, and José María Arguedas, to name some of the
most obvious cases. For Zurita, as for the latter three, a major
part of the work to be done is with the language.

One of the features which distinguish Zurita within this tradition is the intensive and multiple use of land, landscape, and,
in a more general sense, space, including both the cosmological and the social, as a main vector for interventions in the
language and the culture. The statement 'Pero mi amor ha
quedado pegado en las rocas, el mar y las montañas' [but my
love has become stuck to the rocks, the sea, and the mountains]
may be taken as a key formulation in this respect. Love, in coun-
terposition to violation, becomes a constant as feature of the
land, the most permanent of spaces. The process, involving
emotion, perception, language, and landscape, is complex, and
needs to be understood in relation to what is specifically
American in Zurita's handling of space. This Americanness

---

[1] Interview, in Juan Andrés Piña, *Conversaciones con la poesía chilena* (Santiago, 1990), 230.

includes an ontological primacy in which space is not the setting for occurrence but itself occurrence; a sense of the land as expression of social hope (democracy, love, paradise); and of landscape as expression of emotion. These characteristics, which have to do with the land as relatively uncoded space and with the city as a space still capable of invasion by nature, may be contrasted with the more stable European triad of city, garden, wilderness. Zurita's poetic techniques in relation to this material include the familiar metaphoric one of making the land anthropomorphic, a virtually automatic characteristic of common speech and even of geographical description, as when 'features' of a landscape are talked about as if it were a human face. But Zurita introduces an unfamiliar dimension, where the land is treated quite literally as a face, rather than representing one. This is an inscriptive use of non-human space, not as something to be humanized but as a surface upon which signs are made or recognized. And so writing, speech, the skin of the body, the land, and the sky are placed on the same plane, in a radical relocation that breaks with inherited poetics of space (*modernista* or *vanguardista*) and makes Zurita's a late twentieth-century work.

The phrase 'pegado en las rocas, el mar y las montañas' [stuck to the rocks, the sea, and the mountains] appears in *Canto a su amor desaparecido* [Song to his | her | their disappeared love],[2] the book which Zurita published in 1987, in response to the experience, including his own, of imprisonment and torture, but also with the aim of reaching beyond that experience to a sense of love as a permanence beyond death. The notion of the cosmological role of love relates to his deliberate use of Dante as a model, evident in the titles of Zurita's books and in a multitude of quotations and echoes. But there is also a Latin American tradition here, in which Neruda and Martí are among the key figures: Neruda with the permanence of word and stone as a continuity, discovered through love, countering a genocidal history, and Martí with the notion of love and place as indispensable foundations for a genuine American identity. For Martí, the union of love and place in a particular time and circumstance (Cuba, in the late

---

[2] *Canto a su amor desaparecido* (Santiago, 1987). Hereafter references to this book will take the form *C* followed by page number. *Anteparaíso* (Madrid, 1991), will be referred to as *A*.

nineteenth-century struggle against Spanish colonialism) was the only basis for self inside nation to become universal, a notion expressed in a line which Zurita quotes in modified form: Martí's 'Yo vengo de todas partes, I y hacia todas partes voy' [I come from everywhere I and I go everywhere][3] becomes 'Yo vengo de muchos lugares' [I come from many places] (*C* 13), juxtaposed with 'De un bayonetazo me cercenaron el hombro y sentí mi brazo al caer al pasto. I Y luego con él golpearon a mis amigos' [they cut off my arm at the shoulder with a bayonet and I felt the arm when I fell on the grass. I And then they took the arm and hit my friends with it] and with 'Mira tiene un buen cul' [look he/she's got a good arse], the erotic violence of the military in their mission to clean up the nation.

The phrase 'pegado en las rocas, el mar y las montañas', grammatical complement of 'mi amor', is heard first as 'pegado *a* las rocas' (*C* 12, my italics), the variation of the preposition making the spatial relationship multiple: there is both an adhesion to the surface of the earth—'ha quedado adherido en las rocas' (*C* 13)—and some degree of penetration or incrustation of that surface resulting in the marking of it by love.[4] The prepositional indefiniteness is typical of a constant variability of location in Zurita's work, whereby no object can be placed at any one point. The effect is not sentimental haze but a non-Euclidean multiplicity, where precision is in the movement and does not submit to the authority of the point over the line. But besides this possibility of a cosmos without fixed stars or constants, Zurita's work also includes a mapping of constants, in the form of Christian symbols. His use of space occurs at an intersection of these two main procedures.

In his discussion of nature as the central foundational element of Latin American literature, Roberto González Echevarría frames his analysis within the terms of land as that which needs to be coded legally and, in a more primary sense, scripturally, to give a basis for civilization.[5] What his essay omits,

---

[3] José Martí, *Versos sencillos*, in José Martí, *Ismaelillo, Versos libres, Versos sencillos*, ed. Ivan A. Schulman (Madrid, 1982), 179.

[4] On the idea of incrustation as writing or graphism, see William Rowe, 'La oralidad y las trazas visuales: *Hijo de hombre* de Augusto Roa Bastos', in *Hacia una poética radical* (Rosario, 1996), 78–84.

[5] 'Doña Bárbara Writes the Plain', in *The Voice of the Masters* (Austin, Tex., 1988), 33–63.

however, is Carl Sauer's vital distinction between physical landscape and cultural landscape, the former being the purely physical and non-human, and cultural landscape the appropriation
and marking of land by human actions.[6] Without some such
distinction, we are already inside the frame of Nature, with all
the unification and stabilization that European and predomi-
nantly eighteenth-century term implies, and what is left out is
not only the non-human but also those native American traditions of space-time which the colonial mind suppressed in
order to sustain the myth of virgin territory. That the non-
human is what precedes territory is a major presupposition of
the poetics of Neruda's *Residencia en la tierra*, and in fact always
occurs in his poetry when he enters the area of the uncoded, of
that which has no name. This is also the case with América 'sin
nombre todavía' [as yet without a name] in the first foundational canto of *Canto general*, where we move in both directions
between the non-human and nature named and territorialized:

> Tierra mía sin nombre, sin América,
> estambre equinoccial, lanza de púrpura,
> tu aroma me trepó por las raíces
> hasta la copa que bebía, hasta la más delgada
> palabra aún no nacida de mi boca.[7]

> [Land of mine without a name, without America,
> stamen at equinox, purple lance,
> your aroma rose in me through the roots
> into the cup I drank, into the slenderest
> word not yet born from my mouth.]

The movement is between smell and word, the unnamed and
the symbolic, the language ranging between the purely sensual
and that which belongs to specific symbolic traditions. In Zurita
also, the land is an uncoded area, furrowed by the pulse of
speech and emotion and prior to their social organization. The
differences from Neruda are of course great. Zurita's lack of
sensual specificity and generic approach to landscape lead to
an extreme of uncodedness which by the same token is open to
extreme possession by the symbolic.

The generic thrust, as in words like 'rocas', 'mar',

---

[6] Carl Sauer, *Land and Life: A Selection from the Writings of Carl Ortwin Sauer*
(Berkeley, 1963), 321.

[7] *Canto general* (Buenos Aires, 1963), 10.

'montañas', includes a dehistoricizing effect, whereby the land becomes a surface cleared of historical memory. There is an apparent contradiction here, in that Zurita's book is among other things an affirmation of memory. But the issue is the necessity for places where memory can be inscribed, in order to be available at all. The land, cleared, can become another skin, a site of perception that can be imagined as unviolated: thus events can be inscribed and read, without the amnesia caused by trauma and without the selectivity which public discourses impose upon memory, so as to make certain events un-rememberable. The land becomes an alternative body, resistant to the repressive effects of pain: an opposite situation to that of Kafka's character in the story 'In the Penal Settlement',[8] where a machine inscribes the letters of the Law into his flesh.

The making of the land into another skin occurs most vividly in repeated insertions of the skin of a mestizo face into the Atacama Desert and vice versa. That relocation upon a single plane is powerfully reinforced by the inclusion of Zurita's deliberate burning his own face,[9] as mark on the land/skin, making it into sign; that primary movement from thing to sign is a recurrent fascination in his work, as a process of renewal, new life, new vision. Again, this means that history has, in some senses, to be undone; but through the force of wounding, pain, and their conversion into love, not through programmes of willed amnesia, the desert produced by Walter Benjamin's 'destructive character',[10] or the dreams of Jacobin violence. Hence Zurita's violence against his own face, his self-defacement, needs to be understood as an action a person undertakes when already penetrated by totalitarian violence at a level which cannot be undone by analysis, thereby converting violation into a possibility of tenderness. It is also, perhaps, an act of defiance and responsibility, by establishing a bottom line with one's own hands.

If land is another skin to which love adheres, love is defined as a continuum of the erotic and the social, in that other, Whitmanian sense of adhesive, as what draws human beings

---

[8] 'In the Penal Settlement', in *Metamorphosis and Other Stories* (Harmondsworth, 1961).

[9] See Piña, *Conversaciones*, 209.

[10] Walter Benjamin, 'The Destructive Character', in *Reflections* (New York, 1986), 301–3.

together. The word *amor* varies between the possessives 'mi amor' and 'su amor', where the latter—as in the book's title—locates love, polysemically, as both theirs, his, and yours, in multiple reference both to the mothers and others close to the disappeared, and to those who died in prison and torture. Differences between singular and plural continue, but each passes through the other within a continuum of love that includes the living and the dead:

> Entera su enamorada canté así. Canté el amor:
>
>> Fue el tormento, los golpes y en pe-
>> dazos nos rompimos. Yo alcancé a
>> oírte pero la luz se iba.
>> Te busqué entre los destrozados,
>> hablé contigo. Tus restos me mira-
>> ron y yo te abracé. Todo acabó.
>> No queda nada. Pero muerta
>> te amo y nos amamos, aunque
>> esto nadie pueda entenderlo. (*C* 11)
>
> [I sang his/her/their love like this. I sang love:
>
>> It was torment, kicks, and
>> we were broken into pieces. I managed to
>> hear you but the light was fading.
>> I looked for you among the destroyed,
>> I spoke to you. Your remains looked
>> at me and I embraced you. Everything ended.
>> Nothing is left. But I love you
>> dead and we love each other, although
>> no one can understand this.]

The *yo* becomes *su*, but particular, as love, as opposed to willed sentiment, is. So that continuation after death moves from memory towards desire.

The phrase 'pegado a las rocas al mar y a las montañas', in its various repetitions, enriches the relationships between love and the earth's surface in such a way that they become not only a counterforce to specific historical abuse but also more extensively a primary condition for being in the world at all. That relationship resists notions of redemption and salvation, with their programmatics of inherited debt to be paid. The need for that condition of love arises within an intensive juxtaposition of violation and tenderness, exemplified in the following:

– Pero todo será nuevo, te digo,
– oh sí lindo chico.
– Claro—dijo el guardia, hay que arrancar el cáncer de raíz,
– oh sí, oh sí.
– El hombro cortado me sangraba y era olor raro la sangre.
– Dando vueltas se ven los dos enormes galpones.
– Marcas de T.N.T., guardias y gruesas alambradas cubren sus
– vidrios rotos.
– Pero a nosotros nunca nos hallarán porque nuestro amor
– está pegado a las rocas, al mar y a las montañas.
– Pegado, pegado a las rocas, al mar y a las montañas. (*C* 13)

[—But everything will be new, I tell you,
– ah yes beautiful boy.
– Yes—said the guard, the cancer must be pulled out by the root,
– oh yes, oh yes,
– The shoulder they had cut bled and the blood was a strange
    smell.
– You can see the enormous sheds spinning round.
– Marks of TNT, guards, and thick barbed wire cover their
    broken windows.
– But they will never find us because our love is stuck to the
    rocks, the sea,
– and the mountains.
– Stuck, stuck to the rocks, the sea, and the mountains.]

In one sense the land is that place which torture cannot penetrate, a surface it cannot mark. But the land in Zurita cannot be taken as a single, concrete space. It is itself in a process of becoming which involves simultaneously a becoming of self. The latter occurs here in dizzying switches between violation and tenderness; the shock they cause derives from sudden and unsignalled transitions between words which are acts of violation and others which express openness to tenderness. One finds oneself thrown, as reader, from extremes of defensive closure to extremes of tender vulnerability. The poem takes the risk of actually confronting the erotics of violence, instead of using it as a means to capture readers into passivity, as is characteristic of a large proportion of writing on violence in Chile and Argentina. Zurita seeks by means of a counter-erotics to rescue the ultimate undefended zone of trauma from invasion by erotic violence—no small undertaking. The passage just quoted continues with

– Pegado, pegado a las rocas, al mar y a las montañas
  – Murió mi chica, murió mi chico, desaparecieron todos.
                             Desiertos de amor. (*C* 14)

[—Stuck, stuck to the rocks, the sea and the mountains.
– My girl has died, my boy has died, they all disappeared.
                             Deserts/deserted of love.]

The tension of opposed meanings in the word 'desiertos' is extreme: on the one hand, there is the emptiness of total loss. At the same time, there is an opposite sense that draws on a prophetic-utopian discourse of the transformation of desert into fertile land and on the notion of the inscription of love upon the land, the bareness of the space becoming a positive. Another passage, already quoted, where a severed arm is used to beat others, continues with:

– corrí al urinario a vomitar.
– Inmensas praderas se formaban en cada una de las
– arcadas, las nubes rompiendo el cielo y los cerros
– acercándose. (*C* 13)

[—I ran to the lavatory to vomit.
– Immense meadows formed in each one of the
– arches/retchings, the clouds breaking the sky and the hills
– coming near.]

The word 'arcadas' (=retching/arches) dramatizes an extraordinary concurrence of self violated and self restored by projection of inner life on to the land. In that action, land becomes landscape.

This gives the context of the revisiting of sites of imprisonment, torture, and death which the poem traces: 'Canté la canción de los viejos galpones de concreto' [I sang the song of the old concrete sheds], the sheds also sites of niches for the dead, 'Unos sobre otros decenas de nichos los llenaban' [dozens of niches, one above the other, filled them]. What is then mapped is not only a particular personal and collective experience in Chile but the countries of America as having arrived at their shape through similar experiences. Each *galpón* becomes a country: 'En cada uno hay un país, son como niños, están muertos' [In each one there is a country, they are like children, they are dead]. The clichéd patriotic narrative of dead human beings expressing the essence of a national territory is opposed by countries becoming violated human beings,

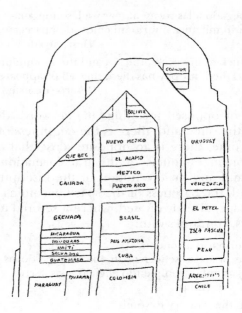

Fig. 2 Zurita's map of the niches.

instead of human beings sacrificed in order to create a national
identity. In fact Zurita's remapping overturns the whole notion
of 'national' territory; instead of territory and its symbols
preserved by violence against foreigners and 'the enemy
within', country is where human beings have become the
unwilling site of violation and abuse.

There are thirty niches, set out on the page as blocks of
twelve lines, each in two columns, making six niches to the
page. Obviously, they can be read in different spatial orders, as
tombstones can. There are also two diagrammatic maps—like
maps of cemeteries—each taking up a single page. All Latin
American nation-states are included, as well as other 'countries', including Easter Island, or regions not corresponding
with national territories, such as 'las hambrientas llanuras
chilenas, argentinas, chamarritas y pampas' [the hungry plains
of Chile, Argentina, blankets and pampas] or 'los Andes de los
países' [the Andes of countries] (*C* 22, 23). The 'países

centrales' [developed nations] also have their tomb, marked, as are all the tombs, by pain. The 'nicho arauco' is one of several which show the discrepant thrust of Zurita's geopolitics, acknowledging native rights over American space and the many ways in which current national boundaries are arbitrary and colonial. The USA is included, both as a whole and in those regions which are marked by native and/or Hispanic traditions, such as what he calls 'país Colorado del desierto' [Red country of the desert]. Another of the tombs/niches is called Canada: the cemetery is the whole continent, and what is laid to rest there is above all a history of destruction and violation. The Argentina niche may be taken to exemplify the compressed tombstone narratives:

> Nicho Argentina. Galpón 13, nave y nicho remitido bajo el país Perú y sobre el país Chile. De tortura en tortura, desaparecimiento y exterminio quedó hueca, como los países nombrados, y la noche no tuvo donde caer ni el día, Amén. País desaparecido del horror tras los cuarteles. Desde allí el viento silbó sobre la pampa inexistente y apagándose se vieron las masacradas caras, Amén. Lápida 6. Piel blanca sólo dice.
>
> (*C* 19)

[Niche Argentina. Shed 13, nave and niche consigned beneath the country Peru and above the country Chile. From torture to torture, disappearance and extermination became empty, like the countries named, and the night had nowhere to fall nor the day, Amen. Disappeared country of horror behind barracks. From there the wind blew over the non-existent pampa and dying down the massacred faces were seen, Amen. Tombstone 6. White skin it says only.]

The name Argentina—naming, in Zurita's poem, is a prerogative of these rites of burial—is first placed within the spatial and typographical arrangement of the *galpones.* Then it is positioned in a geographical field, via the prepositions *bajo* and *sobre.* This mapping, however, does not correspond to the layout of Zurita's diagrams: there are gaps between the land itself and the different mappings of it (the map is not the territory).

Location becomes a function of 'tortura', and temporality is spatialized: the history of the past two decades is related in a condensed language which moves towards the cosmological. Finally, history thus spatialized is dramatized in a longer view, which includes, crucially, the genocidal absence of Indians from Argentine identity.

Each niche is a composite of fragments, in condensed epitaphic style, which echo the fragments-phrases that make up other niches. The process of composition consists in rapid transitions, not signalled syntactically, moving typically from personal emotion to land perceived outside, to land within the *galpón* and again to land outside, vaster, continental now, to military barracks in the sea and finally to islands:

> Tumba nicho nevado 27 de los países. Creció, creció del amor que tuvo, anota la tumba. Heladas, del amor que tuve subieron las cadenas de picos nevados y fue entonces el penacho blanco que desde el mar se ve. En Galpón y nicho están montañas y mares. El más grande es la altura de las montañas América del Sur y América del Norte. No, son cuarteles rodeados de mar, son las islas rodeadas de mar ay no. No te vas.
> (*C* 23)

[Tomb niche snow peak 27 of the countries. It grew, it grew from the love it had, the tomb states. Frozen, from the love I had the chains of snowy peaks rose up and then it was the white plume that can be seen from the sea. In Shed and niche are mountains and seas. The greatest is the height of the mountains South America and North America. No, they are barracks surrounded by sea, they are the islands surrounded by sea ay no. Don't go.]

Each space becomes other and at the same time returns, not in repetitive circularity but with emotional intensification of affect and semantic expansion. The historical, the geographical, the cosmological, and the experience of violation are condensed on to a single surface which situates a reading and a writing. In the niche named Canada (and which names Canada) whiteness and ice penetrate perception, becoming an equivalence (not a representation) of domination, torture, and genocide, the map of perception becoming memory, as niche in the continental map. Zurita's epitaphs, with their vast scale, are also counter-overcodings which contest that dominant making of national identities that plays so freely and loosely with populations like the Indian or the gaucho or landscapes like the tropical, and make them available as cultural capital to unscrupulous regimes.

Those authoritarian narratives of colonialization and modernization which have sought to eradicate all traces of idolatry and superstition (European words for the native cosmos) have been demolished with enormous energy by Latin American writers. Among them is Juan Rulfo, whose novel *Pedro Páramo* insists that the dead whom the writing of history omits are still a place (as in native American traditions), where memory resides, in defiance of programmes of amnesia. In Zurita's *Canto a su amor desaparecido*, the dead are a continuing place, beneath the TV masts which have taken the place of 'los viejos galpones', the mass media entering to remove the traces, except that, in Zurita's vision, images of the continuity of love invade the TV screen too. The place is still there, despite what is said ('esas épocas ya pasaron' [those epochs have finished]) and despite the 'grandes glaciares' [great glaciers] which 'vienen a llevarse ahora los restos de nuestro amor' [come now to take away the remains of our love] (*C* 15); the time-space of the dead lovers continues, and discovers a continuation of torture, despite denial by official versions.

The time-space of the niches is not that of chronological time added to space plotted from fixed coordinates. Thus, to return to the word *país*, it is used for spaces, territories, collectivities, experiences; the place of torture becomes cemetery (there were none for the tortured and 'disappeared'), becomes the continent, in precise opposition to that notion, proposed by the military, of a cancer to be cut out in order to cleanse the social body. 'En cada nicho hay un país, están allí, son los países sudamericanos' [in every niche there is a country, there they are, they are the South American countries]: the three verbs, distributive, localizing, and ontologizing, make the mapping its own event, not expression of what has already been defined elsewhere. The nature of this event includes writing, reading, and hearing. The niches are both themselves letters of a script and offer signs which are 'anotados' [noted] and 'señalizados' [made into signs] (*C* 20), and which are simultaneously read and heard: the usual relationship between the written and the spoken, where the written purports to transcribe and supersede the spoken, is countered by placing them alongside each other:

> Letras, letritas, dice, tumbas del
> amor ido dice. Yo te sostuve con mi
> mano y lo viste. Países idos dice. (*C* 17)

> [letters, little letters, it says, tombs of
> love gone it says. I held you with my
> hand and you saw it. Countries gone it says.]

Together with these inscriptive movements, there is also a metaphoric tendency in Zurita's approach to language and space. In the interview already quoted, he states,

Lo que más me conmueve, aunque suene grandilocuente, son las pasiones y la emotividad humana. Siento que esas emociones a veces son tan contrastantes, otras veces son tan abismales, otras veces son tan planas, que la más grande imagen que podemos tener de ellas no se encuentra tanto dentro de nosotros mismos, sino que están en estos espectáculos. Las cordilleras y las playas yo las veo como metáforas de las pasiones humanas y de allí siento su fuerza, lo que me da la dimensión de una cierta grandeza o de una intensidad en esos sentimientos y esas pasiones.'[11]

[What move me most, though it may sound grandiloquent, are human passions and feeling. I feel that those emotions are sometimes so contrasting, and at other times so vast, or so flat, that the largest image we can have of them is not inside ourself, but in those spectacles. I see the mountain ranges and beaches as metaphors of human passions and that is where I feel their force, which gives me the dimension of a certain grandeur or intensity in those feelings and passions.]

The metaphoric tendency in the poems tends to fix the land inside inherited modes of perception; it reaches its extreme in *Anteparaíso*, where, in the opening section, the beaches of Chile take on the transferred attributes of Christ crucified as traditionally described. Nevertheless, Zurita's interview statement describes a non-metaphoric force in his language: the concern with a pure flow of emotion, irrespective of its meaning, and with the land as the site and shape of that flow,

---

[11] Piña, *Conversaciones*, 221.

without anthropomorphic movement—which separates Zurita from the Romantic inheritance. Where his language is metaphoric, it is closer to Dante's sense of nature as emblematic.

Zurita describes his attitude to landscape as an urban one:

Yo soy un ser urbano, siempre fui un hombre de ciudad y mis contactos con los paisajes fueron muy esporádicos. Es probable que por este hecho de ser alguien tan urbano, los paisajes aparecen aquí como una nostalgia, más que una realidad física donde el hombre aparece inserto en él.[12]

[I am an urban being, I was always a person of the city and my contacts with the land were very sporadic. It's probably because of my being so urban that the landscapes appear here like something nostalgic, rather than a physical reality inside which there are human beings.]

If this emptied landscape, for which the term nostalgia seems inappropriate given Zurita's utopian vision, is susceptible to purely intensive movements of emotion, then this is a function of Zurita's highly unusual combination of spatial multiplicity and linguistic polysemy. However, the extreme openness of method gives greater penetrative force to the Christian symbolic when it does enter. This is something that happens more in *Purgatorio* [Purgatory] and *Anteparaíso* [Anteparadise], books that were written before and after *Canto a su amor desaparecido*.

THE RENEWAL OF LANGUAGE

Writing on the condition of culture and identity in Chile after the coup of 1973, the sociologist J. J. Brunner draws attention to the combined effect of military authoritarianism and free-market ideology in the following terms:

The actual symbolic-expressive emptying of society produced by the combined operation of the market and repression, both of them mechanisms that operate with a low threshold of communication in that they do not require (and even exclude) interpersonal elaboration of collective projects and of organised reciprocities, is filled in the new order by the diffusion of 'lightweight ideologies', especially through television.[13]

---

[12] Ibid.

[13] J. J. Brunner, *Un espejo trizado: ensayos sobre cultura y políticas culturales* (Santiago, 1988), 94.

Raúl Zurita's poetry is written inside and against that situation, and in so far as what Brunner describes is recognizably an experience of other countries than Chile, Zurita's work, though emphatically Chilean, can be read as an intervention in a more widely shared condition.

The period between Pinochet's coup and the transition to democracy in Chile was characterized by the decay of communication: caught between two communicative regimes, one which sought to prolong the language and the values of the previous Popular Unity government (broadly socialist) and the other which sought to impose those of the military government (authoritarian and neo-liberal), the society lacked a sense of truth: 'there is no truth of actual facts, whatever these might be, since the facts themselves have been incorporated into the struggle to define reality.'[14] With two opposed communicative orders 'struggling to impose themselves and control the production of meanings, truths, public topics, and schemes of understanding and evaluation in the society', the country became 'an implosion of images, none with sufficient force to produce a general and shared meaning'. The effect was to divide people, both from each other and within themselves. For Zurita, this condition, where the only possible conversation is a trivial one, can be defined as a lack of transparency in the realm of conversation; conversation ceases to be a place of agreed (even if opposed) meanings and people lose confidence in the spoken word.[15] Transparency is not to do with the absence of social conflict but with the functioning of language as a site of mutuality. If the military regime, by producing a culture of fear that brought surveillance and censorship even into the interstices of private life, caused a collapse of transparency, an important question, implicit in Zurita's essay of 1983, remains: what was it in the state of the language that allowed this to happen? It is precisely here—within the space opened up by that question—that Zurita's poetic work intervenes. And it does so in terms of longer durations and less obvious dimensions of

---

[14] Brunner, *Un espejo trizado: ensayos sobre cultura y políticas culturales*, 75.
[15] Raúl Zurita, *Literatura, lenguaje y sociedad (1973–1983)* (Santiago, 1983), 4–8; translations from this text are by Catherine Boyle. See also Catherine Boyle, 'Touching the Air: The Cultural Force of Woman in Chile', in S. Radcliffe and S. Westwood (eds.), '*Viva*': *Women and Popular Protest in Latin America* (London, 1993), 170.

language than those circumscribed by the battle of communicative stances unleashed in 1973.

Zurita points out that the Pinochet regime sought to make it impossible to say anything against it:

En un primer momento se descubre la censura (administrada), impuesta, luego se la internaliza (autocensura) y finalmente pasa a desbordar cualquier estrategia que sobre ella se pueda tener. No se tratará ya de privarse de hablar de algo por temor a un posible castigo (en general los análisis de la censura paran aquí), sino que hablar, ejercer la lengua, es ya un castigo. Es allí donde el régimen dobla y subvierte su culpabilidad, ella pasa a ser dominio público de modo tal que todos son culpables aunque no se sepa de qué.[16]

[First one discovers the imposition of censorship on an institutional level, then it becomes internalized (self-censorship) and finally it goes beyond any strategy one might use to control it. It is no longer a question of not being able to speak of something through fear of possible punishment (most analyses of censorship stop here), but of how speaking as such, simply using the language, is already a punishment. That is where the regime replicates and subverts its own guilt; the guilt enters the public domain in such a way that everyone is guilty although without knowing of what.]

Zurita's proposition here is that the regime has succeeded in tainting the language with its violence. Any ideological refutation of the regime, easy anyway, is no longer the point. The issue lies elsewhere. One of the regime's key strategies was the attempt to monologize language, turning its interlocutors, quite literally, into its message:

En efecto, roto el sistema de conversación el interlocutor pasa a ser el mensaje emitido. El interlocutor cuyo sonido es contestado segundo a segundo.[17]

[In effect, once the system of conversation is destroyed, the interlocutor becomes the message that is emitted. Interlocutor whose sounds are answered second by second, followed, sought out.]

In other words, even unspoken thoughts, or the internal sounds that initiate them, are interfered with. If words had only one meaning, then the sayable could be reduced to a schematics of state legitimacy. The vast paranoia implicit in this position was not matched by any collective counter-paranoia among its

[16] Zurita, *Literatura*, 15.　　[17] Ibid. 6.

victims; on the contrary, they were enlisted as its individual bearers.

It is worth at this point considering that other project for a totalitarian language capable of speaking its victims: Orwell's 'Newspeak' in *1984*. In an appendix, Orwell provides us with a commentary on its principles. These consist in the reduction of vocabulary and the subjection of semantics, via rules of morphology, to a closed set of relations between fixed concepts (such as that everything is either positive or negative, an ideal situation for paranoia). All possibilities of drift would be stamped out. Designed for introduction by stages, its final aim is to make it impossible even to think in the old way. Political desires would become permanently fixed inside a predetermined horizon of the possible. One of the effects it has to achieve is to remove any memory of the past from the language. For this purpose it alters the morphology of words and coins new ones. Without such methods of linguistic engineering at its disposal, the Chilean regime's attempts to monologize language had to rely on eliminating the interlocutor, and this, Zurita stresses, was a key weakness:

El discurso oficial, al eliminar uno de los términos de la cadena enunciativa, el receptor que se ve impedido de ejercer cualquier tipo de respuesta, [. . .] provoca una crisis en el interior de la secuencia significativa del lenguaje cuya resultante va a ser la implantación de dos discursos paralelos: el discurso oficializante y el discurso opositor que operará con los mismos términos pero a los cuales se le doblará el sentido.[18]

[Official discourse, by eliminating one of the terms of the enunciative chain, the receiver who finds himself prevented from exercising any reply, produces a crisis inside the signifying sequence of language whose result will be the implantation of two parallel discourses: official discourse and an oppositional discourse that will operate with the same terms but by giving them a double meaning.]

One such term is the word *patria*. Official discourse seeks to possess the word entirely for itself, eliminating the long history of social experiences through which its meanings were shaped. What makes official discourse refutable is precisely the historical formation of meanings. Words remain attached to these

----

[18] Zurita, *Literatura*, 21.

meanings, which have changed over time, despite attempts to eradicate them from memory. Hearing the word *patria* expressed by official militarist propaganda, a person becomes aware for the first time, says Zurita, of all the meanings that are being suppressed. Language becomes dominated by what is unsaid.[19]

Using the regime's words against it is a prime strategy of Zurita's book *Anteparaíso*. But the work of renewing the language against paranoia, communicative entropy, and destructive sociability is a much larger undertaking than that of simply refuting the Pinochet regime. For a start, the action has to begin much further back. The first section of the book, entitled *Las utopías* (The utopias), places the sixteenth-century arrival of Europeans alongside experiences of the twentieth century. Instead of the securities of the heroic, conquering self, Zurita writes a counter-epic of wounded bodies and shattered selves, closer to the painful narrative of Cabeza de Vaca,[20] than the triumphalist chronicles of conquistadors used in schools and State propaganda. The result is not an ideological refutation of the conquest ideology used by the twentieth-century dictatorships against the enemy within,[21] but an alternative passage through the language where the vectors are pain and tenderness and these become the bases of the social (the lower-case roman numerals are reproduced from the original):

i. Empapado de lágrimas arrojó sus vestimentas al agua

ii. Desnudo lo hubieran visto acurrucarse hecho un ovillo sobre sí   tembloroso   con las manos cubriéndose el purular de sus heridas

iii. Como un espíritu   lo hubieran ustedes visto cómo se abrazó a sí mismo   lívido   gimiente   mientras se le iba esfumando el color
del cielo en sus ojos (*A* 42)

[i. Soaked in tears he threw his clothing into the water

19 Ibid. 21–2.
20 See M. Glantz, 'Nakedness as Shipwreck: Alvar Núñez Cabeza de Vaca', *Travesía: Journal of Latin American Cultural Studies*, 1/2 (1992), 86–112, and J. Kraniauskas, 'Cabeza de Vaca', ibid. 113–22.
21 See F. Graziano, *Divine Violence: Spectacle, Psychosexuality and Radical Christianity in the Argentine 'Dirty War'* (Boulder, Colo., 1992).

ii. Naked they might have seen him hunched over himself
trembling   covering with his hands the suppuration of his
wounds

iii. Like a spirit   you should have seen how he embraced himself
pale   moaning   while the colour
of the sky faded in his eyes]

This site of pain, loss, and dissolution of self and world becomes
at the same time a place of utopia and radical renewal. Utopia
emerges from a body opened by grief:

Porque la playa nunca se espejearía en sus ojos sino mejor en el
derramarse de todas las utopías como un llanto incontenible que se
le fuera desprendiendo del pecho   hirviente   desgarrado
despejando la costa que Chile entero le vio adorarse en la iluminada
de estos sueños (*A* 57)

[Because the beach would never shine in his eyes but rather in the
scattering of all utopias like an uncontainable weeping torn out of
his chest   seething   ripped apart   clearing the coast that all Chile
saw worshipped in the illumination of these dreams]

The extraordinary conversion of extreme grief into the capacity to imagine a different future is placed within an emergence
of luminous vision. The wounds themselves are the places
where the world enters self, Zurita's language inviting us to pass
through that same process. From pain and the alterations it
makes in the sensing body, there emerges a luminosity of world
and gaze, in a splendour of the visible made available to vision
washed clear, to use Zurita's phrase ('la lavada visión', *A* 42–3).
Patria is the key theme of the renewed vision: 'la patria resp-
landecía levantándose desde el polvo como una irradiada en las
playas de sus ojos relucientes' [the *patria* shone like one irradi-
ated rising up from the dust on the beaches of their gleaming
eyes] (*A* 44), part of the larger renewal of the West in utopia
and New World—'un nuevo mundo que les fuera adhiriendo
otra luz en sus pupilas' [a new world that caused a different
light to adhere to their pupils] (*A* 56).

The vision of Chile as *patria* occurs within a process of
language that works quite differently from totalitarian ambitions
of linguistic engineering. The tender fragility of the body
extends into an extreme permeability of words, released into
multiple meaning by reduced syntactic and narrative controls. It
is not that syntactic and narrative order is inoperative—in fact in

this sense the writing is fairly conventional—but that the communicative action is not single or unidirectional. Speakers and interlocutors are in constant variation (them, you, us, I, he) in such a way that the words are always an event between shifting interlocutors and not part of a prior communicative scheme. It could even be said that each utterance causes interlocutors to emerge. The full openness of communication permits words to be repeatedly recharged, without finality or subordination to any single discourse. Similarly, the shape of the verses is given by the breath in oral exchange, in an exhalatory movement that contributes a physical loosening of ties to the effect of release from rigid orders of communicative authority.

The loosening of the boundaries of the body—its organization and containment in given social orders—extends into redefinition of the possibilities of the collective:

ii. Porque no fueron las playas la Utopía de Chile sino Usted
    mismo era las costas que buscaron   enceguecidos   como
    ánimas   palpándose entre ellos

iii. Donde ciegos cada vida palpó a tientas otra vida hasta que ya
     no quedasen vidas sino sólo el vacío esplendiéndoles la Utopía
     de entre los muertos   descarnados   tocándose   como el aire
     ante nosotros (A 59)

[ii. Because the beaches were not the Utopia of Chile but You
     yourself were the   coast they searched for   blinded   like souls
     touching each other

iii. Where blind each life touched gropingly another life until there
     were no more lives only the void radiating Utopia to them
     from among the dead   fleshless   touching each other like the
     air before us]

Just as the communicative action lacks any single origin, the emergence of light lacks any single source. The experience is ecstatic, but closer for example to Heidegger's secular use of Eckhart (who enters the Spanish language through San Juan de la Cruz and Santa Teresa) and other figures in the mystical tradition, than to Octavio Paz's mythology of returning gods as solution for social decay in the 1950s.[22] In Zurita there is no appropriation of the ecstatic by religion; instead, the luminous

---

[22] See Michael E. Zimmerman, 'Heidegger, Buddhism, and Deep Ecology', in C. Guignon (ed.), *The Cambridge Companion to Heidegger* (Cambridge, 1993), 240–69.

is multiple in emergence. This requires a prior washing, clearing, and emptying, in turn made possible by pain and wounding, which do not belong to the supernatural but occur as historical events. With the entry of ecstasy into the horizon of the socially possible, historiography is redefined.

Ecstasy should not be confused with inner reverie. In the latter, Georges Bataille writes, '*I* remain: everything escapes if I have not been able to lose myself in Nothingness; what I have glimpsed is brought back to the level of objects known to me.' With ecstasy, there is a suspension of discourse:

If I only gain access to the simple intensity of inner movement, it goes without saying that discourse is only rejected for a time, that it remains at bottom the master. [. . .] the mind attentive to inner movement only gains access to the unknowable depth of things[:] by turning to an entire forgetting of self—not satisfying itself with anything, going always further to the impossible.[23]

Bataille's distinctions give new dimensions to Brunner's terms of social analysis. Zurita's concern is a refoundation of the social in ecstatic vision and not in ideology, that is from a place outside discourse, though capable of discursive elaboration. The crisis of social meaning occurring as 'symbolic-expressive emptying' and the 'implosion of images' is extended into a more radical and total emptiness, where everything is risked. This is not some self-indulgent 'spirituality', but the total cost of a particular regime of the social written into the body of the tortured and embraced as a starting-point. The final page of the 'Utopias' section of the book enters a moment in the experience of being interned for two months in the hold of a cargo ship along with hundreds of others:

> Acurrucados unos junto a otros contra el fondo del bote
> de pronto me pareció que la tempestad, la noche y yo
> éramos sólo uno
> y que sobreviviríamos
> porque es el Universo entero el que sobrevive
> Sólo fue un instante [. . .]
> Sólo fue un raro instante, pero aunque se me fuese la
> vida
> ¡Yo nunca me olvidaría de él! (*A* 66)

---

[23] Georges Bataille, *Inner Experience* (New York, 1988), 114.

[Huddled together at the bottom of the ship
suddenly it seemed that the storm, the night, and myself
were a single thing
and that we would survive
because it is the entire Universe that survives
It was just a moment
It was just a strange moment, but even if I lost my
life
I would never forget it!]

The ecstatic, in Bataille's phrase, is 'a fleeting moment', but does not its force irradiate all others—its totality contesting that other, willed, totality of socio-linguistic engineering? That, certainly, is the thrust of Zurita's book. And that would require one to reformulate Brunner's other term, the social imagination (*el imaginario social*), so as to include in it possibilities of radical change. Zurita's work asserts that susceptibility to being invaded and wounded is also precisely where imagination resides. It also suggests that the power of imagination is not to be confused with heroics.

EXORCIZING THE LANGUAGE

If *patria* is the highest ideal of the social imagination, it does not in Zurita's work partake of the male sacrificial heroism that characterizes the foundational symbols of the Latin American republics. And the communality it presupposes does not rest upon social division and its denial in the higher unity of the nation-state. What is at stake is the cost of the sociability imposed by the State under capitalism: that use of internal and external evaluative comparisons (the family as model of the nation, 'our' national character as opposed to others') which Corrigan and Sayer expose in *The Great Arch* as examples of how the State's statements are material actions 'which cartographize and condition the relations they help organize'.[24] Part of these, they go on to say, is the fact that 'the "Mortall God" is sexed (just as He is classed, raced, tongued, penned, styled, dressed). If He—to adapt both Durkheim and

---

[24] P. Corrigan and D. Sayer, *The Great Arch: English State Formation as Cultural Revolution* (Oxford, 1985), 142.

Hobbes—represents society, it is a very particular form of "Society" that is held up as an object of worship and emulation.'[25] And the denial inherent in this process of idealization includes denial of the 'painfulness' inherent in state formation, that is in 'the forms of cultural relations which states regulate (normally naturalized or presented in terms of increasing "provision" and "access") [and which] hurt as much as they help'.[26]

Zurita deals in counter-idealizations, as a response, for example, to the absence of justice:

> Chile no encontró un solo justo en
> sus playas   apedreados   nadie pudo
> lavarse las manos de estas heridas (*A* 47)

> [Chile did not find a single just person on
> its beaches   stoned   no one could
> wash their hands of these wounds]

The lack of any just person can only be filled by a conversion of pain:

iv. Pero sus heridas podrían ser el justo de las playas de Chile

v. Nosotros seríamos entonces la playa que les alzó un justo desde sus heridas

vi. Sólo allí todos los habitantes de Chile se habrían hecho uno hasta ser ellos el justo (*A* 47–8)

[iv. But their wounds could be the just person on the beaches of Chile

v. We would be then the beach that raised up a just person from their wounds

vi. Only there all the inhabitants of Chile would have become one so as to be themselves the just person]

The *we* afforded by such an event of the imagination differs radically and obviously from the one granted by nation-states that deny the division and pain they reproduce. In fact where the primary is not categories—which have to be obeyed—but light, understood not symbolically but as a capability of active perception in every human being, the dividing and unifying

---

[25] Corrigan and Sayer, *The Great Arch: English State Formation as Cultural Revolution*, 143.   [26] Ibid. 4.

State loses its customary ground. The epic actions of the artist, as Zurita stresses, 'no son sino pequeñas síntesis del esfuerzo que hace todo ciudadano por vivir cada día' [are merely small syntheses of the effort that every citizen makes in order to live each day].[27]

The *patria* passes through repeated obliterations which become resurrections in the vision of those whose pain it is:

iv. Toda la patria fue entonces la resurrección pintándose en sus despojos [. . .]

vi. Por eso Chile entero reverdecía mientras le manaban mojándolo las lágrimas [. . .]

En que la patria borrada fue renaciendo como una playa que les hacía luz de sus despojos (*A* 62–3)

[iv. The whole patria was then the resurrection depicting itself in his remains

vi. That is why all Chile became green again while he became wet with the tears he wept

In which the patria erased was born again like a beach which gave light from its remains]

This is not therefore Hobbes's Mortall God who drains individual energies to maintain his continuity. Zurita's interest is in the continuity of love after the death of love, as a 'corriente subterránea' [an underground flow], and in the resurgence of words after their obliteration. The words concerned are those such as God, or love, 'words that are so much used and yet so powerful, so indispensable and yet so criticised'.[28] This resurrection has nothing to do with the willed continuity of some immobile Horatian monument resting upon the State's own continuity, but is closer to Charles Olson's definition of resurrection, in his poem of the same title, as 'a directed magnitude' or 'the vector of space':[29] not a dead replication but a continuing available movement in space, like the rivers which supply the overarching cosmology, folding time on to itself, in *La vida nueva* [The new life], the final book of Zurita's great project. Not a restoration of the past, but its contemporaneity, as becoming. Not the

---

[27] Piña, *Conversaciones*, 229.
[28] Ibid. 223, 219.
[29] Charles Olson, 'The Chain of Memory is Resurrection', in *Collected Poems* (Berkeley, 1987), 372–9.

cemetery of memory, or of the dictionary, but a rebirth of the
language, as in Huidobro's *Altazor* (which includes a cemetery
where words die and are reborn), or Lorca's account of
personal and artistic death and resurrection in *Poeta en Nueva
York*:

> Comprendí que me habían asesinado.
> [. . .]
> Ya no me encontraron.
> ¿No me encontraron?
> No. No me encontraron.
> Pero se supo que la sexta luna huyó torrente arriba,
> y que el mar recordó ¡de pronto!
> los nombres de todos sus ahogados.[30]

> [I realized they had murdered me.
> They could not find me.
> They could not find me?
> No. They could not find me.
> But it was known that the sixth moon fled upstream,
> and that the sea remembered, suddenly,
> the names of all the drowned.]

For Zurita, works of literature make a store of human possibilities ('grandes preservatorios de todas las pasiones')[31] continually available through words. And nowhere more radically
than in Neruda's *Alturas de Macchu Picchu*:

una radical y absoluta liberación del hombre—o el pueblo—que
escribe ese poema, como alguien que ha logrado dominar absolutamente la lengua de los conquistadores, sortear todas sus trampas. Ahí
se presenta algo a conquistar colectivamente para el futoro, algo así
como que estos pueblos alcanzarán definitivamente su paz cuando
logren reconciliarse con la lengua que hablan. 'Alturas de Macchu
Picchu' es el gran canto en el cual las palabaras, unas con otras,
conviven en la más absoluta dicha y armonía. Nadie ha hecho una
cosa así. Por eso es radicalmente un genio.[32]

[a radical and absolute liberation of the man—or the people—who is
writing this poem, as someone who has achieved complete mastery
over the language of the conquistadors, and has avoided all its traps.
What is presented is something to be conquered collectively for the
future, which is that these nations will find a definitive peace when

---

[30]   Federico García Lorca, *Poeta en Nueva York* (Madrid, 1987), 119.
[31]   Piña, *Conversaciones*, 222.
[32]   Ibid. 231.

they manage to reconcile themselves with the language they speak. *Heights of Macchu Picchu* is the great song in which words live together in absolute happiness and harmony. No one has done anything like that. That is why Neruda is radically a genius.]

Death and resurrection in Neruda's work are, again, both personal and at the same time collective and historical. They entail, most importantly for Zurita,

una reconciliación radical de la lengua española consigo misma. Creo que nosotros hablamos una lengua que está cargada de fantasmas: somos el fruto de la imposición. Es una lengua que en cada una de las palabras que usamos, guarda, por así decirlo, la memoria y las huellas de todo lo que significó esa imposición: la historia de todos los aherrojamientos y la conquista. Una de las grandes dificultades que como países, como pueblo, hemos tenido para lograr construir proyectos sólidos y estables, tiene que ver con una relación con el lenguaje. Esa no es una relación armónica.[33]

[a radical reconciliation of the Spanish language with itself. I believe that we speak a language full of ghosts: we are the product of imposition. It's a language in which each one of the words we use keeps alive, so to speak, the memory and the traces of everything which that imposition meant: the history of enslavement and conquest. One of the great difficulties we have had as countries, as nations, in building solid and stable projects, has to do with a relationship with language. It is not a harmonious relationship.]

Quite clearly, these are central issues for Zurita's own ambition as poet.

Purgatorio, his first book, initiates the work of exorcizing the language. It explores the possibility of being outside 'the logos' altogether, expressing, in the need for that, an extreme distrust of the language. Interestingly, parts of the book were written before 1973, suggesting that Zurita was already grappling with possibilities in the language that would be unleashed later, producing work that was, to use his own terms, out of phase, just as, in the realm of the social imagination, José Donoso's novel *El obsceno pájaro de la noche* [The obscene bird of night][34] was also an anticipation of the coup that would come three years later. To read *Purgatorio* is to have one's relationship with

---

[33] Ibid. 230.
[34] Barcelona, 1970. English translation: *The Obscene Bird of Night* (New York, 1973).

the Spanish language—and with language as such—altered.
The Atacama Desert, a huge strip of land running from northern Peru to some 500 kilometres north of Santiago in Chile, is
used as part of a total clearing action:

  i. Dejemos pasar el infinito del Desierto de Atacama

 ii. Dejemos pasar la esterilidad de estos desiertos

Para que desde las piernas abiertas de mi madre se levante una
Plegaria que se cruce con el infinito del Desierto de Atacama y mi
madre no sea entonces sino un punto de encuentro en el camino (*P*
30)

[i. Let the infinite of the Atacama Desert enter

ii. Let the sterility of these deserts enter

So that a Prayer can rise up from the open legs of my mother and
intersect with the infinite of the Atacama Desert and my mother be no
more than a meeting-point on the path]

The need for birth to intersect with the infinite of the desert
cancels birth as insertion into social cartography and its
symbolic operations. Hayeck, seeking to reaffirm private property as the foundation of sociability, asks the question, how
much of nature is it legitimate for an individual to appropriate?
as if this were an innocent way of starting from scratch. The
question itself is a mythical alibi for an existing ideological
commitment. In Zurita's more radical desire, the very terms
individual and nature are broken down, in the relief of a space
with nothing there, without roads, without codes. It is land, but
it is above the sky, resisting even the mapping of vertical and
horizontal. It is vast, but has zero inertia. Like silence, it is
before or after dichotomies. Zurita's writing here brings about
a huge influx of silence into the Spanish language, breaking
associative chains—the well-worn roads—including those of
cruelty and violent domination.

    But whereabouts is violence in language? Not solely in the
expressive dimension, as in associations for example, but also,
as Alan Pauls shows so effectively,[35] in the welding of meanings
to a violent place from which a word is spoken. Whenever that
word is uttered, it carries the violence of continuing social division with it. The double adhesion of sounds to meanings and

---

[35] Alan Pauls, 'Languages at War', *Travesia: Journal of Latin American Cultural Studies*, 2/1 (1993), 115–28.

these as signs to surfaces—i.e. the basic functioning of language as recognizable signs—is interrupted in *Purgatorio* by being placed inside a desert, an unmarked expanse. The influx of emptiness flows around signs and things, causing the violent weldings to crack. The writing, once again, moves into an area of ecstasy, 'the vision', in Bataille's words, 'of this object in which I lose myself [. . .] which I call the unknown and which is distinct from Nothingness by nothing which discourse can enunciate'.[36]

The unknowing, the nothingness, recall San Juan de la Cruz's work with the Spanish language, but in Zurita's case the materials also include quantum physics. The 'Areas verdes' [Green areas] section of *Purgatorio* experiments with paradoxical space, placing non-verbal space inside discourse and vice versa:

Las había visto pastando en el radiante λὸγοσ?

I. Algunas vacas se perdieron en la lógica

II. Otras huyeron por un subespacio
donde solamente existen biologías

III. Esas otras   finalmente vienen   vagando
desde hace como un millón de años
pero no podrán ser nunca vistas por sus vaqueros
pues viven en las geometrías no euclideanas [. . .]

I. Esta vaca es una insoluble paradoja
pernocta bajo las estrellas
pero se alimenta de logos
y sus manchas finitas son símbolos (*P* 47–8)

[He had seen them feeding on the radiant logos

I. Some cows got lost in logic

II. Others fled into a subspace
where only biologies exist

III. Those others   finally   have been wandering
for around a million years
but can never be seen by their cowherds
as they live in non-Euclidean geometries

I. This cow is an insoluble paradox
it spends the night under the stars
but it feeds on logos
and its finite markings are symbols]

---

[36] Bataille, *Inner Experience*, 114.

The paradoxes include the cow that is in itself not part of any sign system but at the same time feeds on logos, that lighting, as Heidegger calls it, which human beings are bound to but unaware of in the familiarity of recognitions.[37] Further, the cows are imperceptible and perceptible, non-signifying and symbolic at the same time. Which is similar to the existence, in quantum physics, of particles and waveforms, depending on the observer's action, an interaction which gets played out in the relationship between cows and cowherds:

> Ahora los vaqueros no saben qué hacer con esa vaca
> pues sus manchas no son otra cosa
> que la misma sombra de sus perseguidores (*P* 48)

> [Now the cowherds don't know what to do with that cow
> its markings are none other
> than the shadow of its pursuers]

In the meantime, topologically, the markings ('manchas') are both marks upon the surface of the cows and spaces within which the cows exist. The entry into a type of space where signs, becoming particles or mere spatiality, are released from signifying chains also loosens the chains of reference which paranoia needs. The overall effects include a massive release from the universe of discourse.

The cows, which can be taken as standing for the possibilities of existence of objects, move from emptiness into the symbolic and then, emptying the symbols, back into void. The void, like the cows, the cowherds, and even the 'you' ('Ud.') the statements address themselves to, is imaginary; not in the weak sense of compounded from existing recognitions, but in the strong, Kantian senses of the spatio-temporal relations which make understanding possible and of 'productive and spontaneous imagination "as originator of arbitrary forms of possible intuitions" '.[38]

The Kantian implication of Zurita's experiment gives some measure of its scope. But there is none of Kant's confidence in synthesis of consciousness as a reliable constant. Consider these topological features of the writing: imperceptible spaces, spaces still occupied by bodies now absent, full and vacated spaces

---

[37] Martin Heidegger, *Early Greek Thinking* (New York, 1984), 122.
[38] Gilles Deleuze, *Kant's Critical Philosophy* (Minneapolis, 1990), 18, 49.

occupying a single location several times over. One of their effects upon language is to abolish any separation of subjectivity and objectivity and, more than that, to scramble ('comienzan a cruzarse todos los símbolos entre sí' [all symbols start to intersect] *P* 50) and to clear the surface of consciousness of previous incision by the symbolic, suspending any cartography and thereby any representation:

III. Retornando de esos blancos espacios no regidos
    a través de los blancos espacios de la muerte de Ud.
    que está loco   al revés   delante de ellas. (*P* 51)

[III. Coming back from those white ungoverned spaces
    across the white spaces of your death
    who are mad   inside out   in front of the cows.]

UNMEDIATED MADNESS

Madness is a recurrent topic in *Purgatorio*, and the whiteness that tends to accompany it gives a clearing of any signs or marks. This is taken to an extreme on a page which, apart from the title, 'LAS LLANURAS DEL DESVARÍO' [THE PLAINS OF RAVING], contains three propositions:

$N=1$
La locura de mi obra
$N=$
La locura de la locura de la locura de la
N   (*P* 57)
[$N=1$
The madness of my work
$N=$
The madness of the madness of the madness of the
N]

If N stands, as it usually does in maths, for a positive integer, then in the first proposition, madness enters numeration as such and all its possible operations. In the second, where the restrictions are left open, madness, not confined to the speaker, is all cases, and, through the ambiguity of the *de*, extends to all possibilities of any inside or outside: a mad language as opposed to a mad person. The third proposition, like silence, is left entirely open. Zurita himself, in answer to a query from his

English translator, uses the phrase 'total madness'.[39] Is this necessary but highly risky madness in one sense a counter-insanity, to be used as a counteraction to paranoia, given that paranoia notoriously cannot be cured by logical argument? Insanity is the destructive element in the risk and Zurita here takes the advice of Conrad's character Stein in *Lord Jim*, to 'immerse' in 'the destructive element'.[40] The difficulty of any commentary is that it may end up attempting to contain the uncontained and uncontainable (as of the third proposition quoted above). And that the action of containing madness in concepts and propositions may begin to partake of the para-noia of the dominant power-systems—a measure of how chal-lenging Zurita's work is as it exposes attempts to contain it as themselves perhaps paranoid. His action is thus to begin to make visible the spectre—to use his word—of the dominant paranoia from positions that are inside and against.

Purgatorio uses an actual EEG printout—presumably the poet's 'own'—and a psychiatrist's letter referring to 'Raúl Zurita'. But instead of being located inside any discourse, copies of them are placed, unmediated, on the page. The letter, which refers to an EEG and speaks of 'psychosis', has the words Raúl Zurita crossed out and replaced by four handwritten women's names, which include Dulce Beatriz. It is overprinted, at the top with the phrase 'LA GRUTA DE LOURDES' [THE GROTTO OF LOURDES] and at the bottom with 'TE AMO INFINITAMENTE' [I LOVE YOU INFINITELY] (*P* 41). In between the horizontal wave-forms of the EEG, three phrases are written; the third reads 'del amor que mueve el sol y las otras estrellas' [of the love that moves the sun and the other stars] (*P* 67). In this way, a diag-nostic map of electrical brain activity is overscored and resigni-fied as love: in the sense of personal emotion, in the sense of a journey to the Vita Nuova, and in the sense of healing. The timeflow of the EEG becomes a counter-graph, an erotogram.

Zurita uses three main words for madness: *demencia, locura,* and *voladura*. In this order they move from the destructive to the paradisal. But in the writing there is no comfortable linear progression to separate them. Each touches the others

---

[39] S. Jackson, 'The Union of Mathematics and Poetry in the *Purgatorio* of Raúl Zurita', in Raúl Zurita, *Purgatorio*, trans. Jeremy Jacobson (Pittsburgh, 1985), 12.
[40] Joseph Conrad, *Lord Jim* (Harmondsworth, 1962), 163–4.

constantly. Near the end of *Anteparaíso*, the dementia of life in the poor districts of Santiago is given as a precondition for paradise:

PERO ESCUCHA SI TÚ NO PROVIENES DE UN BARRIO POBRE DE SANTIAGO ES DIFÍCIL QUE ME ENTIENDAS TÚ NO SABRÍAS NADA DE LA VIDA QUE LLEVAMOS MIRA ES SIN ALIENTO ES LA DEMENCIA ES HACERSE PEDAZOS POR APENAS UN MINUTO DE FELICIDAD (*A* 194)

[BUT LISTEN IF YOU DON'T COME FROM A POOR AREA OF SANTIAGO IT WILL BE DIFFICULT FOR YOU TO UNDERSTAND ME YOU WOULDN'T KNOW ANYTHING ABOUT THE LIFE WE LEAD LOOK IT'S WITHOUT HOPE IT'S MADNESS IT'S SMASHING YOURSELF TO PIECES FOR JUST A MINUTE OF HAPPINESS]

Volado and *voladura* are used in the meanings of in love, dreamy and crazy alongside the root meaning of *volar*=to fly, with the added connotation of blowing up and demolishing—a typical multiplicity which unfortunately tends to get lost in English translation:

LOS POBRES ESTÁN POBLANDO EL PARAÍSO SÍ TÚ MISMO ME LA ANUNCIASTE LOS POBRES UNA PURA DE AMOR VOLANDO LAS BARRIADAS (*A* 184)

[THE POOR ARE POPULATING PARADISE IT WAS YOU YOURSELF TOLD ME THE POOR A PURE OF LOVE MAKING THE SHANTY TOWNS FLY]

Another condition for entry to the pre-paradisal has to do with the capacity to be penetrated by wounds-statements. There is the voice of 'algo como un ángel' [something like an angel] (P 16) heard before the act of burning his own cheek, an act which is included in the text of both *Purgatorio* and *Anteparaíso*. And then the attempt at self-blinding included in *Anteparaíso*. This action included a wish to get back to the very basis of seeing: 'tocar un instante casi inmemorial en la conciencia humana en que el hombre decide ver' [to touch an almost immemorial instant of human consciousness when man decides to see]. The decision was made in connection with the project to write fifteen phrases in the sky as part of *Anteparaíso*:

esas escrituras en el cielo que yo pensaba hacer serían infinitamente más elocuentes si el tipo que las había inventado no alcanzaba a verlas y tenía solamente que imaginárselas, como una especie de trazado invertido. Es decir, la contradicción entre la máxima apuesta a la visibilidad, como es una escritura en el cielo, y el que su autor no pudiera ver aquello.[41]

[41] Piña, *Conversactiones*, 215.

[those writings in the sky that I intended to make would be infinitely
more eloquent if the person who had invented them was unable to see
them and could only imagine them, like an inside-out tracing. In
other words, the contradiction between maximum visibility, as is the
case of writing in the sky, and the fact that the author could not see it.]

The sky as zone for writing makes use of what has been inherited through various religious traditions as the ultimate place of
authority, source of gods' voices. María Sabina, the well-known
Mazatec shamaness, talks of seeing 'letritas en el cielo', a transposition of spoken power into script.[42] But the sky can also be
taken as an ultimate projection of the human body as an
inscribable surface. As Zurita writes on the final page of
Anteparaíso:

> Fue duro. Está bien, quise hacerlo así;
> más puro y más limpio, para que cuando
> se dibujaran las escrituras en el cielo
> poder imaginármelas infinitamente más
> bellas en su trazado invertido dentro
> de mi alma.
> Dos años más tarde vi las letras
> del cielo y de Dios recortarse sobre mí (*A* 203)

> [It was hard. That's all right, I wanted to do it that way;
> purer and cleaner, so that when
> the writings were inscribed in the sky
> I could imagine them infinitely more
> beautiful in their inverted tracing
> in my soul.
> Two years later I saw the letters
> of the sky and God outlined above me]

Recortarse denotes a cutting action, which the sharpness of the
letters seen depends upon. At the same time, the sky becomes
fused with the imagination, as place of first emergence, in
insane conditions of poverty.

The fifteen phrases were written by five aeroplanes in the sky
of New York, over Puerto Rican districts, in a text 9 kilometres
long which took four hours to complete; the action was
photographed and the photographs reproduced in the book.
The skywriting took place in 1982, the year the book was

---

[42] Jerome Rothenberg and Diane Rothenberg, *Symposium of the Whole*
(Berkeley, 1983), 187–91.

published. The completion of *La vida nueva* has included a similarly vast text-sculpture, a photograph of which is included in the book.[43] A handwritten phrase, 'ni pena ni miedo' [neither sorrow nor fear], was transcribed in August 1993 as letters 250 metres high excavated by earthmoving equipment into the surface of the Atacama Desert, 56 kilometres south of Antofagasta. The peculiarities of the climate will allow them to remain there for thousands of years, visible from enormous distances, like the colossal Nazca lines in the Peruvian desert strip. Both of these actions speak of a need to work on a Michelangelesque scale, making sky and earth into sculptures, an ambition which has some similarity with the work of twentieth-century land- and city-scape sculptors. But they also reveal a necessity: to convert the earth or cosmos into sign, into an image that will hold in times of vast but often hidden destructiveness. Once again, it is the primary, initiatory act of entry into signs that fascinates and offers a prospect of release from the past.

The idea for the skywriting was triggered by a memory of seeing advertisements written in the sky as a child, and is linked with a sense of the disappearance of the book as a unique place for verbal art, just as Joyce had wanted *Ulysses* to be displayed in public space as a vast advertisement. But advertisements only have force inside a social value system; they seduce and tell you of your failure if you do not possess the valued things. Zurita reverses that process: first the advertisement, then the society it requires for its operativity. The phrase scored into the desert is concerned with reconciliation after the experience of military rule. But the content of the phrases in the sky, which repeat the words 'Mi Dios es' fourteen times (e.g. 'Mi Dios es miedo' [My God is fear]), seems less charged with futurity than with an inheritance of past skygods.

However, Zurita's comment on the Christian materials in his work has been to say that for someone who is an atheist they have come as a surprise, unexpectedly. It is possible to read these materials not as symbols connected with an institutional discourse but as means for entering a zone of extreme susceptibility to penetration by signs. The words 'Mi Dios', in phrases such as 'Mi Dios es cáncer' [My God is cancer] or 'Mi Dios es

43 *La vida nueva* (Santiago, 1994), 520–1.

no' [My God is no], whose force is destructive and negative, can
be taken as enacting a scarifying effect and not a religion in the
sense of dogma and programme. The zone in question may be
compared with the Freudian notion of primal (or primary)
repression which has to do with 'the initial presence of some
formations in the unconscious which cannot have been drawn
there by other ones'.[44] This 'first phase of repression' is postu-
lated as the necessary precondition for any consciousness. Less
hypothetically, Merleau-Ponty writes of consciousness as always
in the world, and

that our effective involvement in the world is precisely what has to be
understood and made amenable to conceptualization, for it is what
polarizes all our conceptual particularizations. The need to proceed
by way of essences does not mean that philosophy takes them as its
object, but, on the contrary, that our existence is too tightly held in
the world to be able to know itself as such at the moment of its involvement, and that it requires the field of ideality in order to become
acquainted with and to prevail over its facticity.[45]

For philosophy, substitute poetry and the statement becomes
highly relevant to Zurita's use of a generic vocabulary of idealities. Without some such resource, clarity is impossible; there is
simply, as Artaud wrote, 'a slimy and powerful nausea [. . .]
vegetable and thundering [. . .] [a] vegetable mass'[46]—an experience which Sartre would explore later in *Nausea.*

In Zurita's work the idealities are spatial and most frequently
projected as landscape. The second main section of *Anteparaíso*
is concerned with the immense *cordilleras* [mountain ranges] of
Chile which include the highest peaks of the Andes. Their vast
whiteness is a recurrent intensity. But it is an intensity without
tracings, a zone of madness:

> Blancas son también las voces de los
> que se fueron
> Sí, blanco es el destino que se van
> tragando estas montañas
> [. . .]

    [44] J. Laplanche and J.-B. Pontalis, *The Language of Psychoanalysis* (London,
1980), 334.
    [45] M. Merleau-Ponty, *Phenomenology of Perception* (London, 1962), pp. xiv–xiv.
    [46] Antonin Artaud, *Selected Writings* (Berkeley, 1988), 60.

i. De locura es el cielo de los nevados   gemían
   marchando esas voladas

ii. Imponentes   albísimas   sin dejar piedra ni pasto
    hasta que todo fuera su blancura

iii. Pero no   ni borrachos creyeron que la locura era
     igual que los Andes y la muerte un cordillerío
     blanco frente a Santiago (*A* 89)

> [White too are the voices of those
> who have gone
> Yes, white is the destiny these
> mountains swallow

i. Mad is the sky of the snow peaks   they groaned
   marching these crazy

ii. Imposing   utterly white   leaving neither stone nor grass
    until everything becomes their whiteness

iii. But no   not even drunk did they believe that madness was
     the same as the Andes and death a white mountain range
     in front of Santiago]

Locura moves into whiteness and then into *voladas*, placing destructive delirium alongside a state of being absent-minded, dreamy, in love. The unexpected conjunction of meanings, of destructive irrationality with the necessary capacity to be in love, is part of the risk Zurita takes. As in Rafael Filipelli's film *Hay unos tipos abajo*,[47] set in the period of recent military dictatorship in Argentina, an unexpected capacity for renewal in the midst of destructive paranoia is revealed. What makes this renewal possible, paradoxically, is a state of vulnerability and penetrability. Zurita's repetitive language produces an incantatory effect which is both emptying and penetrative. The whole section is prefaced by a voice commanding sacrifice (' "Anda y mátame a tu hijo [. . .] Lejos, en esas perdidas cordilleras de Chile" ' [Go and kill your son. Far away, in those lost mountain ranges of Chile]; *A* 79).

The whiteness is not of language in general but of certain specific dimensions of it. It is not for instance a whiteness of voice, in the sense of a voice emptied of inflexion and expression, but a characteristic of the statements. They are statements which turn themselves inside out, in that they keep putting the

[47] Buenos Aires, 1982.

possible places of enunciation inside the statement so that any outside is eroded. In so far as the enunciative area gets pulled inside the statement, the idea of any controlling subject of enunciation, any transcendent, overarching speaker or source, becomes impossible. The whiteness is therefore of the place of enunciation, in the sense that you do not know where the statements are coming from, or that there are voices which the hearer cannot locate, making this language more penetrative than ordinary language. The comparisons would be with shamanistic possession or with that effect of schizophrenia known as 'hearing voices'. The very first statement of the book is an unlocatable but forcefully penetrative voice, printed in double-size letters:

oye Zurita—me dijo—sácate de
la cabeza esos malos pensamientos (*A* 29)

[listen Zurita—he said—get those bad thoughts out of your head]

THIS SIDE OF PARADISE

The ambition of *Anteparaíso* is to occupy the spaces of language and imagination that religion, the State, and advertising have taken possession of. It is difficult to find adequate terms to respond to a poetry that is concerned with the emergence of the new and not with repetition or restoration. Despite its use of inherited symbols, the procedures are not mythical in a Freudian or Jungian sense. It does not seek to control primal zones of language and imagination with predictable figurations. The idea of 'a return to the mythical tradition'[48] is a predictable response of institutional criticism. Even the most interesting critical essays, such as those of Cánovas and Foxley, tend to stabilize the work in terms of recognitions of the already-known. Cánovas, for example, univocalizes Zurita's landscapes by offering a metaphoric reading of them,[49] and Foxley seeks a fixed foundation for the work's statements in notions of will, commitment, conviction, self-consciousness,

---

[48] F. Lafuente, '*Anteparaíso*: la poética del mito', in Raúl Zurita, *Anteparaíso* (Madrid, 1991), 18.
[49] Ibid. 18.

and representation, that is, conceiving it as a programme.[50]A key difficulty is the gap between the statements-actions and the existence of any society capable of responding to and incorporating them. This difficulty is on the one hand conceptual—how to think the new—but simultaneously utopian and architectonic, like a great arch of desire.

This transcending movement is conceived as direct intervention in the urban landscape. Zurita was a member of CADA (Collective of Art Actions), which used the bodies of its members alongside the objects of everyday life in the city to create social sculptures which rejected any notion of art as an island set apart: 'The future we desire for art is life itself, the creation of a different society as a great work of art.'[51] The statement is from 1982, but CADA was founded in the late 1970s. With other advanced groups of the time, they shared the aim of going beyond 'the spatial limits of art by moving away from the format of painting (the pictorial tradition) towards the use of the landscape (the social body as a support for artistic creativity)'. 'To establish the outside as a place for art' included mural art as an action for 'relocating the parameters for reading walls as a text of the city',[52] which in the case of Zurita's poetics is extended into relocating the parameters for reading printed poems as urban text. In 1979 he wrote:

What are the supports? No longer a sheet of paper or a photograph or tape or video, no longer an act. The support is our own objective lives [. . .], our South American landscapes, cities or villages where the people search for food in the same way that museum patrons search for beauty: that is the work.[53]

The ideas are exemplified in the action entitled 'Para no morir de hambre en el arte' [So as not to die of hunger in art], a social sculpture in the sense of being

a work or art action that tries to organise, by means of intervention, the time and space in which we live, firstly to make it more visible, and then to make it more livable. The present work [. . .] is a sculpture

[50] C. Foxley, 'Raúl Zurita y la propuesta autorreflexiva de *Anteparaíso*', in R. Yamal (ed.), *La poesía chilena actual (1960–1984) y la crítica* (Concepción, 1988), 270, 280, 282.

[51] Nelly Richard, *Margins and Institutions: Art in Chile since 1973, Art and Text 21* (Melbourne, 1986), 82.

[52] Ibid. 57–60, 53.   [53] Ibid. 78.

since it organises the material of art in terms of volume, and it is social to the extent that such material is our collective reality.[54]

The multiple event, which sought to eradicate the boundaries between genres, included distributing powdered milk among families living in a shanty town, publishing a blank page in a magazine, reading a text in front of the United Nations building in Santiago, and hanging a white sheet over the façade of the Museum of Art. The effects may be compared with the art action carried out by Lotty Rosenfeld, one of CADA's members, consisting in transforming road lines into crosses by painting white lines across them. 'The crosses of Rosenfeld take as their premise the fact that the road sign seems the most inoffensive of signs, and submit it to inversion.'[55] The effect has to do with the inscription and operativity of signs received by the mass gaze, and its possibilities are both local and diffused over the whole domain of social meanings. The key commitment is to transform the bases, the supports, what Nelly Richard in her valuable study calls 'the social structures of historical significance',[56] and not just the aesthetic effect, making CADA's and other similar actions non-sublimatory but transcendental. Zurita's poetics use the de-framing possibilities opened up by these types of action and deploy landscapes and the human body as places of counter-inscription in order to cut across the statements of divisive sociability. The newness of his poetics is that they break through the impasse in Latin American poetry signalled by Eduardo Milán: the difficulties of moving beyond the great innovations of the avant-garde of the early twentieth century and of being available to a broad readership without becoming facile.[57]

Two of CADA's members, Zurita and Diamela Eltit, used self-laceration as a social art action. There are difficulties of response and interpretation here. Richard takes sacrifice and martyrdom as the models and writes of 'the stigmatised body' as a means to 'recapture the communal body of suffering'.[58] But does not a premeditated self-wounding (self-violation) cut through all justifications for painful socialization, exposing

[54] Richard, *Margins and Institutions:* 62.
[55] Ibid. 61.   [56] Ibid. 78.
[57] Eduardo Milán, *Una cierta mirada* (Mexico, 1989), 14–16, 169, 199.
[58] Richard, *Margins*, 66, 68–9.

existing sociability as violation? The wound as public spectacle includes the question: why should someone take a decision to wound themself? The notion of 'communal sacrifice' leaves pain as a legitimization, a necessity, a cost to be paid, as in certain Catholic ideologies, whereas Zurita's burning his face was enacted without any justification. It pointed to the absence of any such thing. Zurita himself links his action with a need to make visible the limits of the sayable: ' "quise distinguir entre [. . .] lo que puede ser dicho y lo que no. Frente a una experiencia personal extremadamente violenta o dolorosa, el deseo de expresarla, aún cuando se llega hasta quemar su propia cara, ya es un signo" ' [I wished to distinguish between what can be talked about and what cannot be talked about. Faced with a personal experience that is extremely violent or painful, the wish to express it, even by going so far as to burn one's face, is already a sign].[59] The 'wish to express' becomes an action at the level of the frame or support of possible expression, and not at the level of representation. The skin being an organ of perception, the wounds are in the surface and process of perception, of being in the world.

For the Chilean liberation theologian Pedro Morandé, sacrifice is still fundamental to modern societies, despite their claims to be secularized. The functional rationality of the market becomes the agency demanding sacrifice of human beings:

Secularization is not, as is often thought, a one-way process. It is a double process. It proclaims the death of God only to build Leviathan to replace Him. But Leviathan cannot signify totality if he is not made into the 'Mortall God'. The secularization of the world is simultaneously the sacralization of the roles necessary for the circuit of functionality.[60]

Zurita's writing cuts across one of the vital supports of this hidden sacrifice: it refuses the language of ideological collectivity, the 'we' effect of modern states claiming there is no alternative, the pseudo-symmetry of the individual and the collective inside a language of collective representations demanding submission. The refusal of a secure but ultimately sacrificial 'we' is, as Zurita points out in his essay, a characteristic of those poets

---

[59] Ibid. 73.
[60] Pedro Morandé, *Cultura y modernización en América Latina* (Madrid, 1987), 134.

in Chile, emerging since the late 1970s, who have broken with
the prevailing literary conventions.

Zurita appears to coincide with Morandé in the view that,
given the need for sacrifice, it is better to return to the popular
Christian notion of the sacrificial, where sacrifice means not the
rituals directed by an institution controlled by Rome but the
key symbolic systems of popular Catholicism.[61] It is clear that
religion, particularly in popular and vulgar ideas of the sacred,
is a key site in Zurita's writing (as it is in current debates in the
social sciences). Nevertheless, religion is not exactly the right
term. More precisely, his concern is with those areas of human
capability that religion takes control of. The difficulty of finding a language to describe them is parallel to the difficulty of
entering these areas while eluding their systematization into
symbols. Vision and ecstasy are words I have used so far: sacrifice is not a necessary part of the experience they refer to.
Another key difference between Zurita's work and religion is its
delirious aspect, whether in terms of self-wounding—something normally done by mad people—or of a love which will not
obey normal limits.

'Pastoral' is the title of the penultimate section of
Anteparaíso. It has the shape of a vast curve or arc of love
sustained over time-space obstacles and becoming by the end of
the section 'amor que mueve el sol [. . .] y las otras estrellas'
[love that moves the sun and the other stars] (*A* 164). It begins
with Chile as a wasted landscape, destroyed by social madness,
and moves through individual love lost and regained, to a transformation of pain into joy, and finally to ecstatic, cosmic love.
In the scenario of burnt fields, the Spanish word is *pastos*, placing the title in the Chilean landscape as green valleys in
contrast to desert and mountains:

ii.   Lloren la locura del quemarse de estos pastos

iii. La locura será así un dolor crepitando frente a Chile (*A* 124)

[ii. Cry the madness of the burning of these fields

iii. Madness will thus be a pain that crackles in front of Chile]

The scenario of suffering, vast in extension and intensity,
becomes also a ritual of mourning. The ritual effect is simulta-

---

[61] Morandé, *Cultura y modernización en América Latina*, 150.

neously spatial-conceptual and rhythmic: it builds up through a multiplicity of syntactic tracks and a propositional accumulation which is not syllogistic, in that subjects and predicates keep changing. Any representational content of propositions is attenuated in favour of their spatial, directional force; there is no beginning or end, just places of intersection and emergence; the inside becomes outside, the subject predicate, the predicate subject, the spoken speaks, the speaker becomes spoken. As with serial music, there is no centre. These are propositional ways of describing the techniques. Their effect is something like being at sea in language, such that the unfettered movement required to survive immersion in that element involves letting go of controls and trusting one's ability to move inside it.

The language achieved causes the erotic and the sacred to enter and extend each other. In part, this comes through using a textual tradition that goes back, in particular, to the Song of Songs (see *A* 133). But Zurita also makes use of vulgar language:

En que hasta la madre se hizo palos de zarza ardiendo sobre los pastizales donde Chile se parió a sí mismo hecho un dolor bajo estos cielos caídos irredentos como paisajeríos malditos que ni tu madre perdonara (*A* 126)

[In which even your mother became brambles burning over the pastures where Chile gave birth to itself made into pain under these skies fallen unredeemed like cursed landscapes that not even your mother would forgive]

The words 'Tu madre' are an insult, 'hasta la madre' adapts the vulgar and violent use of 'mother', and 'parió' directly uses part of another insult that calls the mother whore. The vulgar sense of the sacred within the familiar, conveyed in a combination of elevation and violent abasement, cuts across any appropriation by privileged religious discourse. The entry of *madre* into the poem is as unmediated as possible, without interpretation, using the actual spoken language like the social objects and signs in the CADA actions.

As 'Pastoral' moves towards resurrection, history becomes part of the process, not history from above or even from below, but as 'everyone', without exclusions:

v. Y qué si Chile entero amaneciese resucitado con sus muertos

vi. Todos podrían saber entonces si amaneció el
nuevo día sobre Chile (*A* 145)

[v. And what if the whole of Chile woke up resurrected with its
dead
vi. Everyone could know then whether the new day dawned
over Chile]

The dead too are witnesses, included in 'everyone'. But as in
José Martí's conception of Latin America, it is from the poor
that the future emerges:

v. Porque los pobres serían el milenio enverdecido
vi. Esplendorosos como levantados desde su dolor
como si se borraran sus heridas (A 147)

[v. Because the poor will be that green millennium
vi. Splendorous as if raised up from their pain
as if their wounds had been erased]

But the eradication of wounds is governed by 'as if'; at the
climax of 'Pastoral', where even the torturers are called to
dance 'por nuestro amor, sólo por eso' [for our love, only for
that] (A 150), and the whole universe to speak 'only of love',
pain nevertheless remains:

Griten entonces porque yo sé que tú vives
y por este Idilio se encuentran los perdidos
y los desollados vuelven a tener piel
Porque aunque no se borren todas las cicatrices
y todavía se distingan
las quemaduras de los brazos
También las quemaduras y las cicatrices
se levantan como una sola desde los cuerpos y cantan
Con cerros, cordilleras y valles (A 151)

[So shout because I know that you are alive
and those who are lost find each other through this Idyll
and the flayed have skin once more
Because even if all the scars are not erased
and the burns on the arms
can still be distinguished
Burns and scars also
rise up as one from bodies and sing
With hills, mountains, and valleys]

The tenses shift from conditional, future, and imperative to the
present. This is the actual: not pain abolished as in the false
promises of modernity, satirized by César Vallejo in his great
poem 'Los nueve monstruos' [The nine monsters], but the

wound as new basis of the social, since the new emerges from the place of greatest suffering, of that which, to paraphrase Rilke, we are just able to bear. The body becomes not the victim of wounds to be wished away, as in Ariel Dorfman's shallow notion of reconciliation in 'Death and the Maiden',[62] but the support of wounds as marks of history to be transformed into paradise. The key comparison is with Neruda's *Heights of Macchu Picchu*, its sense of slavery as the bottom line of history and in particular its supreme renunciation of any beauty, including the form and language of the poem in hand, that has violation as part of its cost. In both poets, it is the same word, *también* [also], that carries the thrust of inclusion against all division or exclusion,[63] and in both, that word acquires a vast scale of time and place, in ways that recall Milton's use of the word *all* as fulcrum of epic intentions.[64] Zurita extends Neruda's radically non-sacrificial action: wounds are at the origin, and this includes the 'spirit of the language', that making sense which in even the most inoffensive areas of the language serves to cover over inherited pain.

Anteparaíso is a book that demands completion outside itself, as a promise to be completed in the actual happiness of human beings. Instead of fulfilling a hope in a work of art, as Dante had done, it takes paradise to be possible, as Zurita writes in the introduction, only 'como una empresa colectiva en la cual la vida de cada ser que pisa la faz de esta tierra devenga en la única obra de arte, en el único poema, en la única Pietá digna de nuestra admiración [as a collective task in which the life of every being that walks on the face of this earth becomes the only work of art, the only poem, the only Pietá worthy of our admiration] (*A* 24). This persistence in achieving paradise given all the evidence at hand looks like madness (*A* 23). But the insistence that paradise is not artificial but a human possibility is a peculiarly American thing. It is there all through Pound's *Cantos* and in Juan Carlos Onetti's *Dejemos hablar al viento* [Let the wind speak],[65] where, in a distinctively Latin American inversion, the imagined city has to

---

[62] See Catherine Boyle, 'The Mirror to Nature? Latin American Theatre in London', *Travesia: Journal of Latin American Cultural Studies*, 1/1 (1992), 105–17.

[63] Neruda, *Canto general*, 34.

[64] See William Empson, *The Structure of Complex Words* (London, 1985), ch. 4.

[65] Barcelona, 1979.

burn down before the conditions for paradise can be met. Zurita's journey is likewise an inversion of Dante's:

desde los inmensos espacios del sur del Río Grande yo he tratado de imaginarme el viaje inverso, para pasar no de la promesa al trabajo, no de la Vida Nueva a la Comedia, pero sí—abiertos como una flor desde nosotros mismos—pasar de la Comedia a la Vida, del trabajo a la promesa, del Viejo al Nuevo Mundo. (*A* 24)

[from the immense spaces to the south of the Río Grande I have tried to imagine the opposite journey, to go not from the promise to the work, not from the New Life to the Comedy, but—opened like a flower from inside ourselves—to go from the Comedy to Life, from the work to the promise, from the Old to the New World.]

8

The Subversive Languages of
Carmen Ollé

AGAINST CONFESSION

Over the past fifteen years, there has been a huge increase in the amount of poetry written by women published in Peru. A book of interviews by Roland Forgues with Peruvian women poets is an index of this new phenomenon—in the masculinist ways it attempts to construe this writing and in the refusal of a number of the poets to go along with these. The book's title is *Las poetas se desnudan* [Women poets bare themselves], indicating a paradigm that relegates women's poetry to the erotic and to intimate confession: no place here for the public sphere, for ideas, or, crucially, for the invention of poetic forms. Only the themes matter, and these—as the questions reveal—are preconceived as the confession of what was previously hidden. As the introduction claims,

sólo a partir de la década del setenta y la del ochenta se dará una verdadera revolución estética con el surgimiento de jóvenes poetas quienes, rompiendo con todos los tabúes, en especial el del sexo, no vacilarán desnudarse para reverlarnos los lugares más recónditos de su intimidad.[1]

[a real aesthetic revolution would begin only in the 1970s and 1980s, with the rise of young women poets who, breaking all the taboos, especially the sexual ones, would not hesitate to bare themselves to reveal their most intimate, hidden places.]

In response to the question '¿No crees tú, por ejemplo, que reivindicarse como poeta femenina, sea una manera de reivin-

---

[1] Roland Forgues, *Las poetas se desnudan* (Lima, 1991), 14. All translations from *Noches de adrenalina* are by Anne Archer; all other translations are by Jane Freeland and Deborah Shaw.

dicarse en tanto que mujer?' [Don't you think, for instance, that to claim your rights as a feminine poet is a way of claiming your rights as a woman?], Magdalena Chocano answers: 'No. Porque creo que si uno quiere luchar por sus derechos como mujer no lo va a hacer a través de la poesía. No es la manera eficaz' [No, because I think that if you want to fight for your rights as a woman, then you don't do it through poetry. It's not the most effective way] (252). She then adds that she is in total agreement with the struggle for 'una igualdad, una libertad, una democracia en este país que es un país realmente autoritario y represivo hasta en nuestras actitudes cotidianas' [equality, liberty, democracy in this country, a country that is very authoritarian and repressive even in its daily dealings]. The exchange shows the difficulty of refusing definition as a *poeta femenina*—namely, the difficulty of claiming artistic autonomy—without being condemned as reactionary.

Carmen Ollé, similarly, refuses the prevalent labelling of women poets. One of the questions she is asked goes as follows: '¿Cómo explicas tú, justamente, que en *Noches de adrenalina* que es tu primer libro, tenga tanta importancia lo erótico, y lo erótico tratado en forma, diría, casi clínica?' [How exactly do you explain that in your first book, *Noches de adrenalina*, the erotic has so much importance, and the erotic is treated, I would say, in an almost clinical way?] Here 'clinical' has to be understood as meaning not submitting to the style of seductive confession of intimacy. Ollé answers by turning the question round and placing the erotic as part of larger concerns which include the understanding of the self as process that moves beyond the private: 'Lo erótico es parte de un proceso y análisis de la infancia, de la juventud, del enfrentamiento con la vida, de lamentación sobre la cultura' [The erotic is part of a process and analysis of infancy, of youth, of facing up to life, of lamentation about culture].[2] She is also critical of the term 'poesía femenina':

hablar de poesía femenina puede llevarnos a confundir un poco lo que es el proceso. De hecho las mujeres que escribimos ahora, las que recién hemos salido un poco al aire a partir del 80, hablamos de la mujer. Pero es nuestra propia experiencia como mujeres porque no somos hombres. Pero no me parece que haya tanta diferencia entre la

[2] Forgues, *Las poetas*, 147–8.

poesía hecha por mujeres y la poesía hecha por hombres. Tal vez la particularidad sea que hasta ahora no se habría tomado en cuenta la literatura hecha por mujeres. Por eso nos llama la atención que muchas mujeres escriban ahora, y escriban obre sí mismas.[3]

[To speak of feminine poetry could lead us to mistake what this process is. Certainly we women writing now, who have come out into the open since 1980, talk about women. But our experience is as women because we are not men. But I don't think there's such a great difference between poetry written by women and poetry written by men. Perhaps it seems different because up to now women's poetry hasn't received much attention. That's why it seems striking that many women are writing now, and writing about themselves.]

This stance might suggest that Ollé is somehow the exception among women poets in Peru, but, on the contrary, she is seen very much as the spokesperson of her generation. She is especially unhappy with the imposition of a particular agenda upon women poets by critics: 'Eso me parece terriblemente castrador: que un lector busque un texto porque le dice cosas y no porque le gusta. Es una manera de liquidar en el lector esa capacidad de inocencia para acercarse al texto sin parámetros' [That seems terribly castrating to me: that a reader should seek out a text because it says certain things and not because he enjoys it. This is a way of liquidating a reader's capability for approaching a text innocently and without parameters].[4] This innocence is already compromised by the social formation of the reader as interlocutor, a point I will amplify below. What needs saying at this stage is that the conversations with Forgues reveal difficulties of reception that arise as limits within the larger field of social communication, limits that need acknowledging if that innocence is to be reached which will allow readers to be open to seeing and hearing what previously has been made invisible and inaudible.

Ollé's distance from a particular view of women's poetry does not mean that she is not concerned with what Elizabeth Vargas calls 'individuación femina' [feminine individuation].[5] She states that the most important aim of her poetry is 'tal vez la tentativa de plasmar la conciencia de un personaje femenino

---

[3] Ibid. 150.   [4] Ibid. 158.
[5] Elizabeth Vargas, *Identidad femenina: cuestionando y construyendo estereotipos* (Lima, 1991), 20.

que sea un ser humano complejo, conflictivo, real' [perhaps
the attempt to give form to the consciousness of a feminine
personality who is a complex, conflictive, real human being].[6]
Noches de adrenalina [Adrenalin nights], through an architec-
tural sense of language as public space, participates in the refor-
mulation of private and public that Peruvian feminist authors
underline as really taking off in the late 1970s. Elizabeth Vargas
traces the evolution of thinking in a particular generation of
women: after joining the left-wing political parties in the early
1970s, a situation which meant they had to suppress their particular experience as women, they then turned to the theory of
patriarchy, which made it possible to discover 'no sólo la
riqueza y complejidad del mundo privado, de las relaciones
personales, sino también las deformaciones del mundo
político' [not only the richness and complexity of the private
world, of personal relationships, but also the distortions of the
political world].[7] Underlying this change was a new historical
situation that had taken shape over the past two decades: 'La
transformación del "ama de casa" en sujeto social implica,
entre otras cosas, formarse como individuo integral; dueño de
su presente, responsable de su pasado y constructor de su
futuro' [The transformation of the 'housewife' into a social
subject implies, among other things, developing oneself as an
integrated individual, in command of one's present, responsible for one's past, and builder of one's future].[8]

   Although she has never been a member of a political party,
Ollé belongs to that generation of women and has been
through a similar radicalization. While the shift in power
among women shanty-town dwellers was more dramatic,
because pauperization from the mid-1970s meant that, in order
to fulfil their traditional domestic roles, women had to enter
public struggle and build new social movements,[9] middle-class
women like Ollé were also affected by the discovery that there
was a broader experience of women that cut across class divisions. Ollé was also, if briefly, a member of the Hora 0 group of
poets, who located poetry within experiences of urban margin-
alization, away from the traditional language of the well-off
classes. But her work also moves decisively from language as a

[6] Forgues, *Las poetas*, 158.   [7] Vargas, *Identidad*, 21; see also 19–20.
[8] Ibid. 21.   [9] Ibid. 12–19.

sign of social membership to language as material for creative invention. This concern with language as form and not just as representation makes the discussion of her work particularly challenging, given the need to separate writing by women from the types of justificatory paradigm that Ollé condemns and that tend to affect even the most interesting debates.

In *Women, Culture, and Politics in Latin America*, the editors write: 'the overall corpus of research on women in Latin America shows little focus on woman's intellectual, literary, political, and pedagogical activity.'[10] Nevertheless, when they come to discuss the contribution made by their book to correcting this situation, the emphasis is on 'the issues of women's rights, especially with respect to civil status, family, and participation in literary life', and on women writers 'as cultural innovators' in conflict with 'the inadequacies of the traditional space from which they were allowed to speak and act'.[11] Although these issues are crucial for any serious research on women's intellectual and artistic work in Latin America, the introductory proposals in the book, and to an important extent the various chapters, exclude consideration of inventiveness in language and form as key cultural actions. The problem is not specific to gender studies: it extends more broadly to current practice in literary and cultural studies. But it has a particular force in the study of women writers: if the prime emphasis is on women representing themselves differently from men, or vice versa, the danger is that not enough attention is given to transformations of artistic form, which—because they are alterations of the possible—are key cultural actions.

The most influential proposal of gender as basis of differences in form—not just in representations—is the idea of *écriture féminine*. But the extension of gender categories into form—and equally into language—is problematic, since the result is not only, as many have noted, to essentialize the feminine, but also to disconnect writing from the socio-cultural which traverses it. Put quite simply, *écriture féminine* is not equivalent to writing by actual social and historical women,[12] and it

[10] University of California-Stanford Seminar on Feminism and Culture in Latin America, *Women, Culture, and Politics in Latin America* (Berkeley, 1992), p. vii.
[11] Ibid. 1–2.
[12] Toril Moi, *Sexual/Textual Politics* (London, 1985), 108.

can prevent a proper investigation of forms as engagements with social and cultural experience. One of the most interesting and useful aspects of *Women, Culture, and Politics in Latin America* is, as Catherine Boyle writes, that 'the book takes us into [. . .] an area where gender studies meets cultural studies'.[13] The rarefying effect of *écriture féminine*, at least in the hands of some of its adherents, ghettoizes the excitement and unpredictability of artistic discovery inside knowing academic jargon.

A further concern of my presentation of Ollé's work is with how formulations of gender difference are extremely useful entries into her poetic use of language but that they exist alongside another type of action that moves into non-gendered zones. These are not easy to name and the term I have preferred is 'the productive body'. The area is similar to Kristeva's use of the term '*chora*', which she takes to be previous to the differentiation of male and female.[14] Kristeva asserts that the '*chora* is no more than the place where the subject is both generated and negated, the place where his unity succumbs before the process of charges and stases that produce him':[15] that is, the body as productive rather than symbolized, categorized. Other work that could be cited in this instance includes Deleuze and Guattari's proposition, via the writing of Artaud, of the body without organs,[16] H.D.'s notion of 'jelly-fish consciousness',[17] Bataille's proposals of entry into experience without the authority of belief or knowledge,[18] or the work of the Peruvian poets César Vallejo and Emilio Adolfo Westphalen.[19]

REPRESENTATION AND IMAGINATION

When representations are spoken of, a number of questions

---

[13] Catherine Boyle, *Review of Women, Culture, and Politics in Latin America*, *Bulletin of Latin American Research*, 13/2 (1994), 235.

[14] See Moi, *Sexual/Textual Politics*, 161–5.

[15] *The Kristeva Reader*, ed. Toril Moi (Oxford, 1986), 95.

[16] Gilles Deleuze and Félix Guattari, *A Thousand Plateaus* (London, 1988), ch. 6.

[17] H.D., *Notes on Thought and Vision* (London, 1988), 18–20.

[18] Georges Bataille, *Inner Experience* (New York, 1988), 7–14.

[19] On Westphalen, see William Rowe, 'E. A. Westphalen: la inteligencia poética y el imaginario social', in *Hacia una poética radical: ensayos de hermenéutica cultural* (Rosario, 1996), 124–40.

arise, such as who by, from where, to whom, and in what medium. The questions have to be asked of critics as well as writers. In academic discussions, the referential and representational aspects of language are often taken to be its prime or only function. But reference and representation can only occur as effects thanks to the dialogical working of language. This is because meaning arises in verbal interchange, in conversation. Knowledge cannot be separated from the actual sensuous and persuasive occurrence of language between speakers and hearers. Therefore we need to be concerned with 'the poetic and rhetorical, the social and historical, the pluralistic, as well as the responsive and sensuous aspects of language use'.[20] If social knowledge passes through the poetic dimensions of language, then poetics in a more literary sense are concerned with the interventions of language in the social construction of reality.[21] If you accept this, then literature is no longer out on a limb, as somehow secondary to the social sciences.

There is a particular issue about representation in Carmen Ollé's poetry. She names sexual organs and practices in forbidden ways, ways that are particularly forbidden to women in Peru. But a question arises here about motivation. To take these simply as counter-representations would be to isolate representation from its bases in speaking and hearing and the positions from which these can be done. To dare to refer, to represent in specifically forbidden ways, is to challenge the rules that govern what women are allowed to say. But is this the only motivation? By using that kind of language, is not Ollé also doing something else? This question will be addressed shortly.

First, an account of Ollé's materials—broadly, the cultural/historical context her work engages with—is necessary, before going on to look more closely at the varieties of language that she uses and the possibilities they open up for a reader. One of the problems with this approach is that the materials depend on the languages in which they are handled and should not be separated from them. Nevertheless, to make a partial and temporary separation does help in order to focus subsequently on the language.

[20] J. Shotter, *Conversational Realities: Constructing Life through Language* (London, 1993), 7.
[21] P. Berger and T. Luckmann, *The Social Construction of Reality* (Harmondsworth, 1966), 26–8.

Ollé belongs, loosely, to what came to be known as the generation of 1970 in Peruvian poetry, although she was not included in the most important anthology of those poets' work, *Estos 13*.[22] She was born in Lima, and in the 1970s she lived for several years in Paris with her husband Enrique Verástegui, a prominent poet of that generation. Her first book, *Noches de adrenalina*, was published in Lima in 1981. Her second book, *Todo orgullo humea la noche* [Every pride pervades night with smoke], came out in 1988. Her third and most recent book of poetry is *¿Por qué hacen tanto ruido?* [Why do they make so much noise?] and dates from 1992.

Noches de adrenalina[23] is particularly concerned with location in time and space, in terms of an autobiographical investigation of different times (adolescence and adulthood), places (Lima and Paris), and languages (Spanish and French). A quotation from Gaston Bachelard is used to help bring the complexities of time and place into focus:

> Dónde está el peso mayor del estar allí,
> en el estar o en el allí?
> En el allí—que sería preferible llamar
> un aquí—debo buscar primeramente mi ser? (*N* 11)
>
> [Where is the main stress in being there,
> on being, or on there?
> In there—which it would be better to call
> here—shall I first look for my being?]

The processes of memory and perception are therefore both inward and outward, specific to a sense of self or selves and specific to their location in time and space.

In order to give a clear sense of the components of the book, the different times and places that become interwoven in the text can be separated out. The book starts with the sentence 'Tener 30 años no cambia nada salvo aproximarse al ataque cardícao o al vaciado uterino' [To be 30 changes nothing save one's proximity to a heart attack or uterine extraction] (*N* 9). The sense of thirty years as a threshold is amplified in various statements of the body ageing, especially as the result of giving birth, which include an ironic sense of the female body as

---

[22] J. M. Oviedo (ed.), *Estos 13* (Lima, 1973).
[23] Cited as *N* in page references.

highly constructed, paradigmatic object: 'La sonrisa de la Monalisa indica el camino del envejecimiento | detenido por las cremas' [Mona Lisa's smile shows the course of ageing | stalled by creams] (*N* 20).

The geographical and spatial locations are given by Paris and Lima. The first is defined less as a cultural inheritance (in the sense of high culture) than by the Champs-Élysées or the Mona Lisa becoming 'el ménage | delegado a las jóvenes muchachas del tercer mundo' [the ménage delegated to young third-world maids] (*N* 12), in a Brechtian juxtaposition between cultural monuments and the women—from places like Peru—who do the cleaning. An aspect of life in Paris that gets mentioned frequently is looking after a small child, in particular changing nappies. To be a woman—more precisely a married woman—and an artist is an issue that is given considerable attention near the beginning of the book, where the Parisian scenario is being set out. But when it comes to the question which artists' work affects perception, the list is not Parisian: someone called Evelyne (*N* 13) (possibly the same Dutch woman painter mentioned later), Sylvia Plath, Diane di Prima, Burroughs, Cézanne, Van Gogh, Warhol.

Lima—in memory—is three friends from university days, associated with the world of political militancy, Avenida Venezuela (a working-class area), cheap hotels (including one associated with lost virginity), books read (e.g. David Cooper's *Death of the Family*), and the moulding of bodies into desirable and acceptable shapes: 'recuerdo mi timidez | en Lima la belleza es un corsé de acero' [I remember my shyness | in Lima beauty is a steel corset] (*N* 21). One section consists in a dramatized conversation between several figures in a park in a working-class district. One of the main topics is physical appearance: 'una deformación física nos hace pólvora' [a physical deformity eradicates us], says the *Dama del chiclet* (*N* 31). And a little later: 'La impresión de ser tumbada derramada en una maqueta de plástico' [The impression of being tumbled, spilled into a plastic mould].[24] Here Lima is no longer a place of memory and becomes instead a grotesque spoken drama.

Lines of spatial and cultural tension intersect with the axis of personal time. The main example would be the tracing of the

[24] Translation modified.

characteristics of adult sexual pleasure ('cariños masoquistas' [masochistic endearments] *N* 44), through mother's blush, puberty as exacerbated tensions between purity and dirtiness (*N* 45), seen and scenified by the gaze of mother and doctors, with any move towards nostalgia prevented by irony:

> después de masturbarme quería llorar de miedo y de verguenza
> tenía el tic de la señal de la cruz
> las misas de difuntos eran el coro que necesitaba
> la miseria de mi adolescencia. (*N* 46)

> [after masturbating I wanted to cry with fear and shame
> crossing myself became a nervous tic
> masses for the dead were the chorus needed
> for my adolescent misery.]

These are some of Ollé's materials, with some unavoidable pointing to the form of expression. The book is perhaps as much a dramatization of languages as of locations. Take, for example, one of the main topics, the question of watching oneself/being seen. In language terms, the question of who is seeing/who is being seen becomes who is the speaker/interlocutor when this is being spoken of, and what are their positions. On the back cover of the book there is a handwritten statement signed by Ollé which includes the following: 'quiero llegar a mirarme y abolir complejos y vergüenzas, en la creencia permanente en el valor de las mujeres' [I want to be able to look at myself and abolish complexes and shame, in the permanent belief in the value of women].

The necessity of seeing oneself, as against the gaze of the other (mother, doctor, male lover are the main agents), is dramatized a number of times, with the mirror as central to the action. One of its most complex treatments opens with a meditation on living under a roof as key initiation of all restricted spaces. But after the initial declaration 'Hay que huir de los techos' [Must flee the roofs], the poem proceeds to counterpose actions of escape with the other necessity of being seen or constructed within the social; thus 'poseer un cuerpo completo' [to have a complete body][25] is 'una suerte de arquitectura' [a kind of architecture] (*N* 18)—the complete body becoming socialized space, house, and, in so far as the archi-

---

[25] Translation modified.

tecture becomes exemplary representation, the spectacle has an epic glow ('epicidad'). Completeness or incompleteness of body is distinguished from the effects of make-up ('ningún maquillador lograría tales efectos' [no make-up artist could manage such effects]). Completeness is more fundamental, to do with becoming substantial, as in the phrases 'polvo abstracto' [abstract dust], 'polvo incontenible' [uncontainable dust], but it is not the same as the body that makes and produces:

> Debí volver a casa antes de anochecer pero
> me detuve en un hotel para hacer el amor.
> Bella palabra hacer=poiesis
> se hace un verso el amor y la caca por algo de juego
> natural
> este hacer no necesita patente. (*N* 18)

> [I should have made it home before nightfall but
> I dallied in a hotel to make love.
> Beautiful word to make=poiesis
> one makes a poem love and caca by a sort of
> natural play
> this making doesn't require a patent.]

Creative invention, imagination—not as in Lacan's Imaginary but as in Blake, Kant, or Lezama Lima (to cite a Latin American theory)—as alternative to being seen/recognized, is a very important concern of the book.

The incomplete body becomes, un-epically, in the final part of the poem, the lack of a tooth:

> La enfermera me da los precios de los dientes
> los dientes han subido—me avisa con firmeza
> [. . .]
> Ahora me costaría un ojo de la cara recomponer mi belleza.
> Trataré de no reír lo más que pueda. (*N* 19)

> [The nurse quotes me the price of teeth
> teeth have gone up—she informs me firmly.
> Now it would cost me an arm and a leg to restore my beauty.
> I will try not laughing as hard as I can.]

But the speaker is already laughing, silently, ironically. This is not, however, ironical self-dramatization used to keep ego in safe enclosure. It is an irony that arises in the need for self-containment as the only way to survive and be heard in a given society—the cost of living under a roof. Because to be heard or read means adjusting to an interlocutor who has been trained by that same society to expect that women contain themselves. As Ollé writes in an essay on women poets in Peru:

La necesidad de la compostura, de no perder los papeles entre la gente de la clase media alta en la década del sesenta se vuelve evidente [. . .] El límite es exigente, irreversible, no tolera la desmesura en la mujer.

Y es lacerante porque no hay cabida para la desesperación y existe temor al grito, o lo que es más arriesgado: existe temor a que en el lenguaje poético este grito se panfletario, huachafo, parodia de un grito. Por lo tanto la poeta se ironiza a sí misma y es implacable con sus propias debilidades: la angustia, el vacío.

La pasión de la no desesperación se nos muestra mediante el humor negro, y la descreencia. Queda la herida pero no una que excluye el sufrimiento que es manar, que es dialéctico.[26]

[The need for composure, not to lose your cool among the upper middle classes of the 1960s becomes clear. The boundary is strict, unalterable, it will not tolerate a lack of moderation in women.

And it wounds, because it allows no space for desperation and there is a fear of crying out, or what is even more risky: there is a fear that in poetic language this crying out might be cheap, affected, a parody of crying. So the woman poet becomes ironic and is implacable with her own weaknesses: anguish, the void.

The passionate pursuit of non-desperation manifests itself through black humour, scepticism. The wound remains, but not one that excludes suffering, which is rich, dialectical.]

That is, the body is lacerated not because it is an imperfect fulfilment of the social stereotype of the acceptable but because it is cut into/wounded by the impossibility of releasing despair. Referring to a text by the Peruvian poet Blanca Varela, Ollé writes 'Pocas veces se lee un texto lacerante como "Del orden de las cosas", lacerante en sentido inverso a la pasión, si es posible sentir pasión cuando dejamos de creer en la desperación' [Very seldom can one see a text as lacerating as 'Of the order of things', lacerating in a sense opposite to passion, if it's possible to feel passion when we stop believing in desperation].[27]

[26] Carmen Ollé, 'Poesía peruana escrita por mujeres: ¿Es lacerante la ironía?', *Márgenes*, 7/ 12 (1994), 11–26.
[27] Ollé, 'Poesía peruana', 13.

The body that is lacerated is the productive body, not the represented one. Productive in the sense that being cut into/open is also a capability of energy and feeling (this seems to be what Ollé means by calling the wound 'dialectical'). As the US poet H.D. writes, 'The centre of consciousness is either the brain or the love-region of the body.' The latter can be visualized as 'placed like a foetus in the body'; whereas consciousness centred on the 'realm of the intellect or brain' is something she became aware of 'before the birth of my child'.[28] But if passion is a source of creative invention, it occurs within specific limitations of language. If the wound as creative is one movement, the other, simultaneous one is the (socially and historically) specific interlocutor as cause of containment and laceration.

The subtitle of Ollé's essay is '¿Es lacerante la ironía?' [Is irony lacerating?], and it would be possible to suggest that the ability to receive that type of irony is a characteristic of a feminine reading. Ollé, however, chooses not to genderize reading in this case and states instead that 'como lectores no alcanzamos la madurez' [as readers we are not mature].[29] Her own poetry places its interlocutors/readers in the double position of being agents of the containment of women and of suffering it; that is, readers are not gendered but invited to discover the construction of gender as passing through them as both agents and sufferers.

The demand that women be moulded, malleable, is not one that comes from a particular place in the society. In the essay, Ollé mentions the upper middle class, but in *Noches* there is no such particularity—witness the voice of the dental nurse, whose legitimacy comes from its place in a total social rationality (*techos*), not from one social sector, and which is made to sound grotesque not because contrasted with other sociolects but because of the simple irony that being complete is unaffordable.

In the scene in the park in Lima, Ollé experiments with a different method, using an avant-garde style of grotesque drama, with working-class areas of Lima as scenario, in order to try out a language capable of expressing desperation—that of women in Lima. The main dramatic event is the shooting of a lover by a woman; the speakers are women intellectuals, readers of Simone de Beauvoir, for example; their language is

---

[28] H.D., *Notes*, 20, 21. [29] Ollé, 'Poesía peruana', 12.

hard, violent, without vulnerability, except where a kind of litany interrupts, recounting the moment when mothers show menstrual blood to their first daughter as initiation into being 'mujeres de carne y hueso tan integras para hacer el amor' [women of flesh and blood, so integral for lovemaking]— except that all the syllables are interrupted by and inseparable from childspeak: 'MUpuJEpeREpes DEpe CAparRNEpe Ypi HUEpesopo [. . . etc.] (*N* 34). 'Los pa-pe-pis o pos' go on sounding in the memory of one of the speakers (*N* 35), and cannot be prised apart from the content of the utterance, the infantilization inexpungible.

To say languages in the plural can mean several different things. Analytically speaking they can be set out as follows:

1. Different sociolects.
2. The differential placing of speakers and interlocutors.
3. Different poetic options such as narrative, dramatic, lyrical, and intellectual modes.

(1) and (2) have been referred to. The third set of possibilities needs brief comment. A significant proportion of the book consists in autobiographical narrative. As a way of writing poetry, this was first explored in Peru by the generation of 1960 and further developed by Ollé's own generation. Her use of dramatic form goes back to the avant-garde of the 1930s (for example César Moro and César Vallejo in Peru), a connection which is also evident in Ollé's lyrical (in the sense of condensed, non-narrative) passages (e.g. *N* 30). The fourth mode, the intellectual, is unusual. It includes not only materials from say Bachelard and Bataille in direct quotation but also an ongoing elaboration of abstract and analytic statements (e.g. 'en cariños masoquistas el sufrimiento es el yugo' [in masochistic caresses suffering is the yoke] 44), which act as a diagnostic of the conditions explored and as a body of thought, a place to be. There is one point, however, when this intellectual component shows its limits. In a passage which looks ironically at the effect of racial and social models in eroticism, there are the following four lines:

disponerse en el viaje a ser azaetada por el viento
como por la pasión
todo el que goza es verdadero y sus consecuentes
silogismos (*N* 23)

[To be prepared on the journey to be pierced by the wind's
    arrows
as by passion
everyone who experiences pleasure is true and its consequent
syllogisms]

where the move from passion as epic (*saeta*=arrow) to passion
as irony takes the energy out of merely intellectual consciousness and shows its tendency to move along pre-given tracks
('silogismos').

To return to the question of speaking and hearing, as
performed by the written text, one might well expect that the
restrictive expectations placed upon women would be characterized as coming from a particular type of voice, belonging to
a particular sector of society—which would make it possible to
present a counter-voice (of the marginalized, the oppressed).
But, as indicated earlier, this is not what happens. The expectation that women should be contained—the main reason for
irony—is not a particular voice of authority but an expectation
that is dispersed through the language as a whole. It is within
the language not as a set of representations—the vocabulary
could be changed but the forcing of women into restrictive
containment would still occur—but as orders given. The orders
take effect without having to assume the form of commands in
the grammatical sense. Consequently, neither the demand for
containment nor its exposure are placed as sociolects or
confined to any one of the poetic forms of expression (e.g. the
narrative or the intellectual).

Ollé responds to the restrictive effect of the language in two
main ways. The first is irony, as already discussed. The second is
by saying 'cosas sucias' [dirty things] (*N* 17)—what must not be
said because it is dirty, impure, dangerous. Here, as mentioned
at the beginning, the references are to female genitals,
menstruation, and sexual practices, including tabooed ones.
Clearly, an important motive is a defiance of the ban on speaking, and a reclamation of what is denied. But the lacerating
irony also comes in here, bringing into play the limits of possible reclamation. Take these uses of the word *partes*:

¿Nuestras partes se cercenan por falta de belleza
o de carácter?

Como antes aún sigo en estado de alerta ante cualquier

extraño ante cualquier contacto presintiendo que debo
relucir o impresionar con mis lecciones de piano como
ahora con mis partes. (*N* 23)

[Are our parts less for lack of beauty
or of character?

Now as then I am in a state of alert with any
stranger with any contact sensing that I must
excel or impress with my piano lessons as
now with my parts.]

In the first case the meaning is *partes íntimas* or *pudendas*, but in
the second there is an ambiguity: *partes* as euphemism for genitals or *partes* as qualities, accomplishments? The equivalence is
ironical, and speaks of being placed in an impossible (desper-
ate) situation.

But there is also *suciedad* as a condition of desire. The curves
and folds of a naked body '¿Qué son sino el caracol?' [What
are these if not the slug?] (*N* 36), which, in other circumstances ('en una hoja de hortaliza'), 'nos asquea' [on a leaf of
lettuce, disgusts us]. The technique of enquiry into inner
experience is similar to that of Bataille, whose writing is
explored at some length in another section (*N* 16–17). Later,
dirty nappies are included in the sights and smells that can
cause repulsion (*N* 40) but this repulsion is placed as belonging to the mind ('mente'). And the mind is capable of transforming *lo sucio* into *lo limpio* through a certain type of memory
(*N* 41). Such mental processing takes us away from *suciedad* as
a shape of desire.

Thus the concern with the unclean is not limited to social
definitions of the clean or its genderization. *La suciedad* is
different from being not perfect, the wrong shape; it breaks the
certainty/passivity of the viewer of 'estampas eróticas' [erotic
prints] (*N* 49). Does it offer a possible way of breaking other
moulds? Certainly it is not the certainties of social representation that are the source of this sense of the unclean, but the
other productive, inventive body—the body of imagination—
which is involved when 'en esta mística de relatar cosas sucias
estoy sola | y afiebrada' [in this mystique of telling dirty things I
am alone | and feverish] (*N* 17). Does this go beyond irony, or is
there an uncertainty, a possible irony in the phrase 'esta mística
de relatar cosas sucias'?

BETWEEN SOUND AND SILENCE

If *Noches de adrenalina* was concerned with how to move from being seen to seeing oneself, *¿Por qué hacen tanto ruido?* [30] works with the difficulties of hearing and being heard, and the whole book is an invitation into ways of listening that go against the grain—of the Spanish language in Peru as the majority have been trained to hear it, and of Peruvian poetry in the ways it is usually read.

The difficulty of being heard, which arises from all the noises that interpose themselves, includes the difficulty of hearing one's own inner life. If the voices of mother and other authorities, and of a lover who is a poet, plus the sounds of neighbours and the general social noise, are constantly interfering, then the movements of inner life become distorted or blotted out. The following passage responds to that situation not just as an existential problem but as a question of poetics:

Deletreo mi espíritu en estas circunstancias: está vacío. Vacío significa lleno de nada. No hay en la naturaleza algo que se parezca a mi espíritu, ni el frío de la niebla, o un árbol sin hojas, pues ellos son paisaje. Mi espíritu no tiene paisajes, ahí nada se siembra, tampoco se marchita. Allí se ha querido instaurar el orden, la limpieza, la disciplina de las cosas que no existen, porque en todo lo que existe hay un bello desorden, una querida suciedad, un olor a algo. Mi imagen no huele ni hace ruido. (*PQ* 13)

[I decipher my spirit in these circumstances: it is empty. Empty means full of nothing. There is nothing in nature which resembles my spirit, neither the cold of the mist, nor a tree without leaves, for they are landscape. My spirit has no landscape, there nothing can grow nor does it die. There is an attempt to establish order there, cleanliness, the discipline of things that do not exist, for in all that exists there is a beautiful disorder, a cherished dirtiness, a smell of something. My image neither smells nor makes a noise.]

There is not just a refusal of pastoral or Romantic organicism but also a sense of there being no resonance with the world of external things. To be without that disorder of things that exist for the senses may involve an emptying or even death of the

[30] Lima, 1992. Textual references are given as *PQ*.

imagination but not the end of writing, 'ya que no hay un punto cero que no sea también nodal, esa es la imposibilidad del silencio' [because there is no zero point which is not also nodal, that is the impossibility of silence] (*PQ* 13). Nodal in physics signifies an intersection of astronomic movements or of sound vibrations. Thus emptiness in Ollé's sense is also always the becoming of something. And to fail to resolve the existential is not artistic failure; on the contrary, not to achieve silence (that would be 'terapia' [therapy]) but instead 'sólo el ruido' [only noise] is the conditon of 'la gran maña' [the great trick] of art. Noise thus becomes a complex social and spiritual condition of art. And emptying the inner life can become a process of ascesis, the better to hear—and not just to hear, since change in any one of the senses involves the others. The process, and the style, recall César Vallejo's poem 'Voy a hablar de la esperanza' [I am going to talk of hope], and a key feature of the similarities is a dismantling of the language of symbolism, both in the specialized literary sense and as an influence within the wider language as ordinarily spoken.

The difficulty of hearing and being heard occurs not just because of the noise of the society, as in the lover's complaint that he is being atttacked because of his poetry (*PQ* 31), but also because both the inherited poetic language and the wider language are suffused with a particular imagery of desire that controls not so much what can be desirable (the object), as the inner life of the person desiring. These issues are worked out through a double journey, on the one hand existential and on the other artistic. Both are haunted by despair and the danger of remaining trapped in the past. The existential involves the painful break-up of a relationship, where a key difficulty is that of love based on an idealized image nurtured in childhood and adolescence, an image that induces passivity; a sense of emptiness following the break-up, troubled by dreams and memories; an emergence of new desires, those of maturity; and a decision deliberately to close the door, which is where, thematically, the book closes. The poetic journey passes through symbolism, a formative influence in childhood reading, as expression and containment of solitude and the inner life, to a sense of emptiness on the one hand and of the everyday material world on the other, the world which symbolism and Platonism exclude. The final stage is to articulate the values of a new poetics, which, embodied as form, are what make the writing of the book possible: to deploy artistic invention against despair and stasis.

Ollé moves on from the method used in *Noches*: to delineate in *la suciedad* the body of love, freeing it from the idealizing representations that restrictively confine it, and that for women growing up in Lima in the 1950s and 1960s meant a material and linguistic 'corsé de acero' [corset of steel]. Her concern with inventing possible forms of expression of a woman's desire now involves a contrastive delineation of Ignacio, the poet-lover. His confidence in poetry and in a particular form of expression of his desire go together: at one point he compares himself with Hölderlin (*PQ* 22), and at one of the most tense moments of the breakdown of the relationship declares: 'quiero y quise y siempre querré que seas como la Nora de Joyce: mi puta' [I want, I wanted, and I shall always want you to be like Joyce's Nora: my whore] (*PQ* 78). Ignacio represents that other attitude where the relationship between desire and its expression is not problematic but confident, seamless. Two ways of writing, which are also ways of hearing and reading, emerge: in the first there is an unbroken road from desire to beauty, the pulsations of the body becoming, in language, cosmic. 'Desde el sur me enviaba cartas quejándose de su soledad, amándome como sólo él sabía, como Dante a Beatriz, como Petrarca a Laura' [He sent me letters from the south complaining of his solitude, loving me as only he knew how, as Dante loved Beatrice, as Petrarch loved Laura] (*PQ* 65). Ollé does not resort to easy dismissal, and more than once speaks of Ignacio's beauty, but, as in her essay on Peruvian poetry written by women, finds in irony a way of making audible the restriction of what is permitted to women and its enactment in the language. The second way of writing involves making perceptible the obligatory 'compostura' [composure] that women writing in Peru have to assume, the lack of any place for 'desesperación' [desperation], since it will be heard as 'huachafo' [tacky] and 'panfletario' [propagandist], and exposing the diminution of poety written by women to erotic and of the erotic to the sexual.[31]

There is, consequently, no question of a prestigious literary tradition to be inherited as there is for Ignacio (Dante, Petrarch, and so on). The situation for Ollé is quite the oppo-

---

[31] Ollé, 'Poesía peruana', 1, 2, 4.

site: that dominant tradition gets in the way of being heard, and the need is to find ways of breaking with it. Once again life and writing are in close connection: 'Lo irracional en mí radicaba en que lo poético sólo servía para que me dominaran' [The irrational in me centred on the fact that the poetic only helped others to dominate me] (*PQ* 22). Whereas Ignacio, who makes himself represent 'the poetic', turns it into an exclusive action: 'Lo irracional en Ignacio era no poder soportar la racionalidad de los otros' [The irrational in Ignacio meant not being able to bear the rationality of others] (*PQ* 22).

César Vallejo enters here as ally for a reformulation of poet-ics. Ollé's title *¿Por qué hacen tanto ruido?* can be heard as a reminder of '¿Quién hace tanta bulla?' [Who's making such a racket?], the first line of the first poem of Vallejo's *Trilce*, famous, at least to critics, because of their renewed attempts to find an interpretative key to it. Vallejo's poem links noise, formally, with an excess of meanings that cannot be controlled, making a parodic counter-luxury to Baudelaire's 'luxe, calme et volupté'.[32] Thematically, Vallejo defines noise in terms of *guano*, excrement, money, and lack of respect, enumerating some of the factors that foul up the sense of cosmic correspondences which symbolist poetics rely upon. The result is that the paths of interpretation multiply and become clogged—witness the unilluminating deluge of critical essays on *Trilce* no. I.

Symbolism has had considerable effect on twentieth-century Peruvian poetry. The language of poetry, from Eguren to Sologuren, to name the major line of transmission, has to an important extent been symbolist. Ollé's decision to break with that tradition can be compared with Vallejo's, but her method is different. In terms of semantic field, Vallejo's *bulla* is merely noise, whereas Ollé's *ruido* includes sound as well as noise: its ambiguities force an entry between dualisms of sound and silence. Ollé's writing opts for quietness, a zone in between sound and silence, where the usual frontiers between what can and cannot be heard become changed. The idea of eluding symbolism is most explicit when, in response to a windy night that 'se parece a un poema de Nerval, exquisitamente román-tico' [resembles a Nerval poem, exquisitely romantic] (*PQ* 29),

[32] See 'L'Invitation au voyage', in *Les Fleurs du mal* (1857 edn.: XLIX; 1861 edn.: LIII).

she delineates a contrasting imaginary poem: 'un poema como una oreja que se corta sin hacer ruido, un simple cartílago que cae a tierra, que no es ningún símbolo sino un simple corte delicado' [a poem like an ear which is cut off with no noise, a simple cartilage which falls to earth, not any kind of symbol but a simple delicate cut] (*PQ* 29). This is clearly meant to be an antidote to the attraction to 'los poemas misteriosos de todos los simbolistas' [the mysterious poems of all the Symbolists] (*PQ* 34, see also 71), acquired in childhood.

But the method itself is less willed than that imaginary poem. It relies on an emptying of the space of writing so that resonance and echo between one thing and another, or between 'mi espíritu' and the world, are minimized. Against the luxury of Baudelaire or Nerval, ascesis and discipline of the imagination are deployed. But the issue is not just literary: there is also the question of the persistent forms of intensity inherited from a Catholic childhood and what, as a poet, to do with them. One option is the therapeutic action of 'limpieza' explored by Rodolfo Hinostroza—Ollé takes the word from the title of his book, *Aprendizaje de limpieza*—also a prose work by a poet.[33] Its disadvantage is that, by systematically emptying the symbolic, through psychoanalysis, it risks, to use Ollé's phrase, the death of the imagination.

Another side to Ollé's method is the decision to allow into her writing the ordinary and the practical, the unresolved difficulties of everyday life and work which are excluded by Ignacio's purity (she reads Ignacio's letters, from his 'exile' in the south, as moving towards 'un encuentro definitivo con Dios' [a definitive encounter with God] *PQ* 87). But inclusion of the 'non-poetic' does not of itself mean change. One of the shortcomings of the critical discourses which began to proliferate in Peru and elsewhere in the late 1960s and early 1970s was the idea that poetry had to be anti-elitist by embracing everyday life: the equivalent in poetics of populism in politics. What this does not answer is the need for the invention of new forms.

In a crucial passage, Ollé writes:

Me sofoca la cultura, la vitalidad que viene envuelta en esa pócima, es como recogerme en un paisaje en el que no puedo nutrirme de sol

[33] Rodolfo Hinostroza, *Aprendizaje de limpieza* (Lima, 1978).

o echarme blandamente en el pasto. O como mi desnudo rollizo que no es pictórico sino vacilante ante el espejo.

Me sofoca que nada suceda hoy y luego escribir esa experiencia de que nada suceda hoy, ver cómo algo existe en ese pedazo de tiempo en al que nade sucede, sólo porque lo observo por un retrovisor. Estoy viviendo a través de lo que leo.

Siento la angustia de acercarme a la hoja en la máquina de escribir y sorprender la imagen que no aflora. Todo lo hace la fantasía, pero mi imaginación es como un cuchillo sin filo, corta a dentelladas trozos de realidad porque algo la impulsa desde su bloqueo.

Es imposible no decir nada. Me observa, se sienta a mi lado y ve cómo no puedo hilvanar sino frases cortas. (*PQ* 37)

[Culture suffocates me, the vitality hidden in this concotion, it's like taking shelter in a landscape where I am unable to take nourishment from the sun, or throw myself softly into the grass. Or as if my plump nudity is not artistic but hesitant before the mirror.

I'm suffocating by the fact that nothing is happening today and then writing that experience, that nothing is happening today. To see how something exists in the scrap of time in which nothing is happening, only because I observe it in a rear-view mirror. I'm living through what I read.

I feel the anguish of approaching the sheet in the typewriter and surprising the image which does not emerge. Fantasy can do anything, but my imagination is like a blunt knife, it bites into fragments of reality because something pushes it from its blockage.

It is impossible to keep silent. He is watching me, he sits by my side and sees how I am only able to string together short sentences.]

A number of difficulties combine: writer's block, Ignacio's gaze, and the weight of inherited language and forms of perception. The block connects with a failure of the body seen to meet the ideal. Separation from the ideal is necessary: 'Beber no es ningún símbolo' [There is no symbol in drinking], as she writes one night after Ignacio has left (*PQ* 84). But Ollé's way does require the interrogation of childhood idealizations and their artistic consequences. Of these she repeatedly uses the word Platonism. The diagnosis includes a list of men capable of eliciting 'mi capacidad de entregarme a una imagen [. . .] cuando era adolescente' [my capacity to give myself up to an image as an adolescent], among them not just 'el cura alemán' [the German priest], but also, with some irony, 'el pintor de la casa, el albañil de al lado' [the painter who did the house, the bricklayer from next door] (*PQ* 78). This interference of the 'alter ego' in love has become, in the relationship with Ignacio, 'un rabioso masoquismo platónico por la imagen que él proyectaba en mi fantasía [an angry platonic masochism provoked by the image that he projected in my fantasy]. In opposition to the transcendentalizing of desire in idealized figures, in exclusive synthetic images, Ollé exposes 'mi puterío platónico' [my platonic whoring] (*PQ* 78)—a phrase with plenty of irony in it, given the usual, puritanical, connotation of 'platonic love'.

But Platonism is not just an autobiographical matter, it is also a burden of symbolist poetry. As James Higgins writes in his essay on Martín Adán, a key figure in the Peruvian symbolist tradition, 'to live exiled in the world', fate of the soul in the Neoplatonic tradition, becomes in Adán's poems a condition of the poet in Peru.[34] However, Adán was not a Neoplatonist in any simple, unproblematic way; his writing enacts a struggle between the ideal world of Neoplatonism and the actual environment of twentieth-century Peru, between 'perfección ideal' [ideal perfection] and 'dimensión sensible' [sensual dimension], as Edmundo Bendezú notes.[35] Ollé's book is not, either, a simple junking of Platonic capacities, but a decision to prise them away from stasis and submission to a tradition. One of the most powerful moments in her book is when a surge of desire to make love with Ignacio opens the senses to the beauty of the material world of a Lima street ('Cualquier cosa alentaba mis sentidos. La lozanía de los escolares con sus medias remangadas, luciendo en sus dedos sortijas de plástico multicolores' [Anything would excite my senses. The vitality of the school kids with their socks around their ankles, showing off multicoloured plastic rings on their fingers] *PQ* 69). Renunciation of 'ese sueño' [this dream]—because Ignacio has left—does not destroy the capacity of aliveness to the real or turn it to nostalgia. What is gained is understanding of the process—which makes this book utterly different from a confessional autobiography—and as a result Platonism goes through a 'descomposición': 'pensaba en su belleza que exaltaba también la del mundo material' [I thought of his beauty which also exalted that of the material world]; (*PQ* 69).

---

[34] James Higgins, *The Poet in Peru* (Liverpool, 1982), 149; see also 1, 147, 153.
[35] Edmundo Bendezú, *La poética de Martín Adán* (Lima, 1969), 140; see also 133–41.

Those beauties become the beauty of understanding, a resource against the seductiveness of Platonism, which is the danger of drowning in 'Plato's honey head', to use Melville's phrase.[36] This understanding is brought to bear upon reading Yeats's 'Byzantium', which is taken as exemplary of symbolism and the struggle with Platonism. Ollé makes particular mention of Yeats's first line, in which 'unpurged images' make their passage into night to become changless artefacts.[37] If Yeats traces the distance between Platonic ideality and 'human complexities', and moves within that tension, Ollé finds that understanding Yeats's poem, finding the form of her own experience, and preserving the capacity to move (figured as a game of chess) converge: 'para comprender "Bizancio", para contenerme en lo que amo y no amo y desaparece' [to understand 'Byzantium', to contain myself in what I love and what I do not love and disappears] (*PQ* 85), a route ('una ruta') has to be found, one which is also adequate to handling the enemy queen, the most energetic piece.

The aesthetic decisions of *¿Por qué?* consist in a choice of moves. The route is towards 'lo desconocido' [the new, the unknown] (*PQ* 85), but depends on staying with the incompleteness of experience as opposed to willed resolution, which would include the Platonic or the therapeutic. There is a choice of restraint, as opposed to confession or self-legitimization, with an extraordinary absence of ego as its result. There is a choice of slowness, as opposed to lyrical speed, and of quietness, allowing the actual turns of inner feeling to be heard. There is a desire of movement, as opposed to a luxury of sensuality folded upon itself: the 'lozanía' of the schoolchildren, though semantically close to *lujo*, is not luxury but aliveness. The writing moves without laying down a line of logic that signals or excludes deviations from itself. This is its openness, its nonexclusiveness. The transition from one topic to another is not a sequence in time. Ollé herself calls its genre hybrid (*PQ* 51). The long sentences are achievements of responsibility for an

[36] Herman Melville, *Moby-Dick* (New York, 1967), 290.

[37] Yeats's poem begins: 'The unpurged images of day recede; | The Emperor's drunken soldiery are abed; | Night resonance recedes, night-walkers' song | After great cathedral gong; | A starlit or a moonlit dome disdains | All that man is, | All mere complexities, | The fury and the mire of human veins' (*Collected Poems* (London, 1950), 280).

existential/artistic process, and in that sense quite different from Octavio Paz's transcendent 'instante poético' [poetic instant]: as Ollé writes, with some irony, 'Me leía a Octavio Paz: "Piedra del [*sic*] sol". Me leía expresamente un pasaje sobre los amantes. Cómo quisiera aún ser esa mujer' [I read Octavio Paz: 'Piedra del sol'. I intentionally read an excerpt about lovers. How I wish I still could be that woman] (*PQ* 34).

Conclusion

The best way of concluding this book is to use it as an instrument for further explorations. For that purpose, I suggest below the names of other poets for possible reading. First, though, the question of exclusions perhaps needs some comment. There are two types of exclusion in this book. On the one hand, there are certain types of poetry which I judged unsuitable for inclusion on the grounds that, in order to do justice to them, they would require specialized study and there was not space for that. These are the poetry that makes extensive use of native materials and language, and visual poetry. An example of the former would be the Mapuche poet Lienlaf. For its part, visual poetry in Latin America has mainly been associated with the Brazilian *Concretistas* but there have been important traditions of visual poetry in Spanish America, for example in the Cuban journal *Signos*. The other type of exclusion I refer to has a different purpose. This is where I have not included those who are considered to be major poets or where there is no poet from a country with a major literary tradition, such as Mexico. The criterion has been to select poets who open new possibilities of language and poetic form, rather than those who prolong existing traditions, however successfully.

The aim has been, in each chapter, to suggest in detail ways of reading a particular poet, and to do this in such a manner as to make that reading an opening to reading other poets, and to gaining a sense of the vast and varied field of what poets have written during the past half-century in Spanish America. With what success, readers will judge.

Finally, I would like to mention here the names of other poets whose work readers may find worth exploring. Inevitably, limitations of my information come into play here. The most serious absence from the book is that of Brazilian poets: to have included them would have made the book twice as long and it seemed to me there was no sense in including just one. João

Cabral de Melo Neto, Haroldo and Augusto de Campos, and Edimilson de Almeida Pereira are among those I suggest a reader should look at. The list that follows is of poets writing in Spanish. After each poet or group of poets, the country they come from is given in brackets. Hugo Gola, Edgar Bayley, Juan Gelman, Néstor Perlongher (Argentina). Jaime Saenz (Bolivia). Enrique Lihn, Jorge Teillier, Diego Maquieira (Chile). Fernando Charry Lara (Colombia). Alberto Blanco (Mexico). José Coronel Urtecho, Pablo Antonio Cuadra (Nicaragua). Javier Sologuren, Carlos Germán Belli, Pablo Guevara, Antonio Cisneros, Rodolfo Hinostroza, José Watanabe (Peru). Eduardo Milán, Enrique Fierro, Ida Vitale (Uruguay).

Bibliography

GENERAL

ADAMS, HENRY, *A Henry Adams Reader*, ed. Elizabeth Stevenson (New York, 1958).

ADÁN, MARTÍN, *De lo barroco en el Perú* (Lima, 1968).

ADORNO, THEODOR, *Minima moralia: Reflections from Damaged Life* (London, 1978).

ARGUEDAS, JOSÉ MARÍA, *Obra completa* (Lima, 1983).

ARTAUD, ANTONIN, *Selected Writings* (Berkeley, 1988).

BAKHTIN, MIKHAIL, *The Dialogical Imagination* (Austin, Tex., 1981).

BARTHES, ROLAND, *Image-Music-Text* (London, 1977).

—— *Writing Degree Zero* (London, 1967).

BATAILLE, GEORGES, *Inner Experience* (New York, 1988).

—— *Literature and Evil* (London, 1985).

BENDEZÚ, EDMUNDO, *La poética de Martín Adán* (Lima, 1969).

BENJAMIN, WALTER, *Charles Baudelaire: A Lyric Poet in the Era of High Capitalism* (London, 1983).

—— *Illuminations* (London, 1973).

—— *Reflections* (New York, 1986).

BERGER, P., and LUCKMAN, T., *The Social Construction of Reality* (Harmondsworth, 1966).

BEVERLEY, JOHN, and ZIMMERMAN, MARK, *Literature and Politics in the Central American Revolutions* (Austin, 1990),

BLAKE, WILLIAM, *Poems and Prophecies* (London, 1972).

BLANCHOT, MAURICE, *L'Espace littéraire* (Paris, 1955). English translation with an introduction by Ann Smock: *The Space of Literature* (Lincoln, 1989).

BLOOM, HAROLD, *The Western Canon* (London, 1995).

BORGES, JORGE LUIS, *Otras inquisiciones* (Buenos Aires, 1960).

BOURDIEU, PIERRE, *The Field of Cultural Production* (Cambridge, 1993).

BOYLE, CATHERINE, *Review of Women, Culture, and Politics in Latin America, Bulletin of Latin American Research*, 13/2 (1994).

—— 'The Mirror to Nature? Latin American Theatre in London', *Travesia: Journal of Latin American Cultural Studies*, 1/1 (1992).

BROTHERSTON, G., and DORN, E. (eds.), *Our Word: Guerrilla Poems from Latin America* (London, 1968).

BRUNNER, J. J., *Un espejo trizado: ensayos sobre cultura y políticas culturales* (Santiago, 1988).

BURROUGHS, WILLIAM, *Electronic Revolution* (Expanded Media Editions, n.d.).

—— *The Naked Lunch* (London, 1964).

CASTILLO, OTTO RENÉ, *Poemas* (Havana, 1971).

CONRAD, JOSEPH, *Lord Jim* (Harmondsworth, 1962).

CORBIN, HENRI, 'Le Temps cyclique dans le Mazdéisme et dans l'Ismaélisme', *Eranos-Jahrbuch XX* (1951; Zurich, 1952). English translation: *Cyclical Time and Ismaili Gnosis* (London, 1983).

—— *Creative Imagination in the Sufism of Ibn 'Arabi* (Princeton, 1981).

CORRIGAN, P., and SAYER, D., *The Great Arch: English State Formation as Cultural Revolution* (Oxford, 1985).

CORTÁZAR, JULIO, *Nicaragua tan violentamente dulce* (Barcelona, 1984).

CREELEY, ROBERT, *A Sense of Measure* (London, 1970).

—— *The Collected Poems of Robert Creeley* (Berkeley, 1982).

DELEUZE, GILLES, *Kant's Critical Philosophy* (Minneapolis, 1990).

—— *The Logic of Sense* (New York, 1989).

—— *Nietzsche and Philosophy* (London, 1983).

—— *Dialogues* (London, 1987).

—— and GUATTARI, FÉLIX, *A Thousand Plateaus* (London, 1988).

—— —— *Anti-Oedipus* (Minneapolis, 1977).

—— —— *What is Philosophy* (London, 1994).

DONOSO, JOSÉ, *El obsceno pájaro de la noche* (Barcelona, 1970).

EMPSON, WILLIAM, *The Structure of Complex Words* (London, 1985).

FEYERABEND, PAUL, *Against Method* (London, 1988).

—— 'History of the Philosophy of Science', in *The Oxford Companion to Philosophy* (Oxford, 1995).

FORGUES, ROLAND, *Las poetas se desnudan* (Lima, 1991).

FOUCAULT, MICHEL, *Technologies of the Self* (London, 1988).

—— *The Order of Things* (London, 1974).

FRANCO, JEAN, *César Vallejo: The Dialectics of Poetry and Silence* (London, 1976).

GARCÍA CANCLINI, NÉSTOR, *Culturas híbridas: estrategias para entrar y salir de la modernidad* (Mexico City, 1989).

GARCÍA LORCA, FEDERICO, *Poeta en Nueva York* (Madrid, 1987).

GINSBERG, ALLEN, *Your Reason and Blake's System* (New York, 1992).

GIRONDO, OLIVERIO, *Obras, i: Poesía* (Buenos Aires, 1968).

GLANTZ, M, 'Nakedness as Shipwreck: Alvar Núñez Cabeza de Vaca', *Travesia: Journal of Latin American Cultural Studies*, 1/2 (1992).

GOLA, HUGO, 'Experiencia y lenguaje', in *Nombres*, 3 (1993).

GONZÁLEZ, MIKE, and TREECE, DAVID, *The Gathering of Voices: The Twentieth-Century Poetry of Latin America* (London, 1992).

GONZÁLEZ ECHEVARRÍA, ROBERTO, 'Doña Barbara Writes the Plain', in *The Voice of the Masters* (Austin, Tex., 1988).

GRAMSCI, ANTONIO, *Selections from Cultural Writings* (Cambridge, Mass., 1991).

GRAZIANO, F., *Divine Violence: Spectacle, Psychosexuality and Radical Christianity in the Argentine 'Dirty War'* (Boulder, Colo., 1992).

GRICE, PAUL, *Studies in the Way of Words* (Cambridge, Mass., 1989).

GUIBERT, RITA, *Seven Voices from Latin America* (New York, 1973).

GUIGNON, C. (ed.), T*he Cambridge Companion to Heidegger* (Cambridge, 1993).

HABERMAS, JÜRGEN, *The Theory of Communicative Action* (London, 1984).

H.D., *Notes on Thought and Vision* (London, 1988).

—— *Trilogy* (London, 1973).

HEIDEGGER, MARTIN, *Being and Time* (Oxford, 1962).

—— *Early Greek Thinking* (New York, 1984).

HEISENBERG, WERNER, *Physics and Philosophy* (London, 1989).

HERAUD, JAVIER, *Poesías completas* (Lima, 1973).

HIGGINS, JAMES, *The Poet in Peru* (Liverpool, 1982).

—— *Visión del hombre y de la vida en las ultimas obras poéticas de César Vallejo* (Mexico City, 1970).

HINOSTROZA, RODOLFO, *Aprendizaje de limpieza*, (Lima, 1978).

HUIDOBRO, VICENTE, *Altazor* (Madrid, 1931).

—— 'Arte poética', in *El espejo de Agua* (Buenos Aires, 1916).

HUXLEY, ALDOUS, 'Tragedy and the Whole Truth', in *Music at Night and Other Essays* (London, 1949).

KAFKA, FRANZ, *Metamorphosis and Other Stories* (Harmondsworth, 1961).

KAMENSZAIN, TAMARA, *El texto silencioso: tradición y vanguardia en la poesía sudamericana* (Mexico City, 1983).

KEATS, JOHN, *The Letters of John Keats* (Oxford, 1960).

KOLOCOTRONI, V., et al. (eds.), *Modernism: An Anthology of Sources and Documents* (Edinburgh, 1998).

KRANIAUSKAS, JOHN, 'Cabeza de Vaca', *Travesia: Journal of Latin American Cultural Studies*, 1/2 (1992).

KRISTEVA, JULIA, *The Kristeva Reader*, ed. Toril Moi (Oxford, 1986).

LAPLANCHE, J., and PONTALIS, J.-B., *The Language of Psychoanalysis* (London, 1980).

LAWRENCE, D. H., 'Chaos in Poetry', in *Selected Literary Criticism* (London, 1956).

—— *Love among the Haystacks and Other Stories* (Harmondsworth, 1960).

—— *The Complete Poems* (Harmondsworth, 1977).

LEZAMA LIMA, JOSÉ, *El reino de la imagen* (Caracas, 1981).

LIENHARD, MARTÍN, *La voz y su huella* (Lima, 1992).

LODGE, DAVID (ed.), *Modern Criticism and Theory: A Reader* (London, 1988).

LUDMER, JOSEFINA, *El género gauchesco: un tratado sobre la patria* (Buenos Aires, 1988).

LYONS, JOHN (ed.), *Poems of Love and Revolution* (London, 1983).

McLUHAN, MARSHALL, *The Mechanical Bride: Folklore of Industrial Man* (New York, 1951).

MACSWEENEY, BARRY, *Pearl*, in *The Book of Demons* (Newcastle, 1997).

MALLARMÉ, STÉPHANE, *Selected Poetry and Prose*, ed. Mary Ann Caws (New York, 1982).

MÁRQUEZ, ROBERT (ed.), *Latin American Revolutionary Poetry* (New York, 1974)

MARTÍ, JOSÉ, *Ismaelillo, Versos libres, Versos sencillos*, ed. Ivan A. Schulman (Madrid, 1982).

MARTÍN-BARBERO, JESÚS, *Communication, Culture and Hegemony: From the Media to Mediations* (London, 1993).

MAXWELL ATKINSON, J., and HERITAGE, J., *Structures of Social Action: Studies in Conversation Analysis*, (Cambridge, 1984).

MELVILLE, HERMAN, *Moby-Dick* (New York, 1967).

MERLEAU-PONTY, MAURICE, *Phenomenology of Perception* (London, 1962).

—— *The Primacy of Perception* (Chicago, 1989).

MILÁN, EDUARDO, *Una cierta mirada* (Mexico City, 1989).

MILLER, HENRY, *The Colossus of Maroussi* (Harmondsworth, 1963).

MOI, TORIL, *Sexual/Textual Politics* (London, 1985).

MORANDÉ, PEDRO, *Cultura y modernización en América Latina* (Madrid, 1987).

MOTTRAM, ERIC, *Towards Design in Poetry* (London, 1977).

NERUDA, PABLO, *Tercera residencia* (Buenos Aires, 1961).

—— *Residencia en la tierra* (Buenos Aires, 1966).

—— *Canto general* (Buenos Aires, 1963).

—— *Antología esencial*, ed. Hernán Loyola (Buenos Aires, 1971).

NIETZSCHE, FRIEDRICH, *The Birth of Tragedy and the Genealogy of Morals* (New York, 1956).

—— *The Will to Power* (New York, 1968).

O'HARA, FRANK, *Selected Poems* (New York, 1974).

OLSON, CHARLES, *Collected Poems* (Berkeley, 1987).

—— *Collected Prose* (Berkeley, 1997).

ONETTI, JUAN CARLOS, *Dejemos hablar al viento* (Barcelona, 1979).

OPPEN, GEORGE, *Collected Poems* (New York, 1975).

—— 'Cultural Triumph', George Oppen Papers, University of California at San Diego, Box 27, Folder 39.

ORWELL, GEORGE, *1984* (London, 1989).

OSORIO, NELSON (ed.), *Manifiestos, proclamas y polémicas de la vanguardia literaria latinoamericana* (Caracas, 1988).

OVIEDO, J. M. (ed.), *Estos 13* (Lima, 1973).

PAULS, ALAN, 'Languages at War', *Travesia: Journal of Latin American Cultural Studies*, 2/1 (1993).

PAVESE, CESARE, *El oficio de poeta* (Buenos Aires, 1970).

PAZ, OCTAVIO, 'The Word as Foundation', *Times Literary Supplement*, 14 Nov. 1968.

—— *Libertad bajo palabra* (Mexico City, 1968).

PIÑA, JUAN ANDRÉS, *Conversaciones con la poesía chilena* (Santiago, 1990).

PLATO, *Meno*, trans. W. K. C. Guthrie (Harmondsworth, 1956).

—— *The Republic* (Harmondsworth, 1955).

POUND, EZRA, *ABC of Reading* (London, 1961).

—— *Literary Essays* (London, 1954).

PROUST, MARCEL, *Sur la lecture* (Arles, 1988).

RADCLIFFE, S., and WESTWOOD, S. (eds.), '*Viva*': *Women and Popular Protest in Latin America* (London, 1993).

RAMA, ÁNGEL, *Transculturación narrativa en America Latina* (Mexico City, 1982).

RICHARD, NELLY, *Margins and Institutions: Art in Chile since 1973*, *Art and Text*, 21 (Melbourne, 1986).

RILKE, RAINER MARIA, *Duino Elegies*, trans. J. B. Leishman and Stephen Spender (New York, 1963).

—— *Das Buch der Bilder* (Leipzig, 1913).

ROTHENBERG, JEROME, *Revolution of the Word: A New Gathering of American Avant Garde Poetry 1914–1945* (New York, 1974).

—— and JORIS, PIERRE, *Poems for the Millennium* (Berkeley, 1995).

—— and ROTHENBERG, DIANE, *Symposium of the Whole* (Berkeley, 1983).

ROWE, WILLIAM, 'E. A. Westphalen: The Poet's Intelligence and the Social Imaginary', *Travesia: Journal of Latin American Cultural Studies*, 4/1 (1995).

—— *Hacia una poética radical: ensayos de hermenéutica cultural* (Rosario, 1996).

—— and SCHELLING, VIVIAN, *Memory and Modernity: Popular Culture in Latin America* (London, 1991).

RUSSELL, BERTRAND, *A History of Western Philosophy* (London, 1961).

SAER, JUAN JOSÉ, *Nadie, nada, nunca* (Mexico City, 1980). English translation: *Nobody nothing never* (London, 1993).

SAUER, CARL, *Land and Life: A Selection from the Writings of Carl Ortwin Sauer* (Berkeley, 1963).

SERRES, MICHEL, *Hermes: Literature, Science, Philosophy* (Baltimore, 1982).

SHOTTER, J., *Conversational Realities: Constructing Life through Language* (London, 1993).

SHUMWAY, NICHOLAS, *The Invention of Argentina* (Berkeley, 1991).

SMITH, CYRIL, *Marx at the Millennium* (London, 1966).

SPENCER BROWN, G., *Laws of Form* (London, 1969).

STEIN, GERTRUDE, *Selected Writings* (New York, 1972).

SUCRE, GUILLERMO, *La máscara, la transparencia* (Caracas, 1975).

TEDLOCK, DENNIS (ed.), *Popol Vuh* (New York, 1996).

TEILHARD DE CHARDIN, PIERRE, *The Phenomenon of Man* (London, 1959).

TEITLER, NATHALIE, 'The Reconstruction of the Body in the Poetry of Alfonsina Storni', Ph.D. thesis, University of London, 1999.

University of California-Stanford Seminar on Feminism and Culture in Latin America, *Women, Culture, and Politics in Latin America* (Berkeley, 1992).

VALLEJO, CÉSAR, *El arte y la revolución* (Lima, 1973).

—— *Poemas escogidos*, ed. Julio Ortega (Caracas, 1991).

—— *Obras completas*, ed. R. González Vigil (Lima, 1991).

VARGAS, ELIZABETH, *Identidad femenina: cuestionando y construyendo estereotipos* (Lima, 1991).

VIÑAS, DAVID, *Indios, ejército y frontera* (Mexico City, 1984).

VIRILIO, PAUL, *Open Sky* (London, 1997).

VOLOSINOV, V. N., *Marxism and the Philosophy of Language* (New York, 1973).

WESTPHALEN, E. A., *Otra imagen deleznable* (Mexico City, 1980).

WILLIAMS, WILLIAM CARLOS, *The Autobiography of William Carlos Williams* (New York, 1967).

—— *Collected Earlier Poems* (New York, 1988).

—— *Selected Essays* (New York, 1969).

WITTGENSTEIN, LUDWIG, *Tractatus Logico-Philosophicus* (London, 1963).

YEATS, W. B. *Collected Poems* (London, 1950).

YURKIEVICH, SAÚL, *Fundadores de la nueva poesía latinoamericana* (Barcelona, 1971).

ZANETTI, SUSANA, et al., *Las cenizas de la huella: linajes y figuras en torno al modernismo* (Rosario, 1997).

ZERAN, FARIDE, 'Gonzalo Rojas y la miseria del hombre', *La época*, 28 May 1995.

ZUKOVSKY, LOUIS, 'Program: "Objectivists" 1931', *Poetry: A Magazine of Verse*, 37/5 (1931).

—— *Bottom: On Shakespeare* (Berkeley, 1987).

ZURITA, RAÚL, *Literatura, lenguaje y sociedad (1973–1983)* (Santiago, 1983).

SELECTED BIBLIOGRAPHIES

Nicanor Parra

Works

Poemas y antipoemas (Santiago, 1954).
La cueca larga (Santiago, 1958).
Versos de salón (Santiago, 1958).

Canciones rusas (Santiago, 1967).
Obra gruesa (Santiago, 1969).
Sermones y prédicas del Cristo de Elqui (Santiago, 1977).
Nuevos sermones y prédicas del Cristo de Elqui (Valparaíso, 1979).
Chistes para desorientar a la poesía (Madrid, 1989).
Poemas para combatir la calvicie (Mexico City, 1993).

Critical Studies

BENEDETTI, MARIO, 'Nicanor Parra, o el artefacto con laureles', in Alfonso Calderón (ed.), *Antología de la poesía chilena contemporánea* (Santiago, 1970).

FLORES, ÁNGEL (ed.), *Aproximaciones a Nicanor Parra* (Barcelona, 1973).

GOIC, CEDOMIL, 'La antipoesía de Nicanor Parra', in Cedomil Goic (ed.), *Historia y crítica de la literatura hispanoamericana*, iii: Época contemporánea (Barcelona, 1988).

GROSSMAN, EDITH, *The Antipoetry of Nicanor Parra* (New York, 1975).

MILÁN, EDUARDO, 'Hojas de Parra', *Vuelta*, 137 (Mexico, 1988).

MONTES, HUGO, and RODRÍGUEZ, MARIO (eds.), *Nicanor Parra y la poesía de lo cotidiano* (Santiago, 1974).

MORALES, LEÓNIDAS, *La Poesía de Nicanor Parra* (Santiago, 1972).

SCHOPF, FEDERICO, 'Introducción a la antipoesía de Nicanor Parra', in *Del vanguardismo a la antipoesía* (Rome, 1986).

YAMAL, RICARDO, *Sistema y visión de la poesía de Nicanor Parra* (Valencia, 1985).

Ernesto Cardenal

Works

Gethsemani, Ky (Mexico City, 1960)
Epigramas (Mexico City 1961; Buenos Aires, 1972).
Oración por Marilyn Monroe y otros poemas (Medellín, 1965).
Salmos (Buenos Aires, 1969).
Hora 0 (Mexico City, 1960).
Poemas de Ernesto Cardenal (Havana, 1967).
Vida en el amor (Buenos Aires, 1970).
Poemas (Barcelona, 1971).
Homenaje a los indios americanos (Buenos Aires, 1972).
Canto nacional (Mexico City 1973).
Oráculo sobre Managua (Buenos Aires, 1973).
Poesía escogida (Barcelona, 1975).
El evangelio en Solentiname, 2 vols. (Caracas, 1976–8).
El estrecho dudoso (Madrid, 1980).
Vuelos de victoria (Madrid, 1984).

Los ovnis de oro (Mexico City, 1988).
Poesía (Madrid, 1989).
Los ovnis de oro: Golden UFOs [bilingual edition] (Bloomington, Ind., 1992).
Cántico cósmico (Madrid, 1992).
Cardenal, Ernesto (ed.), *Poesía nicaragüense* (Havana, 1972).

Critical Studies

BORGESON, PAUL, *Hacia el hombre nuevo: poesía y pensamiento de E. Cardenal* (London, 1984).
CALABRESE, ELISA (ed.), *Ernesto Cardenal: poeta de la liberación latino-americana* (Buenos Aires, 1975).
CORONEL URTECHO, JOSÉ, 'Prologo' to Ernesto Cardenal, *El estrecho dudoso* (Managua, 1966).
MERTON, THOMAS, 'Prólogo' to Ernesto Cardenal, *Vida en el amor* (Buenos Aires, 1970).
PRING-MILL, ROBERT, 'Acciones paralelas y montaje acelerado en el segundo episodio de *Hora O'*, *Revista iberoamericana*, 118–19 (1982).
VEIRAVÉ, ALFREDO, *Ernesto Cardenal: el exteriorismo; poesía del nuevo mundo* (Chaco, 1974).
ZIMMERMAN, MARC, 'Ernesto Cardenal after the Revolution', in *Flights of Victory: Vuelos de victoria by Ernesto Cardenal* (New York, 1985).

Gonzalo Rojas

Works

La miseria del hombre (Valparaíso, 1948).
Contra la muerte (Santiago, 1964; 2nd edn. Havana, 1966).
Oscuro (Caracas, 1977).
Transtierro (Madrid, 1981; 2nd edn. expanded, 1984).
Del relámpago (Mexico City, 1981; 2nd edn. expanded, 1984).
El alumbrado (Santiago, 1986). Other edn.: *El alumbrado y otros poemas* (Madrid, 1987).
Materia de testamento (Madrid, 1988).
Antología personal, prologue by Eduardo Vázquez (Mexico City, 1988).
Antología del aire (Mexico City, 1991).
Cinco visiones (Salamanca, 1992).
Río turbio (Madrid, 1996).

Critical Studies

CHARRY LARA, FERNANDO, 'Poesía de Gonzalo Rojas', *Eco*, 190 (1977).

CODDOU, MARCELO, *Poética de la poesía activa* (Madrid, 1984).
—— *Nuevos estudios sobre la poesía de Gonzalo Rojas* (Santiago, 1986).
GIORDANO, ENRIQUE, *Poesía y poética de Gonzalo Rojas* (Santiago, 1987).
LOYOLA, HERNÁN, 'Gonzalo Rojas o el respeto a la poesía', *Anales de la Universidad de Chile*, 135 (1975).
PACHECO, JOSÉ EMILIO, 'Oscuro', *Vuelta*, 8 (1977).
ROJAS, NELSON, *Estudios sobre la poesía de Gonzalo Rojas* (Madrid, 1984).

Jorge Eduardo Eielson

Works

Reinos, separata de *Historia*, 9 (Lima, 1945).
Canción y muerte de Rolando (Lima, 1959).
Mutatis mutandis (Lima, 1967).
El cuerpo de Giuliano (novel) (Mexico City, 1971).
Poesía escrita (Lima, 1976).
Poesía escrita (Mexico City, 1976; 2nd edn, corrected and enlarged, 1989).
Noche oscura del cuerpo (Lima, 1989).
Il linguaggio magico dei nodi (Milan, 1993).
El diálogo infinito: una conversacion con Martha L. Canfield (Mexico City, 1995).
Antología (México City, 1996).
Poesía escrita (Bogotá, 1998).
La scala infinita (Milan, 1998).

Critical Studies

CANFIELD, MARTHA, 'Las fuentes del deleite inmovil', in *Poesía escrita* (Bogotá, 1998).
FERNÁNDEZ COZMAN, CAMILO, *Las huellas del aura: la poética de J. E. Eielson* (Lima, 1996).
MARTOS, MARCO, 'Poesía escrita', *Revista de crítica literaria latinoamericana*, 3/6 (1977).
ORTEGA, JULIO, 'JEE', in *Figuración de la persona* (Barcelona, 1971).
OVIEDO, JOSÉ MIGUEL, 'Poesía escrita', *Vuelta*, 16 (Mexico City, 1978).
PAOLI, ROBERTO, 'Exilio vital y exilio verbal en Eielson', in *Estudios sobre literatura peruana contemporánea* (Florence, 1985).

Juan L. Ortiz

Works

En el aura del saúce, 3 vols. (Rosario, 1970).
Obra completa (Santa Fe, 1996).

Critical Studies

CONTARDI, MARILYN, 'Trece versos de El Gualeguay', *Poesía y poética*, 18 (1995).

—— 'Sobre El Gualeguay', in J. L. Ortiz, *Obra completa* (Santa Fe, 1996).

DEL BARCO, OSCAR, 'Notas sobre Juan L. Ortiz', *Poesía y poética*, 18 (1995).

DELGADO, SERGIO, 'La obra de Juan L. Ortiz', in J. L. Ortiz, *Obra completa* (Santa Fe, 1996).

GOLA, HUGO, 'El reino de la poesía', in J. L. Ortiz, *Obra completa* (Santa Fe, 1996).

KAMENSZAIN, TAMARA, 'Juan L. Ortiz: la lírica entre comillas', in *El texto silencioso: tradición y vanguardia en la poesía sudamericana* (Mexico City, 1983).

SAER, JUAN JOSÉ, 'Juan', in J. L. Ortiz, *Obra completa* (Santa Fe, 1996).

VEIRAVÉ, ALFREDO, *Juan L. Ortiz: la experiencia poética* (Buenos Aires, 1984).

Ana Enriqueta Terán

Works

Presencia terrena (Montevideo, 1949).
Libro de los oficios (Caracas, 1975).
Casa de hablas (Caracas, 1991).

Critical Studies

OROPEZA, JOSÉ NAPOLEÓN, 'La imagen, intercambio de esencias', in E. Terán, *Casa de hablas* (Caracas, 1991).

Raúl Zurita

Works

Purgatorio (Santiago, 1982). Trans. Jeremy Jacobson (Pittsburgh, 1985).
Literatura, lenguaje y sociedad (1973–1983) (Santiago, 1983).
Canto a su amor desaparecido (Santiago, 1987).
El amor de Chile (Santiago, 1987).
Anteparaíso (Madrid, 1991).
La vida nueva (Santiago, 1994).

Critical Studies

CÁNOVAS, RODRIGO, 'Lectura de *Purgatorio*: por dónde comenzar', *Hueso húmero*, 10 (1981).

CÁNOVAS, RODRIGO, 'Zurita Chilensis: nuestro dolor, nuestra esperanza', in *Lihn, Zurita, Ictus, Radrigán: literatura chilena y experiencia autoritaria* (Santiago, 1986).

Foxley, C., 'Raúl Zurita y la propuesta autorreflexiva de Anteparaíso', in R. Yamal (ed.), *La poesía chilena actual (1960–1984) y la crítica* (Concepción, 1988).

MILÁN, EDUARDO, *'Canto a su amor desaparecido'*, *Vuelta*, 136 (1988).

PIÑA, JUAN, ANDRÉS, *Conversaciones con la poesía chilena* (Santiago, 1990).

VALENTE, IGNACIO, *'RZ: Purgatorio'*, *El Mercurio* (16 Dec. 1979).

—— 'Zurita en la poesía chilena', *El Mercurio* (31 Oct. 1982).

Carmen Ollé

Works

Noches de adrenalina (Lima, 1981).
Todo orgullo humea la noche (Lima, 1988).
¿Por qué hacen tanto ruido? (Lima, 1992).
Las dos caras del deseo (novel) (Lima, 1994).
'Poesía peruana escrita por mujeres: ¿Es lacerante la ironía?', *Márgenes*, 7/12 (1994).

Critical Studies

FORGUES, ROLAND, *Las poetas se desnudan* (Lima, 1991).

Index